THE

WORLD

WE

LIVE IN

TIME INCORPORATED

Editor-in-chief
HENRY R. LUCE

President
ROY E. LARSEN

———————

"The World We Live In" Series and Book were produced
under the general direction of

EDWARD K. THOMPSON, *Managing Editor*
PHILIP H. WOOTTON, JR., *Assistant Managing Editor*
JOSEPH KASTNER, *Copy Editor*

by the following editorial staff:

Editor
KENNETH MACLEISH

Art Director
CHARLES TUDOR

Writer
LINCOLN BARNETT

Chief of Research
MARIAN A. MACPHAIL

Text and Picture Research by
NANCY GENET, DAVID BERGAMINI, WARREN YOUNG, MARION STEINMANN,
JAMES GOODE, PATRICIA GRAVES, ROBERT CAMPBELL,
ELEANOR PARISH, TERRY HARNAN

Paintings by
RUDOLPH F. ZALLINGER, CHESLEY BONESTELL, RUDOLF FREUND, JAMES LEWICKI,
ANTONIO PETRUCCELLI, JAMES PERRY WILSON and ROBERT GARTLAND,
SIMON GRECO, WALTER LINSENMAIER, RICHARD EDES HARRISON

Photographs by
FRITZ GORO, ALFRED EISENSTAEDT, GJON MILI, ANDREAS FEININGER,
LOOMIS DEAN, ROMAN VISHNIAK, J. R. EYERMAN
(The names of other photographers whose pictures appear
in this book will be found in the List of Illustrations)

———————

Publisher
ANDREW HEISKELL

Assistant Publisher
ARTHUR R. MURPHY, JR.

"The World We Live In" series appeared in LIFE at intervals of approximately two months from December 8, 1952 to December 20, 1954. It consisted of thirteen parts. Each one of these parts was researched by one assistant editor or reporter, who devoted an average of eight months to the exacting job of gathering, evaluating and organizing data for the writer, supplying the art director and artists with material for paintings and working with photographers in the field. "The World We Live In" book is basically a compilation of the thirteen parts of the series. Certain minor editorial alterations have been made in text and pictures. An introduction, index, bibliography and list of illustrations have been added.

Working closely with the above staff in the production of the series were the following individuals and departments: Ray Mackland, Picture Editor; Irene Saint, Newsbureau Chief; Helen Deuell, Copy Chief; LIFE's foreign and domestic correspondents, picture bureau and copy desk.

THE WORLD WE LIVE IN

BY THE
EDITORIAL STAFF OF

AND LINCOLN BARNETT

TIME INCORPORATED
NEW YORK · 1955

ACKNOWLEDGMENTS

LIFE is indebted to the following scientists and institutions for their generous assistance in the preparation of "The World We Live In" series:

(Roman numerals after each name indicate the particular article or articles on which that person or institution collaborated.)

R. TUCKER ABBOTT—Smithsonian Institution   VII
DR. LEASON H. ADAMS—Carnegie Institution of Washington   I, III, IV
DR. HENRY R. ALDRICH—Geological Society of America   III
E. H. ALEXANDER—New York Botanical Garden   IX
DR. DEAN AMADON—American Museum of Natural History, N.Y.   VIII
CHARLES ANDERSON—USAF Cambridge Research Center   IV
DR. HENRY N. ANDREWS—Washington University   V
JOHN C. ARMSTRONG—University of Miami
   (formerly with American Museum of Natural History)   II, V, VII
DR. CHESTER A. ARNOLD—University of Michigan   V
DR. ROBERT ARTHUR—University of California
   Scripps Institution of Oceanography   II
WILLIAM VON ARX—Woods Hole Oceanographic Institution,
   Woods Hole, Mass.   II
DR. WALTER F. BAADE—Mount Wilson and Palomar Observatories   XIII
COLONEL P. D. BAIRD—Arctic Institute of North America   X
DR. STANLEY BALL—Yale University   VII
A. W. F. BANFIELD—Canadian Wildlife Service   X
DOROTHY BROWN BECKEL   X
DR. WILLIAM BEEBE—New York Zoological Society   VII
DR. LYMAN BENSON—Pomona College   IX
DR. FRANCIS BIRCH—Harvard University   I
DR. J. BRIAN BIRD—McGill University   X
MARSHALL BISHOP—The Lerner Marine Laboratory,
   Bimini, Bahama, B.W.I.   VII, VIII
DR. CHARLES M. BOGERT—American Museum
   of Natural History   V, VIII, IX, XI
DR. BART J. BOK—Harvard University   XIII
DR. IRA S. BOWEN—Mount Wilson and Palomar Observatories   XIII
DR. CHARLES BREDER—American Museum of Natural History   VII, VIII
DR. PERCY BRIDGMAN—Harvard University   I
DR. HARRISON BROWN—University of Chicago
   Institute for Nuclear Studies   I, II, IV
DR. ROLAND W. BROWN—National Museum, Washington, D.C.   VI
DR. MURRAY F. BUELL—Rutgers University   XII
DR. KONRAD BUETTNER—USAF School of Aviation Medicine
   at Randolph Field   IV
M. W. BYRNE—Government Public Relations Office, Australia   VIII
COLONEL PAUL CAMPBELL—USAF School of Aviation Medicine
   at Randolph Field   IV
GROUP CAPTAIN A. G. CARR—Royal Australian Air Force   VIII
DR. MELBOURNE R. CARRIKER—University of North Carolina   XII
T. DONALD CARTER—American Museum of Natural History   IX, X, XI
DR. KENNETH E. CASTER—University of Cincinnati   V
DR. MONT A. CAZIER—American Museum of Natural History   XII
JOSEPH CHAMBERLAIN—USAF, Cambridge Research Center   IV
WILLIAM CHAPMAN, Low Isles, Australia   VIII
DR. FENNER CHACE—Smithsonian Institution   VII
DR. H. G. CLAMANN—USAF School of Aviation Medicine
   at Randolph Field   IV
AUSTIN H. CLARK—Smithsonian Institution   II, VII
WILSON CLARKE—American Museum of Natural History   VII, VIII
DR. THOMAS CLEMENTS—University of Southern California   IX
DR. WILLIAM CLENCH—Museum of Comparative Zoology,
   Harvard College   II, VIII
DR. PRESTON CLOUD—U.S. Geological Survey   VIII
DR. DORIS COCHRAN—Smithsonian Institution   VII, VIII
DR. ARTHUR DODD CODE—University of Wisconsin   XIII
DR. G. ARTHUR COOPER—National Museum   V
CAPTAIN J. Y. COUSTEAU—The Marine Biological Laboratory,
   Woods Hole, Mass.   VII
DR. RAYMOND COWLES—The University of California at Los Angeles   IX
CYRIL COX, Heron Island, Australia   VIII
AGNES CREAGH—Geological Society of America   III

DR. SEARS CROWELL—Indiana University   VII
COLONEL FRANK J. CUNNINGHAM—Canadian Department of Northern
   Affairs and National Resources   X
DR. B. W. CURRIE—University of Saskatchewan, Saskatoon, Canada   IV
DR. REGINALD DALY—Harvard University   I
DR. WILLIAM DAWSON—University of Michigan   IX
DR. ELIZABETH DEICHMANN—Harvard University   II
DR. H. G. DEIGNAN—Smithsonian Institution   VIII
DR. ROBERT DIETZ—U.S. Navy Electronics Laboratory,
   San Diego, Calif.   II
DR. THEODOSIUS DOBZHANSKY—Columbia University   V
DR. ERLINE DORF—Princeton University   V
DR. CARL O. DUNBAR—Yale University   III, V, VI
DR. DAVID H. DUNKLE—National Museum   V
GEORGE ERNST, Cairns, Queensland, Australia   VIII
DR. MAURICE EWING—Columbia University   I, II
WILLIAM FIELD—American Geographical Society   X
DR. RICHARD FOSTER FLINT—Yale University   IV
DR. R. H. FLOWER—New Mexico Institute of Mining and Technology   V
DR. HERBERT FRIEDMANN—Smithsonian Institution   VIII
DR. PAUL GALTSOFF—U.S. Bureau of Fisheries, Woods Hole, Mass.   VII
DR. GEORGE GAMOW—George Washington University   I, XIII
LESLIE GARLICK, Murray Islands, Australia   VIII
NATHANIEL GERSON—USAF Cambridge Research Center   IV
DR. WILLIS J. GERTSCH—American Museum of Natural History   XII
E. THOMAS GILLIARD—American Museum of Natural History   V
JAMES GILLULY—U.S. Geological Survey   III
DR. EARL GODFREY—National Museum of Canada   X
EDWARD GOLDBERG—University of California
   Scripps Institution of Oceanography   II
DR. JOSEPH GREGORY—Yale University   V, VI
DR. ROSS GUNN—U.S. Weather Bureau   I, IV
NICHOLAS GUPPY—N.Y. Botanical Garden   XI
DR. FRITZ HABER—USAF School of Aviation Medicine
   at Randolph Field   IV
DR. LYLE E. HAGMANN—Rutgers University   XII
JAN HAHN—Woods Hole Oceanographic Institution   II, VII, VIII
SIR EDWARD HALLSTROM—Taronga Park Zoological Trust, Australia   VIII
HAROLD HANSON—Natural History Survey of Illinois   X
FRANCIS HARPER   X
DR. BERNHARD HAURWITZ—New York University   IV
DR. RALPH HAVENS—U.S. Naval Research Laboratory   IV
DR. BRUCE HEEZEN—Columbia University   II
DR. D. C. HEISKES—Surinam Museum, Dutch Guiana   XI
DR. J. BRACKETT HERSEY—Woods Hole Oceanographic Institution   II
PHILIP HERSHKOVITZ—Chicago Natural History Museum   XI
DR. CARL L. HUBBS—University of California
   Scripps Institution of Oceanography   VII, VIII
DR. E. O. HULBERT—U.S. Naval Research Laboratory   IV
I. A. DE HULSTER—Surinam Landsboschbeheer, Dutch Guiana   XI
DR. MILTON L. HUMASON—Mount Wilson and
   Palomar Observatories   XIII
CHARLES B. HUNT—U.S. Geological Survey   III
DR. PATRICK HURLEY—Massachusetts Institute of Technology   I
DR. G. EVELYN HUTCHINSON—Yale University   II, IV, V
DR. LIBBIE HYMAN—American Museum of Natural History   VII, VIII
DR. COLUMBUS ISELIN—Woods Hole Oceanographic Institution   II
DR. MARTIN W. JOHNSON—University of California
   Scripps Institution of Oceanography   II, VII
DR. BERWIND P. KAUFMANN—Carnegie Institution of Washington   V
MARSHALL KAY—Columbia University   I
DR. REMINGTON KELLOGG—Smithsonian Institution   VII
PHILIP B. KING—U.S. Geological Survey   III
DR. EDWIN KIRK—U.S. Geological Survey   V
DR. J. BROOKES KNIGHT—National Museum   V
MAX KOHLER—U.S. Weather Bureau   IV
DR. GERARD P. KUIPER—University of Chicago   I, II, IV, XIII
DR. HARRY LADD—U.S. Geological Survey   II, VIII
DR. I. MacKENZIE LAMB—Farlow Herbarium, Harvard University   X
FRANCESCA LaMONTE—American Museum of Natural History   VII
DR. ROBERT B. LEIGHTON—California Institute of Technology   XIII
MICHAEL LERNER—The Lerner Marine Laboratory,
   Bimini, Bahamas, B.W.I.   VII, VIII
DR. J. C. LINDEMAN—Botanisch Museum en Herbarium,
   Utrecht, Holland   XI
DR. ARMIN K. LOBECK—Columbia University   III
CHESTER R. LONGWELL—Yale University   III
DR. CHARLES LOWE JR.—University of Arizona   IX
DR. BASSETT MAGUIRE—New York Botanical Garden   XI
WINSTON MAIR—Canadian Wildlife Service   X

Dr. Joanne Starr Malkus—Woods Hole Oceanographic Institution   IV
T. H. Manning   X
Dr. H. A. Marmer—U.S. Coast and Geodetic Survey   II, III
Marou, Native Representative, Murray Islands, Australia   VIII
Jules W. Marron Sr.—New Jersey Division of Fish and Game   XII
Frank J. Mather—Woods Hole Oceanographic Institution   VII
Dr. Ernst Mayr—American Museum of Natural History   V
Dr. George C. McVittie—University of Illinois   XIII
Dr. Peveril Meigs—Quartermaster Research and Development Center,
   Natick, Mass.   IX
Dr. Henry Menard—U.S. Navy Electronics Laboratory,
   San Diego, Calif.   II
Dr. Robert Menzies—University of California
   Scripps Institution of Oceanography   VII
Angelina Messina—American Museum of Natural History   VII
Captain Stewart Middlemiss, Barrier Reef Airways, Australia   VIII
Dr. A. K. Miller—State University of Iowa   V
Dr. Rudolph L. Minkowski—Mount Wilson and
   Palomar Observatories   XIII
Dr. Hilary B. Moore—University of Miami   VII
Ralph C. Morril—Yale University   VI, X
Dr. Edwin T. Moul—Rutgers University   XII
Dr. Robert Murphy—American Museum of Natural History   VIII
Dr. Walter Munk—University of California
   Scripps Institution of Oceanography   II
Dr. Jerome Namias—U.S. Weather Bureau   IV
Dr. Maurice Nelles—Borg-Warner Corp.   VII
Dr. Norman Newell—American Museum of Natural History   II, VIII
Herbert B. Nichols—U.S. Geological Survey   III
John T. Nichols—American Museum of Natural History   VII, VIII
Dr. N. L. Nicholson—Canadian Department of Mines
   and Technical Surveys   X
Professor C. B. van Niel—Hopkins Marine Station,
   Pacific Grove, Calif.   I
Kenneth Norris—University of California Scripps Institution
   of Oceanography   II
C. O'Leary—Director of Native Affairs, Queensland, Australia   VIII
Norman Oliver—USAF Cambridge Research Center   IV
John Pallister—American Museum of Natural History   XI
Dr. Allison R. Palmer—U.S. Geological Survey   V
Dr. Albert Parr—American Museum of Natural History   II
Dr. William Petrie—Defense Research Board of Canada   IV
Dr. Marian H. Pettibone—University of New Hampshire   VII
Dr. Allan Phillips—University of Michigan   IX
Dr. Walter Phillips—University of Arizona   IX
Dr. Grace Pickford—Yale University   VII
Dr. Nicholas Polunin—Gray Herbarium, Harvard University   X
Dr. A. E. Porsild—National Museum of Canada   X
J. A. Posgay—Woods Hole Oceanographic Institution   VII
Richard Pough—American Museum of Natural History   IX
Dr. Russell W. Raitt—U.S. Navy Electronics Laboratory,
   San Diego, Calif.   II
Dr. Norris Rakestraw—University of California
   Scripps Institution of Oceanography   II
Dr. W. J. Rees—British Museum, London   VII
Dr. Roger Revelle—University of California
   Scripps Institution of Oceanography   I, II
Dr. Francis A. Richards—Woods Hole Oceanographic Institution   II
Dr. Gordon Riley—Yale University   VII
Dr. S. Dillon Ripley—Yale University   XI
Dr. Luis R. Rivas—University of Miami   VII
Dr. H. P. Robertson—California Institute of Technology   XIII
Dr. Donald P. Rogers—New York Botanical Garden   X, XI
Dr. Alfred Romer—Harvard University   VII
Colonel Graham Rowley—Canadian Department of Northern
   Affairs and National Resources   X
William Rubey—U.S. Geological Survey   I, II, III, IV
Colin C. Campbell Sanborn—Chicago Natural History Museum   XI
Dr. Allan R. Sandage—Mount Wilson and Palomar Observatories   XIII
Ivan T. Sanderson (zoologist and author)   XI
Dr. Bobb Schaeffer—American Museum of Natural History   V, VI
William Schevill—Woods Hole Oceanographic Institution   II
Dr. Arnülf Schlüter—Max Planck Institute   XIII
Dr. Knut Schmidt-Nielson—Duke University   IX
Dr. John B. Schmitt—Rutgers University   XII
Dr. Per Scholander—Woods Hole Oceanographic Institution   VII
William C. Schroeder—Woods Hole Oceanographic
   Institution   VII, VIII
Dr. Leonard P. Schultz—Smithsonian Institution   VII, VIII
Dr. Martin Schwarzschild—Princeton University   XIII

Dr. Mary Sears—Woods Hole Oceanographic Institution   VII
Dr. Ralph Shapiro—USAF Cambridge Research Center   IV
Dr. John S. Shelton—Pomona College   III, IX
Dr. Francis Shepard—University of California
   Scripps Institution of Oceanography   II
Dr. Demitri Shimkin—U.S. Bureau of Census   X
Dr. George Gaylord Simpson—American Museum of Natural History   V
Rear Admiral Edward H. Smith—Woods Hole Oceanographic
   Institution   VII, VIII
Dr. F. G. Walton Smith—University of Miami   VII
W. J. J. Snijders—Surinam Landsboschbeheer, Dutch Guiana   XI
V. E. F. Solman—Canadian Wildlife Service   X
Kenneth Stager—Los Angeles County Museum   IX
Dr. Vilhjalmur Stefansson   X
Henry Stommel—Woods Hole Oceanographic Institution   II
Professor Carl Stormer—Institute of Theoretical Astrophysics,
   Oslo, Norway   IV
Dr. Arthur M. Strahler—Columbia University   II, III, IV
Dr. Hubertus Strughold—USAF School of Aviation Medicine
   at Randolph Field   IV
Dr. Otto Struve—University of California at Berkeley   XIII
John Teal   X
Dr. Curt Teichert—Melbourne University, Australia   VIII
Dr. Llewellyn Hilleth Thomas—Columbia University   XIII
Chankey Touart—USAF Cambridge Research Center   IV
Harry J. Turner—Woods Hole Oceanographic Institution   VII
Dr. Harold C. Urey—University of Chicago
   Institute for Nuclear Studies   I
Professor Leif Vegard—Institute for Aurora Borealis Observation,
   Tromso, Norway   IV
Peter Versteegh—Surinam Landsboschbeheer, Dutch Guiana   XI
Peter van der Voorde—Surinam Landbouwproes Station,
   Dutch Guiana   XI
Hugo Wahlquist—California Institute of Technology   XII
Dr. Selman A. Waksman—Rutgers University   XII
Dr. George Wald—Harvard University   VII
Dr. Bruce Wallace—Long Island Biological Association, N.Y.   V
Dr. A. L. Washburn   X
Dr. John Wells—Cornell University   VIII
Dr. Harry Wexler—U.S. Weather Bureau   IV, IX
Dr. Fred L. Whipple—Harvard University   I, IV
Dr. Robert White—USAF Cambridge Research Center   IV
High Commissioner to London Sir Thomas White (Australia)   VIII
Dr. H. C. Willett—Massachusetts Institute of Technology   IV
Dr. John Tuzo Wilson—University of Toronto, Canada   I
Jay S. Winston—U.S. Weather Bureau   IV
F. G. Wood—Marine Studios, Marineland, Fla.   VIII
Colonel Walter Wood—Arctic Institute of North America   X
Dr. A. O. Woodford—Pomona College   III
William Woodin—Tucson Desert Museum   IX
Dr. J. L. Worzel—Columbia University   II
Ellis Yochelson—U.S. Geological Survey   V
Dr. C. M. Yonge—University of Glasgow, Scotland   VIII
Ronald Younger—Australian News and Information Bureau,
   New York   VIII
Dr. Claude E. Zobell—University of California Scripps Institution of
   Oceanography   VII

ACKNOWLEDGMENTS FOR INSTITUTIONS

The Allan Hancock Foundation, University of Southern California   VII
The American Geographical Society   III
Canadian Defence Research Board, Department of National Defence,
   Department of Transport and National Film Board   X
Field and Stream   VII
Hudson's Bay Company of Canada   X
The Marine Biological Laboratory, Woods Hole, Mass.   II, VII, VIII
The Marine Studios, Marineland, Fla.   VII
National Audubon Society   XII
The National Park Service   III
Peabody Museum, Yale University   VI
Queensland (Australia) Navigation and Lighthouse Service   VIII
Royal Canadian Air Force and Mounted Police   X
Tucson Weather Bureau   IX
U.S. Army and Navy   X; U.S. Coast Guard   II
U.S. Navy Hydrographic Office   II
U.S. Navy Weather Squadron Two   IV
U.S. Weather Bureau   X

The poem which appears on page 246 is reprinted from
Complete Poems of Robert Frost with the permission of
the publishers, Henry Holt and Company, Inc.

TABLE

OF

CONTENTS

SCULPTURED IN STONE by wind and water, the unremitting agents which fashion the features of the land, Utah's monumental Delicate Arch stands bright-lit by a harsh desert sun—a magnificent detail of the world we live in.

AN INTRODUCTION

by VANNEVAR BUSH

President of the Carnegie Institution of Washington
Wartime Chief of the Office of Scientific Research and Development

FOR as long as man has lived in the world he has been interested in knowing something about it. When he lived in a cave, his very existence depended on such knowledge; for if he mistook a saber-toothed tiger for a tapir or a woolly mammoth for a musk ox, he was likely not to get back to his cave. His world was a simple one, extending only a few miles in any direction. But he peopled it in his imagination with mystic beings that blew the winds and caused the eerie sounds he heard and waved their arms from the trees as the dreaded night approached.

Today we are still interested in our world, though for different reasons. Self-protection against the forces of nature has not ceased to be of concern to us, but it has become less important as a motive for inquiry than our endless curiosity and inquisitive spirit. The race of man has become dominant on the earth primarily because of its urge to know and its phenomenal ability to learn. Some of us, to be sure, are interested chiefly in the works of man—in automobiles and gadgets, in the squalling of loudspeakers, or in the curve of a baseball. Some of us study nature romantically to escape from oppressive thoughts of what may result from our uncontrollable creations. We find a placid relief in contemplating the beauties of nature—the flight of birds and butterflies, the graceful motions of trout and deer, the trembling of an aspen leaf over a stream or the hopeful light of the east a moment before the sun rises—and such relief is indeed salutary in these troubled times. All of us ought, at least, to be interested in curbing our prodigal depletion of the power and material resources of our world and enlarging the niggard legacy we are likely otherwise to leave for future generations. Yet our interest in the world, even when it is narrow or specialized, stems mainly from a craving to know and understand, which has developed through ages of evolution as an essential part of our character.

Understanding is not a simple matter in our time. Science has extended the world of our experience and shown it to be almost infinitely complex. Astronomers, with their giant telescopes on Mt. Wilson and Mt. Palomar and their recently perfected radio telescopes, have extended our view of the universe far beyond our solar system, beyond the Milky Way, out into space more than a billion light years away, disclosing events and situations so stupendously remote in both time and space that we hesitate to concede to them full reality. It was but a few years ago that we saw through our light telescopes and confirmed through our radio telescopes the dramatic collision of two giant galaxies that occurred more than two hundred million years ago. In the light of such events we are tempted to echo Sir Thomas Brown's observation that "The created world is but a small parenthesis in eternity."

While astronomers have looked farther and farther out into the limitless reaches of space, geologists and paleontologists have delved into the history of the earth and its creatures, tracing evolution through hundreds of millions of years. Chemists and physicists in their exploration of the very small have gone beyond the molecule and the atom to find that all we experience in a material way comes from the interaction of particles so tiny and elusive that billions of them go to make up the smallest particle we can actually see, even with the aid of the electron microscope. Geographers and explorers have brought us knowledge of hitherto forbidden places in the frozen areas about the poles. Oceanographers have plumbed by sonar sounding and charted the vast mountain ranges and abyssal valleys that lie hidden miles under the surface of the sea.

Great stores of knowledge have been accumulated by specialists, but they remain largely in the minds and libraries of the specialists. In coping with this mighty plethora of fact what we most need for the guidance of multitudes of men and for the development of wisdom is synthesis and interpretation. We need to have brought together the knowledge that has been garnered in many fields of investigation. We need to have its complexities made intelligible and its significance for ordinary lives expounded.

THE conventional boundaries between sciences are neither fixed nor absolute. There has been an increasing tendency in every science to explore those areas that lie near the boundaries, and this has inevitably led to a good deal of crossing over the lines. We have physical chemists, chemical physicists, biochemists, astrophysicists—all concerned with problems involving two or more major disciplines. But most research scientists who work in a border province have to specialize in their province almost as narrowly as those who work within a single discipline. They concentrate on a particular problem, straddling the border, just as the research scientist within a more conventional field concentrates on a particular problem lying within that field. Few of them have the art or the inclination to write a broad interpretative work on a single whole discipline, let alone on two; and fewer still will essay to write a popular book, cutting across many disciplines, that will meet the need for information and understanding of a public that is curious about the world but is mainly occupied with other concerns than the study of science.

Thus, those who summarize and interpret perform a great service for all of us. There are many scientists who write well and who contribute greatly to our progress by condensing the essential aspects of scientific fields for the guidance of their fellow scientists. A few, a very few, can interpret for studious laymen. But only the true journalist of science can fully satisfy the public need. And competent science journalists are exceedingly rare. For they must not only have familiarized themselves with all the essential data supplied by every department of science; they must have mastered the most difficult art of communicating in brief space, by evocative words and illuminating pictures, the fundamental meaning of those data. It is their task to bridge the gap between research workers who extend the boundaries of knowledge and the rest of us who wish only to comprehend the meaning of it all. Too often there is spread before us, in science fiction and books that popularize science, only the spectacular and the bizarre, presented with scant regard for accuracy, or distortions that conceal rather than reveal the true wonders of the universe.

IT is for this reason that I have hailed the efforts of LIFE in producing the remarkable series of articles called "The World We Live In," now presented in book form. Here is a new approach to popular education in science. The editors have brought to bear the power of an organization that knows how to accomplish great feats in the realm of journalism—in finding out what is most important in the events and personalities of our day and setting them forth vividly and forcefully. Their book is indeed the product of journalism but it is journalism with a difference. In its brief dimensions it cannot pretend to be either exhaustive or profound. It is neither a treatise nor a monograph, but a modest volume of text richly illustrated, which, by presenting a lucid, interesting and withal accurate account of the world we live in, will captivate the imagination of millions of non-scientific people who would otherwise not concern themselves with its subject matter. No pains were spared to make it accurate. Many scientists were consulted and gave their best advice to make its statements true and correct in scale. The result is natural history in modern dress.

Lincoln Barnett, author of the text, has told his story in a stimulating, vigorous manner. The book cuts freely through the realms of astronomy, geology, biology, paleontology, geography, oceanography and meteorology. In a word, it runs the gamut of all sciences that relate to our universe.

It graphically describes the most widely accepted theory as to how the earth, a child of the sun, came into being between three and five billion years ago. It traces the physical changes that have occurred in the earth's structure—the hardening of its crust, its inundation by water erupted as vapor or squeezed up from the interior of the earth as it cooled and contracted, the recurrent upheavals that have produced mountains and ocean beds, the successive periods of glaciation, the slow leveling influences of erosion by water, ice, and wind. It points up the rare combination of circumstances that made possible the development of life on our planet—the nature of the land, the abundant presence of water, the atmosphere. For Earth alone in the solar system, and possibly in our entire galaxy, is blessed with vast oceans—in which life was first begun—and an atmosphere sufficiently dense to protect living things from the extremes of temperature that normally prevail throughout the rest of the universe. The book describes the ocean floor, only recently charted in any detail. It explains the ocean currents, tides and surface disturbances; the canopy of air and its never ending turbulence; the cycle of evaporation and precipitation which alone keeps the continents watered and productive. It depicts in broad strokes the history of life through geologic ages and elucidates with simple, clear illustrations the basic principles of genetics that account for the evolution of all living things. It tells of how in the pre-Cambrian era, a billion and a half years ago, life began with the soft-bodied creatures of the sea; how toward the end of the Paleozoic era (some 200 million years ago) the reptiles became dominant, developed and differentiated, giving rise to the widely variant species of dinosaurs and turtles; and how finally in the Cenozoic era (commencing about 75 million years ago) the race of mammals prevailed in all lands.

The book pictures the widely different environments offered by nature and the amazing adaptation of various species of life in each. Some of its most fascinating portions are those that describe and vividly picture the strange conditions of life in those parts of our contemporary world that are outside our ordinary experience. There are the remarkable color photographs and descriptions of desert regions with their arid sands and dry caked earth—not uninhabited as the term suggests, but peopled with many small creatures and covered sparsely and unevenly by fantastic plants, whose normal parched and faded aspect yields suddenly to the influence of spring showers and freshets, transmuted into radiant color hardly to be matched in any other surroundings. At the opposite extreme there are the rain forests of the tropics, where growth is so dense that it piles up in layers with great emergent trees rising high above the general level of its roof. At yet other environmental extremes there are the great and forbidding wastes of the frozen tundra and the amazing life forms of the luxuriant coral reefs. Then against the background of the world's splendid and exotic features a theme of nostalgia is developed in the idyllic portrayal of the "Woods of Home," with its tall hardwoods, its clear streams, the changing colors of its foliage and its winter snows.

In sum, the book is a magnificent contribution, which should delight as well as instruct a vast number of people. LIFE is to be congratulated on a great achievement.

THE EARTH
IS BORN

PART I

THE EARTH IS BORN

Spawned by a cloud of dust and forged in elemental fire, the young planet on whose face we dwell provides a shelter for life within a hostile universe

Earth! Thou mother of numberless children, the nurse and the mother,
Sister thou of the stars, and beloved by the Sun, the rejoicer!
Guardian and friend of the moon, O Earth, whom the comets forget not,
Yea, in the measureless distance wheel round and again they behold thee!
SAMUEL TAYLOR COLERIDGE, *Hymn to the Earth*

PRISONED in his paved cities, blindfolded by his impulses and necessities, man tends to disregard the system of nature in which he stands. It is only at infrequent moments when he finds himself beneath the stars, at sea perhaps, or in a moonlit meadow or on a foreign shore, that he contemplates the natural world—and he wonders.

Yet it is his essence to wonder. On some primeval hilltop perhaps half a million years ago the first man raised his eyes to the sky and wondered. At that instant, transcending himself and nature, he left behind the animal forebears from which he sprang: the questioning spirit of man was born, and with it the initial spark of his philosophy, religion and science. His earliest graves, in caverns of age-old rock, bespeak his awareness of the mystery of existence and of realities beyond immediate space and time. In the regularities of nature—the march of days and seasons—and in the irregularities—the caprices of lightning and volcanoes—he saw the will of supernatural beings. Only yesterday, as his own brief history is computed, did he win the key to nature's outer ramparts. This was the idea of causality, telling him to seek in natural causes the explanation of natural events.

Today it seems incredible he ever penetrated the disguises of the visible world at all. To his eye the earth is flat; the ground on which he walks seems stationary. How did he find himself clinging to the surface of a sphere—spinning about its axis at 1,000 miles an hour, whirling around the sun at 20 miles a second, riding through space on the rim of the Milky Way at 170 miles a second, slipping, sliding, wobbling, dipping among the stars in half a dozen other intricate motions? What could he think of this strange craft bearing him he could not know where—how explain the awful vibrations of its deck, or the alarming sounds and vapors that recurrently issued from below?

In every age he could only guess. The ancient Egyptians imagined the universe an enormous room; the earth was its floor, the sky a vast ceiling supported on four great columns and hung nightly by the gods with the lamps of the stars. In the miraculous flowering of Greek learning a few men of great intellect arrived somehow at many of the right answers. Pythagoras (around 530 B.C.) deduced that the earth was a sphere, and Aristarchus of Samos (310–230 B.C.) that it revolved around the sun. Eratosthenes, curator of the library of Alexandria (276–196 B.C.) computed its circumference with an error of less than 150 miles. It is one of the ironies of history that these insights were lost for 15 centuries through war and other stupidities of men and nations. Not till the great age of Copernicus, Galileo and Newton did science begin to rediscover ancient truths and disclose the humbling actualities of our situation in the universe. We know now that far from being the center of the cosmos, our earth is only a minor satellite of a second-rate star on the outer fringe of our local galaxy, the Milky Way. And as our small solar system is to the Milky Way, so the Milky Way is to the galaxies of outer space.

But with knowledge of our insignificance has come, too, a suspicion of uniqueness. In many ways our earth is an oddity. The solid elements of which it is composed are rare; for 99% of all the matter in the universe consists of the two lightest elements, hydrogen and helium; all the other elements together account for only 1% of the total substance. Since the cosmic temperature ranges from more than 35,000,000°F. in the interior of stars down to the absolute zero (−459.6°F.) of outer space, we can think of the material universe as made up almost entirely of luminous gases in a highly ionized and unstable state, with here and there perhaps a few errant motes of cold dust and stone. Only in very narrow temperate zones of space like our orbit can matter liquefy to form such delicate rarities as water, animals and plants.

It is the apparent loneliness and singularity of our planet in a hostile universe that evoke the deeper questions: How was the earth created? When did it come into being? What is its fate? The concept of a random universe, existing without origin or destiny, is meaningless to the human animal who lives in a dimension of time. Man has always postulated a Creation, and Genesis speaks with universal accents in its mighty opening phrases: *"In the beginning God created the heaven and the earth. And the earth was without form, and void; and darkness was upon the face of the deep . . ."* In its assault on these uttermost questions modern cosmogony impinges on the ancient realm of religion. The striking fact is that today their stories seem increasingly to converge. And every mystery that science resolves points to a larger mystery beyond itself.

For most of his short history egocentric man has assumed that his planet was scarcely older than himself. Indeed he often resisted the clues that periodically came to light—fossil remains impressed in rock, defining forms of life quite unlike contemporary forms, or utterly out of place. In 450 B.C., Herodotus noticed fossil shellfish deep in the Libyan desert and correctly inferred that the Mediterranean had once encroached far inland. Two thousand years later Leonardo da Vinci discovered similar remains in Italy and reached the same conclusion. But in 1650 Archbishop Ussher of Ireland firmly announced that studies of Scripture had proved that creation took place in the year 4004 B.C. on Sunday, October 23. For a century or more thereafter the date was official and it was impiety to suppose an earlier origin. Fossil discoveries were deprecated as devices planted by the devil to delude man. When new remains continued to turn up, a conviction grew that they were "relics of that accursed race that perished with the Flood."

Yet by the turn of the 19th Century a few lonely pioneers were creating a new science: geology. Chipping away at hillsides and in valleys where streams had cut deep gorges exposing antique strata of rock, they soon noted a relation between the separate layers and the fossils they contained. Each level held its own characteristic plant and animal remains, and they differed strikingly from layer to layer. And so they began dimly to sense vast vistas of time, punctuated by profound changes of climate, topography and life. How else could one explain sea shells in the heights of the Rockies, marine deposits on the plains of Kansas, remains of fig trees in Greenland or glacial debris in Australia and Brazil? In 1858 Darwin's epic work not only revealed that terrestrial life had undergone an irreversible evolution but supplied a coherent system of geologic chronology: the calendar of fossils pushed back the time of creation untold millions of years.

THE LIFE OF THE EARTH is shown from its probable origin in a primeval cloud of cosmic dust to its final entombment in the void. At center the planet is pictured condensing out of the original cloud. For more than four billion years it rolls through the starry cosmos, through ages of mountain building, ages of ice. In the foreground is the young earth today. As it journeys through time and space, its continents change their shape. At some distant time the sun will redden and swell, boiling away the earth's seas and atmosphere. Then, as the solar fires wane, the scorched planet will circle, cold and lifeless, around the dying sun.

EARTH'S INTERIOR (*left*), if laid bare by a slice from pole to pole, would reveal a structure like that of some titanic fruit. The outer skin is a rock crust 10 to 30 miles thick. Beneath it lies an inner shell 2,000 miles thick. The core is a ball of molten iron twice as thick as the moon.

EARTH'S CRUST consists of two layers: a top layer composed mostly of folded granite, of which the continents are built; and a "basement" of basalt, a black rock heavier than granite. Mountain roots reach into the red-hot rock of the inner shell. Fingers of basalt are old volcanic fissures.

However, the reading of the rocks remained a formidable task. All across the scarred, pitted, folded face of the earth, the record of the past has been obscured or obliterated by the scouring of glaciers, repeated outpourings of volcanic lava, and eons of erosion by rain and frost. It was not until the discovery of radioactivity around 1900 that the age of the earth could be fixed with approximate precision. For the radioactive elements, such as uranium, thorium and radium, decay at fixed rates, ending up eventually as lead. So it is possible to weigh the amount of uranium in any bit of radioactive rock against its residue of lead and thus calculate how long ago the deposit was formed.

Careful analyses of radioactive rocks in all parts of the world have disclosed some that are three to four billion years old, thus pointing to the conclusion that the earth's crust must have solidified at least four billion years ago. Other approaches to the problem—calculations of the ratio of salt in the ocean to the amount of salts annually conveyed by rivers to the sea, as well as recent studies of stellar combustion and galactic movements—all indicate a beginning, a creation fixed in time. The date always falls within certain crude limits, never less than two billion years, never more than four or five. And so the earth did not exist always. Yet it is older far than man ever surmised until now. It is when one turns from the question *When* to the question *How* that science enters the deep waters. Any study of origins must begin with a knowledge of present state; and it is the paradox of geophysics that its greatest mysteries lie just under our feet. Although the implements of astronomy have taught us much about the stellar universe up to a radius of two billion light years, our knowledge of what lies beneath us terminates a few fathoms down. The greatest depth to which man has ever penetrated the earth is 21,482 feet (in an oil well in California), only a thousandth of the distance to the terrestrial center. For this reason geophysics is of all sciences the least dogmatic and the most beset by conflicting interpretations of the fragmentary evidence at hand.

Heat measurements in mines and deep borings in the earth's crust show that the temperature increases at an average rate of about 1° F. for every 60 feet of depth, although the rate of increase varies in different parts of the earth. Below 30 miles it reaches the melting point of rocks (2,200°) and it is here that the lavas of volcanoes are commonly formed, whence they work upward through cracks in the solid layers above. This steep temperature gradient does not continue, however, all the way to the center. Recent discoveries disclose that much of the heat of the upper strata emanates from radioactive elements which occur in concentrated deposits near the surface. Farther down, the temperature curve tapers off, so that its maximum at the core may be around 8,000° or about that of the surface of the sun.

The picture most generally accepted by geophysicists today envisages the planet as composed of three main concentric spheres. The earth cannot be built throughout of the kind of rocks we see on the surface, for such a composition would account for less than half of its known mass of 6,600 million million million tons. Investigations have shown, moreover, that its density increases toward the center, and furthermore that its central core is probably in a liquid state. Many considerations argue that the deep heart of the earth must be a gigantic ball of molten iron (with perhaps some nickel and other elements), 4,000 miles in diameter or about the size of Mars. Yet the physical properties of this great ball are unknown, for the stupendous pressures at the core (46,500,000 pounds per square inch) would crush the iron molecules into a strange dense substance technically a "liquid" yet unlike any liquid known to man. Surrounding the molten iron core and reaching almost to the surface is the earth's great inner shell, 2,000 miles thick, known as the "mantle." Here again sciences combine to suggest its make-up. The mineral which satisfies most requirements is a high pressure phase of some iron-magnesium silicate like olivine, a heavy, greenish crystalline substance. The mantle seems, paradoxically, to be both rigid and plastic, white hot where it meets the core and probably at least red hot throughout. Above the mantle lies the thin crust of man's world, relatively no thicker than the skin of an apple to the fruit. This too is divided into layers. Its underlayer or "basement" seems to be a shell of basaltic material (like the black rock often found in lava), 10 to 20 miles thick, which lines the ocean basins and undergirds the land. Topmost of all stand the granitic continents on which we live. Some geophysicists describe them as "floating," for granite is lighter than basalt, as basalt is lighter than olivine and olivine lighter than iron. So our great land masses are, curiously, the lightest of the materials that compose the terrestrial sphere.

This strange anatomy, with its descending layers of ever heavier elements and ever higher temperatures, suggests that the earth was once molten. While recent authorities believe the earth cohered from cold matter which has since been heated by some mechanism—perhaps the release of radioactive energy—the opposite view has been the classic one. Since before the dawn of science man has thought of earth as a child of the sun and regarded fire as the primordial substance. The philosopher Heraclitus said, "This world was ever, is now, and ever shall be an ever-living Fire."

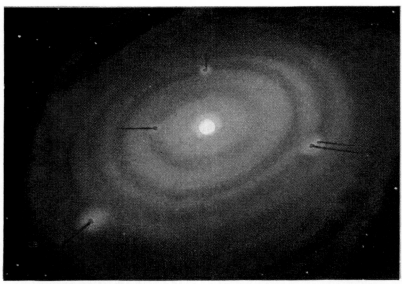

THE SOLAR SYSTEM IS BORN out of a rotating cloud of gas and dust. Gravity makes the cloud contract; the nucleus grows hot and becomes the sun; whorls in the outer disk become planets and moons. Dark streaks are planets' shadows.

THE FORMATION OF THE PLANET

HOWEVER details differ, all theories of terrestrial origin follow two main lines of thought, each with a long tradition. In 1749 the French naturalist Buffon proposed that a comet once crashed into the sun, sending up great splatters of solar gas which then condensed into the planets. In later adaptations of this theory the comet became a star and the collision a near-collision, near enough so that the gravitational attraction of the trespassing star raised giant tidal waves on the body of the sun. At the point of closest approach the wave crests broke away into space, cooled and became planets, half of them attached to the invader, the others remaining with their mother sun.

Against this "tidal theory" stands the no less venerable "nebular hypothesis" suggested by the philosopher Kant in 1755 and elaborated by the French mathematician Laplace in 1796. In this picture the sun was once surrounded by a rotating nebula, or envelope, of gas and dust, the possible residue of some wild solar explosion. Centrifugal force caused the nebula to bulge at the equator and cast forth a series of rings. The rings then coalesced into the separate objects of the solar system.

Generations of astronomers have revised and discarded various modifications of these two basic ideas. The currently popular theory is a refinement of the nebular hypothesis. As almost all astronomers now agree, it assumes, first, that all the stars evolved from primordial clouds of sparse gas and cosmic dust, drifting randomly in space. Compelled by gravitation, they massed, contracted, rotated. Internal pressures and temperatures rose until in the last white-hot stages of collapse they began to radiate as stars. Most of these vast turbulent clouds tended to divide, condensing around two vortices and thus giving birth to the binary (double) stars that make up more than half the stellar population. Others, like our North Star, separated into triplets that appear to the eye as one.

But in certain instances—perhaps one in 100—different events ensued. (It is here that the modern theory departs from those which presuppose some rare accident; astronomers conjecture that there may be a billion systems like ours within the Milky Way.) Occasionally the distribution of matter and balance of forces were such that, instead of dividing, a cloud formed a single nucleus. One was our sun, an infant star growing and glowing in the center of a rotating disk of inchoate matter the diameter of our solar system. As the disk spun, growing ever flatter, it separated into rings, and within the ring whorls of denser matter accumulated under the influence of gravity. The whorls collided, intermingled, collecting ever larger masses of matter into ever larger aggregates. In time— perhaps it took 100 million years—the nuclei of the larger whorls which were composed mostly of the heavy elements, condensed into the planets, the lesser into subplanets, satellites and the wandering comets of the outer rim. Inside the whorl from which our earth congealed, a still smaller one coagulated into our moon.

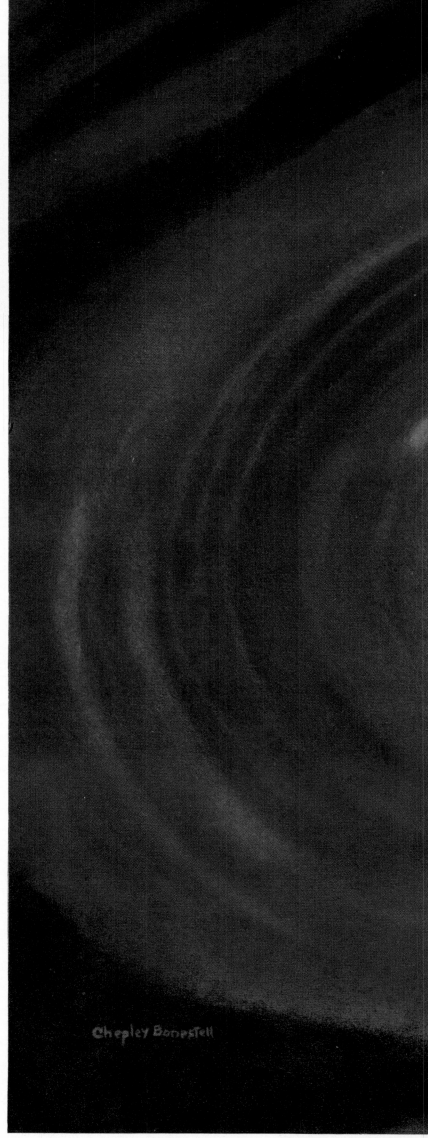

NEW-BORN EARTH AND MOON, reddened by the heat of their own internal fires, spin through the placental cloud of matter that gave them birth. Century after century they have whirled through dim and dusty space, sweeping up

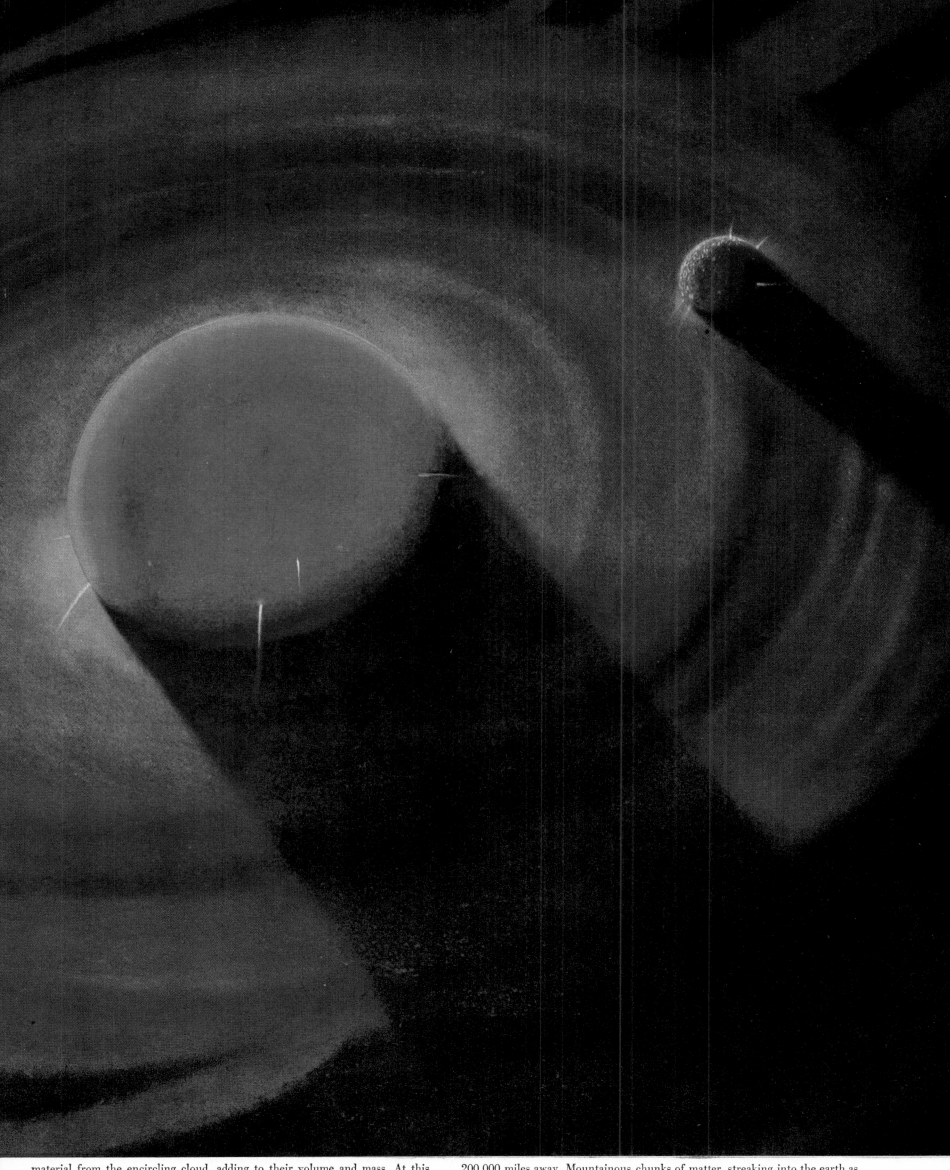

material from the encircling cloud, adding to their volume and mass. At this moment of cosmic time the young moon hovers only a few thousand miles from earth, whence it has since spiralled outward to its present orbit more than 200,000 miles away. Mountainous chunks of matter, streaking into the earth as flaming meteorites, disappear quickly into the molten interior, leaving no scars. But on the smaller, less-heated body of the moon, the wounds remain visible.

RIVERS OF MOLTEN STONE flow across the earth as wild outpourings of lava erupt to the surface through weak points in the cooling crust. Here and there frozen masses of rock rise above the fiery mass, now etched with red and gold mosaics as it cools and forms a surface slag. Through such eruptions lighter silicates in the molten interior are borne to the surface where, cooling and collecting in ever growing aggregates, they gradually build the protocontinents.

THE CONTINENTS CONGEAL

IN the morning of time the newly formed earth was a ball of anarchic matter, haloed by light gases, hurtling down the dusty corridor of its orbit. Some theorists believe that at this interlude of its formation, full grown but as yet featureless, its slowly accumulated substance must have been cold by cosmic standards—perhaps not more than a few hundred degrees Fahrenheit. Others think it must have been heated to incandescence by the squeeze of gravitation and the friction of its passage through the solar cloud. But however theories differ as to whether it cohered from cold or heated matter, most agree that at some time during its first half billion years of existence the earth must have passed through a molten or partially molten stage induced by gravitational compression or the release of energy by radioactive elements. It was at this phase that the heaviest substances sank to the core, the lighter minerals floated to the surface and the others arranged themselves generally in between. Meanwhile great jets of water vapor and carbon dioxide, pent in the interior, welled up and away to form the primal atmosphere. Slowly the crust cooled.

It may have taken a few centuries for the surface rocks to freeze, or a few thousand years, or, as some say, a million years. For as fast as heat radiated from the surface into space, new streams of hot matter rode upward on convection currents (like fluid movements in a caldron of boiling water), only to cool and settle again toward the center. And so it is probable that the first crystallization took place deep in the interior, and that the mantle hardened before the outer crust, sealing in the earth's metallic core the primeval heat that still rages there undiminished to this day.

It was in this epoch that the platforms of the continents took

Meteorites of all sizes bombard the earth incessantly, blasting craters in the hardening rocks. Fountains of water vapor and other gases, hissing through volcanic fissures, rise and mass in thick, dark cloud banks above—the future oceans of the earth. From time to time rain prematurely condenses, tries to fall, and at once boils back into the sky. The markings on the moon, still incandescent, viscous and close at hand, bear little resemblance to those visible today.

shape amid the wildest scenes of geologic time. All across the savage face of the planet smoke and flame arose incessantly and billowed skyward, and fierce fountains of fluid rock spewed forth, spreading new layers of lava on the plutonic plain. As years rolled into centuries, titanic outpourings of white-hot rock, recurring in regions where the terrestrial crust was weakest, may have built up highlands of light protogranite; and around these solid pedestals the continents eventually formed. Or, according to another conjecture, it may have been that the outpourings of light granitic materials were concentrated in a few great pools as they flowed into broad depressions in the crust; later, hardened into stone, they were lifted above the surrounding heavier basalt by pressures from below to become the protocontinents of earth.

No one knows for certain how or when the map acquired its present lineaments. One theory has it that the continents congealed exactly where they rest today; another that they crystallized in a single mass, then separated and moved across the globe—impelled by the earth's rotational force—until they came to rest upon their present sites. (A glance at the map shows that the eastern coastlines of the Americas fit those of Western Europe and Africa like the pieces of a jigsaw puzzle.) But most geophysicists hold that the continents have built up gradually, and that the process of continent building is still going on in volcanic areas today as globs of matter continue to rise and fall in the hot mantle of the earth. Any hypothesis about the formation of the continents is difficult to sustain, however, for every assumption must rest in turn on other assumptions about the formation of the planet as a whole and its present internal composition. Perhaps the deepest challenge confronting geophysics today is to explain why all the earth's granite has been concentrated in a few continental masses, divided by vast tracts of graniteless ocean floor.

THE PRIMEVAL OCEANS are created when the temperature of the surface rocks falls below the boiling point of water. The great overhanging cloud masses that enshroud the young planet in impenetrable darkness condense and pour their waters into the basins and valleys of the earth. It rains for century on century. And as these greatest of all rains fall they begin the unending process of erosion, sweeping the earth's minerals down to the ever-hungry, ever-saltier sea.

THE PRIMEVAL LANDSCAPE takes form slowly over unknown millions of years after the first cooling of the earth's crust, as the bleak aboriginal rock is sculptured by two great antagonistic processes: the process of mountain building and the process of erosion. No sooner do new mountains arise than the falling rain begins to chisel them away, leveling their pinnacles, furrowing their ridges and shoulders, carving steep-sided canyons and widening valleys along their

THE COMING OF THE WATERS

AFTER the land cohered, the seas were made. As the rocks slowly hardened, water vapor and other gases released in the process of crystallization escaped from the hot interior of the planet, rose into the cool outer atmosphere and collected in enormous cloud masses that shrouded the earth in perpetual darkness. Sometimes in the upper reaches of the cloud canopy rain started to fall—only to boil and turn again to steam as it approached the scorching surface below. For possibly 1,000 years sunlight never penetrated this dense, self-renewing pall of sullen clouds. It must have taken at least that long, and probably much longer, for the new-formed crust of the earth to cool from the freezing point of rocks (1,000°–2,000°) to the boiling point of water. For while the ever-dissipating cataracts of rain sped the escape of heat from the simmering rocks, the dense blanket of clouds above served as an insulating barrier between the hot earth and the cold heights of outer space.

But at last the day came when the rains fell and did not boil away. And the falling waters then hastened the cooling of the atmosphere and quickened the condensation of the clouds. No one can say how long this greatest deluge of all time went on—perhaps for centuries. But when at last the clouds thinned, the primeval oceans glittered in the rays of the bright new sun. Many eons elapsed before the sea basins became full as they are today. In the beginning perhaps only 20% of the present volume of ocean waters lay in the low valleys and shallow depressions of the young earth's surface. But through geologic time water vapor has continued to effuse from volcanoes and fumaroles, adding to the moisture of the atmosphere and thus to the content of the seas. Since that first great flood the level of the earth's waters has risen and fallen many times; coastlines have changed; the seas have crept inland and receded; and the profile of the continents has been repeatedly revised.

As the earth's interior continued to cool, it contracted, shrinking away from its outer crust as a dried apple shrinks within its skin. And like the apple skin the earth's crust wrinkled, and the wrinkles were mountains. Other mountains appeared too wherever convection currents in the hot mantle folded the face of the land, as light molten materials near the surface converged on regions where heavy masses of rock were sinking.

In their infancy these first mountains must have had relatively smooth walls with rounded summits and gentle ravines. But their soft contours were quickly disfigured by the sculpturing action of air and water. Even before the rains began to fall, the humid primordial atmosphere, laden with corrosive gases, began to disintegrate the surface rocks, weakening them for the impact of the flood. The fierce rains came, their acid waters ate away the highlands with voracious speed, incising and eroding the landscape, producing changes which the bland rains of today would take millennia to effect. How many mighty ranges rose and fell in this first eon of prehistory no one can assert; their roots lie buried miles deep in the earth, strewn in the sediments of the sea, lost in the ruins of time.

lower slopes. And all the time, as the forces of destruction do their work, volcanoes bring forth new supplies of lava from the uneasy depths, hurling ever thicker covers of molten rock upon the primal crust. At some unknown point in this shadowy era, and through some unknown process, life appeared. One of the earliest forms of life is visible in this painting; the purple bacteria which give color to the lake shown at left, just as they redden certain lakes on earth today.

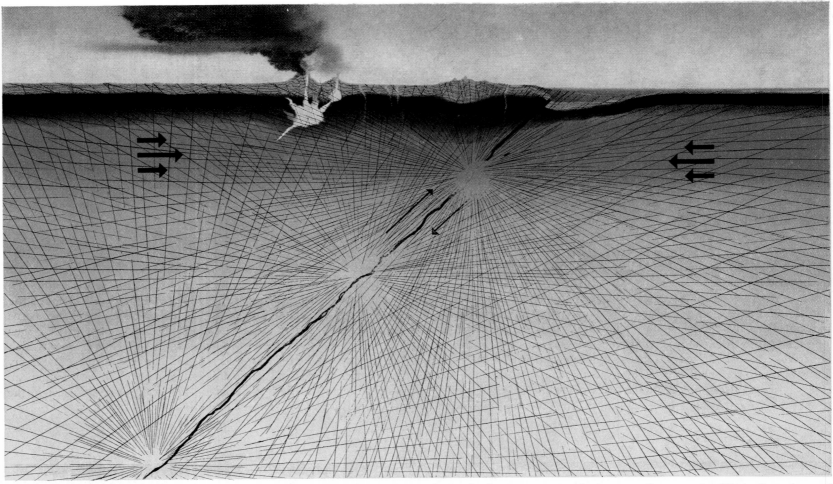

MOUNTAINS ARE CREATED by some such process as the one shown above. As the earth cools it contracts, producing tremendous horizontal stresses (triple arrows) which warp the crust. Along the coasts this pressure forces the higher land masses to override the ocean floor, creating "faults," or planes of weakness, angling downward for 350 miles. Here frequent slippages (diagonal arrows) occur, accompanied by earthquakes (radiating lines) and volcanic action.

THE BUILDING OF MOUNTAINS

THROUGHOUT geologic time, periods of violent mountain building, when the earth's crust readjusted itself to thermal contraction and the changing stresses of its load, have alternated with longer periods of calm, when the implacable rains drilled away at the mountaintops, leaching out their minerals, carving canyons and gorges, sweeping the substance of the mountains down to the insatiable sea. Then for millions of years the earth lay flat and the oceans rose from their basins and encroached on the continents, and the land was level and featureless, save for slow rivers and shallow inland seas—until once again the crust revolted and new mountains arose.

Somewhat more than one billion years ago there came an age of prodigious upheaval which geologists call the Laurentian Revolution because the roots of some of the great mountains that were reared then still lie embedded in the Laurentian Hills of eastern Canada. All over the world the earth's crust revolted, warping upward and downward to form oceanic deeps and vast mountain chains. Here and there the process of crustal uplift was accompanied by earthquakes and volcanic outbursts. The Laurentians, in particular, were born of a succession of volcanic activities more furious than any the earth has since known—vast upwellings of molten rock that engulfed two million square miles of the region around Hudson Bay in a cover of lava two miles thick. Although changed, the lava is still there today—the great granite floor of the Canadian Shield. The Appalachian Chain came into existence 200 million years ago, a range then splendid as the modern Alps but now long since leveled by erosion, so today only its underlying folds remain to suggest the snow-crowned peaks that once marched unbroken from Newfoundland to Alabama.

All the high mountains of the modern earth—the Himalayas, Rockies, Alps, Andes—were created within the last 60 million years. Scarcely one million years ago the youngest of all, the Cascade Mountains of our own West Coast, arose out of the sea accompanied by outbursts of volcanism whose traces are everywhere visible in the West. Nor has it ceased yet. All around the Pacific, volcanoes form a ring of fire. There is evidence that the Himalayas and other mountains are still growing. For we are living even now in a revolutionary age of mountain building. All of human history has been enacted during one of the earth's brief interludes of splendor when mountains transfigure the planet's ordinarily flat countenance. There have been at least 10 mountain-building epochs since the beginning—perhaps many more.

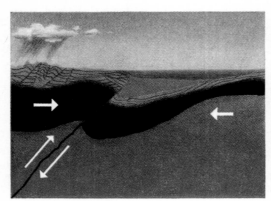

THE SEA FLOOR SAGS as stresses and slippages continue, creating coastal deeps. Here thick sediments collect, adding to pressure along the fault.

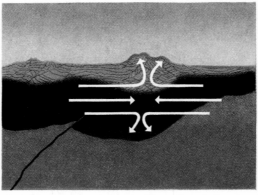

THE CRUST CRUMBLES when the fault gives way, crushing sea floor and continent together and thrusting them upward to form a mountain range.

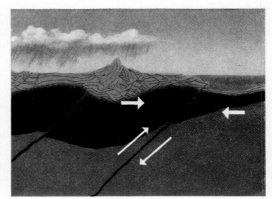

A NEW FAULT APPEARS under the new continental shelf and the cycle repeats. Meanwhile rains sculpture the new mountains and wear the old away.

THE OCEAN FLOORS, originally flat basalt plains lying one to five miles below the granite mass of the continents, were deformed in time by the same internal forces that produced many of the features of the land. Mountain ranges and deep submarine gorges creased the depths. Volcanic cones rose, ejected lava, sometimes formed islands and sometimes disappeared. In this picture appear two of the peculiar flat-topped mounts that still rise from the mid-Pacific floor.

GLACIERS MOVE ACROSS THE EARTH throughout geologic time, sculpturing the final scene—planing the floors of valleys, scouring the soil from fertile lands and leaving behind them new rivers and lakes. The first ice age probably refrigerated the earth a billion or more years ago. Since then glaciers have advanced and retreated many times. Each time the ice sheets, often 4,000 feet thick like the one shown above, have changed the face of the land, crushing trees

and vegetation and forcing animal life inexorably toward the Equator. When they reached land's end they sheared away in grim, glittering cliffs, glowering briefly above the sea, then crashing piecemeal into the open water in giant icebergs.

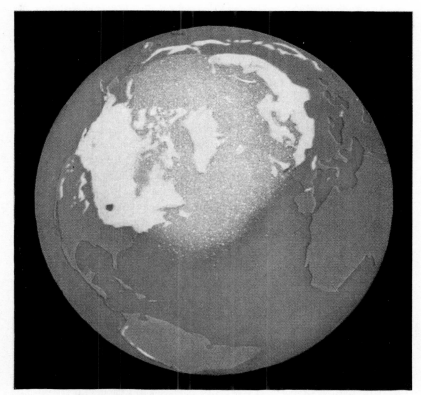

THE LAST GREAT ICE CAP, which began spreading southward a million years ago, glaciated northern Europe, Asia, America, and the high places of both hemispheres. It began its last shrinkage 10,000 years ago and is still receding today.

THE MARCH OF THE GLACIERS

WE live today in a glacial age. Wherever tall mountains stand there is snow and ice; and geology reveals that many epochs of mountain building have been accompanied by one of glaciation. Mountain chains impede the flow of air, and land bridges that arise in times of continental uplift divert the warm currents of the oceans, producing local climatic extremes. During the Appalachian Revolution, which affected both northern and southern hemispheres, ice caps covered Africa up to the Tropic of Capricorn, and South America to within 10° of the Equator. Yet the vagaries of glaciers suggest that their recurring presence cannot be explained as an effect of mountain building alone.

The causes of the earth's periodic ice ages constitute one of the deepest enigmas of geo-history. Some scientists have explained them by atmospheric factors—changes in the chemical composition of the air, or lingering clouds of volcanic ash that might filter out the sun's warm rays for periods of time. Others have suggested astronomical causes, like fluctuations in the intensity of solar radiation, or shifts in the position of the earth with respect to the sun. Yet no one factor suffices; perhaps all of them must operate together.

The last and possibly greatest series of all ice ages began one million years ago. Glaciers covered more than one fourth of the earth's land surface. In our hemisphere they extended south as far as Louisville, Ky. Sheets of ice two miles thick bestrode the mountains of New England, hollowed out the Great Lakes, shaped the Mississippi and Missouri river valleys, stripped the soil from eastern Canada and deposited it in our Midwest. At least four times the glaciers advanced and retreated during this last epoch of refrigeration.

Today we are just emerging from the last great advance which reached its climax about 10,000 years ago. About one tenth of the earth's surface is still permanently glaciated. Greenland and Antarctica, where in other ages vegetation thrived, lie capped by five million cubic miles of ice. Glaciers still armor the mountains of Alaska, New Zealand and Scandinavia as well as the loftier Himalayas, Andes and Alps. Yet in the last 200 years there has been a marked retreat. Hotels in Switzerland, built at the turn of the century to command scenic vistas of ice, today have no glaciers in view. The Arctic and Antarctic ice packs recede yearly. Probably the earth's climate will become increasingly warm for several millennia. Should present ice caps melt completely the profoundest consequence will be the raising of sea level by more than 100 feet—enough to submerge New York, London, Paris and most of the coastal areas of earth.

DESTINY OF THE EARTH

IN ages to come the relentless alchemy of glaciers, wind and water, and the imprisoned fury of the primal fires within the earth's thin crust will repeatedly revise the features of man's world. For the earth is still young. Though man has known but a thousandth part of the time since living things first stirred in pre-Cambrian seas, though life itself is but the most recent chapter of geologic time—yet the earth is still young. Its existence will doubtless continue as long as the sun's, and the sun is a long-lived, slow-burning star. The best testimony of astrophysics suggests that the solar fuel supply will last for many billions of years. Barring some rare catastrophe like a stellar collision, the earth should continue to wheel in its orbit so long as the sun remains unchanged. Astronomers used to believe that in the end the sun would simply fade, like a dying ember, and that as its brilliance dimmed, terrestrial life would succumb to the chill of space, the oceans would freeze, the continents revert to barren rock. But they know more today about the processes that keep the stars alight. And they suspect that stars do not die peacefully. It appears that man, or whatever he may become, is destined to perish not of cold, but by fire, and that the earth will finally feel the fervors, as Heraclitus believed, of primordial flame.

Perhaps three to 10 billion years from now the hydrogen that lights our sun will begin to run low, and as it dwindles certain dynamic processes will come into play to make the sun expand. Millennium by millennium the sun will swell, at first slowly, then more rapidly, evolving about 15 billion years from now into what astronomers call a "red giant," like Betelgeuse or Antares—diffuse, distended stars 80 to 100 times their original size. In this stage its monstrous, swollen body will fill the entire orbit of the planet Mercury. The temperature on earth will rise to 1,300°. Red light will bathe its tortured surface. All living things will shrivel, the oceans will boil away and the very atmosphere will be driven into space. Then, for countless centuries to come, the scorched and lifeless planet will turn on the grill of the dying sun. The end is pictured in Revelation in one of the striking parallels between Biblical and modern scientific prophecy: "*And the fourth angel poured out his vial upon the sun. . . . And men were scorched with great heat . . . and the cities of the nations fell.*" If by some miracle of ingenuity man somehow succeeds in surviving underground, it is conceivable that the earth could blossom once again, for the sun will finally shrink as once it swelled, and the temperature on earth will fall. But as the sun grows smaller it will shine ever more faintly, until eventually, 30 to 50 billion years from now, its last fires will flicker out forever and unending night will reign.

In the enormous span that lies between our present epoch and the future holocaust, however, nature's great recurring rhythms will repeat themselves, as they have times without number in the past. Each day the rains and running waters will sweep eight million tons of the land's substance into the sea, until all the towering peaks we know lie crumpled on the ocean floor. But new summits will arise. And again, at intervals so vast as to be meaningless in man's meager dimension of time, the earth's face will buckle, volcanoes will roar, glaciers will abrade the plains and forests, leaving new lakes and rivers in their wake, and the seas will rise and fall. Man's world is hence but a tiny interlude in terrestrial time. And on a still vaster scale, discerned by the philosopher Sir Thomas Browne three centuries ago, "The created world is but a small parenthesis in eternity."

THE MIRACLE
OF THE SEA

THE MIRACLE OF THE

> To me the sea is a continual miracle,
> The fishes that swim—the rocks—the motion of the
> waves—the ships with men in them,
> What stranger miracles are there?
>   WALT WHITMAN, *Miracles*

MEN have always recognized the sea as a supreme wonder and paradox of the natural world—at once a thing of beauty and terror, a barrier and a highroad dividing and uniting mankind, a source of life and a fearful and capricious destroyer. The sea poets of every land have sung in exaltation of its sunlit moods and in awe of its fury and fathomless deeps.

Today in the light of man's increased awareness of the universe it has become clear that the sea is in many ways a miracle. We know now that we are dependent on the sea not only for certain accessories of existence but for the very character of existence itself. The entity called life emerged from the sea; the basic fabric of all living things was initially determined by it; the entire system of nature composing man's "environment" is governed by it. More than any other physical feature of the planet it is the sea that makes the earth unique.

If somewhere in space an extraterrestrial astronomer should examine our solar system he might name our planet Sea rather than Earth (a word connoting land or soil). For the characteristic that would impress itself most vividly, setting us apart from other satellites of the sun, is the great glistening sheath of water that permanently envelops nearly three quarters of the globe. No other world in range of man's vision has a sea. Mars discloses ice caps, some moisture, perhaps vegetation, but no sea. Mercury appears to have no water at all. Venus lies veiled behind dense clouds which, unlike the clouds of earth, probably contain neither oxygen nor water. The outer planets are too cold to have a sea—the temperature of Jupiter rests at 216° F. below zero, that of Saturn at 240° below.

But our earth is nearly drowned in water. Only 29% of its entire crust climbs above the great oceans that hide all the rest of the planetary surface under a liquid overlayer approximating two miles in depth. South of the equator the seas engulf 81% of the hemisphere. If all the land areas of earth—continents, islands, mountains—were somehow torn from their foundations and hurled into the sea, they would displace only 1/18th of the total volume of water in the ocean basins. And if all the irregularities in the earth's crust were somehow ironed out, reducing the planet to a perfectly smooth sphere, the seas would then completely submerge the globe beneath a uniform cover about 8,000 feet deep.

As he does with so many other aspects of his dependence on the manifold of nature, man takes for granted the abundance of water with which the earth is endowed. For, in a special sense, the miracle of the sea is the miracle of water. Only a few men of deep perception have ever realized this. St. Francis of Assisi, on his deathbed, composed a prayer containing the lines, "Praised be Thou, my Lord, for sister water, which is very useful and humble and precious and chaste," and thus with the insight of saintly humility affirmed his gratitude for a surpassing gift. Similarly, in desert regions or times of drought, men have acknowledged the worth of water. But the thought is always of fresh water—as if the salt sea, the ultimate source and reservoir of virtually all the earth's waters, fulfilled no function in the acquittal of man's needs.

Yet, in the universe as a whole, liquid water of any kind—sweet or salt—is an exotic rarity. Even in the lesser dimension of man's own terrestrial existence, water stands as one of the most remarkable compounds in nature, upon whose unique properties most of the features and processes of his physical environment—the atmosphere, the weather, the soil, and all living things—ultimately depend. For example, nearly all material substances expand when heated and contract when cooled (*e.g.*, the mercury in a thermometer). And so does water—save for a crucial anomaly: upon freezing it reverses the contraction process and expands by 9%. And this is the reason that ice floats on the surface of all lakes and rivers, instead of sinking to the bottom.

Although the properties of salt water differ somewhat from those of fresh water, sea ice also floats—a fact of crucial importance to the climate and ecology of the world. For if ice sank as it formed, the cold seas of the earth would be frozen solidly, save for a thin layer of surface melt water in the summer months—and so the constant interchange of warm and cold oceanic currents that serve to moderate and regulate the diverse temperatures of the planet would be profoundly impaired.

There are other peculiarities of water, still not fully understood, that affect the whole edifice of life on earth. Its heat capacity—highest of all liquids and solids in nature save for ammonia—enables it to absorb and store vast quantities of heat, so that the oceans are in effect great reservoirs of solar energy, helping to prevent climatic extremes. Water dissolves more substances than any other liquid—and it is this property that helps make the sea a repository of minerals and sustains the processes of erosion and sedimentation—the never-ending washing away and sweeping away of minerals and salts, sand, silt and soil from the land to the sea. These substances remain forever in the sea, providing rich nourishment for the minute organisms on which all marine life depends.

Perhaps most important of all, the freezing point and boiling point of water are, by comparison with related compounds, extraordinarily high; hence it can subsist in the liquid state within the temperature range given to the planet Earth. For contrary to common belief the liquid state is exceptional in the natural world; most of the matter in the universe seems to consist either of flaming gases, as in the stars, or frozen solids drifting in the abyss of space. Only within a hairline band of the immense temperature spectrum of the universe —ranging through millions of degrees—can water manifest itself as a liquid.

It is surely no accident that life as we know it exists only within this same tenuous temperature band. While certain insulated animals are capable of surviving in the frozen wastes of earth and a few simple organisms live comfortably in hot springs, the temperature limits of living matter fall well within the temperature limits of water. Nor should this cause surprise, for all living things not only use water but are largely made of it. The human body is about 70% water, of which one third is in the blood and other body fluids, and two thirds lies within the walls of living cells. It is, moreover, a fact of deep evolutionary significance that the chemical composition of man's blood is similar to that of sea water—in it swim all the elements of the sea though dispensed in different proportions. One reason is that we came originally, all of us, from the sea.

And the waters of the land originate—and come daily—from the sea. The great ocean basins of the planet hold some 300 million cubic miles of salt water. From this vast store 80,000 cubic miles of water are sucked up each year by evaporation and then returned by rainfall and the flow of rivers. More than 24,000 cubic miles of rain descend each year over the continents, replenishing the sweet water lakes and streams, springs and water tables on which all the animals and plants of the land depend for life. Out of this intricate skein of natural processes and the miraculous properties of water, the slender thread of organic existence has been spun. So in the end the miracle of water is the miracle of the sea.

PART II

SEA

The enveloping mantle of water, unique to the planet Earth, governs the entire system of nature in which man dwells

"BEHOLD THE SEA, The opaline, the plentiful and strong. . . ." Here along a rocky California coast the white spume of angry surf glows in the sunlight of a winter dawn. Stirred by the winds of an offshore gale, these foaming breakers batter sand and rock in the endless battle between sea and land, as the waves of other oceans batter other shores around the earth. Yet another day, another season, this turbulent sea will lap gently at the foot of the strand.

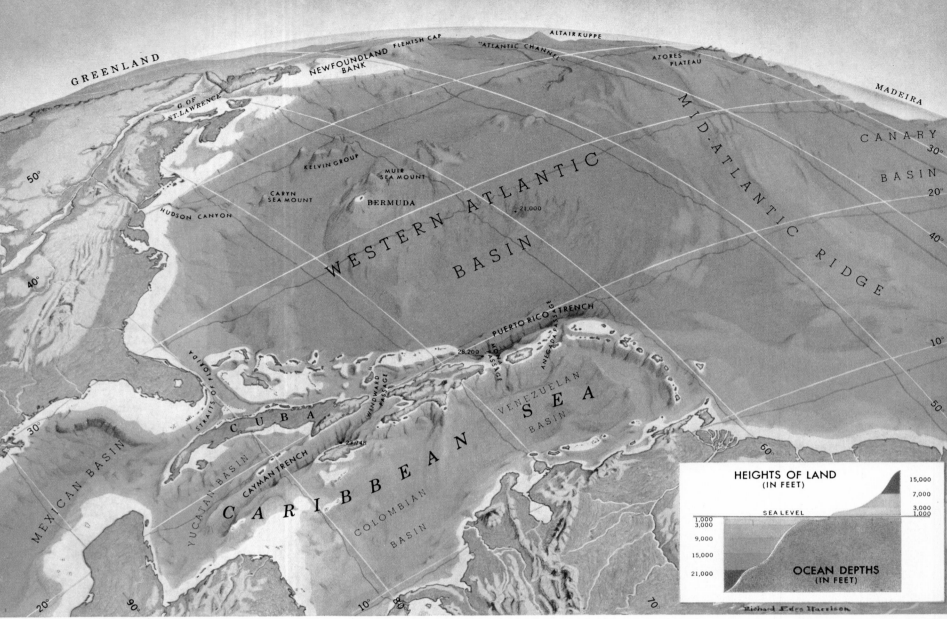

Within the map:
GREENLAND
NEWFOUNDLAND BANK
FLEMISH CAP
"ATLANTIC CHANNEL"
ALTAIR KUPPE
AZORES PLATEAU
MADEIRA
G. OF ST. LAWRENCE
CANARY BASIN
KELVIN GROUP
MUIR SEA MOUNT
CARYN SEA MOUNT
BERMUDA
21,000
WESTERN ATLANTIC BASIN
MID-ATLANTIC RIDGE
HUDSON CANYON
MEXICAN BASIN
STRAITS OF FLORIDA
CUBA
YUCATAN BASIN
CAYMAN TRENCH
22,748
WINDWARD PASSAGE
PUERTO RICO TRENCH
28,200
MONA PASSAGE
ANEGADA PASSAGE
VENEZUELAN BASIN
CARIBBEAN SEA
COLOMBIAN BASIN

HEIGHTS OF LAND
(IN FEET)
15,000
7,000
3,000
1,000
SEA LEVEL
1,000
3,000
9,000
15,000
21,000
OCEAN DEPTHS
(IN FEET)

Richard Edes Harrison

FROM MEXICO TO THE AZORES the Atlantic extends northeastward over the flat floor of the western basin, the volcanic rise at Bermuda, the submerged mountains of the Mid-Atlantic Ridge. Color scale at right shows the relative elevations of the land and depressions of the sea. The North Atlantic's deepest hollows are in the Cayman Trench (23,748 ft.) and in the Puerto Rican Trench (28,200).

THE ATLANTIC, owing to its many arms—like the Caribbean and Mediterranean—has more miles of coastline than the Pacific and Indian Oceans combined. In this view from the upper atmosphere the Mid-Atlantic Ridge can be seen winding down the middle of the ocean, dividing it into several basins. Most of the ridge lies 9,000 feet below the surface, though its highest peaks emerge as islands.

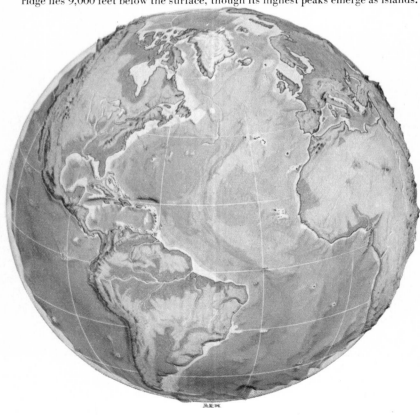

THE EXPLORATION OF THE SEA

TO the question, "How were the seas created?" there have been many answers. The author of the 95th Psalm sang simply, "The sea *is* His and He made it." Today scientists reply that the earth's waters came from volcanoes—from the interior of the terrestrial sphere. Sealed in the heart of the young planet from the beginning, water vapor and other gases erupted to the surface as the interior cooled, forming a dense pall of clouds which subsequently dissolved in the greatest deluge of all time. Most authorities agree that this first great flood could not have filled the ocean basins as they are filled today, or indeed supplied much more than 20% of the water that now laps high on the continental ramparts. But for thousands of centuries thereafter, as the earth's interior continued to cool and contract, new water was squeezed to the surface and disgorged by volcanoes through fissures in the ocean floor until, perhaps a billion years ago, the seas rose to their present levels.

The first men to set sail on the great waters outside the Pillars of Hercules believed that the ocean was infinite, flowing forever around the world like a great river, the final and inviolable frontier of the known. The Greeks called it *Oceanos Potamos*, the Ocean River. Until barely yesterday—a mere heartbeat ago in terrestrial time—the Atlantic horizon marked the terminus of Western man's affairs, the edge of the void. Beyond, in Milton's words, lay only "a dark/Illimitable ocean; without bound,/Without dimension; where length, breadth, and highth,/And time, and place, are lost."

And in a modern sense Oceanos *is* limitless. There are no separate oceans, there is only the sea, single and all-encompassing, girdling the planet, moving ceaselessly from deep to deep. In the watery wastes between Cape Horn and Antarctica the oceans are literally one; here a fated ship could conceivably sail east or west until time's end without ever coming within sight of land. But northward the continental land masses trisect the sea longitudinally into three great "gulfs" and it is these that geographers recognize as individual oceans; the hourglass-shaped Atlantic, the heart-shaped Indian Ocean, and the elliptical Pacific. Some scientists identify the ring-shaped Antarctic as a fourth ocean; the Arctic or North Polar Sea is conventionally assigned to the Atlantic.

Today the mystery that long enshrouded the surface dimensions of the sea has been dispelled, for ships have crossed and crisscrossed its farthest mist-hung wastes. But the dimension of depth remains to stir men's imagination and conjecture. Though in respect to the terrestrial globe the oceans represent but a thin film of water, it is the land beneath this film that beckons now as the last dark boundary of the planet—"throne of the Invisible."

Until the last half century few could even imagine the configurations of the oceanic abyss. Common assumption envisaged the sea basins as featureless—flat, drowned plains, stretching for league after lightless league across the great hollows between the continental walls. Knowledge of undersea topography was limited to shoal waters, for the operation of measuring depth with hemp ropes and sounding leads—the only method known prior to 1870—was a cumbersome and costly one. It often took several hours or an entire day for a single finding. Even after the development of more efficient wire gear the picture of the deep ocean floor remained fragmentary. By 1895 the world's navigation charts included only 7,000 soundings in depths greater than a mile (one per 12,000 square miles) and only 550 in depths of more than three miles.

So, for all the proud claims of 19th Century science, man could not truly say he knew the profile of his own planet—but only that three tenths of it which appeared above water. Then in 1920 came one of the most important developments in the annals of hydrography—sonic soundings, the method of measuring depth of water by timing the interval necessary for a sound impulse to travel to the bottom and back. Thus instead of taking hours, measurements were made in seconds, even in the deep sea. And soon soundings from many parts of the oceans began accumulating—faster than they could be plotted on hydrographic charts.

THE PACIFIC engulfs nearly half of the earth, extending from the nearly land-locked North Polar Sea to the endless ring of waters around the Antarctic continent. The ocean floor is serrated with many island festoons, incised by deep trenches, and embossed with more than 500 newly discovered submarine mountains. Below Alaska rises one of the longest, highest escarpments on earth.

FROM NEW GUINEA TO THE ASIAN COAST the Pacific floor reveals contours more varied and rugged than any on the planetary surface. The earth's deepest abysses are in the Philippine Trench (34,578 ft.) and the Mariana Trench (35,640 ft.). The Mariana Islands constitute a volcanic mountain range 500 miles long. In the distance lie the shoal waters of the great continental shelf of Asia.

IN A CANYON'S MOUTH at base of a continental slope, jellyfish, viperfish, sea devils, sea cucumbers, quill worms move through lightless depths a mile below last glimmer of sun. Cataract in background is a slump or seaslide of green mud and sand, similar to one that broke the Atlantic cables in 1929.

ON A MOUNTAIN LEDGE, nearly two miles down, squid, prawns, sea spiders, ribbon worms, glass sponges subsist precariously in a still colder frontier world of everlasting night. The rock pinnacle at left is an outcrop of volcanic basalt. The snowlike sediment frosting it is an organic marine ooze.

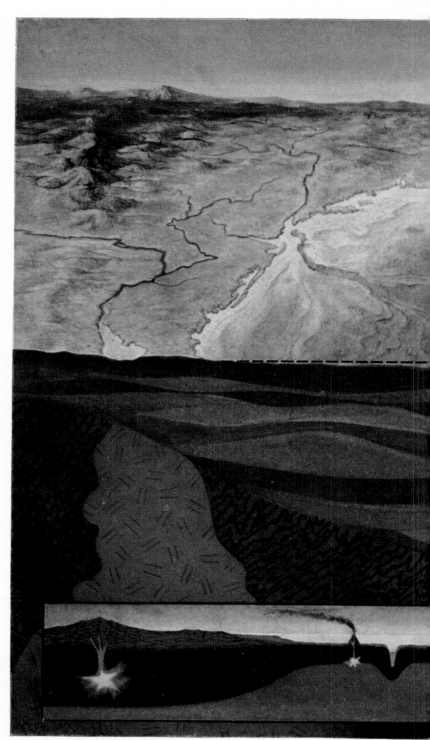

ATLANTIC SEASCAPE, drained of its waters, exhibits plains and mountains, canyons and escarpments mightier than any visible to man. At left is a characteristic Atlantic continental shelf, built of thick masses of sediment, slanting

THE PROFILE OF THE ABYSS

TODAY many unseen contours of the deep sea basins have taken form, and it is possible to visualize sections of the planet Earth as it would appear if stripped of its leveling mantle of water. Its image bears little resemblance to the familiar cartographer's globe or to the conceptions of those who pictured the sea floor as an undifferentiated plain. The submarine landscapes of the planet exhibit all the variety of those above the surface, together with a scale and grandeur such as the eye of man has never viewed in his domain of light and air. As on land there are mountain ranges, volcanoes, cliffs, plateaus and plains. Valleys and deep gorges furrow the floor. But the dimensions are more majestic—many mountains are higher, many ranges longer, many canyons and gorges immensely deeper. If the earth's topmost pinnacle, Mt. Everest (29,002 feet), were dropped in the deepest part of the ocean, it would lie submerged with a mile of water above its summit.

But there are differences between drowned and dry land regions other than those of scale. All the mountains and elevations of land wear the scars of the never-ending surgery of wind, rain and running water. Yet except for the occasional surgery of undersea landslides and the mild erosive action of deep currents, the mountains of the

PACIFIC SEASCAPE, whose generalized features are shown above, warps downward into abysmal trenches and is studded with flat-topped sea mounts or Guyots which marine geologists believe to be drowned volcanic islands. Around the bases of some sea mounts are moatlike depressions, hinting that the underlying rock may have sagged beneath the weight of the Guyot above. Erosion debris and coral skeletons on their flat tops suggest that they lay exposed to air and the planing

mud washed down from the land by rivers and rain. According to one calculation, some 3 billion tons of material from land is dumped annually into the sea.

In ocean basins the sea floor is covered with finer fabric: the marine oozes and red clay. Pink, white, yellow, red, green, brown—the oozes are the organic remains of incomputable numbers of minute sea creatures whose calcareous or silicious shells and skeletons have drifted down from above, century after century, in numbers meaningless to man. Mingled with them are certain more esoteric deposits—fragments of lava and pumice ejected by submarine volcanoes, lumps of manganese and iron, and mysterious magnetic spherules believed to be fragments of meteorites from outer space. Many of the mid-ocean basins are streaked with occasional layers of sand. How did the sand arrive in the middle of the deep sea? Alternative theories suggest that it was transported by wind or by turbidity currents meandering across the deep sea floor.

Of all the unseen scenery of the sea, perhaps none has so evoked the wonder and curiosity of marine geologists as the great mountain ranges whose treeless, snowless, sunless peaks and pinnacles rise out of darkness into darkness, wrapped in eternal night. The greatest of these is the Mid-Atlantic Ridge, which winds down the middle of the North and South Atlantic oceans from Iceland almost to Antarctica,

virtually unbroken throughout its enormous length, save for one major gap, the Romanche Trench, close to the equator. First discovered nearly a century ago during the laying of the transatlantic cable, the ridge is now known to be the mightiest single mountain system on earth—at least 10,000 miles long and 500 miles wide, more than twice the width of the Andes, and with many peaks loftier than most continental mountains. Although for most of its length its summits lie a mile or more below the surface, here and there a peak emerges into the world of air. These are the scattered islands of the Atlantic —Ascension Island, the Rocks of St. Paul, the Azores. The highest of all, Mount Pico of the Azores, towers 7,613 feet above the surface of the sea and plunges 20,000 feet below the surface.

Lesser ridges emboss the Pacific and Indian Ocean beds. The Hawaiian Islands represent the peaks of a 1,600-mile-long range that divides the Central Pacific Basin. The Hawaiian volcano Mauna Kea is the highest mountain on earth, a great lava dome rising about 31,000 feet directly from the Pacific floor, though only its final 13,823 feet appear above the sea. Virtually all mid-ocean islands are built of volcanic, basaltic material and thus differ geologically from offshore islands like Britain, Cuba and Newfoundland, which are actually appendages of the granitic continents beside which they stand. Most of the mountains of the sea are believed to be of volcanic origin, and

in truer horizontal scale, showing how the continents extend above and below the ocean floor. In the foreground a geological section shows the granitic and sedimentary rock of the continent, the underlying basalt of the ocean bed, and the volcanic fissures up which molten rock erupts to form submarine mountains and islands. Overlying the basic rock are layers of varicolored clay and marine ooze about 2,000 feet thick. The dotted line indicates the surface of the sea.

River and all its tributaries, which may arise from great canyons off Greenland. No one today can explain the origin of submarine canyons. Their proximity to rivers—as with the 150-mile canyon off the Hudson and the 145-mile canyon off the Congo—suggest that they might have been carved by river water at a time when a widthdrawal of the sea exposed the continental slopes. Yet some of these gorges lie more than three miles below the surface, and no one accepted theory of rising and falling sea levels can account for a recession to so great a depth. Some authorities have proposed that the canyons might have been incised by faults in the earth's crust, by earthquakes, by submarine mud flows or landslides, or by the erosive action of deep-lying, silt-laden "turbidity" currents. On occasion these forces may interract to produce some of the most dramatic events that occur beneath the sea, as on November 18, 1929 when a severe earthquake shook the continental rampart south of Newfoundland. In consequence, masses of sediment, loosened by the shock, came tumbling down the continental slope in great mud-dark cataracts which swept out across the ocean floor, snapping transatlantic cables up to a distance of 300 miles from the coast.

At the base of the continental slopes, drowned in the eternal cold and darkness of opaque miles of water, lies the deep ocean floor, nadir of man's world, comprising half of the total surface of the planetary sphere. In a sense the term floor is misleading, for only in certain places, like the great eastern Atlantic basin and a vast volcanic plain in the Indian Ocean southeast of Ceylon, does the deep sea bottom exhibit the flatness and homogeneity one associates with a floor. All the ocean beds are ribbed and corrugated, grooved by elongated trenches, separated by mountain ranges and subdivided by transverse ridges and island chains into groups of smaller basins. So each ocean has many floors—as many as it has basins—each with its own contours, each carpeted with varied layers of sediment.

Over the basic rock underlying all the ocean bottoms these sedimentary layers—product of a billion years of deposition of organic and inorganic debris, flaking slowly downward from the surface waters —average a half mile in depth. They come chiefly from two sources— from the erosion and disintegration of rock on land, and from animal and plant remains. Some oceanographers have estimated that they accumulate from the surface at the rate of one inch per 2,500 years, others that in certain areas deep currents flowing along the bottom may from time to time deposit as much as 10 feet in a single day. Yet the sediments vary from basin to basin and sea to sea. In parts of the Pacific they lie less than 1,000 feet thick over the basalt basement, and in parts of the Atlantic they have piled up in great deposits nearly two miles in depth. On the continental shelves and canyon deltas the deposits consist largely of coarse particles—sand, silt and

ocean floor stand untouched and immutable in the calm depths, insulated against time and change by the cover of the sea. Only those loftiest mountaintops that rise above the surface and that men call islands feel the bite of wind, surf and rain.

Though the ocean basins differ from one another topographically as much as Africa from Asia, or North from South America, they share certain massive features in common. Each is divided into three great areas or domains: the continental shelves, the continental slopes and the deep sea floor.

The shelves are the thresholds of the continents, the transition zones between land and water, during past ages alternately flooded and exposed to air with the rise and fall of the sea. While a few sections of continental coastline and many islands plunge abruptly into the depths, most of the earth's land masses are skirted by broad belts of shoal waters, sloping gently downward to depths of 200 to 600 feet, running outward from the land for a distance of 10 to 200 miles. Off young mountainous coasts, such as the western shores of North and South America, the continental terraces are likely to be narrow. But off lowland coasts and the mouths of great rivers they slant seaward mile after gentle mile. The most extensive shelf on earth, with an area of more than a million miles, lies off the southern coast of Asia. The widest shelf on earth stretches northward 800 miles from

Russia into the Arctic Sea. Scarred by scattered ridges, drowned river valleys and glacial troughs, the broad, muddy, sandy floors of many shelves bear reminders of vanished epochs when the seas rode lower and they belonged to the land. It is near the shelves and in the shoal waters around islands and coral reefs that the rich and multifarious life of the sea chiefly abounds. (Later portions of this book deal in detail with the subject of marine life.)

At the outer brink of the continental shelves the submerged terraces of the land drop away in immense slopes often 100 miles long, plunging 12,000 to 18,000 feet into the abyss—the longest unbroken escarpments on the face of the planet. Though some precipices are steeper, no mountain walls on land fall in so continuous a sweep from summit to base. In a few areas where the sea floor has warped downward into offshore deeps or trenches the continental slopes plummet as much as 30,000 feet in a single stupendous decline. The facades of these ocean ramparts are not smooth but deeply seamed and fissured with canyons and gorges, often deeper and grander than those of the land, cutting back into the continental shelves and fanning out below upon the ocean floor in complex radial branches or in lengthy channels which may spread out for a thousand miles. In the Atlantic between Bermuda and the Azores oceanographers have recently discovered a system of channels as vast as the Mississippi

action of waves. At the center of the panorama is a typical oceanic trench, 10 miles wide, 25,000 feet deep, edged on the left by rolling hills of a 30-mile-wide submarine ridge. At the bottom of the trench lie untold layers of sediment, perhaps six miles deep. To the right the continental slopes climb to a characteristic Pacific-type borderland, differing from the Atlantic-type shelf in that it is grooved and furrowed with subsidiary basins and ridges. At the extreme right

thus, too, differ fundamentally from many of the mountains of dry land. Although volcanic activity often accompanied the building of the continental ranges, many of the great land systems rose slowly over the centuries through the imperceptible folding and faulting of the surface crust. The long geometrical patterns of the underseas ranges suggest they were formed by the opening of extended faults or fissures in the ocean floor. Through these crustal cracks hot molten rock welled up to build the long mid-ocean ranges and island festoons of the earth's seas.

In addition to great ridges and volcanic chains, the oceans conceal another form of submarine mountain the like of which man's eye has never viewed: the "Guyot" or flat-topped sea mount. No marine geologist had ever envisaged such a structure or suspected its existence until naval vessels equipped with Fathometers found more than 150 of them in the Central Pacific during World War II. Since then more than 500 have been charted in the Pacific and a few in the Atlantic plains. Like the offshore canyons the Guyots present a major challenge to oceanographic theory. They appear to be volcanoes whose tops were planed smooth by wave action at some period when they stood above the sea. Yet today their truncated tops lie submerged beneath a half mile to a mile of water—"drowned ancient islands," as their discoverer called them. It may be that ocean levels have risen

since they first sprang from the depths. But it is more likely, authorities agree, that they sank, either from their own weight or because of some general catastrophic collapse of the contiguous ocean floor.

As there are valleys on land, so there are valleys under the sea. But many of the valleys of the ocean floor are deeper, more forbidding far, more alien to the experience of man than even the wildest Himalayan gorge. Every ocean has its deeps—long, narrow crevices or chasms in the sea floor where the bottom falls away as though some titanic force had sucked the crust inward toward the earth's core. No mountain peak thrusts as far above the sea's surface as these great oceanic trenches fall beneath it. Curiously they appear near the continental slopes or along the edge of island arcs rather than isolated in mid-ocean. No one can say what stupendous stresses caused the sea floor to warp downward into these chasms. But their proximity to island chains and volcanoes suggests that there may be a reciprocal relationship between the upheaval of mountains and the down-thrusting of deeps, as though the earth's crust always maintained a changing balance of elevation and depression, height and depth. Some authorities believe that the oceanic deeps may actually represent future appendages of the continental shelves. For into these lightless troughs, century after century, turbidity currents carry sediment from land and the ocean floor, piling it layer on layer, possibly mile on mile. And so in

a range of continental mountains and a land canyon drawn to the scale of the Grand Canyon of Arizona emphasize the difference in dimension between the contours of the land and the majestic hidden mountains and valleys of the sea.

time the imbalance of stresses might have caused the abyssal floor to buckle, thrusting the masses of sediment upward to form a new mountain range or island chain. Some of the earth's coastal mountains reveal sedimentary rocks containing fossils from the sea. And many of the continental edges disclose long parallel arcs of diversified rocks, some of them believed to be of deep ocean origin—like growth rings in the tree of geologic time. But in the present state of man's knowledge, no theory fully defines either the origin or destiny of the oceanic trench. It takes its place with other unsolved riddles of the sea, yet transcends them in mystery and awe. For the deeps are ultimate fastnesses of Earth, eternally cold, eternally dark, crushed beneath pressures of seven tons to the square inch.

The complexity and wonder of the sea resides, however, not only in the realms beyond man's view, but in its everlasting motion—the visible rise and fall of tides, the furrowing of its surface by wind and wave, and the subtler streaming of its great currents, flowing from pole to pole, east to west and west to east, from sandy shelf to dark abyss, keeping "eternal whisperings around/Desolate shores." In a wave lapping a familiar beach there may be droplets that once came from the Antarctic Sea, or droplets from the hot saline waters of the Persian Gulf, or from Baffin Bay, the Coral Sea or the Straits of Madagascar. And so in a real sense "deep calleth unto deep."

ATOP A GUYOT, or flat-topped sea mount 1,200 feet down, hatchet fish, eel larvae, lantern fish and sea fans dwell in an intermediate zone high above the ocean floor (*background*). Strange doughnut-shaped object on ground is a sea biscuit. Brink of the Guyot is paved with dead coral remains.

ON AN OFFSHORE BANK, 600 feet down, marine life flourishes prolifically in a twilight domain too dark for plant life but favorable to creatures like porpoises (*top*), the goggled rat-fish and prickly skate (*center*) and sea cucumbers, hermit crabs and starfish (*below*). Plantlike objects are actually animals.

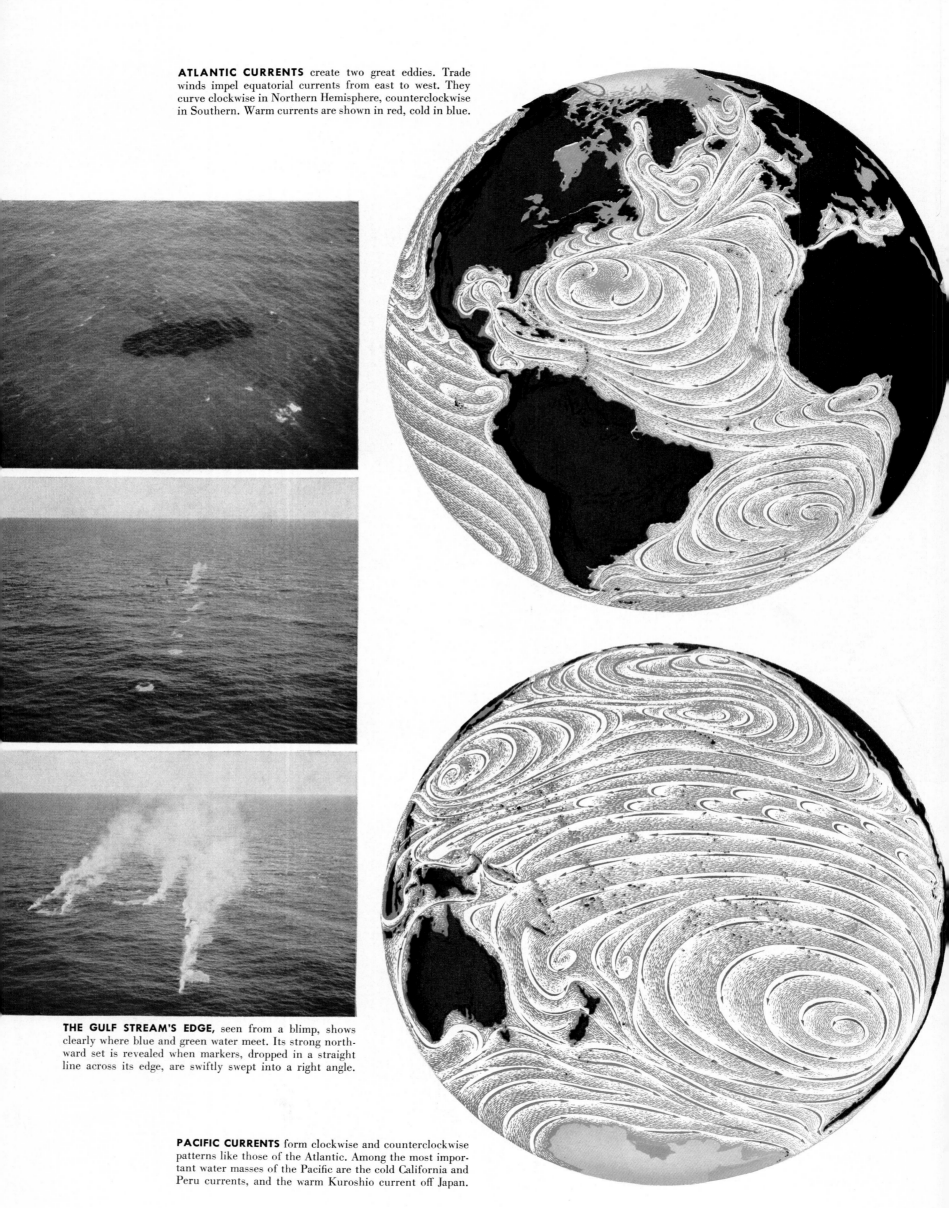

ATLANTIC CURRENTS create two great eddies. Trade winds impel equatorial currents from east to west. They curve clockwise in Northern Hemisphere, counterclockwise in Southern. Warm currents are shown in red, cold in blue.

THE GULF STREAM'S EDGE, seen from a blimp, shows clearly where blue and green water meet. Its strong northward set is revealed when markers, dropped in a straight line across its edge, are swiftly swept into a right angle.

PACIFIC CURRENTS form clockwise and counterclockwise patterns like those of the Atlantic. Among the most important water masses of the Pacific are the cold California and Peru currents, and the warm Kuroshio current off Japan.

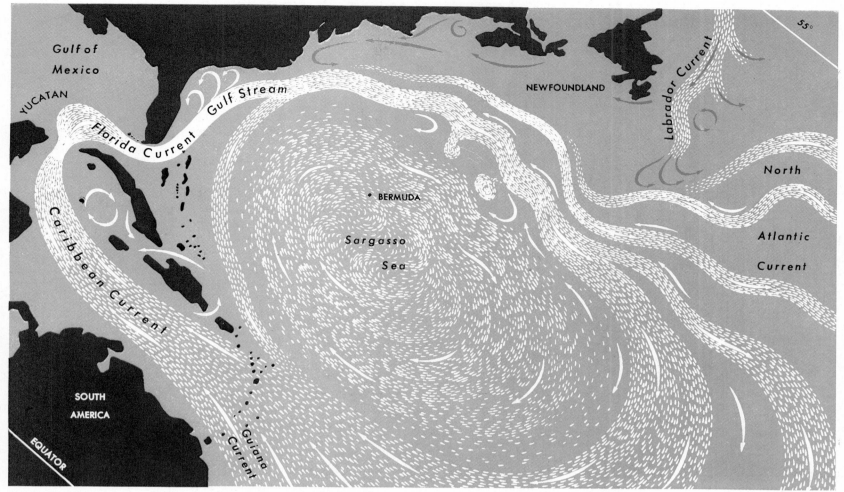

THE GULF STREAM is actually a series of warm streams curving from Yucatan to Europe around the rim of the Sargasso Sea. Fed by the Guiana and Caribbean currents, it speeds past Florida, widens, and then becomes four streams, one of which skirts the cold Labrador current to produce fog over the Grand Banks.

THE CIRCLING CURRENTS

THE forces that unite the oceans and keep them in reciprocal motion are intricate and interlocking, but essentially they are three in number: the wind, the rotation of the earth, and the changing density of water (which varies with its temperature and salt content). Climate, gravity, and the friction of the water against the earth also play smaller parts in perpetuating the motion.

Although local winds may be created by local conditions, the steady planetary airstreams directed by the rotation of the earth are the Trade Winds, which blow out of the northeast just above the equator and out of the southeast just below it, and the Westerlies, which are closer to the poles and blow in directions opposite to the Trades. It is the Trades that give the initial impulse to the great westward-rolling equatorial currents from which most of the oceans' complex surface movements evolve. In every ocean the equatorial currents, riding from east to west with the Trades, are bent gradually to north and south by the force of the earth's rotation. As they near the continental barriers, they swing southward in the Southern Hemisphere, creating a great counterclockwise eddy; in the Northern Hemisphere they turn northward forming a clockwise swirl.

From each of these major systems a complex of secondary current systems then develops, each of them profoundly affecting the climate and economy of the adjacent lands. The most famous is the great North Atlantic Current known to mariners for more than four centuries as the Gulf Stream. Until recently it had been envisaged as a single integrated "river" within the sea, sweeping in a steady arc from Florida to the coast of Norway. But now oceanographers believe that it consists of four narrow streams, separated by countercurrents, and meandering in wavy paths which continually change position and even occasionally break off into broad eddies 100 miles wide. Varying with place and season the current may transport as much as 72 million cubic meters of water per second (almost 1,200 times the volume of the Mississippi) at a maximum speed of six miles an hour.

But it is not the winds alone that keep the seas in motion. There are invisible slopes within the water, sloping surfaces created by variations in temperature and salinity, which are caused for the most part by rain and evaporation of water by the sun. Ocean temperatures at the surface range from 28° F. in the polar regions to 90° F. in the steaming basin of the Persian Gulf. Cold water is denser than warm water and therefore settles to the bottom, where day and night, the year around, the temperature remains at about 31° F. But salt content also affects the density of water. Red Sea water, for example, with a salinity ratio of 41 parts of salt to 1,000 parts of water, has a far greater density than that of the Baltic where rivers and rain keep the salt content low. And so throughout the earth's seas, unseen streams of water are continually welling upward and downward or gliding along secret ever-changing slopes of temperature and salt.

There are many currents in the sea that derive their energy from density differences alone. Most famous of these, perhaps, are the density currents that pass through the Straits of Gibraltar. In the Mediterranean basin rainfall is sparse and temperatures are high, so that month after month, under warm sun, water evaporates rapidly. It becomes ever saltier, ever more dense, and sinks to form a briny layer beneath the surface. This layer of salty water flows outward over the sill at the Straits of Gibraltar and thence downward into the deep sea until it reaches a depth of 3,000 feet, at which level it is no longer heavier than the waters around it. It then spreads horizontally across the Atlantic, finally losing its identity in the vicinity of Bermuda. As the Mediterranean deep water flows outward across the sill, the lighter, less saline water of the Atlantic flows inward on the surface to replace it. During the last war German submarines used this two-way current at the Straits to enter and leave the Mediterranean with engines silenced—riding in with the top Atlantic water, drifting out over the sill with the heavy water.

And so, one can visualize the great current patterns of the sea as two rotary systems. On the surface, blown by winds, are rotating sheets of water on whose rims lie the narrow, swift currents like the Gulf Stream, moving at speeds up to six mph. Below the surface are the deep density currents, groping their way poleward through the blind depths in superimposed layers, now rising, now settling along their invisible slopes. Some oceanographers estimate that a given particle of water in such a density current might take 10 years to slide from the surface layers at the Arctic to the abyssal depths near the Equator; others guess 2,000 years.

THE PULSE OF THE TIDES

IN addition to the progressive, continuous movements of the planetary waters, energized by winds and the earth's rotation, the oceans manifest more obvious periodic or reversible rhythms—the daily rising and falling of the tides, some of whose effects are shown in the pictures at left and opposite. First discussed in recorded history in the middle of the Fifth Century B.C. by that acute Greek observer, Herodotus, the diurnal tides remained a mystery—often attributed to the breathing of some giant sea monster—until Sir Isaac Newton related them to his theory of gravitation in 1687. Yet even today the complexity of tidal phenomena is such that no simple explanation suffices. The one familiar fact is that in many areas of the world, such as along the Atlantic Ocean, the tide rises higher and ebbs lower when the moon is either full or new: the spring tide. When the moon is in its first or third quarter the fluctuations are less marked: the neap tide. These variations derive from the fact that the earth's waters respond to the gravitational pull of *both* sun and moon, but the pulls are unequal. The moon, being closer to the earth, exerts a force more than twice as powerful as the sun's. During a new moon or a full moon, all three bodies—earth, moon and sun—are in line, so the gravitational influence of sun and moon abet each other to produce the spring tides. But during the moon's first and third quarters, sun, moon and earth stand at right angles to each other, neutralizing each other's influence and thus producing the lesser pulsation of the neaps.

Yet this is by no means the complete answer. The speed of tidal movements is determined by the depth of the water. Each inlet, bay and cove on earth exhibits its own unique rhythms and scale of rise and fall. At some places like Nantucket and Tahiti the tide lifts only a foot. At others like the Bay of Fundy in Nova Scotia it surges upward more than 40 feet, or, as in certain parts of the Amazon, it may form a 10-foot wall of water, or "bore." In most parts of the Atlantic the tides wax and wane twice a day, in some regions of the Pacific and Indian Oceans only once every day. These aberrations remained among the unexplained anomalies of the sea so long as the ocean floor was envisaged as a broad flat plain. But we know now that each ocean has many basins, and that within each basin the water tends to oscillate—to slosh back and forth like the water in a dishpan or a bathtub when it is disturbed. The size, shape and depth of each basin governs the period of oscillation, and it is this factor that produces irregularities in the time and magnitude of the tidal rhythms. When the harmonic movement of the waters in any basin happens to coincide with the pulse of the sun and the moon, the tides swing to extremes; when the rhythms fall in opposition they neutralize each other and tides are weak. A locality situated at either end of a basin will experience higher tides than one at the central node, in the same way that the ends of a seesaw experience more motion than the middle. The Bay of Fundy lies at the end of a basin whose period of oscillation is in step with solar and lunar rhythms. Its local contours, moreover, are such that the waters surge through a wide mouth into ever-narrowing estuaries. Twice a day 3,680 billion cubic feet of water rush in and out of this funnel, producing the greatest tides on earth.

LOW TIDE at Mont St. Michel, historic fortified abbey off Brittany, exposes 11 miles of sand and mud flats twice daily as falling water retreats across a smooth and imperceptibly sloping shore in one of the greatest tidal fluctuations on earth.

HIGH TIDE envelops the abbey's walls six hours later. Contrary to legend, the water comes in not in a fearsome wall but in a shallow flood advancing at the speed of a fast walk. Yet many have been overtaken by the tide here and drowned.

TIDAL TUNNELING through the vertical walls of chalk at Flamborough Head in Yorkshire, England has created vaulted caves which are fully exposed at low water. The arch at left was formed when a cave collapsed, leaving its entrance standing.

TIDAL MARSH near Brunswick, Ga. displays an intricate filigree of twisted channels into which the waters of the sea course each day at high tide and then withdraw. On low-lying shores such as this the rhythmic rise and fall of the tide often creates new land. Years ago this area was covered by the sea. Then an off-shore bar was built by sand-laden surf. Behind it sediment deposited by waves and washed down by streams from shore slowly accumulated to form a marsh.

A **BREAKING WAVE** arches above the sands of South Beach, Martha's Vineyard. Engendered by some distant storm at sea, it has traveled unknown miles to its destiny on this shelving strand. The breaking process begins a few yards offshore when the wave "feels bottom" and, slowed by the friction of its contact with the sea floor, changes shape. What had been a long, flat swell mounts upward, first into a rounded ridge, then higher into a narrow steep

THE RESTLESS WAVES

TIDES and currents serve man in many ways; waves have always been his enemies. Of all movements of the waters none have wrought more destruction or evoked more terror than waves—whether tossing white frothy manes in the open sea (*below*) or crashing on a wind-swept shore (*above*). To most people the term "wave" denotes any vertical rise or swelling of the sea. Actually there are three types of waves, differing in form and circumstances. A wave, when it first forms in wind-blown water, is called a "sea." When it has advanced out of a storm area and is traveling across calm water under its own momentum, it is called a "swell." And finally, when it reaches land and breaks, it is called "surf."

Water responds to extremely gentle movements of air. A zephyr wafting at a speed of no more than half a mile an hour is sufficient to start an oscillation of the surface strata that swiftly rises into a train of ripples. When the breeze freshens to two miles an hour the ripples evolve into waves that will then build themselves up so long as the air stream continues to press on their rear slopes and pull from in front. The size they eventually attain depends on three quantities: the velocity of the wind, the duration of the blow and the "length of fetch," which is the extent of the water over which the wind can travel without obstruction. For example, a 37-mile gale blowing across a bay only 12 miles wide could not produce waves more than 7 feet high; the same wind sweeping across 300 miles of water would raise 19-foot waves. In the oceans a 60-mile gale, raging for two days over a 900-mile expanse of open water can develop waves 40 feet in height, which is about the observed maximum. Winds of greater velocities, such as accompany hurricanes and typhoons, make the ocean surface fearsomely turbulent but do not engender extremely high waves because they blow the tops off the waves and are continually changing direction; it is the steady wind that incites nature's highest seas. Occasionally seamen report monstrous, pyramidal giants

STORM WAVES are created by the steady blowing of strong winds over a wide expanse of sea. The height which a storm wave may attain depends both on the violence and the duration of the gale and the extent of open water over which the storm rages. Most seas are only five to 12 feet high, even in a stiff blow, but a fierce two-day storm in mid-ocean may produce 30-foot waves, like the one shown here. Waves 50 feet high—and even higher—have been reported, though they are rare.

crest, laced with foam and sparkling with reflected sunlight (*left*). The crest hurries landward at a speed greater than that of the wave's forward slope. It hovers, curls forward (*center*) and then thunders with a final concentrated

explosion of power and fury onto the sand (*right*). Depending on wind conditions and the configuration of the beach, surf may take the form of lapping wavelets, spilling breakers or plunging rollers like those shown above.

of 80 to 100 feet, but these are isolated freaks caused by the chance collision and union of two or more wave trains.

Once a wave has been set in motion it will continue to run across the sea, even in a flat calm, traveling for thousands of miles: it has become a swell. As it progresses, its height (from trough to crest) diminishes, but its length (from one crest to the next) increases. Its speed also increases, so that eventually it is cruising faster than the wind that originally set it in motion. The great waves that occasionally arise from submarine earthquakes or landslides have been known to attain velocities of almost 500 miles per hour.

Contrary to popular belief, it is not the component water of a wave that thus sweeps over the sea, but only the wave form. An advancing swell may be envisaged rather as an undulation, like the wave pattern that shimmers over a field of standing grain before a gust of wind. The heads of grain bow in rhythmic sequence but remain attached to their separate stalks. Yet the analogy is not quite accurate, for in the case of water waves each individual particle of water does in fact move

forward slightly at about 1 or 2% of the velocity of the wave form.

Every droplet or particle of water in a wave swings in a circular orbit, as though riding on the rim of a wheel rolling in the direction of the wave's advance. The size of the orbit equals the height of the wave for surface particles; farther down the orbits diminish in size. When the wave reaches the edge of land, its size changes until its depth is half its length. Then the circular orbits of the water particles are flattened into ellipses, and the wave arches up and breaks as surf.

The energy contained in a breaking wave is tremendous. Measurements made with wave dynamometers have shown that waves sometimes strike with a force equal to the pressure of 6,000 pounds per square foot. The energy content of a four-foot swell, moving along a 100-mile front, would supply power to a city the size of Seattle for 24 hours. Storm waves battering coastal areas have been known to catapult stones through lighthouse windows 100 feet or more above the sea, to shatter piers and sea walls built of steel and concrete, and hollow great caverns in the walls of rock cliffs.

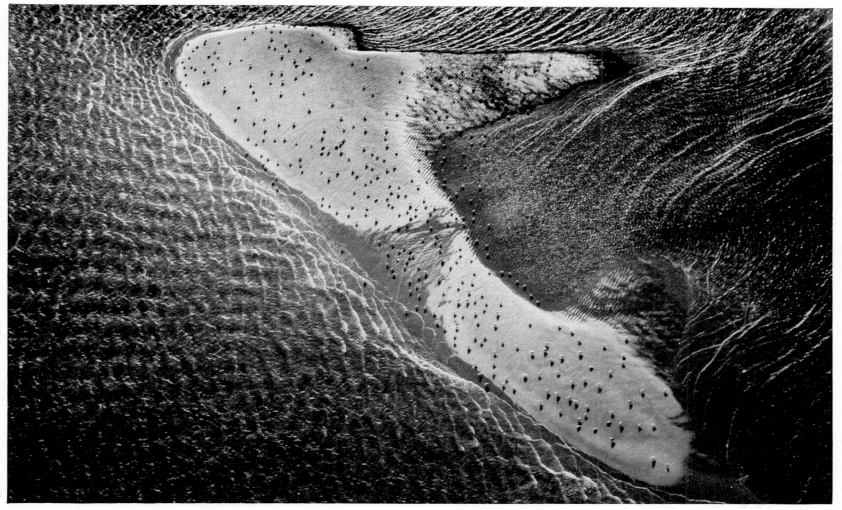

SWELLS are the aftermath of strong winds far out at sea. Waves of this kind, which are self-perpetuating echoes of spent storms, are driven by their own momentum across vast areas of windless water. Low, widely spaced and fast moving,

they cross the sea in ordered pattern to break at last on the shores of distant continents. Here, long swells from the open Atlantic (*lower left*) are shown curling around the ends of a sand bar off Cape Hatteras, where scores of seagulls roost.

THE SEA AS A BUILDER constructed these limestone ridges on the Great Bahama Bank. Over countless years the precipitation of chemicals in the water and the drifting down of the shells and skeletons of minute lime-bearing marine organisms created deposits which solidified into sedimentary rock. The ridges, shown here at high tide, are covered with sand and mud and creased with ripple marks formed by currents. The channels across the banks are 10 to 15 feet deep.

PEBBLE RIDGE in Devon, England has been built up by wave-tossed cobbles such as often are found along rocky coasts or at the foot of cliffs. During spring tides the surf often crashes upon the crest of the ridge, hurling stones 50 feet inland.

THE SEA AS A SCULPTOR

IN many phenomena of nature an uneasy balance of creation and destruction is maintained; and this is especially true of the sea. The hammering of waves may either erode a shore (*bottom, right*) or rebuild it (*top, right*). The shapes of the margins of continents and islands are mere temporary configurations appropriate only to contemporary maps; for every headland, beach and cliff on earth is either in the process of being built or eaten away. In general it is the big storm waves—throwing tons of water upon the shoreline, hurling boulders and cobbles against rock cliffs, and sweeping finer particles out to sea —that destroy. Moderate waves are builders; for the gentle swash and backwash of their waters carry numberless grains of sand, now landward, now seaward, now obliquely up the beach slope; then, having spent their force, they recede, leaving the grains where they fell.

Geologists now know a few sequences in the unending story of marine architecture. One is the sequence that takes place along "shorelines of emergence," where an uplift of the land or a lowering of sea level has exposed a part of the continental shelf. Here the shore is smooth and gently sloping, like the shelf itself, and the action of the sea tends to create new capes and swales and to form sandbars—barriers behind which tidal marshes develop. Many new miles of land may be built this way. The famous long beaches of the southeastern United States are typical constructions of the sea upon an emerged shoreline. But along "shorelines of submergence," like the jagged coasts of Maine and Scotland where the rim of the continent has sunk or the sea has risen to inundate inland valleys, different processes occur. Here the sea's action is a beveling operation, a slow planing down of peninsulas, headlands, rough crags and islands. Sometimes, across the mouths of bays or at bayheads, the waves construct beaches out of the waste products of the abraded cliffs. But in the end, when the sea's work is done, the shoreline presents a straight wall of marine cliff like the coasts of Dover or Calais.

In this long process the innumerable chisels of the moving sea may carve the bedrock into a variety of strange, grotesque or beautiful forms—sea caves, sea arches, hanging valleys, spouting horns and the lonely columnar monoliths called stacks. The sculpturing work of the waves is often amazingly swift, for each rock fragment or boulder that gives way is arrogated by the sea and turned as a battering ram against

LONG BAR BEACH, Flagler Beach, Fla., is characteristic of flat coastlines. Such beaches originate from formation of an offshore bar, often thrown up by storm waves. Thereafter more sand is deposited by light surf and coastwise currents.

CRESCENT BEACH in Dorset, England is a feature of rugged and indented coasts where the land slopes steeply into the water. The waves attack weaker zones of the rock cliffs, cutting series of arcs within which sand then accumulates.

A MONOLITHIC MONUMENT carved out of sloping limestone strata by the incessant surge of the sea along the Welsh coast, the Green Bridge of Wales is a natural arch in process of becoming a stack—an isolated, sea-girt tower of stone. Here, on a shoreline incised by many watercourses and progressively submerged as the sea rises relative to the land, fantastic forms are hewn in the forbidding, near-vertical cliffs bordering a gentle, mildly-contoured countryside.

the land. In many parts of the world soft rock coastlines are eroding at rates as high as 15 to 30 feet a year. But for every cliff that crumbles under the sledges of the sea, somewhere in the world a new curved beach is moulded by the drifting sand brought by quiet waves, a new sandy delta is formed by the sediment of branching streams, a new coral reef grows in the clear waters of a tropic lagoon, or a new island appears as some hidden submarine volcano breaks the surface. And so the boundary between sea and land is an ephemeral one. No coast on earth is the same for two successive days. Every wave that strikes the shore loosens here a pebble, replaces there a grain of sand.

Yet these changes, discernible in man's brief temporal scale, are insignificant beside the vaster changes that have occurred in the past and will occur again repeatedly until the end of time. For beyond local shifts in shoreline many worldwide transgressions and regressions of the ocean waters have occurred in rhythmic sequence throughout geologic history. Again and again the continents have been submerged beneath shallow seas. Some 250 million years ago during the geological epoch known as the Carboniferous Period, much of the central United States was one vast marsh; and 350 million years ago, in the Ordovician Period, the greatest inundation of all time reduced North America to a group of islands. Between such epochs there have been times when the land masses rode high above the seas, when most of the East Indies were part of the Asiatic mainland, and Alaska and Siberia were joined by a bridge across the Bering Strait. Many of the great marginal and inland water bodies of earth today—the North Sea, the Baltic, Hudson Bay and parts of the China Sea—are mere temporary invaders, usurping for a relatively brief moment the low areas of the continental shelves.

What forces produced these majestic floods, these immense, slowly recurring rhythms of the sea? Historical geologists believe that the answer involves two variables: 1) changes in the amount of water in the sea; 2) changes in the shape and depth of ocean basins. It is

SHELVES AND STEPS disclose the stronger layers in these rock cliffs near Point of Buckquoy in the Orkney Islands north of Scotland. In some exposed parts of the British Isles the coast is being eaten away at the rate of 15 feet a year.

GRANITE COLUMNS rise from Land's End, the most westerly point of England. Here waves and weather have gouged vertical fissures in the bedrock, forming these columns, which ultimately are undermined and tumble into the sea.

ROCK NEEDLES, REMNANTS OF AN ANCIENT CLIFF, TOWER ABOVE CANNON BEACH, ORE. AT SUNSET ▶

known for example that water is still emerging from the earth's interior through volcanic action; every time a submarine volcano erupts, a certain amount of new or "juvenile" water is discharged into the sea. But the quantity is inadequate to explain the huge fluctuations that have left their record in the past. Glaciers, however, have played a significant role in the changing levels of the ocean waters. For each drop of rain that falls on land and freezes is a drop of water lost to the sea. During the last million years recurring ice ages, when the glaciers thickened and advanced across the land, were reflected in falling sea levels. But between each ice age there were warmer periods when the glaciers melted and the seas rose again about the land. These alternating ages of refrigeration and warmth left their traces both in the scars of wave erosion on cliffs high above present sea levels and in the glacial grooves and drowned river valleys of the now-submerged continental margins. Today, as the icecaps of Greenland and Antarctica ("fossil" remains of the last great glacial age) slowly melt, ocean levels are again rising, at a rate of about eight inches per century. If all existing glaciers dissolve and the earth again becomes ice free, sea level would stand 65 to 165 feet higher than it does at present, and about one quarter of existing land areas would be submerged.

Yet even this 165-foot melt-water rise cannot account for the stupendous floods of the Ordovician and Cretaceous periods when the seas rose perhaps 600 feet and drowned about half the lands of earth. Still less can it explain the mile or more of water overlying the submarine flat-topped mounts that must once have known the air and felt wave action. The recurring exchange of waters between glaciers and the sea cannot provide the whole answer. Hence most authorities insist that the essential contours of the deep ocean floor must, from time to time, have been deformed by forces unknown. Volcanic cataclysms, rearing new mountain chains like the Hawaiian Islands, would have displaced thousands of cubic miles of water. Or perhaps the primeval fires that lie pent in the deep core of the planet created alternating convection currents or other pressures that caused the ocean floors to pulsate in age-long rhythmic intervals, now pumping water onto the continents, now drawing it back into the deeps.

One may ask, therefore, if a time may come when all the land areas of earth will be drowned in "the rising world of waters dark and deep." It is in contemplating this question that the intricate balance of natural forces fills the mind with deepest awe. For the antagonistic processes of mountain-building and erosion, crustal upheaval and crustal collapse, that have alternated throughout geologic history, are in a sense self-regulating. The higher the eminences of the land, the faster erosion levels them and sweeps their detritus to the sea. And the lower the land, the slower the work of erosion and delivery of sediment to the ocean floor. It is clear too that the earth's thin sensitive crust continually shifts its load, so that whenever the continental masses grow thin and light a new uplift occurs. Each leveling of the continents, each transgression of the waters is followed inevitably by an upward warping of the land and a recession of the sea.

So long as these forces are held in balance—so long as new mountains arise and volcanoes spew forth molten rock and the continental shelves respond to changing pressures—the land will remain above the waters and man will have a place to live. This is perhaps the ultimate miracle of the sea, as the author of Ecclesiastes implied when he said: "All the rivers run into the sea; yet the sea is not full."

THE FACE
OF THE LAND

PART III

THE FACE OF THE LAND

Its ever-changing features are molded by warring forces
that thrust up mountains and ceaselessly wear them away

There is nothing constant in the universe,
All ebb and flow, and every shape that's born,
Bears in its womb the seeds of change.

OVID, *Metamorphoses*

VIEWING the world of nature as a domain to be conquered and exploited for material ends, man looks with pride on the changes he has wrought about him. The stony encrustations of his cities and towns overflow and atrophy the green countryside. His steel rails and concrete roads dissect the prairies and reshape mountain passes. His towering dams block river valleys and create huge new lakes.

As he makes minor alterations to suit his needs man seldom discerns that the natural world may be undergoing vaster changes through agencies beyond his control and at a rhythm too slow for him to perceive. He once thought that the features of the earth existed always—an illusion derived not only from the brevity of human memory, but from the brevity of human history. Although the great mountains and valleys, plains and plateaus of the earth are older far than history, they did not exist always, nor will they persist until the end of time. Every hill and highland, cliff, crag and rock is being eaten away by rain, frost, wind and ice; and in time the mightiest mountains will be leveled and washed away into the sea. The "everlasting hills" of the poet do not exist—there are no everlasting hills.

Yet this does not mean that in the end the earth's surface will be reduced to a flat, featureless plain. For with every mountain that is obliterated from the earth, a new one comes into being. The face of the land is self-renewing and ever-changing, as mobile and inconstant in the long perspective of geologic time as its hovering cloud canopy appears in man's tiny temporal range. Even the earth's greatest relief features—the continental platforms and ocean basins—whose main outlines were molded in the planet's infancy do not preserve a wholly immutable relationship, but continually yield and recapture areas of their ever-shifting rival domains. And as the continental outlines recurrently change their pattern, now surrendering to the sea, now invading it, so the vertical profile of the land rises and falls in age-long cycles of upheaval and disintegration.

Every inch of the earth's surface is subject to immense antagonistic forces of construction and destruction, of lifting up and wearing down. The forces of uplift, originating deep in the interior of the planet, compel the crustal rocks periodically to buckle and bend upward, creating highlands, plateaus and mountain ranges. In opposition, the indomitable forces of the atmosphere strive incessantly through erosion to erase the earth's high places and to transport their substance by wind and running water to the valleys and the sea. Together these internal and external forces of creation and demolition have shaped the face of the planet since time immemorial. They are the coarchitects of every land form on the earth today.

In some areas of the earth the forces of construction appear momentarily to hold sway. Here the land is restless, shaken by earthquakes, perforated by active volcanic fissures which recurrently pour forth molten lava, cinders and ash, erecting new mountains that may change the horizon in a few months or years. Here too at a vastly slower tempo other mountains may be taking form—some by folding of the earth's crust, others by fracturing of the crust and

the uplifting of whole sections of the surface rock. Everywhere in such areas the rocks are freshly tilted and deformed; the mountains, high and precipitous, hunch sharp shoulders to the sky.

But wherever the forces of destruction are dominant, the landscape wears a different countenance. The hammering of rain, the surgery of running streams, the scouring of glaciers, persevering through eons of time, working together to cut down and eradicate the heights and promontories of the planet, produce in the end plains and lowlands, velds and prairies, steppes and flatlands, some studded perhaps with low, rounded hills or ridges of residual rock, others incised with broad valleys down which languid streams meander to the sea.

It was only two centuries ago that scientists began seriously to wonder what forces shaped the complex and enigmatic face of the land. In the beginning they fell into the human error of attributing to nature impulses and caprices as frenetic as man's own. It appeared that a deep canyon or rocky gorge must necessarily be the product of some ancient earthquake, a rift opened violently by a splitting asunder of the earth's crust; or that a wild vista of scarred and jumbled mountain peaks with sheer precipices, dizzy pinnacles and spires must be the monstrous wreckage of some huge catastrophe that shook the earth. Such inferences were understandable, for the most memorable events are violent ones; and since our civilization evolved around the rim of the Mediterranean—a region subject to earthquakes and volcanic action—the first earth scientists were inevitably "cataclysmists" or "catastrophists." Even as perceptive a man as Baron Cuvier (1769-1832), founder of the science of paleontology, saw in the existence of folded rocks and other geologic deformations arguments for catastrophism and asserted that a few thousand years before, some stupendous upheaval devastated the face of the land. "The dislocation and overturning of the older strata," he wrote, "show without any doubt that the causes which brought them into the positions which they now occupy were sudden and violent. . . . Living things without number were swept out of existence . . . whole races were extinguished. . . . The evidences of these great and terrible events are everywhere to be clearly seen by anyone who knows how to read the record of the rocks."

Not until geologists began to study exposed rock in ravines and mountain walls did they discover order in the apparent chaos and realize that it might be possible to deduce from the contours of the land what agencies ordained that in one place high peaks would penetrate the clouds and elsewhere plains would extend the horizon for mile after level mile. As clues reiterated, scientists came to understand that every feature of the earth, however disguised or disfigured by the ravages of time, was the product of a majestic scheme of opposing forces affecting the entire planetary sphere. They learned that the features of the earth's face could be adequately accounted for by cumulative processes, operating not only in the past but in the visible present. The valleys of the earth, they found, were not torn open by violent paroxysms of the planet's surface but were slowly excavated by running water over immense periods of time: the rain gully of today is the canyon of tomorrow. They discovered in the present the key to the past and, by the same token, the key to the future. "We find no vestige of a beginning," wrote the pioneer geologist, James Hutton of Edinburgh in 1785, "no prospect of an end."

UPLIFTED LAND, a fold of layered rock raised by subterranean pressure, created Sheep Mountain on Wyoming's Big Horn River. Millions of years ago the once-level sediments of an ancient sea bed were arched up into a massive dome far greater than the present mountain. Assailed by frost, wind and rain, its top was worn away. But its inner spine and a rampart of concentric hogback ridges remain as monuments to the ceaseless conflict between earth-shaping forces.

A VOLCANO, snow-crowned Mt. Hood, towers high above Lost Lake, Ore. Extinct or dormant, Mt. Hood is a composite volcanic cone, built by alternations of quiet lava flows and violent eruptions of cinders and other fragmentary material.

A BLOCK MOUNTAIN near Las Vegas, Nev. was reared by fracturing of the surface rocks and the uplifting and tilting of a small segment of the earth's crust. The front wall of the mountain has been deeply scarred and seamed by erosion.

A CINDER CONE in Lassen Volcanic National Park, Calif. was created by fierce eruptions of lava and gas from volcanic fissures perhaps a thousand years ago. Its regular contours are characteristic of this type of mountain. When gas-charged

STIRRINGS IN THE EARTH

THE processes of mountain-building have been more difficult to interpret than those of valley sculpture, owing in part to the common misconception of the earth's crust as static and unyielding. Yet the earth is by no means either static or unyielding. Its rotation about its vertical axis causes it to bulge at the equator and flatten at the poles (creating a difference between equatorial and polar diameters of 26.6 miles). It is now known, moreover, that there are tides in the earth's crust as well as in the sea, for just as the transit of sun and moon across the oceans draws the earth's waters upward in gravitational response, so they cause the land to bow upward in a slight tidal movement of about eight inches at the equator. Far greater, however, than these daily tidal stirrings are the earth-shaping movements of the planet's crust, some abrupt, some slow. There are

probably few areas in the world that have not been moved many times. Everywhere around the globe there is evidence that the land surface is a mobile thing, governed by powerful forces and subject to vast disturbances which change the contours of continents and build great edifices of rock, like the mountains shown above.

The most obvious of crustal movements, which in the past have most deeply stirred the imagination of men, are earthquakes. Actually the outer layers of the crust quake constantly in response to the strains imposed by city traffic, waterfalls and even the moving tides of the sea; terra firma is an illusion. But apart from such minor tremors thousands of violent and destructive earthquakes have occurred in recorded history. Although they originate most frequently in certain well-defined areas of the earth, chiefly around the rim of the Pacific Ocean, no region is entirely exempt. Sudden fractures or displacements of the crustal rock along planes of weakness which geologists call "faults" often revise the landscape in a few moments

lava is extruded rapidly and with explosive violence, it is fragmented, quickly hardens, and showers down around the volcanic vent in a more or less symmetrical cone. Thereafter it tends to preserve its form, relatively immune from erosion by water, for even the heaviest rainfall is readily absorbed by the porous cinders of its soilless surface. The graceful cone shown here rises about 700 feet above the surrounding terrain. It last showed symptoms of activity in 1851.

of earthshaking upheaval. In 1906 a horizontal shifting of ground along the San Andreas Fault not only brought devastation to the city of San Francisco, but for a stretch of 270 miles along the fault severed fences and offset roads by as much as 21 feet. Faulting may also cause vertical displacement of the crust; in the great Alaska earthquake of 1899 a section of the coast was lifted nearly 50 feet.

Earthquakes represent the final, abrupt and violent yielding of the rocks to stresses that have been building up over long periods of time —a sudden release from tension like the fracture of a bent stick. But sometimes the compressive forces in the crust act so deliberately and over such long periods of time that the rocks do not break. Instead they buckle, warp or fold. When this occurs the land is gently elevated into domes or depressed into basins and valleys.

One of the deepest mysteries of geophysics is the source of the enormous forces that deform the earth's face, rupture its bedrock and throw up mountain chains. A classic theory explains the buckling of the crust as the consequence of the cooling and contraction of the earth's hot interior. Today scientists feel that this cannot be the whole answer, and indeed, a completely satisfactory explanation for the process of mountain-building has not yet been evolved. One clue may derive from investigations which have indicated that the density of rocks in mountains is less than that of the rock which underlies them. A mountain may thus be envisaged not as a tremendous burden on the earth's crust, but rather as an iceberg whose lighter substance, rising above and extending beneath the surface, is in effect "floating" on the heavier rock beneath. And so it would appear that all around the globe the earth's crust maintains a balance between highland and lowland, a state of equilibrium which geologists call *isostasy* (from the Greek: "equal standing"). As mountains are gnawed away by erosion and their debris washed away into the sea, renascent highlands slowly rise; for the earth adjusts temporary states of imbalance in its crust through the slow plastic flow of deep-lying rock.

HOW MOUNTAINS ARE BORN

ALTHOUGH to observers of normal sensibility mountains may exhibit certain esthetic differences, the mantle of soil and vegetation that covers most areas of the land conceals its underlying geologic structure from the untrained eye. Yet the geologist, by studying deformations and discordances of exposed rock, can generally determine what constructional processes brought the many different land forms into being (*painting at right*) and thus explore the genealogy of the great relief features of the earth.

There are three principal categories of mountains: volcanic mountains, block mountains and folded mountains. The first type is the easiest to identify. Most volcanoes look like what they are, enormous, conical heaps of congealed lava and ash. The earth today has more than 500 active volcanoes and several thousand which are either extinct or dormant, ranging in size from small mounds to the high graceful eminences of Vesuvius, Etna and Fujiyama.

In addition to still recognizable summits, volcanoes of the past have left their traces in varied forms. Crater Lake, Oregon marks the remains of an ancient volcano that apparently collapsed. The lonely rock towers that stud the deserts of Arizona and New Mexico constitute the lava plugs or necks of ancient volcanoes whose outer slopes have been eroded away. Here and there across the land stand long ridges of igneous (once-molten) rock known as dikes, the remnants of eruptive fissures in the sides of vanished volcanoes through which lava once discharged and hardened. In some instances the lava spread between layers of other rock in horizontal strata, forming an intrusive sheet or "sill"—the Hudson River Palisades are the exposed edge of a sill. Small hills and mountains also evolve from upwelling of magma (fluid rock from the deep interior) which has penetrated between layers of native rock, forming lens-shaped masses with flat floors and domed upper surfaces; such formations are known as laccoliths. Larger intrusive formations are known as batholiths; they are often composed of granitic rock and may be seen in the deeply eroded cores of most old mountain ranges.

By far the greatest proportion of the earth's mountains came into being, however, by bending of the earth's crust. In most instances this process is accompanied by fracturing of the rocks, producing breaks ranging from small offsets to great faults hundreds of miles long. Vertical displacements sometimes erect cliffs or "fault scarps" 50 feet high in a single grinding paroxysm, and when faulting recurs in the same place over long periods of time, entire mountain fronts may be reared. Mountains elevated by this process are known as fault-block mountains. In the Great Basin of Nevada faulting on a stupendous scale has broken the land into a chaos of gigantic blocks and basins. The Sierra Nevada of California represent a single tilted block 400 miles long and 60 miles wide. Its gentle western slope constitutes the tilted upper surface of the mass; the eastern wall, uplifted by repeated displacements over numberless centuries, is a gigantic fault scarp towering more than two miles above the desert below. Geologically speaking the Sierra peaks are young mountains, and there is evidence that they are still growing.

Many of the great mountain chains of the world—the Alps, Andes, Rockies—are not simple fault-block mountains, but folded mountains, formed of rocks that have buckled as well as fractured, and fallen into ordered ridges and furrows like the corrugations of a washboard or the swells of the sea. A striking feature of folded mountains is the frequent presence on their summits of marine fossils, testifying that some of the earth's loftiest peaks arose from the floors of ancient, vanished seas. Indeed geologists believe that a necessary precondition for the construction of folded mountain chains must have been the existence of a geosyncline, a great shallow basin or trough, in which sediments were laid down eon after eon, layer after layer, thousands of feet thick. Under this great load, the earth's crust first warped downward and eventually, under huge lateral pressures, buckled, thrusting the accumulated mass of sediment deep into the earth and upward toward the sky. The enormous thickness of the sedimentary strata in the Appalachian Mountains—in some places six or seven miles thick—indicates that the great inland sea which once extended from Newfoundland to the Gulf of Mexico must have been collecting sediment and slowly sinking for nearly 300 million years before the final great upheaval that brought the Appalachians into being.

FORCES OF UPLIFT, originating in the earth's interior, shape the face of the land by causing the crustal rocks to fracture and fold, creating highlands, hills and mountain chains. In this painting the varieties of land forms produced by the earth's constructive processes are depicted in an imaginary terrain from which all soil and vegetation have been stripped away, laying bare the basic

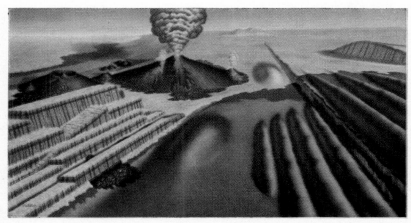

UNERODED LANDSCAPE IS SHOWN HERE FOR COMPARISON WITH SCENE AT RIGHT

HOW MOUNTAINS ARE WORN AWAY

PERHAPS the strangest anomalies among the highlands of the earth are the "mountains of erosion," hewn by running water, wind and frost from once-great plateaus. Many of the mesas of the Far West are such residual mountains, hard and resistant remnants of larger but less durable land masses. The Catskills of New York are also remainders of a formerly extensive plateau, most of which has been removed by erosion. In time, geologists believe, the great Colorado Plateau will disappear and strange rocky buttes and towers will stand on a plain thousands of feet below the level of the present plateau—and men will call them mountains. But these too will eventually vanish, for there is no eminence on earth that is not subject to erosion and will not ultimately be effaced. In the endless conflict of earth-shaping forces, erosion is the slow, the unwearying, the inexorable destroyer.

To the geologist the term erosion means essentially the transport of rock particles from high places to low places. A necessary prelude to erosion is weathering—the process by which the earth's bedrock is disintegrated and decomposed, and in the end converted into soil. The chief agency of weathering is the atmosphere, the invisible envelope of gas that surrounds the terrestrial sphere. Penetrating crevices wherever rock is exposed, the various ingredients of the atmosphere —oxygen, carbon dioxide, water vapor—enter into chemical combinations with various elements of the rocks, causing them to crumble and decay. Water leaches out their soluble components; acids from rotting vegetation abet the process. Chemical decomposition is often accelerated by mechanical factors, such as the prying apart of rocks by the roots of growing plants. In cold and temperate climates, however, one of the most important agencies of mechanical disintegration is frost-wedging. When water freezes it expands by about 9% of its volume. Seeping into crevices and crannies in the rock during the warmth of day and freezing at night, water exerts surprisingly great pressures capable not only of splitting open small stones but of prying great slabs from the faces of cliffs.

The results of weathering depend both on the chemical content of the rock and the climate which acts upon it. Limestone, for example, decomposes when exposed to water but stands up well in a dry climate. Many of the highest mountain peaks in arid sections of the West are composed of limestone. The shape of most land forms on earth is thus predetermined by the resistance of their underlying rock to the particular kind of weathering to which it is exposed.

As soon as fragments of rock have been loosened by weathering, the agents of erosion begin to carry them away. In this process the main energizing force is gravity. The soil cover of slopes and hillsides is continually, imperceptibly creeping downhill. Occasionally the movement may be visible as in the case of sudden landslides, rockfalls and mudflows, or the abrupt collapse of entire cliffs and embankments. Often scars may appear, as when one part of a hillside moves more rapidly than the rest and slumps away in sections. But however stable the appearance of any slope, however thickly it may be covered with a protective canopy of plants and trees, nevertheless the entire soil mantle of every slope on every continent of the earth is moving steadily downward, carrying most of its plant cover with it. One may think of the earth's soil, therefore, as a kind of viscous liquid which even on a moderate slope tends to flow under the pull of gravity.

FORCES OF EROSION, originating in the atmosphere, continually strive to level the face of the land by stripping away its soil cover, disintegrating exposed rock, and transporting loose particles from uplands to valleys and the sea. In this painting the same landscape that appears on the previous pages is depicted after the destructive forces of rain, running water, wind, frost and ice have been at

the level plain in the center foreground over an intrusion of once-molten rock, known as a batholith. At the right of the volcano, a small dome, or laccolith, has been formed by the intrusion of a lens-shaped mass of molten rock between two layers of sedimentary rock. In the right foreground the earth's crust has wrinkled to form a range of folded mountains similar to the Appalachians. Be-

hind them at right and in the center background are examples of tilted block mountains with steep faces and gently graded back slopes. The long escarpment, running from the foreground toward the horizon, is a fault line, along which the crustal rocks have ruptured and been displaced. In the distance at left a coastal plain has been created by a slow emergence of the continental shelf from the sea.

architecture of the bedrock. Three principal mountain types—block mountains, volcanoes and folded mountains—are shown, from left to right, as they would appear in a world free from the ravages of weather and erosion. In the left foreground fractured and uplifted angular sections of crustal rock form a group of block mountains, from the base of which a lava flow extrudes onto the surface.

Behind them, at left, are an inactive volcano with a cratered top and several small cinder cones marking the site of once-active fissures. Farther to the right an active volcano, shown in cross section, ejects smoke, ash and lava from its central cone and two subsidiary vents. Running across the picture, a cutaway section of the crust reveals the underlying strata, which are bowed upward from

work for incomputable years attacking the various land forms reared by the earth's internal processes. The block mountains in the left foreground are now furrowed and dissected by running streams into triangular facets and V-shaped canyons; glaciers gnaw at the higher places, carving ridges and Matterhorn peaks. Behind them the dormant volcano of the first painting has come to life, while the

formerly active cone has expired and been reduced by erosion to a volcanic plug or neck of resistant lava, and a series of radiating ridges or "dikes"; its secondary crater, to the right, is now a *caldera* filled with water (like Crater Lake, Ore.). The dome in center foreground has been eroded in characteristic fashion. Its top has completely disappeared, exposing a jumbled core of older strata surrounded

by an oval pattern of hogback ridges. In the right foreground the range of folded mountains has been deeply cut by running water, which has stripped the crests of the ridges and carved valleys between them. The old fault line, now largely covered by soil, is deeply notched with waterfalls and canyons. The tilted block mountains at right background bear scars made by water and ice. In the center background a continental glacier is receding, leaving behind vestiges of its passage—small hills (drumlins) and ridges (moraines). The streams flowing from its lower edge at right form the headwaters of a river which, like many of the earth's rivers, begins its life in a steep-sided valley, and ends it in the slow meanders of a broad and gentle flood plain of its own construction (*right, foreground*).

HOW WATER SHAPES THE LAND

WATER is the great leveler. Every drop of rain that falls on exposed soil is an advance agent of erosion, acting as a miniature bomb and blasting a tiny crater in the ground at its point of impact. Though raindrops have been hymned by poets and blessed by men in times of drought, it is known now that raindrop erosion represents the first step in the destruction of land, scalping the crests of hills and loosening particles of soil that are subsequently carried away by streams. Over the land masses of the earth about 28½ inches of rain descend annually, varying from two inches in Death Valley to about 450 inches on the slopes of the Himalayas. Some rainfall returns to the atmosphere by evaporation, some seeps into the ground, but about 9,000 cubic miles of water runs off the land into the seas each year.

On every slope the initial rills, formed by the concentration of rainwash, converge into brooks, then into streams, then into rivers, all flowing to the sea through channels excavated by themselves.

Though the work of a watercourse may be imperceptible to man in a lifetime, over the years stream erosion is more effective as a land-leveling force than all other agencies of erosion combined. The erosive power of a stream is governed both by the amount of water it carries and the grade down which it moves. Although running water churns up and washes away soil and rock fragments, it is not this action alone that carves great valleys. For every stream carries along a load of sediment—which, by scraping against the bedrock of the stream bed, cuts away banks and enlarges the channel down which it flows. The destructive force of running water increases with the velocity of flow. Doubling the velocity of a stream may increase its abrasive power four times, and its capacity to transport rock fragments by an even greater factor. Under flood conditions certain large streams and rivers not only double their velocity but may increase it ten- or twentyfold.

When a stream tumbles over a waterfall, enormous amounts of energy are developed. The water that roars from the brink of Niagara Falls, for example, descends into its plunge pool below at a velocity of 50 mph, as a result of which the pool is continually deepened and

AN ALLUVIAL FAN, built of sediment washed down by the rain-swollen mountain streams, spreads out across the level floor of California's Death Valley.

ROCK SPIRES in Utah's Bryce Canyon were sculptured by rainfall and running water out of ancient limestone strata. The water worked in two ways, melting away the lime and wearing away the rock by abrasion. Differences in resistance of the strata produced the strange pillared amphitheater at the left.

widened, undercutting the cliffs above. From time to time the cap rock at the brink tumbles off, thus moving the falls gradually upstream. They have receded seven miles from the original crest at a rate of about 3½ feet a year.

Since young streams cut almost straight downward, their first incisions take the form of V-shaped valleys, like the gorge of the Yellowstone River. But in time the steep walls of every ravine surrender to weathering and mass-wasting; little by little a river canyon widens as it deepens, so ultimately steep gorges become gentle valleys down which quiet rivers meander to the sea. The period required for such transformations is enormously long. It has been estimated, for example, that the watershed of the Mississippi River has been lowering at the average rate of one foot every seven to nine thousand years. This means that in the million years of human evolution an average of 150 feet of rock has been eroded from the entire surface of the Mississippi basin. The younger, swifter Colorado River has carved the Grand Canyon a mile deep, eight miles wide at the rim—in about the same period of time.

A V-SHAPED VALLEY, carved by the swift-flowing Yellowstone River, Wyo., is a perfect example of stream erosion. Slicing through layers of volcanic rock, the river took an estimated 150,000 years to reach its present depth of 740 to 1,200 ft.

WIND-ERODED ROCK near Moab, Utah records the cutting power of moving air. Abrading a sandstone butte weakened by water seepage, the wind has blasted it away, grain by grain, gouging holes and tunneling through to the other side.

THE WORK OF WIND

WATER, however, is not the only leveling force which operates in nature. In the arid regions of the earth, wind is a conspicuous and constant agent of erosion. Wherever the soil mantle is dry and vegetation scarce, as in desert regions, the wind may completely strip the ground of all loose material, exposing the bedrock below. Indeed, most deserts consist less of sand than of rock, scoured bare by wind and weathering. In some sections of Death Valley, Calif. the dry, relentless wind has blown away virtually all sand, leaving a floor of small stones tightly fitted together into a "desert pavement."

In transporting loose particles of weathered rock the wind becomes in effect a sand-blasting machine. Just as the erosive action of streams is augmented by their moving load of sediment, so the erosive action of the wind is intensified by the load of sand particles it transports. A strong, debris-laden wind blowing steadily against vertical rock faces will eventually undercut cliffs and sculpture balanced rocks, pedestal rocks, mushroom rocks and other weird residual forms. In some areas of the world, notably the American Far West and North Africa, wind scour has scooped out large depressions many square miles in area and several hundred feet deep. Violent sandstorms have been known to cut down wooden telegraph poles and destroy the transparency of windowpanes in a single savage blast.

WIND-ERODED SOIL produces strange plant forms in Death Valley, Calif. The wind swept desert soil away from the roots of these "arrow weeds," leaving them atop dry hummocks with thirsty tendrils clawing downward to the vanishing soil.

SAND DUNES in Death Valley are molded and etched with ripple marks by the dry wind. The source of the sand is the granitic rock of the Cottonwood Mountains that border the valley. Weathered, then washed down the mountainsides by

rain and running streams, rock fragments, soil and other debris collect in an alluvial fan at the foot of the mountains (*left*). The sediment, dried by the hot sun, is then strewn by the wind across the valley floor in constantly shifting dunes.

In this picture the wind blows from left to right, transporting the sand up the gentle windward slope of each dune and dropping it on the steeper lee side. The dunes are constantly replenished from the store of the regenerating alluvial fan.

A VALLEY GLACIER, second largest in the great Columbia ice field of the Canadian Rockies, creeps down the flanks of Mt. Athabaska, cutting its own channel, grinding and polishing the rocks over which it moves. The glacier transports quantities of fallen rock which it deposits in lateral moraines—ridgelike formations on either side—and in a terminal moraine at the bottom (*left, foreground*). The melt-water streams at its foot form the source of the Athabaska River.

A U-SHAPED VALLEY in Crawford Notch, N.H. exhibits the planed walls and rounded floor characteristic of valleys that have been converted from their original V-shape by glacial action. The thin white strips are a railroad and a highway.

THE WORK OF ICE

OF all the forces of erosion that attack the earth's high places, the most powerful, though limited in area, are glaciers. Through their enormous mass, glaciers radically revise the shape of entire mountain ranges. Glaciers exist wherever there is perpetual snow, for they are formed initially of snow, piled up, compressed and compacted into glittering tongues of ice. When a snowfield, high on a mountain slope, reaches a depth of about 100 feet, it begins to creep downward under its own weight. Although ice is a crystalline solid, it nevertheless has the property of flowing as a plastic substance.

As the glacier creeps away from its sheltering mountain wall where the snowfield first accumulated, a crevasse opens behind it, sometimes filling with fresh snow during the winter and melting with the spring thaws. With each advance of the glacier the ice that has frozen to the mountain wall tears away huge segments of rock. By annual repetitions of this process the glacier eventually carves out a "cirque" or amphitheater at its head, some so deeply excavated that their floors eventually become, with changing climates, the basins of lakes. Several cirques often surround a single mountain peak, giving it the wild jagged aspect of the Matterhorn or the Teton Range of Wyoming.

A GLACIATED LANDSCAPE in the Canadian Rockies bears many of the scars impressed by moving ice in ages past. All the mountains have been hewn by ice and frost into sharp and craggy configurations. In the center of the picture are two small step lakes or tarns, scooped out and filled with melt water by a vanished glacier. Lake Louise, at left, is a finger lake, also a typical vestige of glaciation. The crumbled rock in the foreground has been shattered by frost action.

The erosive action of a moving glacier has been said to combine that of a plow, a file and a sled. Creeping down a valley it plows up the soil, pushing it ahead and to either side. Meanwhile from exposed ledges above, rock fragments shattered by frost tumble down the valley walls onto the glacier's broad back. Eventually this debris becomes an integral part of the glacial mass. As the great river of ice flows downhill, it grinds the rock debris frozen within across the valley floor, cutting, scraping, filing and polishing. At the same time its rough, unyielding flanks grate against projecting crags and spurs and gradually wear them away. In the end all glaciated valleys acquire a characteristic profile. Where valleys cut by young streams are V-shaped, glacial action converts the V to a U by planing sides and floor, so that eventually the valley is a rounded trough with wide smooth walls.

The sculpture of alpine or valley glaciers is dwarfed, however, by the work of the great ice sheets that covered more than one quarter of the land areas of the planet. Spread over millions of square miles, thousands of feet thick, these stupendous ice masses overlay mountains and valleys alike, and during successive advances and retreats transformed the face of the land on a colossal scale. The mountains of New York and New England—the Adirondacks, the Green Mountains, the White Mountains—and the highlands of Scotland and Ireland were completely enveloped in ice. Crushed beneath this vast weight, they re-emerged with none of the intricate scars wrought by valley glaciers, no knife-edged ridges, pyramidal peaks or cirques, but rather with smooth summits and rounded ridges. The action of the great ice sheets was not one of sculpture but of crude abrasion, a beveling of whole mountain masses. In addition to remodeling the highlands the ice sheets created lakes and rivers by the thousands in North America, Europe and northern Asia. They expanded the rock basins of the Great Lakes and filled them with melt water, and diverted the Ohio and Missouri Rivers to their present channels.

When glaciers melt away, they leave deposits behind—rough ridges of boulders, sand and silt called moraines, and small hills, shaped like the inverted bowls of spoons, called drumlins. Many elevations in Wisconsin and Michigan and all the high ground of Martha's Vineyard and Nantucket are moraines that marked the terminal of a continental ice sheet. Bunker Hill, outside Boston, is a drumlin.

Nor has the influence of the prehistoric ice sheets on man's environment yet ceased, for their vestiges remain today in the shrinking icecaps that overlie Greenland and Antarctica. The five million cubic miles of ice stored in the polar caps are slowly melting, surrendering their locked-up waters to the rising seas. If the process continues, many of the low-lying continental areas of the earth will be inundated, as they have been recurrently at other times in the past.

HISTORY OF A REGION

NEW YORK CITY, built precariously on a block of ancient rock a few feet above the present level of the Atlantic Ocean, may in time fall victim to a rising, ice-fed sea. Yet this event, however catastrophic to men, will be simply another link—and not even a new one—in the endless chain of geologic history. For in the region where New York now stands an inland sea long ago lapped about an island chain of active volcanoes like those of the present East and West Indies. Then for millions of years debris, stripped from the volcanic slopes by weathering and the incision of running streams, poured into the sea, filling its shallow basin, transforming it first into a swamp, then a low plain beneath which the sediments of the ancient sea floor compressed into level strata of sedimentary rock. In time crustal pressures, bearing in from east and west, folded and uplifted those new-formed layers into a chain of mountains: the original Appalachians. All across the region the restless earth continued to

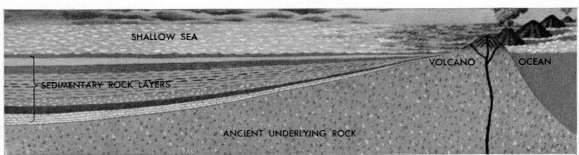

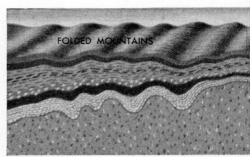

THE NEW YORK AREA, 300 million years ago, was occupied by a chain of volcanic islands with ocean to the east, a shallow inland sea to the west. Debris washing down the volcanic slopes filled in the sea basin and caused its floor to sag under the weight of numberless layers of sediment, shown in cross section, foreground.

UPHEAVAL of the crust 200 million years ago forced the sedimentary beds laid down in the ancient sea to buckle and fall into folds,

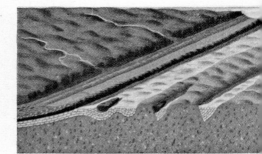

AN EPOCH OF EROSION lasting 140 million years reduced the area to a virtually featureless plain. With crustal forces inactive, running streams washed the original Appalachians into the sea, leaving only their underlying folds as evidence of once-splendid peaks. A few slow streams wandered across the level land.

A NEW UPLIFT about 10 million years ago elevated the plain into a highland. At once streams began to flow faster, attacking softer

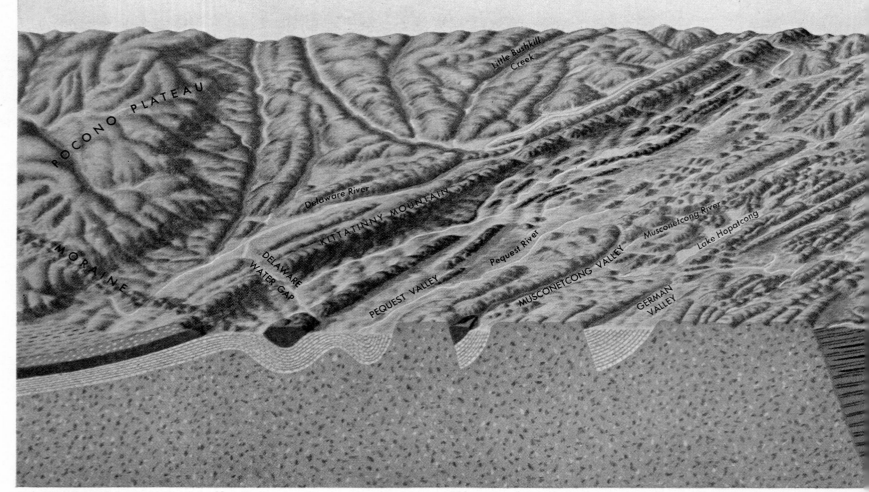

THE CONTEMPORARY SCENE of the New York area, whose topographic features are emphasized here by slight vertical exaggeration, is the product of 300 million years of mountain building, erosion and glacial sculpture. The Kittatinny Mountain at left is the stream-cut remnant of a long ridge of weather resistant rock raised during the period of erosion shown in the center picture above. The three valleys to its right, floored with truncated segments of the sedimentary stir; it cracked and shifted, breaking the regular contours of the folded hills and creating new basins and uplands. New volcanoes burst through points of weakness and molten magma penetrated the surface rocks. Then came a hundred million years of quiet during which the crust lay still and the forces of erosion scourged the face of the land, wearing it down to a flat and undifferentiated plain.

But in time another period of uplift began. Slowly the land warped upward. Its sluggish streams were rejuvenated; new valleys were incised; new hills took form—the present Berkshires, Ramapos and Alleghenies. Finally, a few tens of thousands of years ago, the crushing mass of the continental ice sheet crept down from the north to impress on the area the last of the great alterations that produced the current landscape, smoothing the hilltops, deepening the valleys, striating the bedrock and leaving in its eventual retreat the low mounds and ridges of its terminal moraines. Today erosion is again reducing the highlands to the level of the coastal plain. Yet no one can predict that another uplift will not occur in some future age. For no feature of the land is abiding, no state of nature permanent.

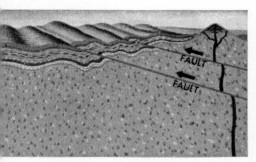

creating the primeval Appalachian Mountains. In the east faulting occurred and sections of the land were displaced over long distances.

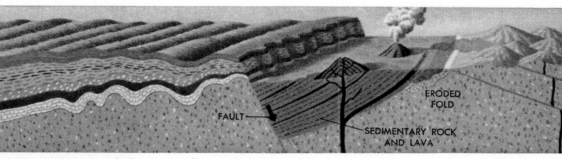

HUGE FAULTS appeared about 170 million years ago, causing some land to settle and form basins which at once began to fill with sediments from the uplands.

Lava from volcanoes intruded between the sedimentary layers. Meanwhile forces of erosion carved some of the original highlands into residual mountain forms (*right*).

rock, creating a new pattern of ridges and valleys. In the east (*right*) a new-born stream began to excavate the Hudson River valley.

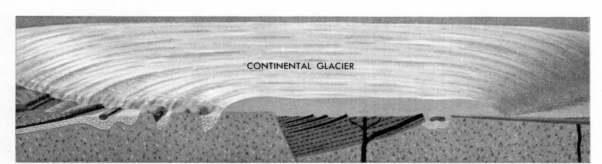

THE ICE AGE applied the finishing touches to the landscape. At intervals for a million years glaciers crept out of the north, crushing and abrading the contours of the land. When the last one receded some 20,000 years ago, it left behind new land forms, among them the outwash plain at right which became part of Long Island.

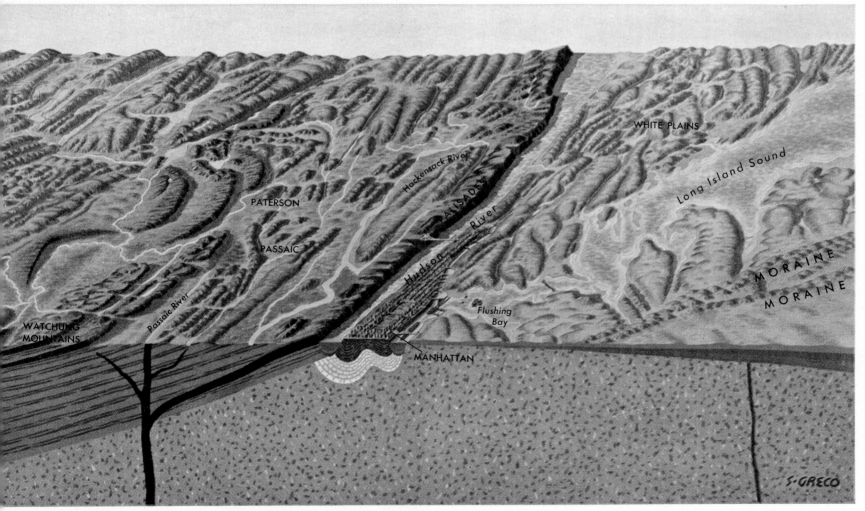

folds produced by warping 200 million years ago (*top, center*), were carved when rivers cut down into the soft strata. The Watchung Mountains and the Palisades along the Hudson River are the exposed edges of great sheetlike layers of igneous rock which spread out as magma from volcanic stems 170 million years ago (*upper right*). The low ridges rising 100–150 feet above the Long Island flatlands are the terminal moraines left behind by the melting continental glacier.

TIME AND CHANGE

KNOWING the processes by which mountains and valleys are constructed and destroyed, geologists find it possible to recapitulate the evolution of every land form on earth and guess its probable future. In so doing they often epitomize a landscape in living terms as "young," "mature" or "old," referring not so much to its actual age as to the visible effects wrought by the combined forces of erosion. Thus, in the eastern half of the U.S., where destructive forces predominate over those of construction, the softened and subdued visage of the land is "old" in appearance if not in years. Today New England is a region of low promontories and rounded ridges, planed and scoured by millenniums of rain, ice and frost. The valleys of the Northeastern and Middle Atlantic states are broad and gentle, possessed now not by swift, rushing streams but by slow, serpentine rivers. In many places the lowlands are carpeted with a thick cover of rich, arable soil which is a characteristic of humid, softly contoured places. For it is only on benign slopes, protected by vegetation from the destructive pull of gravity, that soil can resist the forces of erosion and accumulate in a fertile mantle year after year, century after century.

In the West, where the forces of erosion work no less relentlessly, the earth's internal forces are far more active than in the East. Vast areas of the Western states are strewn with lava, cinders, ash and other debris of recent volcanic activity. The Columbia Plateau in the Northwest is one of the earth's greatest volcanic constructions, an immense lava field covering an area of more than 200,000 square miles and in places a mile thick, built by stupendous outpourings of molten rock. Lassen Peak, in California, is a dormant volcano that may erupt again at any time. Virtually all the mountains of the Far West are high and young, with barren rock and little soil cover; their pinnacles and spurs stand raw and rough-edged, not yet softened and rounded by wind and rain.

In particular the West appears to be a region of great crustal uneasiness. Displacements recur frequently along great fault lines, producing earthquakes and upheaval of the surface rocks. Not long ago scientists of the U.S. Coast and Geodetic Survey discovered that linear strains have been building up along the huge San Andreas Fault ever since the San Francisco earthquake of 1906. Horizontal movements have been especially obvious; at the present time the earth mass along the west side of the fault is moving in a northwesterly direction at the rate of two inches a year. Hence they believe that the great rift will slip again some day, producing another earthquake perhaps as great as that of half a century ago. A new instrument designed to measure long-term strains in the earth's crust is now being tested by seismologists, who hope it may eventually make possible the prediction of future quakes. Elsewhere other slippages along other faults have produced great earthquakes in California at frequent intervals for many years past.

And subtler crustal movements—broad regional uplifts, depressions and warpings—are imperceptibly altering the shape of the land. The Baldwin Hills area of the Los Angeles plain has been arched upward at the rate of three feet per century. The Buena Vista oil field in the San Joaquin Valley is rising at the rate of four feet per century. Trivial as these uplifts may seem, in a relatively brief interval of geologic time they could change the profile of California. If they continue for 25,000 years (discounting erosion), the Alamitos Plain will be a tableland 300 feet above the sea and the Buena Vista Hills will have grown 1,000 feet. If they continue for 200,000 years—only one fifth of the span of man's existence on earth—the Buena Vista Hills will be as high as the Cascades. If they continue for two million years—a not excessive interval when one recalls that the uplifting of the Himalayas, the Alps and the Rockies required at least that much time—the California highlands will attain the height of Mt. Everest.

Thus everywhere on the planet there are signs that the earth's crust is not altogether stable. Surveys made by the U.S. Coast and Geodetic Survey over the last 20 years have shown that along the 1,000-mile stretch from Massachusetts to Florida the coast is being

AN "OLD" LANDSCAPE stretches along New Hampshire's Saco River. The upheaval that produced Mt. Washington (in distance) occurred 200 million years ago. From then on wind, ice and water worked to soften the profile of the land.

submerged at a rate of about .02 feet per year. There is reason to believe that this change in the relationship between land and sea is due not only to a rise in sea level but also to basic movements of the continental block. All around the world the uplift of mountains and plateaus is offset by the slow downward warping of shorelines and inland basins. The entire country of France, for example, appears to be tilting slowly northward, rising in the south, sinking along the Channel coast. If this movement continues, the waters of the Atlantic will ultimately inundate great areas of France from the Belgian border to Brest. Yet at the same time the Baltic coast of Sweden is rising at the rate of one-half centimeter per year. If this rate of uplift were maintained for 10,000 years it would tilt all the water out of the Baltic Sea and turn its shallow floor into dry land.

Although the active movements of the earth's crust are localized—upheavals occurring now in one place, now in another—the antipathetic processes of erosion are continuous and worldwide. Given time, every land mass on the face of the earth would be destroyed and reduced to sea level by the chisels of rain and the wedges of frost, the abrasive breath of the wind and the massive tread of glaciers. If unopposed these forces would have swept all the land into the sea eons ago. But the disquietude of the earth's crust proclaims that the internal forces responsible for the re-creation of the land are as active today as ever they were in the geologic past. Present rates of crustal movement, if long continued, are sufficient to produce mountains as great as any that now stand on earth. So new uplands will arise, new plateaus will be warped toward the sky. And each uplift will create new rushing torrents to begin the work of obliterating the land.

It is only recently that scientists came to understand the antipathy of these natural forces of construction and destruction, and thus perceived that nothing on earth is eternal—no mountain or river, no continent or sea. Yet the flux of nature has been visible to some poets and philosophers of ages past. Two thousand five hundred years ago the Greek philosopher Heraclitus said, "There is nothing permanent in the world except change."

THE CANOPY
OF AIR

PART IV

THE CANOPY OF AIR

The invisible atmospheric ocean that surrounds and protects our sphere creates winds and coursing clouds and gives breath to all living things

> The vapor, which the Greeks and our own nation call by the same name, air—this is the principle of life, and penetrates all the universe, and is intertwined with the whole.
>
> PLINY THE ELDER (23–79 A.D.)

FOR all his hard-won knowledge of the physical world, man continues to regard himself as a self-sufficient being dominating the surface of his planet. Virtually never does he picture himself in his genuine circumstance as a temporal creature dwelling fish-like at the bottom of a sea, doomed and helpless without the life-giving medium into which he has been cast.

Yet in actuality man does live at the bottom of a sea hundreds of miles deep—on the floor of the great ocean of air that engulfs the planet—where he subsists as precariously as a marine organism in its natural element of water. Deprive him of it briefly and he expires, gasping, like a trout lifted from the silvery stream. Raise him a few miles from the bottom and he dies violently of his own internal pressures like an abyssal fish plucked from the lightless deep. He cannot say, in a strict scientific sense, that he lives on top of his world—but only between two layers of it.

In the perspective of physical science the earth must be envisaged not as a single globe but as a series of concentric spheres. The lithosphere (from the Greek *lithos*, meaning stone) is the hard rocky shell of the planet. The lithosphere in turn is covered for nearly three-quarters of its surface by the hydrosphere, or oceanic sheath of water, averaging about two miles in depth. A third major sphere of the planet—the biosphere—is an intermediate domain, tenuous as the film of a soap bubble, on which all living things stand exquisitely poised amid the fragile relationships of organic necessity and physical environment. Animals exist on the dark ocean floor six miles down; spores have been found drifting in thin air six miles aloft. But man and most terrestrial life abide in an even narrower band between the lower levels of the air and the upper storeys of the sea. Encompassing all three spheres in a transparent, mobile and impalpable envelope hundreds of miles thick is the atmosphere, upon which every form of life ultimately depends.

Without the atmosphere no animal or plant, bird or fish, tree or blade of grass could exist. Indeed the air governs the very quality of the terrestrial environment—the whole character of the world as man perceives it. Without the atmosphere there would be no weather, winds, clouds or rain. There would be no sunlit, sapphire sky, no flaming sunsets, aurora borealis or "rosy-fingered dawn." There would be no fire, for all burning is the union of oxygen with the thing that is burned. There would be no sound, for what man calls sound is simply the vibration of airwaves against the drum and the auditory nerve of his ear. Vegetation could not grow nor birds fly.

Beyond its other properties the atmosphere serves as a great protective canopy that shields the earth from the intolerable violence of the sun by absorbing most of its harmful short-wave emissions. At night, like the glass roof of a gigantic greenhouse, the atmosphere imprisons the heat of day and prevents it from spreading away into space. Were there no atmosphere the maximum daytime temperature of the earth would ascend like that of the moon to a searing 230°F. and plunge after dark to a minimum of −300°F. Finally, like a vast transparent screen or grating, the atmosphere catches and consumes by friction virtually all the 100 million meteors which fall into the earth's gravitational field each day from outer space and which through eons of geologic time would have pocked and pitted the face of the earth as ruthlessly as they have the airless visage of the moon. There was deep insight, more than Shakespeare could realize, in Hamlet's phrase: "This most excellent canopy, the air. . ."

Yet for most of his brief history man has remained unaware of his dependency on the air or even of its existence as a form of matter. Unable to see it, he could not think of it as having physical properties, weight or a crucial role in the manifold of nature. For centuries he thought of matter as having only two states—solid and liquid; the concept of the gaseous state, which is the predominant state of most of the matter in the universe, was beyond his grasp. Only a few of the ancient Greeks, with their miraculous insight into nature, dimly sensed the importance of the atmosphere. Anaximenes of Meletus observed, around 500 B.C.: "Just as our soul, being air, holds us together, so do breath and air encompass the whole world." Empedocles, around 450 B.C., who equated air in importance with the other major "elements"—earth, water and fire—concluded that air must be a material substance by observing that when an empty vessel is inverted and placed in water, the water is unable to fill it. But the discovery that air is actually a mixture of gases and that all the elements in nature may exist in a gaseous as well as a liquid or a solid state had to await certain developments of the 18th and 19th Centuries.

The difficulty in envisaging air as a material substance arose not only from its invisibility, but from its compressibility. Solids have constant shape and volume; liquids have no shape but retain constant volume. (Thus a pint of water is always a pint and always weighs the same amount.) But a gas is so mobile, so compressible, that two pints may weigh less than one, depending on its temporary state of density. An important step toward the understanding of the nature of air and the behavior of gases was the formulation, in 1662, of Robert Boyle's famous principle, stating that at a constant temperature the volume of a gas varies inversely as the pressure—*i.e.*, doubling the pressure on a gas reduces its volume by half. Beginning with the 18th Century, knowledge of the atmosphere and of its components evolved rapidly. Carbon dioxide was identified in 1754, nitrogen in 1772 and oxygen a year or so later. So in time science revealed man in his actual circumstance: a hollow, pulsating animal, drowned in a great shifting cloud of gas—or, as the French chemist Lavoisier conceived him, a kind of animate engine, employing oxygen as fuel and emitting carbon dioxide as the end product of the combustion.

The medium through which man moves is a mixture of many gases, but five predominate in quantity and importance: nitrogen representing 78% of dry air; oxygen, 21%; argon, about 1%; water vapor (a compound of hydrogen and oxygen), .01% to 4%; and carbon dioxide, about .03%. The weight of this great blanket of gas is stupendous, though man is unaware of it because of the equal and countervailing pressure of the air and fluids within his body. The pressure exerted upon him and upon the entire earth is 2,016 pounds per square foot. The whole burden of the atmosphere pressing down upon the earth totals about 5,000,000,000,000,000 tons—the equivalent of a slab of granite 1,000 miles long, 2,000 miles wide and half a mile thick.

FROM 78 MILES UP, in a picture taken from a Navy Aerobee rocket, the thin film of air that sustains terrestrial life appears as a hazy layer at the bottom of the clear outer atmosphere. The heavens look black, for the blue sky extends only to a height of 12 miles. The curvature of the northern horizon may be discerned as well as parts of six states: New Mexico, Colorado, Wyoming, Nebraska, South Dakota and Utah. The diagonal green streak at left is the valley of the Rio Grande.

THE AIR IS REPLENISHED by living creatures using its major gases—nitrogen, oxygen, carbon dioxide—and restoring them to the soil and atmosphere. At left, decaying plants in a bog deposit carbon, release ammonia and nitrogen. The nitrogen is removed from the air by bacteria in the soil and roots of clover. Animals eat the plants and excrete nitrogen compounds which decompose to return nitrogen

AIR'S ORIGIN AND UPKEEP

WHERE did the earth's atmosphere come from? If man is unique in the universe, then the sweet, moist air that embraces him may be unique also. Of all the planets in range of his vision only Mars appears to have an atmosphere somewhat similar to ours, containing a small amount of water vapor and possibly traces of oxygen. Neither of these gases has been detected in the thick clouds of dust that overhang the face of Venus. The atmospheric veils enveloping Jupiter and Saturn seem to be composed largely of hydrogen, helium and noxious methane (marsh gas) and ammonia. Mercury, like the moon, may have no atmosphere at all. But apart from our immediate solar system, the earth's air presents a cosmic anomaly: the elements that largely compose it are rare in the universe and, conversely, the elements most common in the universe are relatively scarce in our atmosphere. Studies show that the overwhelming mass of matter in the outer depths of space consists of the two lightest elements, hydrogen and helium. For every 1,000 parts of hydrogen in the universe as a whole, there exist 100 parts of helium and only ten or twenty of all the other elements combined. If, as many astronomers believe, the earth was created out of a primordial cloud of cosmic gas and dust, one would anticipate some relationship between the distribution of elements on earth and those in the sun and other stars. Yet the earth's atmosphere contains only .00005 percent of free hydrogen and .0005 percent helium. What became of all the hydrogen and helium that may once have been present in vast quantities? And what is the origin of the crucial gases that endow the earth with its beauty and its life?

The answer to these enigmas, according to modern theory, is that our present canopy of air represents a secondary atmosphere that accumulated slowly through millennia of geologic time. During the period when the protoplanet was forming from clouds of cosmic gas, its gravitational field may have been too weak to retain such light,

THE AIR WAS CREATED more than a billion years ago. From methane and other gases deep in their interiors, volcanoes synthesized and exhaled carbon dioxide, water vapor (which broke up into oxygen and hydrogen) and ammonia (which formed nitrogen compounds). Most of the earth's life-giving oxygen probably was manufactured by the earliest plants, green algae adrift in the ancient oceans.

and ammonia to the air. Bacteria change soil ammonia into nitrites and nitrates. A similar ammonia-to-nitrate cycle occurs in the lake at upper left. In the center of the picture household fuels (carbon from underground) and burning forests release carbon dioxide. Trees absorb this gas and give off oxygen, while horses inhale oxygen, exhale carbon dioxide and excrete methane, which is acted on by

soil bacteria to produce more carbon dioxide. At right rain washes carbon dioxide and carbonates from the land into the sea. Here plants absorb the former and give off oxygen. Minute sea animals absorb the carbonates to build their hard parts, also take in oxygen and breathe out carbon dioxide. When they die and decay, carbon dioxide is carried to the surface of the water by upwelling currents.

mobile gases as hydrogen and helium. Or, if any hydrogen and helium did exist in the planet's original atmosphere, they would have been evaporated by solar radiation when the sun condensed into a blazing sphere. But nevertheless within the earth quantities of gases remained locked in chemical combination. For millions of years they bubbled upward from the seething heart of the planet and—exhaled through volcanoes, vents and hot springs—floated above the cooling crust of the young earth. And little by little as they fed and enriched the sparse air, the dark sky brightened and turned blue.

Yet there was one critical omission: free oxygen. This life-giving element does not emanate from volcanoes. Scientists believe, therefore, that the entrance of free oxygen into the atmosphere represented an immensely long, slow process that for untold ages paralleled and depended on the evolution of plant life. For plants are the earth's chief manufacturers of oxygen. They give off oxygen during the day. But at night they take it in. Hence some oxygen was probably present before true plant life evolved. Small quantities may have been formed in the upper atmosphere by the breakdown of water vapor (H_2O) by electrical discharges and solar radiation. In this way enough oxygen could have been added to the air to support most primitive plants. The first plants possibly were green translucent algae, called Corycia, whose fossil remains are 1,400 million years old. Those and similar species may have been the earth's first mass-producers of free oxygen. And as the supply of oxygen in the atmosphere slowly increased, more complex plants evolved and quickened the process—a process that accelerated for millions of years, accompanied by an enormous increase in oxygen-consuming animals to help maintain the balance of production and use.

The composition of the atmosphere today remains essentially what it was in Cambrian times, half a billion years ago. Yet it is forever changing. The mobile gases of which it is composed are continually being absorbed by the soil, the rocks and living things, or lost into outer space. And so the supply of atmospheric carbon dioxide in the atmosphere has to be replenished every 4 to 8 years,

the oxygen every 3,000 years, the nitrogen every 100 million years.

The cycle of use and renewal of the atmospheric gases reveals a miracle of balance involving soil, air, animals and plants, for all living things are made largely of the elements of the air: oxygen, water, carbon and nitrogen. As free oxygen comes from plants, so carbon dioxide is continually renewed by animals, who exhale it, and by a variety of other processes. When plants decay through bacterial action, for example, carbon dioxide escapes back into the air. When man burns fuel, carbon dioxide pours from the chimneys of factories and homes and returns to the atmosphere. Moreover the weathering of rocks and soil yields sediments, rich in carbon dioxide, which are then carried to the sea to swell the vast store produced there by the death and decay of marine plant and animal life. The sea is the earth's great reservoir of carbon dioxide, holding in solution 50 times the amount that hangs aloft in the atmosphere.

The intricate interplay of earth, air and life is most dramatically displayed, however, in the nitrogen cycle. The most abundant of the atmospheric gases, nitrogen is chemically rather inert—it does not combine readily with other elements. Since all plants and animals require nitrogen as food, its chemical inertia has caused mankind untold poverty and hard labor through its reluctance to enter into the soil. But man has had an ally in certain bacteria called "nitrogen fixers" which take nitrogen from the air and convert it into useful compounds in the soil. For all its great advances, science has not yet learned the secret or equaled the efficiency of these nitrogen-fixing bacteria. The nitrates they manufacture in the soil provide food for plants, which in turn provide food for animals, which in their turn restore some nitrogen compounds to the soil in the form of urea and other excretions and, when they die, in dead tissue. Other bacteria then go to work: putrefying bacteria which decompose dead organisms; nitrifying bacteria which convert the resulting ammonia into mineral nitrates; and denitrifying bacteria which liberate free nitrogen and return it to the air to complete the cycle upon which all the varied life of earth precariously depends.

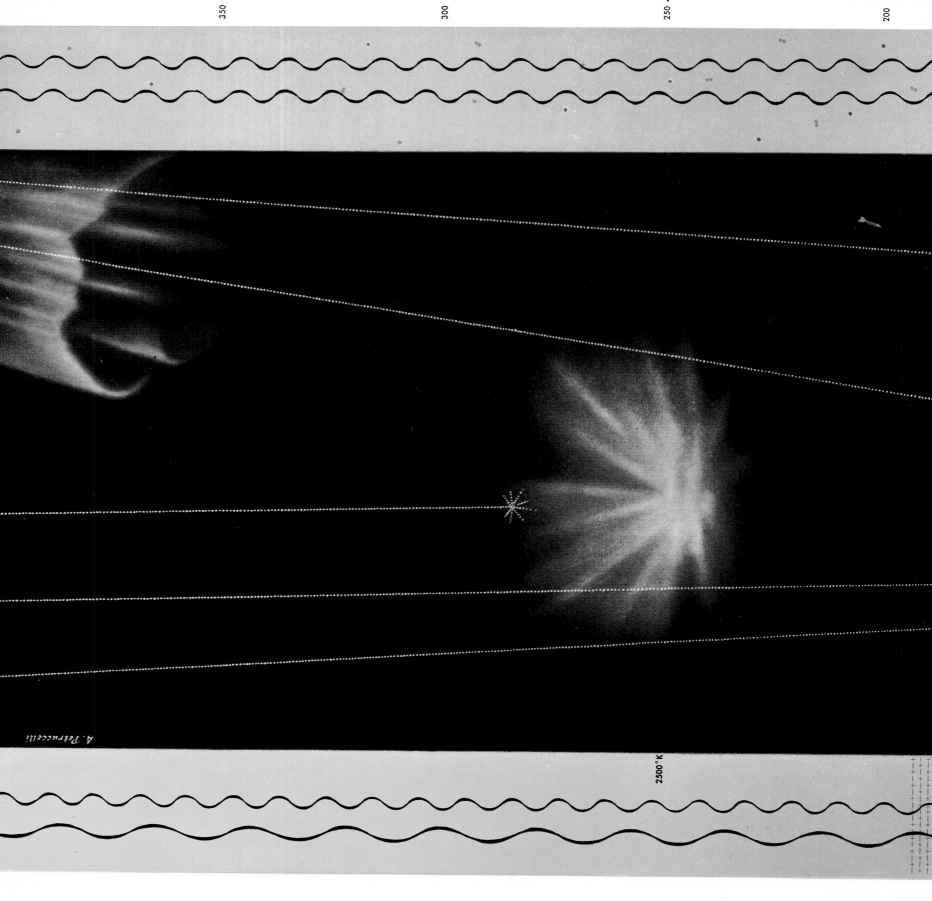

A. Petruccelli

2500° K

ANATOMY OF THE AIR

AIR is a complex and ever varying mixture. Its ingredients vary from place to place and from day to day. Besides the life-giving gases, it contains smaller amounts of the rare gases, helium, xenon, neon; and a few poisonous gases, methane, ammonia, carbon monoxide, nitrous oxide. Up to the realm of the highest familar clouds the atmosphere also holds quantities of foreign matter—pollen, dust, bacteria, soot, spores, volcanic ash, salt particles from the sea and dust from outer space (2,000 tons of "stardust" fall to earth each day).

Although the composition of the air remains more or less constant from sea level to its highest reaches, its density diminishes rapidly with altitude. Six miles up, for example, it is too thin to support respiration; 12 miles up there is not enough oxygen to keep a candle burning. The greater the altitude the fewer the molecules of any gas, and the greater the distances between them. For every million molecules at sea level, there is only one at 60 miles. And while at sea level a molecule cannot move more than four-millionths of an inch before colliding with another, at an altitude of 60 miles it travels about one inch without collision.

At some point several hundreds of miles above the earth the gas particles spray out into space, moving at velocities determined by their last collisions. Some, dragged by gravity, fall back into the ocean of air below; others curve into elliptical orbits and travel like satellites around the earth; others, notably hydrogen and helium, escape forever from the earth's gravitational field. The topmost layer of the atmosphere may be envisaged, therefore, not as the surface of a placid sea, but rather as an indeterminate domain nebulous as a veil of mist rising over the jets of innumerable fountains. Physicists disagree as to the boundaries of this outer fringe or "spray zone" of the atmosphere. Some think it begins 240 miles above the earth and extends to 400 miles. Others place its lower edge at 600 miles and its upper boundary at 6,000 miles. In any event the spray zone is the uttermost frontier of the air. Beyond it lies space.

Apart from quantitative changes, certain

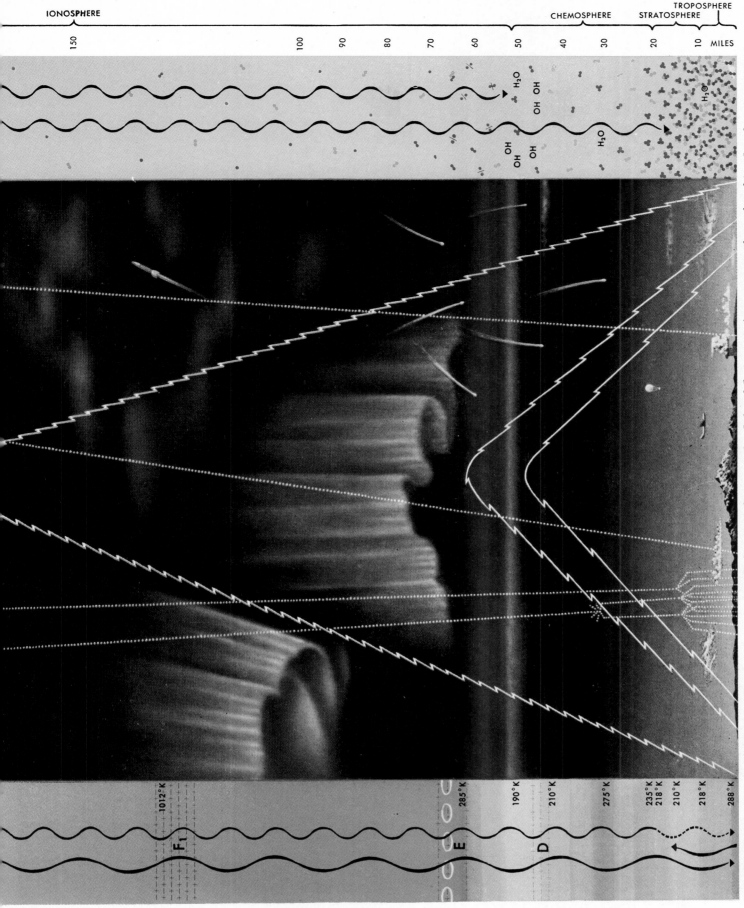

up, solar ultraviolet radiation interacts with oxygen molecules to produce a thin curtain of ozone, a poisonous gas without which life on earth could not exist. Ozone filters out all but a small portion of the sun's lethal ultraviolet rays, allowing only enough through to give man sunburn, kill bacteria and prevent rickets. At 50-65 miles up most of the molecules of oxygen begin to break down under solar radiation into free atoms, or, as in the case of water vapor, to form the incomplete molecule, hydroxyl (OH). Also in this region most of the atoms become ionized (electrically charged).

Perhaps the greatest surprise produced by studies of the atmosphere is that the temperature does not decrease uniformly with increasing altitude, as the experience of earthbound man would suggest. Instead it fluctuates eccentrically at different levels of the upper air. Thus, as shown in the chart at right, it gets steadily colder up to a height of about seven miles; the reason for this is that lower layers of the atmosphere are warmed by heat radiated from the ground. In the stratosphere the decline virtually stops, then at 18 miles descends to a chilly −81°F. (or 210°K. on the Kelvin scale by which scientists measure temperatures of gas). Then the temperature begins to rise, with the accumulation of certain constituents like ozone, which absorb heat directly from the sun. It drops again to a low of −117°F. (190°K.) at about 50 miles, where the ozone disappears. Thereafter it climbs steadily, largely owing to the ionization of particles in the upper atmosphere and their absorption of ultraviolet radiation, reaching 4,188°F. (2,500°K.) at 250 miles. Paradoxically these fantastic temperatures would not be detected by the senses of man, for what he calls heat is simply the energy of molecular or atomic motion. The sense of warmth one feels on a summer day is produced by the bombardment of innumerable air particles whose velocity determines our relative sensations of heat and cold. But in the thin upper air there are not enough particles to impress the skin. So from 50 miles up a man or any living creature, situated in space without the protective cover of the atmosphere, would be broiled to death on one side—the side facing the sun—and frozen to death on the other.

THE EDIFICE OF AIR is detailed in this 400-mile-high section. At the bottom is the troposphere, containing 75% of the atmosphere's weight. Its relative dimensions are shown by Mt. Everest, clouds and high-flying planes, balloons and rockets. Above the troposphere lies the calm stratosphere, and above it the chemosphere where airglow begins. Next is the ionosphere, stretching from 50 to 250 miles, and from 250 miles toward space the almost airless mesosphere. Effects of radiation from the sun (wavy lines) are described in the side panels. At left, ultraviolet (shorter waves) creates several bands of ionization (whose centers of intensity are shown by plus and minus signs). They are known as D, E, F_1 and F_2. Ultraviolet is filtered by ozone at 20 miles. Infrared (longer waves) penetrates to the earth and is reflected as air-warming heat. Temperature variations are here designated in the Kelvin scale (210°K. equals −81°F.) and by color gradations. At right is shown the chemical action of ultraviolet rays, which create hydroxyl (OH) at 50 miles, ozone between 12 and 30. The decrease of air density with altitude is also indicated at right, where atoms are designated by single dots, oxygen molecules by two red dots, nitrogen by two blue dots, ozone by three red dots. The center picture shows the relative heights at which meteors become visible, several forms of aurora, radio waves (jagged lines) bouncing off ionized layers at various altitudes, and showers of cosmic rays (dotted lines).

THE BEAUTY OF THE SKIES

MOST aspects of his environment that man finds beautiful derive ultimately from the atmosphere. Every mood and spectacle of nature that most deeply touches his esthetic spirit springs from the union of light and air. The blue sky and the blue sea, white clouds, green twilight and pearly November mists, rainbows, the flash of lightning—all these flow from the palette of the encircling air.

For the atmosphere intercepts the sun's radiation which contains all the wavelengths of the visible spectrum. It happens that air molecules are the proper size to intercept the short blue wavelengths, deflect them in their flight to earth and scatter them across the sky. The azure "firmament" is thus no glassy dome or vault, but a gauzy, glowing fabric spun of blue light and air. It is, moreover, only about 12 miles high. Beyond, it darkens to violet. Above 20 miles it becomes black and the stars emerge.

The ruddy hues of dawn and sunset are compounded by a similar process. Morning and evening the sun lies low on the horizon, so its rays must traverse many more miles of the earth's atmosphere than at midday. The air molecules, along with water droplets and other particles, filter out most of the shorter wavelengths. The longer wavelengths—vermilion, ruby, rose—predominate in the oblique beams that kiss the earth in the few moments before sundown and after dawn, and it is these that paint the whole world red.

Rainbows, halos, coronas—these too are born of the action of atmospheric components on light: its bending or scattering by raindrops, tiny crystals of ice and cloud droplets. But there are other phenomena of the sky that derive from more complex mechanisms. One is the hazy light that glows in the sky on moonless nights, more brightly near the horizon than in the zenith. Known as "airglow," this faint luminescence is emitted by sodium, oxygen and nitrogen molecules and atoms excited by sunlight during the day. A related phenomenon (*opposite*) is the aurora borealis, which is discussed on the following pages.

THE SETTING SUN glows brilliant red because its oblique rays pass through miles of dense lower air which blocks out all other colors. The foreshortening of the solar face here is caused by the refraction or bending of the sun's rays.

RAINBOWS are caused by the transit of sunlight through falling drops of rain. Each raindrop acts as a tiny prism, breaking down the sun's white rays of mixed light into their component spectral colors. Since each observer sees a rainbow arched around a specific point in the sky directly opposite the sun from his own position, no two people ever see the same bow. Secondary rainbows, like the one at right, are caused by the double reflection of sunlight within the raindrops.

AN AURORA BOREALIS, the corona type which forms a star-shaped pattern, is caused by converging rays high in the sky. The charged particles ejected by the sun (which create the aurora) travel down lines of force in the earth's magnetic field, hitting and exciting the atmosphere's particles. At the magnetic poles the lines of force come together like the spokes of a wheel. It is therefore only in high latitudes near the magnetic poles that auroral rays assume this pattern.

A DRAPERY AURORA develops when parallel streamers of light, spreading upward from horizon to zenith, fall into a graceful pattern that appears to shimmer like the folds of a great curtain hanging from the sky and stirred by a silent wind.

THE MYSTERIOUS AURORA

OF all the pageantry of the atmosphere, the most awesome and, as man has often thought, most fearful, are the auroras—the ghostly streamers of colored light that appear on certain nights, usually in spring and fall, and spread upward from the horizon to the zenith, sometimes projected in shifting rays like searchlight beams, sometimes diffused in shimmering veils and curtains, sometimes dancing and pulsating like the flames of some unutterable cosmic fire.

Auroras seem to be associated with solar flares and gigantic prominences, explosive disturbances in the sun's atmosphere, from which tremendous jets of protons (hydrogen nuclei) and electrons spray outward and speed toward earth at velocities up to 3,000 miles per second. The meeting of this great stream of electrified particles with the earth's magnetic field causes some of the solar particles to be deflected toward the earth's magnetic poles. Auroras always appear, therefore, either in the northern or southern sky, and for the most part in higher latitudes. At a level somewhere between 60 and 600 miles above the earth the solar particles hit the atoms and molecules of the upper air and ionize and excite them, causing them to glow. The colors of the aurora are determined by the wavelengths emitted by the atoms and molecules involved.

A DOUBLE ARC AURORA appears when air particles are disturbed in two zones, one above the other. The colors depend on the particles involved: *e.g.*, green is emitted by atomic oxygen, red by atomic and molecular oxygen, blue by nitrogen.

A HOMOGENEOUS BAND AURORA, in which light is evenly distributed over a wide area without distinct rays, usually forms when an arc aurora turns back on itself. Auroral light is analogous to the light produced by neon tubes. In both

instances it is emitted by atoms or molecules of rarefied gas which have been excited by the impact of electrically charged particles. Auroras appear most frequently in the latitudes of Siberia, Norway and northern Canada (at Hudson Bay they may be seen 240 nights a year) but are occasionally observed as far south as Mexico. This and the other remarkable color photographs of auroras shown on these pages were taken by LIFE's Jay Eyerman in northern Canada.

THE WANDERING WINDS

THE most conspicuous of all properties of the air is its mobility. Long before he understood its composition or role in the sustaining of life, man used the moving air to blow his ships over the sea and trembled at the violence of hurricanes and winter gales. The Old Testament refers to Jehovah walking in majesty on "wings of the wind" and pictures him speaking to Job "out of the whirlwind."

By nature gases are the most mobile of material substances, for their molecules are free and unfettered, not tightly bound as in solids or linked loosely as in liquids. In the atmosphere this mobility manifests itself both in the flow of local winds and in a vast ordered system of air movements that appears to govern weather phenomena around the globe. While the dynamics of these movements are far from clear, contemporary theories agree that the greater winds of earth are impelled by two giant forces: the heat of the sun and the spinning of the planet on its axis. In this process, the sun acts as an engine, the rotation of the earth as a steering mechanism. Were the sun alone at work—if the earth did not rotate—all large-scale winds would blow from a point directly under the sun and spread radially aloft in all directions. But since the earth does rotate, the flow of air from warmer to colder regions is deflected to the east and west. For the atmosphere is not a rigid shell rotating evenly with the earth. On the contrary the planet has only a slack and imperfect grip on its airy mantle.

As a result of this interplay of forces, warm air from the tropics continually mingles with cool air from the poles, moderating climate and preventing violent temperature extremes around most of the world. In each hemisphere warm and cool air masses meet at about 40° Lat., where they form a vast, shifting and unstable boundary, mobile and irregular. Aloft, this boundary is marked by deep folds and undulations, often 4,000 miles across, which alternately advance and retreat northward and southward, but swing in a great orbit around the poles from west to east. It is believed today that most of the weather conditions on earth are related to the behavior of these circumpolar whirls. Recent studies of the northern whirl (little is known of the southern) show that it recurrently expands and contracts, hurling waves of cold air southward toward the equator, sucking warm air northward toward the pole. Simultaneously cells of high and low pressure appear which in turn are related to wind systems at sea level. (Surface winds are also influenced by temperature differences between land and sea, mountains and valleys.)

Near the edge of the northern circumpolar whirl and at an altitude of six to nine miles lies a band of great winds—the swiftest on earth—roaring from west to east in mighty gusts or jets that may attain velocities up to 300 mph. This is the jet stream. In summer, when the circumpolar whirl contracts, it oscillates between 40° and 50° N. Lat.; in winter it wanders as far south as latitudes 25°–35° N. Apart from seasonal fluctuations, the course of the jet stream undergoes cyclical changes. But whether these oscillations create the weather patterns on earth or simply reflect them remains one of meteorology's unanswered questions.

UPDRAFTS AND DOWNDRAFTS create a spectacular wind pattern on the eastern slopes of the Sierra Nevada. Relatively warm, moist air, rolling in from the Pacific Ocean (*off picture at right*), is forced up and over the mountain tops,

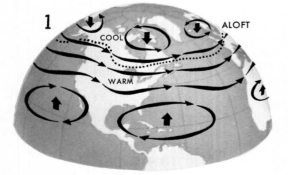

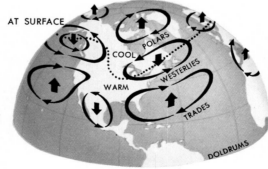

THE GREAT WINDS OF EARTH blow in an ordered cycle of movement that influences weather phenomena around the globe. In this series of diagrams three major phases of the cycle are shown, relating conditions in the atmosphere at 8,000–25,000 feet to wind and weather systems at the earth's surface. The first hemisphere illustrates how, at the meeting point of warm air masses moving poleward and cool polar air moving toward the equator, an irregular undulating boundary is formed, the circumpolar whirl. At the same time, pressure cells are formed: high pressure cells (*arrow pointing up*) in which the winds blow clockwise, and low pressure cells (*arrow pointing down*) in which the winds blow counterclockwise. The second hemisphere shows how these movements relate to belts of high and low pressure at sea level. These belts help shape the three major wind systems of the earth's surface—the Northeast Trades, the Westerlies,

cooling as it ascends and forming a cloud cap atop the highest peaks (*upper right*) 10,000 feet above the valley. On reaching the eastern brink of the range the air plunges down into the valley in a great torrent at a rate of 4,000 feet per minute. It then surges out across the level valley floor in a turbulent, dust-laden wave train whose oscillations cause it to rise again, 5 or 10 miles away from the mountain wall, in a tremendous vertical updraft capped by flat-bottomed roll clouds.

and the Polar Easterlies. In the second phase (*third hemisphere*) the waves of the circumpolar whirl steepen sharply; warm air rides northward on the crests and cold air descends in the troughs as far south as the Gulf of Mexico. Consequently, at sea level (*fourth hemisphere*) the pressure cells take on a north-south alignment, distorting the normal wind system and producing topsy-turvy weather. In the third phase (*fifth hemisphere*) the waves aloft become so steep that they dis-

integrate into vast circular eddies, completely displacing and isolating warm and cool air masses. At sea level (*sixth hemisphere*) areas of warm air are thus trapped in the north, regions of cold air are cut off in the south, and extremely prominent cells of high and low pressure develop. At length, when the earth's air masses have been thoroughly mixed, the cycle swings slowly back to the first phase. As a rule it takes six weeks to run its course, though variations of the pattern occur.

A COLD FRONT forms here when a cool air mass from the land advances into an area of warm air over the sea. The leading edge of the cold mass (tinted blue) undercuts the warm air and thrusts it aloft where it condenses into a line of cumulonimbus clouds. Violent air currents within the cloud mass are defined by arrows. The scene here depicts what is occurring along the front line near the low pressure area shown at far right on the painting on the opposite page.

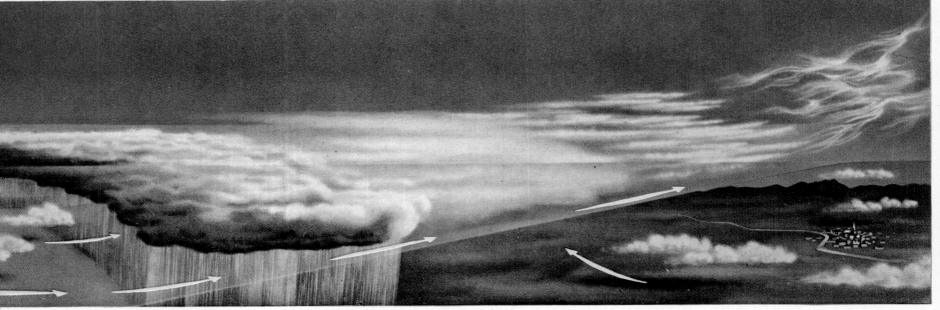

A WARM FRONT develops when the leading edge of a mass of warm air (pink) rides up and over a cool air mass. Ascending and cooling, the warm air condenses into nimbostratus clouds, the earth's greatest rainmakers. Far in the van (*upper right*) float some high cirrus clouds, often precursors of bad weather. The pre-storm wind (*bottom arrow, right*) blows almost perpendicularly to the advancing front. This scene is occurring along the southern U.S. in the picture at right.

THE INCONSTANT WEATHER

THE atmosphere is clearly not a calm ocean of air, but a tossing, unquiet sea, riven and distorted by swift currents, furrowed by tremendous waves. And these waves influence the character of weather across the face of the earth. For whenever the air aloft warps upward to form a great wave crest or ridge, there is likely to be a related high pressure area somewhere on the earth below, and when it sinks into a valley or trough a low pressure area may be revealed by the barometers of man.

A "high" may be envisaged pictorially as a towering mass of air—a hill or mountain of air—rising above surrounding air masses. Because it contains more air than the other masses around it, it exerts greater pressure at its base and within its periphery. Winds spiral outward from regions of high pressure, hence the upper air sinks to fill the gap, warming as it compresses. The weather within highs is, therefore, generally characterized by clear skies, sunshine and pleasant dry air. A "low," on the other hand, represents a depression or valley in the atmosphere, sagging below the level of surrounding air masses and exerting lower pressures on the land beneath it because it contains less air. The weather within low pressure cells is likely to be distinguished by storms because winds blow into lows and the air, then rising to cool heights, condenses into fog or rain.

It is known now that the appearance and movements of highs and lows on earth are related to the cycles of the circumpolar whirl and the jet stream in the upper air. But meteorologists believe that the topography of the earth, the contrasting temperatures of land and sea and the changing seasons may in turn influence the oscillations of the circumpolar whirl. Partly because of the fixed architecture of the earth, certain major regions of high and low pressure manifest themselves in certain parts of the world and recur from year to year. Near the equator, for example, there extends a zone of warm, rising air and low pressure known as the "doldrums." Two other zones of average low pressure appear at 60° N. and S. Lat. Within each of these exist smaller cells of particularly strong action such as the Siberian High, the Canadian High, the North Atlantic (or Bermuda) High, the South Atlantic High, the North Pacific High, the South Pacific High, the Australian High; and the Icelandic Low and the Aleutian Low. None of these zones of action is altogether permanent, however, for each is affected by the changing seasons and the idiosyncrasies of the circumpolar whirl. Thus the continent of Asia becomes a heat trap in warm weather, so that the Siberian High of winter turns into the Monsoon Low of summer.

The distribution and movement of highs and lows around the globe are related to three main zones of bad weather on earth: the Equatorial Convergence and the North and South Polar Fronts. The Equatorial Convergence is created by the collision of the northeast trade

THE UNDULATING ATMOSPHERE moves over the earth in mountains and valleys of air. Here two translucent layers indicate the patterns of highs (up-pointing arrows) and lows (down-pointing arrows) at the surface and at 18,000 feet.

Near the ground these undulations are sharply defined; above, they are flattened and displaced westward. Warm air is shown in red, cold in blue. Yellow arrows give wind direction. Contour lines are isobars, linking areas of equal pressure.

winds of the northern hemisphere with the southeast trade winds of the southern hemisphere. Both of these great wind systems carry masses of warm, moist air. Converging in the region of the equatorial lows or doldrums, they soar upward to cool heights, then condense as rain. The Equatorial Convergence rarely shifts more than 200 miles in small, day-to-day fluctuations. But on occasion, in the summer months when the continental land areas become heated, it moves inland to higher latitudes and occasionally even brushes the fringes of the other two great storm areas—the North and South Polar Fronts.

Fronts are the forward boundaries or leading edges of moving masses of warm or cold air. (The Equatorial Convergence is not a front because its two conflicting air masses have virtually the same temperature.) The Polar Fronts, which oscillate back and forth over many degrees of the middle latitudes, mark the meeting of cold air, streaming out of the polar highs, with the warm breath of the Westerlies slanting up from the subtropics. Clinging close to the earth's surface, the cold air creeps in under the warm air, sometimes thrusting irregular wedges deep into lower latitudes. Meanwhile the warm air rides above, cooling and condensing into clouds, mist and rain. The leading edge of the front is at no time a simple plane surface, but an irregular sloping one, pushing far toward the equator at sea level and extending far poleward in its upper strata. In the struggle between warm and cold air the front tends to buckle and warp, here

retreating, there probing equatorward with long fingers of cold air. Often along these protuberances in the distorted front storm centers form—regions of low pressure that vary from day to day but move inexorably eastward to their meteorological graveyards in the semi-permanent lows off Iceland and the Aleutian Islands.

The manner in which the edges of the great Polar Fronts move determines the distribution and character of the local fronts which appear daily on weather maps around the world. Meteorologists recognize four kinds of fronts: cold, warm, occluded and stationary. A cold front occurs when a cool, swift-moving air mass overtakes warm air and thrusts it suddenly aloft, often to the accompaniment of violent wind and thunderstorms. The turbulence is usually brief and localized, however, and terminates abruptly with a dramatic "broom-in-the-sky" dispelling of clouds. A warm front, which evolves when a warm air mass slowly overtakes and slides over a cooler one, may cover large areas—perhaps several states or even whole sections of the country—with dreary, rainy weather that persists for days. An occluded front develops when a cold front overtakes a warm front and hoists it completely off the ground, so that the line of contact between them is aloft. It brings the characteristic features of both cold and warm front disturbances. And once in a while a cold or a warm front simply stands still. In such instances the front is known as a stationary front, and the weather remains fixed until the front moves on.

AN APRIL SHOWER descends from congested cumulus clouds, hovering over warm land on a humid day. Clouds like this one represent an intermediate type between fleecy fair weather clouds and the ominous cumulonimbus shown below.

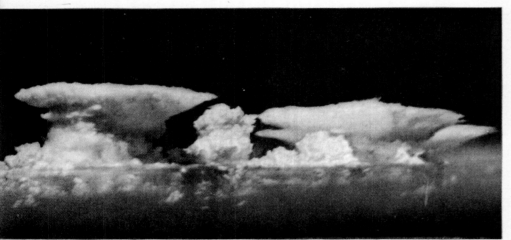

THUNDERHEADS develop from other cumulus forms when rising air carries them to great heights. Their anvil tops, towering 20,000–30,000 feet high, are flattened by stable layers in the atmosphere which prevent them from rising higher.

THE INNER WALL OF A TYPHOON is formed by a great rotating mass of dense clouds, whirling at high speed around a central "eye" or area of calm. In this Air Force photograph the top of the eye can be seen in the upper left corner.

A THUNDERSTORM in Arizona breaks when the violent updrafts and downdrafts that rend its interior create conditions that result in the manufacture of rain and the development of electrical tensions between different parts of the cloud. A

STORMS, LIGHTNING, RAIN

IT is in zones of low pressure, like whirlpools in the atmospheric sea where warm and cool air meet, that the tempests of earth are begotten—from the quick passing squall to the wildest storms man knows: the hurricanes of tropic seas.

A hurricane's inception is tranquil. Somewhere in the doldrums where the hot sun has glared down day after day on a sluggish, windless sea, still air begins to rise. And as this light air floats aloft, new air drifts in to replace it and joins the rotary swirl. Thick clouds mass overhead, torrential rains descend, lightning cuts the darkling air, and the fierce winds whirl around the central "eye" of the storm with velocities up to 150 mph. The great storm will then move across the sea until perhaps a fortnight later its stupendous energies are spent.

No less spectacular, though more familiar to most men than these furious cyclonic convulsions of the air, are thunderstorms. Like all atmospheric disturbances, they evolve from the interplay of sun and water and, paradoxically, from the loveliest of all clouds, the fleecy white cumulus of sunny summer days. Under certain conditions of

typical thundercloud is divided into three zones: lower, central and upper. Of these the central zone is the most active; it is predominantly negative in charge. The upper zone tends to be positive, the lower zone nearly neutral.

Eventually the growing negative potential of the active central zone far exceeds the positive charges elsewhere within the cloud. When this potential grows to between ten and one hundred million volts, a flash of lightning is produced.

temperature, humidity and wind movement, cumulus clouds build up into lofty, anvil-topped cumulonimbus formations, which tower 20,000–30,000 feet into the upper air. Palpable and castlelike in appearance, these giant cloud masses are actually dynamic cells of turbulent energy, seething with hidden forces. Their turreted battlements and inner ramparts are torn by violent updrafts and downdrafts, within which droplets of water are continually being swept aloft and plummeted earthward, now frozen into hail or snow, now evaporated into invisible vapor, now melted again to rain.

The processes by which a cloud manufactures rain remain obscure; it appears that several mechanisms may operate, varying with the temperature of the cloud. In the cold upper strata of lofty clouds it is believed that water vapor congeals on tiny floating crystals of ice which continue to grow until they are heavy enough to fall. On reaching warmer levels they melt and descend as rain. At lower levels raindrops may form through the simple coalescence of minute droplets into larger ones. But there appear to be other requirements. One theory demands the presence of microscopic nuclei, in the form of dust or salt particles, upon which the water vapor can condense to form the cloud droplets. Another theory holds that electricity plays an essential

role in rain formation. Until it starts to rain a cloud has no electrical field, for although each tiny water droplet carries an electrical charge, it is surrounded by a sheath of ionized air molecules carrying an opposite charge which neutralizes it. It is believed therefore that a cloud can shed rain only when some agency intervenes to upset the electrostatic balance—perhaps a sudden updraft that sweeps the neutralizing ions to the upper part of the cloud and thus permits the charged droplets to coalesce and fall, gathering other drops in their descent.

At times the negative charge within a cloud builds up to a point where it must be relieved by a discharge within the cloud or else from the cloud to earth. The exchange of electricity between cloud and earth takes the form of several swift, two-way impulses of which the strongest are usually from earth to cloud, hence the brightest visible lightning flashes are probably traveling up rather than down. The light is produced by the ionization and excitation of molecules of air in the path of the bolt. Behind each stroke lightning leaves a wake of heated air. The sudden expansion of this air creates a train of wavelike vibrations that radiate in all directions. When these vibrations reach the ears of man, he calls them thunder.

79

A SEA OF STRATUS CLOUDS gleams in golden morning light. Formed by warm air sliding over a cool surface, stratus clouds are "layerlike" and smooth above and below. Their base may lie anywhere between ground level and 3,000 feet.

A VEIL OF CIRRUS CLOUDS is touched with the fire of the setting sun. Highest of all the familiar clouds, their slender, tufted filaments, composed of fine crystals of ice or of drifting snow, often ride eight miles or more above the earth.

ALTO-CUMULUS CLOUDS usually ride between 8,000 and 18,000 feet, above summer cumulus (*right*) and below the cirro-cumulus (*right, below*). They may be formed by wavelike currents of air or by the breakdown of stratus layers.

WATER VAPOR AND CLOUDS

ALTHOUGH the frowning thunderhead represents the most spectacular of cloud structures, the blue ocean of air is continually flecked and dappled, white-capped and gray-mottled, with a variety of ever-changing vapor patterns that alter with geography and season and produce much of the beauty and diversity of the sky. However they may vary, from the feathery veils of high cirrus to the billowing cottony fluffs of summer cumulus, all clouds are woven of the same diaphanous substance—water vapor made visible, hovering in the air at altitudes determined by the winds, temperature and sun.

If all the water vapor in the atmosphere were precipitated in a single sudden downpour, it would cover the globe with a layer of water only one inch deep. Yet this sparse but unique gas represents one of the most crucial components of the air, without which the earth would have neither life, as man knows it, nor changing weather. Without water vapor the earth would be suffocated beneath rolling clouds of wind-blown dust and would experience more rigorous extremes of temperature. For the movement of water vapor, both vertical and horizontal, constitutes one of the earth's most important mechanisms of heat transfer. Twice a year, for example, 10,000,000,-000,000 tons of air roll across the equator from the summer to the winter hemisphere, carrying along billions of tons of water vapor that help to moderate and equalize the difference between the hot and cold areas of earth. The ability of water vapor to absorb radiation, especially long-wave radiation from the earth's surface, plays a vital role, moreover, in maintaining the temperature balance that sustains all terrestrial life. Of the total amount of radiation leaving the surface of the earth, only about 15% is lost to outer space. The rest is trapped by the atmosphere, largely through the agency of water vapor.

On clear, dry days water vapor is invisible. But from time to time it makes itself seen—now falling in the form of rain, hail or snow, now coating the limbs of trees in a glistening armor of ice, now hanging like jewel-drops in a cobweb, spangling the grass with morning dew or frost. And when it condenses into tiny droplets (so minute

CIRRO-CUMULUS CLOUDS soar at altitudes above 18,000 feet. Like all the high clouds, they are composed of ice crystals rather than water droplets. This formation, known as "mackerel sky," may indicate the approach of a warm front.

FAIR WEATHER CUMULUS is the most frequent and familiar cloud formation of the lower atmosphere. Each cloud tops a column of air that has risen from the sun-warmed ground to condensation level. They range from 3,000 to 10,000 feet.

A BANNER CLOUD streams from the summit of Mt. Baker, Wash. Such clouds adorn many of the earth's highest mountains. They are formed by the sudden cooling of air as it is thrust up over the peak.

CUMULUS MAMMATUS is a rare formation created by localized downdrafts within a thundercloud. In

it would take five billion to fill a teaspoon) and enshrouds the earth in a pearly, translucent mantle, men call it fog—or, riding aloft, a cloud.

The transition of water vapor from the invisible to the visible state depends primarily on temperature. For warm air can hold more water in transparent vapor form than cold air. When saturated air is sufficiently cooled, condensation occurs. There are several ways in which this process may take place. After sundown, for example, the earth yields back the heat of the day, cooling the lower layers of air and

causing dew and ground fog to form in valley bottoms or over flat marshes and moors. Sometimes, too, winds carry warm air over cool surfaces, creating fog and sheets of low stratus cloud. Thus in wintertime moist breezes from the sea may blow inland over a frozen landscape and produce the wet fogs characteristic of many coastal regions. Or in summertime warm air from the land may blow out across cool offshore waters, and then the fog will overhang the sea—as off the coasts of Newfoundland, Labrador and Maine. On a smaller scale the

LENTICULAR CLOUDS form over mountains, where currents of moist air are thrust aloft, cooling and condensing as they ascend. Here, at Taos, N. Mex., the wind is blowing from left to right. The cloud starts to condense on the windward side of the mountain at left, and thickens to maximum depth over the summit.

this photograph the under side of the main cloud is shown, studded with udderlike protuberances.

FREAK CLOUD may have been formed when erratic eddies sucked streamers from the body of a larger

cloud. Such accidental structures are unstable and usually evaporate quickly into surrounding dry air.

same process may be seen in the sweating of a glass of ice water or any cold drink on a humid summer day.

A somewhat different mechanism of cloud formation is known as convection—the rising and cooling of air—and it is this that engenders both the fierce hurricane and the soft cumulus of tranquil summer days. If air currents were visible, one might look across a landscape on a warm July afternoon and see innumerable columns of sun-heated air rising from the ground, each supporting a white cumulus cloud. For each cloud represents the visible capital of a convective column of ascending air beneath it. The height at which the cloud forms indicates the temperature level at which invisible water vapor condenses into visible droplets. Somewhat in the same way, warm air traveling in a horizontal direction may ride up a mountainside on the back of the wind, cooling as it rises and condensing as it cools. It is for this reason that many of the great mountains of earth wear on their summits, on windy days, a cap of white cloud.

Then the air flows downward to the right, drying as it descends. A lenticular or lens-shaped structure is thus formed. At right center the air starts upward again and forms a similar cloud over the peaks at right. Such clouds have been likened to waterfalls: fixed in position, but composed of ever-changing material.

DESTROYED BY DROUGHT, an ancient Pueblo Indian town stands in silent ruin under the Southwestern sun. Ten centuries ago Pueblo Bonito prospered in New Mexico's then fertile Chaco Canyon. A multistoried apartment building of 800 rooms, it housed 1,200 people—all dependent on field-grown crops. Then, as a dry climate grew drier, the meager margin of essential moisture vanished. By the end of the 12th Century, Pueblo Bonito stood empty and abandoned.

CLIMATE AND HISTORY

MORE than any other aspect of nature, the stately procession of clouds, floating full-sailed across the sky, changing shape and color with the changing angle of the sun, massing and dissolving at the caprice of the winds, has imparted to mankind a sense of evanescence, of the mutability of beauty, life and daily circumstance. "Fickle, short-lived clouds," Wordsworth called them, contrasting their ephemeral existence with the permanence of the "everlasting stars."

To man the basic framework of the world—the sun, the sea, the mountains—has always seemed an eternal stage on which the transitory cycles of life and the inconstant moods of weather are fleetingly projected. Owing to the limits of his temporal vision he often fails to detect vaster, slower changes in the physical world about him—like the rise and fall of ocean levels, the rise and fall of mountains. Ever aware of day-to-day fluctuations in the weather, he tends to assign a certain permanency to climate. For weather is merely the condition of the air at a particular time and place, a single state in the series of states that constitute climate, which is the average weather of any locality. Yet in the grand perspective of Earth history, the aberrations of climate down the centuries appear as eccentric as the day-to-day vagaries of the weather. One cannot assume that Brazil has always been as hot as it is today, or the Sahara always as dry, or that the temperature mean of England is the same now as it was in the reign of Alfred.

At the present time the earth's overall climate is far more rigorous, and distinguished by greater extremes of heat and cold, than it has been throughout most of the last one and a half billion years of geologic time. For most of its existence the climate of Earth has been comparatively uniform and genial, and temperature differences relatively small; its polar regions were ice-free, fairly temperate and fertile; animals ranged more widely and plants spread over areas that are barren today; oceans covered great areas of the present continental masses, and warm currents flowed to the poles through broad channels. This benign state of affairs, which prevailed for the greater span of terrestrial time, is the normal climate of our planet. Intervening interludes of severe but brief climatic change are considered by geologists and climatologists as "abnormal," and they represent less than one-fifth of geologic history. The last such period began about a million years ago and reached its most recent peak some 10,000 years ago when the great ice sheets started to recede from a line passing near the present locations of Syracuse, Milwaukee and Des Moines. Climatologists disagree as to whether we are living today in the final phases of an ice age or merely in a temporary cycle of recession within the greater glacial epoch. In any case the entire history of man has been enacted in "abnormal" times; he has never known the "normal" climate of his planetary abode.

At least four times within the last million years the icecaps have advanced and retreated, and the earth's multifarious animal and plant life advanced and retreated with them, like armies maneuvering along a changing front in a titanic struggle for existence. All over the face of the earth, local climate and living conditions responded to the march of the glaciers. In the tropics and sub-tropics their advance and recession seem to have been reflected in alternating periods of wet weather and dry. Each invasion of the ice thrust the rain belt farther south, converting deserts in Africa, Arabia and Asia into fertile grasslands and savannas. Then with the retreat of the ice they became arid once again.

Even within historical times cyclical changes in climate have been recorded and often profoundly influenced the course of history. Recurring intervals of wet and dry climate produced fluctuations in desert and forest growth, which before the advent of the road-building Romans affected the distribution of human society. Some climatologists believe today that the abandoned pueblos of the American Southwest (*opposite page*), the mysterious Maya ruins in Yucatán and the lost city of Angkor in Indochina can be explained as the relics of civilizations that succumbed to a climatic change. The Southwestern towns were apparently decimated by increasing dryness. Both the Maya and Cambodian cultures developed to a high level during successive centuries of relatively dry weather; then rainfall increased and the tropical forests advanced and literally engulfed

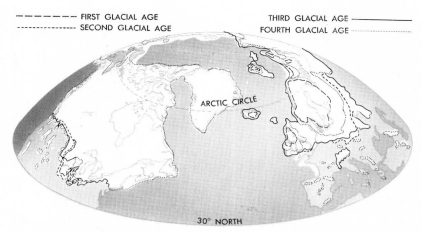

––––––– FIRST GLACIAL AGE   THIRD GLACIAL AGE –––––––
············· SECOND GLACIAL AGE   FOURTH GLACIAL AGE ·············

THE LAST GREAT ICE AGE, which began about one million years ago, was marked by four major advances of the glaciers, punctuated by periods of recession. Although in many areas the frontiers of maximum encroachment remain uncertain, the crude boundaries shown here are generally accepted by geologists. Wherever a single line appears, it means that the limits of greatest advance of the different periods coincided too closely to be resolved. Coastlines at the time of the last advance are indicated by a lighter tone. The entire history of man has been enacted within this glacial epoch. The last major advance began about 50,000 years ago. For the past 10,000 years the glaciers have been receding.

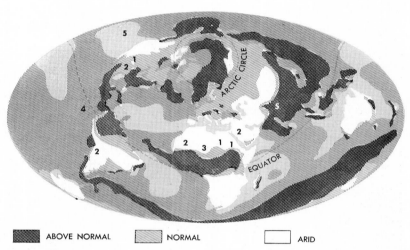

■ ABOVE NORMAL   □ NORMAL   □ ARID

JULY RAINFALL varies around the globe from season to season and place to place. Areas of heavy rainfall (over four inches per month), normal rainfall, and aridity (less than one inch per month) for an average July are indicated on the maps above and below by different shadings. The numerals indicate regions of weather extremes, as follows: 1) Hottest places; Death Valley, Calif., a region in Libya where temperatures of 134°–136°F. in the shade have been recorded, and the port of Massawa on the Red Sea. 2) Driest places; the Sahara, Palestine, the U.S. Southwest and Chile. 3) Sunniest; the Sahara. 4) Calmest; in the region of the doldrums near the equator. 5) Wettest; Hawaii and Assam in India.

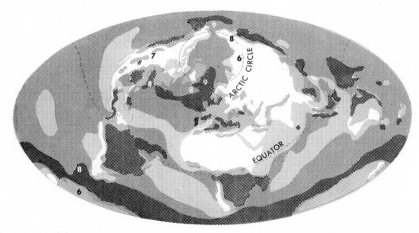

JANUARY RAINFALL often reverses the July pattern, particularly in Africa, whose upper central portion changes from above normal to arid, and in Asia, which is mostly dry throughout the winter. In South America, where January falls in mid-summer, aridity generally gives way to drenching rain. Numerals indicate: 6) The coldest places; Verkhoyansk, in Siberia (−90°F.) and Antarctica. 7) The snowiest; the Sierra Nevada. 8) The windiest; places in the belt of violent westerly winds lying between 40° and 50° south latitude known as the Roaring Forties, the North Atlantic near Iceland, Kamchatka, and Mt. Washington, N.H. 9) The stormiest; areas near Iceland and the Aleutian Islands.

the great cities. The varying rains affected not only forests, but lakes and rivers, producing alternating eras of drought and flood. Some authorities suggest that a great flood in the Second Century B.C. may have induced the Cimbri to migrate from Jutland south to Gaul.

It has been observed that eras of discovery, invasion and conquest in northern latitudes have often coincided with periods of glacial recession and warm climate. At the time of the Norman Conquest, England was a grape-growing country; Greenland, which was settled in 986, provided pasturage for cattle and sheep. But in the next three centuries references to vineyards in England vanished from literature, and the graves of colonists in Greenland became ever shallower as the ground froze more. During the 15th and 16th Centuries—most vigorous of all epochs of exploration and commercial expansion—the glaciers retreated once again. They advanced anew in the 1600s and continued to push southward in some areas until 1850—a period during which some villages in the Swiss Alps were obliterated by the encroaching ice.

Some authorities believe that high civilization and a certain type of climate go hand in hand. The optimum climate for human activity appears to be characterized by moderate temperatures and frequent barometric depressions providing both adequate rainfall and the stimulation of changeable weather. It was in such climatic circumstances that the great civilizations of Greece and Rome evolved. Their eventual decline and the shifting of civilization to the north may have been the result of a northward shift of the circumpolar rain belt and the consequent desiccation of the Mediterranean area. One scholar has correlated the rise and fall of Roman culture with rainfall, showing that precipitation was abundant during the vigorous life of the early republic, then diminished for a while, became abundant again during the heydays of Caesar and Augustus, and from 80 A.D. on declined steadily in step with the decline of the empire.

The variable climate productive of high civilizations of the past is found today, among other places, in Great Britain, France, Germany, the Scandinavian countries, Japan, parts of the Soviet Union, and parts of the U.S. and Canada. Yet for the last century temperatures have shown an upward trend. This has been particularly true in the last four decades, during which glaciers have been in retreat all around the world. The reasons for this gradual warming of the earth cannot be defined with certainty. One suggested explanation is an increase in the carbon dioxide content of the atmosphere. Along with water vapor and ozone, carbon dioxide helps to trap the earth's heat within the greenhouse of the atmosphere and prevents it from radiating away into space. In the last half century the carbon dioxide ratio in the atmosphere has increased by 10%, a phenomenon which some attribute to expanding industry, pointing out that six billion tons of carbon dioxide pour from factory chimneys every year. Other authorities believe that a more important factor may be the decimation of forests, which consume great quantities of carbon dioxide, and the disturbance of the soil which exhales it.

However he may ultimately revise or pollute the atmosphere in which he dwells, man appears now to confront a more immediate problem in learning to survive without any atmosphere at all—i.e., in outer space. The difficulties of space travel would be less complex if gravitation were the only obstacle to be overcome. But it is the rapid disappearance of the atmosphere with increasing altitude that magnifies all hazards. Any space ship in which men hope to live must carry part of the earth's atmosphere along with it. Should its skin be perforated in flight by a meteor, its occupants would die violently in a crescendo of physical reactions. They would lose consciousness for lack of oxygen; they would drown in their own body fluids; their blood and all other intercellular and extracellular liquids would literally boil. Even barring such a dire contingency, the problem of air conditioning a space ship would remain—oxygen would have to be carried along, foul exhalations chemically absorbed, and the air mechanically circulated. In man's natural environment the air around him is kept in circulation largely by convection—his exhaled breath and the sheath of air that surrounds his body drift away because they are warmer and lighter than the contiguous air. As a consequence his perspiration can evaporate and dry air can constantly circulate above his skin, helping to maintain his uniform body temperature. But outside the earth's gravitational field there would be no difference in the weight of warm and cool air; convection would cease and members of a space ship crew might be stifled in a noxious cloud of their own manufacture. And there are other problems involving temperature and exposure to dangerous solar radiation that derive directly from the absence of the protective atmosphere.

So in dreaming of a passage beyond his natural medium of existence man will indeed be casting himself into an environment for which he was never designed. Ancient cosmologists were not altogether wrong when they regarded the blue vault of heaven as the palpable roof or ceiling of the world. For the blue sky does indeed mark the upper boundary of the useful, life-giving atmosphere—the surface of the airy ocean on whose floor man dwells and above which he may not rise unarmored into the hostile and limitless domain of interstellar space. In its combination of beauty and mystery, the ever-changing canopy of air that encompasses and shelters the earth, that gives it light and warmth, color and rain, and provides the breath of all living things, has always stirred the emotions of perceiving man. "Sometimes gentle, sometimes capricious, sometimes awful," wrote John Ruskin of the sky, "never the same for two moments together: almost human in its passions, almost spiritual in its tenderness, almost divine in its infinity."

THE PAGEANT
OF LIFE

PART V

THE PAGEANT OF LIFE

Through the wondrous workings of evolution all the creatures of the earth developed out of distant and shadowy beginnings in the warm primeval seas

> Let the waters bring forth
> the creeping creature having life . . .
> GENESIS 1:20

FOR perhaps one half of the long span of earth history the planet Earth lay barren and lifeless under its canopy of air. The waters of its oceans rose and fell with the pulse of the sun and moon and stirred with the respiration of the winds. But in them no living thing moved. Above them the great continental platforms loomed rocky and bleak, devoid of green as the landscapes of the airless moon.

Then at some indeterminate point—some say two billion years ago, some a billion and a half—the entity called life miraculously appeared on the surface of the deep. What form it took, what concatenation of physical circumstances brought it into being, science cannot specify—nor indeed reply with assurance to the question, "What is life?" All that can be said is that through some agency certain giant molecules acquired the ability to duplicate themselves. From such shadowy beginnings there emerged the wondrous procession of living things—the incalculable hordes of flying, swimming, crawling and ambulatory creatures that have moved across the face of the planet down eons of terrestrial time, and the incomputable generations of shrubs and trees, grasses and mosses, ferns and flowers that have clung to its stony crust, softening and brightening it with a mantle of dappled green.

As a form of life uniquely endowed with the capacity to perceive himself in relation to his environment, man has ever questioned where he came from, how he achieved his present eminence at the apex of the animal kingdom. In the span of his existence he has evolved many theories of his own origin, most of them set forth in terms of his varied theologies. It was only yesterday, however, that he began to interpret a few of the clues that he has found engraved, like the ciphers of some arcane codescript, in the rock tablets of the earth's crust. For in a literal sense the crust of the earth is a book of rocks (see chart, p. 73) inscribed with the long history of life on our planet.

Until the middle of the 18th Century Western man believed in the special creation of every living creature after his kind. Although fossils had been observed since Greek times, they generally were deprecated as isolated freaks of nature. Most living things disappear completely when they perish, crumbling into dust and leaving not a trace behind. Hence the preservation of a fossil is a rare event. Yet fossils have been unearthed by the millions revealing a proliferation of animal life on earth for untold ages past. Most disturbing were the occasional remains of bizarre creatures the like of which no man had ever viewed. Not until the science of paleontology came into being around 1800 did pieces of the puzzle begin to fall in place. But huge gaps remained, deep questions cried for an answer. Why did creatures appear in one epoch, flourish and then disappear? Why did plant and animal forms differ so greatly from one rock stratum to another? From the evidence one idea seemed inescapable—the idea of progression and change from age to age.

In 1859 Darwin published *The Origin of Species*, outlining his classic theory of evolution. Like many works of scientific inspiration it rested on underlying concepts that had provoked the speculation of other thinkers in the past. His own grandfather, Erasmus Darwin, had theorized about the formation of species, as had the French naturalist Lamarck. Darwin's genius lay in his painstaking accumulation of masses of evidence and his distillation of that evidence into a few fundamental principles. To begin with, he had noted that man, in breeding animals and plants to bring out desirable characteristics, often profoundly altered their structure and habits. From the wild horse he had produced the draft horse and the race horse; he had developed many varieties of corn, dogs, poultry and wheat. Once established, new lines appeared to perpetuate themselves. Could the same events occur in nature? Could a single line of animals change so much over millions of years that they would bear no resemblance to their progenitors? Darwin's answer was yes, and he supported it with deductions embodying the essence of his evolutionary theory.

Viewing the animal kingdom as a whole, he observed that all organisms produce more than one offspring, so the populations of all species should be increasing constantly. Then why were the seas not packed with fish, since a single female fish may lay as many as 100,000 eggs at one spawning? Why were there not more elephants, since a single pair of even this slow-breeding species might produce millions of progeny in the space of a few centuries—if all survived? Obviously many offspring must die in the struggle for existence.

Darwin adduced evidence to show that competition is always fiercest *within* species rather than between them. Since each species reveals considerable variation among individual members it is logical to assume that individuals endowed with variations favorable to them in the struggle for existence are most likely to survive. When they reproduce they may pass their special endowments on to their progeny. Species are thus plastic entities that imperceptibly and over long periods of time change through a process of natural selection. In the immense vistas of geologic time it is possible to imagine that a tiny, lemur-like mammal could ultimately develop into man.

Darwin's theory was quickly recognized as one of the great scientific achievements of all time, for it illuminated the whole grand panorama of animal life on earth, past and present. Within a generation after its initial publication, all substantial opposition to its major tenets vanished—among scientists at least. The theological implications led to longer disputes, though Darwin was a religious man and it was not he but some of his followers who wished to dispense with God. Today, while there remain fundamentalists of all faiths who regard Genesis as a literal document open to no interpretation, the main stream of thought in Western theology has embraced evolution as the scientific account of creation. Nor is this interpretive tradition new. Long ago St. Augustine discussed various ways in which the work of the Six Days might be understood, and St. Thomas Aquinas distinguished between the initial creation of matter and the establishment of natural laws that have continued to effect change in the physical world. In Darwin's mind the miracle of creation lay in the infusion of those wondrous laws of nature that, unfolding, called forth the great pageant of life on earth. "There is grandeur," he wrote, "in this view of life . . . having been originally breathed by the Creator into a few forms or into one; and that, whilst this planet has gone cycling on . . . from so simple a beginning endless forms most beautiful and most wonderful have been, and are being evolved."

A 500-MILLION-YEAR-OLD FOSSIL reveals in clear detail the outlines of an 8-inch trilobite, a hard-shelled, multilegged animal that thrived in the warm primeval seas. Extinct now, trilobites constitute more than 60% of the fossils found in the first chapter of the book of rocks. Though the biggest of them never exceeded 27 inches in length, they were nevertheless the giants of their age and dominated life on earth for a span 75 times as long as man's whole existence.

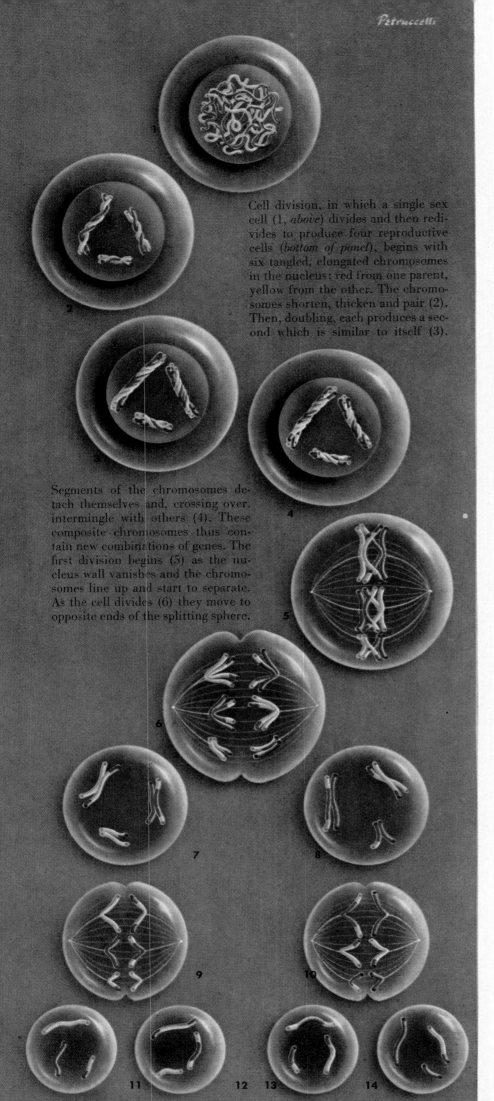

Cell division, in which a single sex cell (1, *above*) divides and then redivides to produce four reproductive cells (*bottom of panel*), begins with six tangled, elongated chromosomes in the nucleus: red from one parent, yellow from the other. The chromosomes shorten, thicken and pair (2). Then, doubling, each produces a second which is similar to itself (3).

Segments of the chromosomes detach themselves and, crossing over, intermingle with others (4). These composite chromosomes thus contain new combinations of genes. The first division begins (5) as the nucleus wall vanishes and the chromosomes line up and start to separate. As the cell divides (6) they move to opposite ends of the splitting sphere.

The two new cells formed by division (7 and 8) each contain three pairs of chromosomes. At this stage the sex cells behave differently from ordinary body cells inasmuch as they split again (9 and 10) to create reproductive cells with single, unpaired chromosomes (11, 12, 13 and 14). These are immature germ cells, each one different from the others and from the parent cell. Their new characteristics will be passed on when they combine as sperms and eggs to produce distinct new individuals.

THE ENDLESS THREAD OF LIFE

DOWN the unimaginable corridors of geologic time the thread of life has passed from generation to generation, ever varying but unbroken. For the essence of life is that it is continuous. Only life can transfuse life, and each living organism on earth acquired its heritage from another like itself.

The processes by which life renews itself are among the most exquisite and esoteric workings of nature. A century ago, when Darwin was developing his theory of evolution, far less was known about them, and it appeared for a time that the whole edifice of his work might collapse for want of an explanation of the actual mechanisms of inheritance. Not until the development of the science of genetics in the 1900s were the foundation stones of Darwin's house made secure. For genetics explained for the first time how the characteristics of plant and animal species have been transmitted down the continuing generations.

So long as the answers were sought in the gross structure of living creatures, the enigma of heredity remained unsolved. It was only after biologists turned to the basic units of living matter, the cells, that understanding began to emerge. While varying greatly in form and function, most cells are microscopic in size, averaging about .0005 inches across. Some living creatures, like amoebas and bacteria, are made of but a single cell. The body of an adult human being contains trillions. Within the nucleus of each cell lies a mass of tangled, threadlike structures called chromosomes. The number present varies among species but it is usually constant for each. Thus the fertilized egg of a fruit fly carries eight chromosomes, the fertilized ova of human beings 48, and the eggs of some crayfish 200.

It is the chromosomes that govern every individual's physical inheritance. For each chromosome is composed of still smaller segments called genes which control the specific hereditary traits that combine to mold the total creature—that predestine him to be a fairly faithful copy of his parents, to be, for example, a man or an antelope, and, if a man, to be endowed with eyes and skin of a certain color or hair of a certain texture. Minutest of all units of living matter, genes are far too small to be seen through even the strongest microscope, but their control of heredity and development has been proved by thousands of experiments.

When a living cell divides, its chromosomes also divide, so that each cell in the total organism contains exactly the same two parental chromosome sets. There is, however, one exception to this rule. In the case of reproductive cells a special form of division occurs, allocating only a single set of chromosomes to each sperm or each egg. This may consist of either set from the parental cell or a mixture of the two. In the process of division the chromosomes often exchange groups of genes, thus astronomically increasing the number of potential arrangements of genetic units. If, as is speculated, a single chromosome contains up to 1,000 genes, a creature like man, with 48 chromosomes, may have nearly 48,000 genes representing a complex integration of ancestral traits passed down through untold generations. Hence when sperm and egg fuse the possible variations of gene distribution are almost infinite. Because sexual reproduction makes possible so fantastically flexible an interchange of inheritance factors, it is no wonder that no offspring is a perfect copy of any progenitor, no wonder that of the 2½ billion human beings on earth no two (save identical twins) are precise duplicates.

But there is still another process continually at work introducing new characteristics by producing new genes. This is the phenomenon of mutation. Sometimes a gene undergoes a mysterious alteration, causing it to induce unusual (and occasionally harmful) effects. All creatures carry such mutant genes; when some change in the environment makes a mutation advantageous, the creature who reveals it will be favored for survival (*opposite page, below*). In each species, therefore, natural selection modifies successive generations, adapting them to the fickle conditions of existence. Operating inexorably through eons of time, these subtle but constant factors have brought forth the ever-changing panorama of life on earth. "If a single cell, under appropriate conditions, becomes a man in the space of a few years," wrote Herbert Spencer, "there surely can be no difficulty in understanding how . . . a cell may, in the course of untold millions of years, give origin to the human race."

FEMININA

ROTHSCHILDI

NIGRA

SPLENDIDISSIMA

STEPHANIAE

EVOLUTION THROUGH ISOLATION

In the working of genetics, many factors operate to produce variations among species and to create new ones. One is isolation. A notable example of its effects is exhibited by birds of paradise in New Guinea. These birds live in mountains above the 6,000-foot level, separated from the others by deep valleys. The parent stock was probably similar to *Nigra*. But since the modern birds never live below 6,000 feet and do not fly from mountain to mountain, their habitats have become islands where each of the five populations has developed its own genetic resources. Thus isolated, they have evolved into the five distinct species shown above.

EVOLUTION THROUGH ADAPTATION

Underlying the factor of isolation are the processes of natural selection and adaptation. Individuals best adapted to their environment survive and propagate others like themselves. On the White Sands Desert there are whiptail lizards which are hunted by a bird called a road runner. Originally all the lizards may have been the same color. Some hid among sand dunes, others in the desert's silt flats. In time mutations produced different shades of skin. The lizards with the best protective coloration survived and thus two distinct types evolved: gray lizards which live on the light-colored sand and brown lizards which live on the darker silt.

GROUP OF FLAGELLATES
CHOANOFLAGELLATES
SEAWEEDS

GROUP OF PROTOZOANS
VOLVOX

PLANULA

SPONGES

FLATWORM
GUTLESS FLATWORM
ANCESTRAL JELLYFISHES

SEGMENTED WORM
ANCESTRAL ECHINODERM

ANNELID
ANCESTRAL MOLLUSK

JELLYFISH

POLYPS

THE MORNING OF LIFE

FOR at least three-quarters of the book of ages engraved in the earth's crust the pages are blank. While the oldest rocks bespeak the rise and fall of ancient mountains and the advance and retreat of primeval seas, so far as life is concerned they stand all but mute. The first creatures whose outlines are clearly etched in fossil remains date from the period called the Cambrian, which dawned 500 million years ago.

Yet evidence exists that the evolutionary epic began at a far more distant time—at the outset of the stupendous span of the Pre-Cambrian era a billion and a half years earlier. Many of its rocks contain carbon traces of probably organic origin. And by its end life was already highly evolved. Such complex structures as the nervous system, digestive tract and sensory organs had already appeared when the continuous fossil record began. Why then are there virtually no traces of the first one and a half billion years of life on earth? Biologists believe that all the animals which dramatically emerged in the Cambrian rose slowly out of soft-bodied creatures having neither bones nor thick shells with which to leave an imprint in the sediments of time. Though the rocks offer little evidence, it is possible to deduce roughly what these first organisms looked like by envisaging vanished forms from the larval and adult stages of tiny, often transparent animals and plants that still teem in the waters of the earth today (*see painting at left*).

As to how life itself was first created science can only speculate. It is theoretically possible that on some distant day at the very dawn of time, when the earth's rocks were still hot and oceans and air seethed with chemical turbulence, certain organic compounds were synthesized in the sea by solar radiation and by unknown catalytic agents into a complex molecule capable of generating units like itself. In time these primordial molecules may have combined into clusters to form an organism analogous perhaps to a bacterium. Then somehow more complex entities evolved and acquired the art of photosynthesis—of utilizing the energy of the sun. These may have been blue-green algae, whose limy deposits have been found in the oldest of Pre-Cambrian rocks. They were probably the first authentic members of the plant world.

Yet both bacteria and blue-green algae represented evolutionary blind alleys. The modern creature which is probably most like the common ancestor of all other living things is a microscopic glob of transparent jelly, half plant, half animal, called a flagellate. Early in the history of the earth flagellates must have peopled the oceans with one-celled plants and one-celled animals called protozoa. As a group the latter now show remarkable diversity. Indeed in their development most of the mechanics of living—sexual reproduction, digestion, locomotion—had been solved. The abyss between primordial organic molecule and protozoan was at least as great as that between protozoan and man, and took perhaps as long to span.

Just how more complex creatures evolved from these veiled beginnings remains another obscure chapter in the history of life. The gulf between one-celled animals and the first organized multicellular creatures may have been bridged by colonial flagellates like *Volvox* made up of many hundreds of individual and semi-independent cells joined together in gelatinous masses. With the advent of true multicellular organisms, ever more complicated animal structures became practicable in the struggle for existence. For within each individual different groups of cells could specialize as organs for different functions. In succession up the evolutionary ladder there must have appeared forms like the sponge, a loose aggregate of cells living in the most elementary interdependence; like planula, now found only as a stage in embryonic development; the jellyfish and polyp, most primitive creatures to possess true mouths and stomachs; like the gutless flatworm, with the first nervous system and the first brain; the true flatworm; the segmented worm and mollusk with the first true body cavities; and the simplest annelids, ancestors of earthworms and eventually of the hordes of the insect world. Sometime in the late Pre-Cambrian there must have appeared a small but important worm-like creature, the ancestral echinoderm, from which there ultimately branched two subsequent lines—one direct but relatively minor, embracing starfish, sea urchins and the like; the other probably collateral but destined to be the heirs of the earth, the vertebrates.

THE SEAS GROW CROWDED

FROM the dawn of the Cambrian period, through the Ordovician, to the end of the Silurian 175 million years later, the quickening life of the planet remained in the warm primeval oceans. The dry lands stretched stark and desolate from sea to sea, their drab rocks naked save for a few green films of algae along the shores. It was a time of high waters and genial climate. Over great areas of all the continents the waters encroached, creating many shallow inland seas. And as age flowed into age, the forms of life multiplied, bringing new populations to the sunlit bottom sands.

By comparison with the ineffable span of the Pre-Cambrian era, the Cambrian period (500–425 million years ago) was relatively brief. Yet within it life waxed with astonishing diversity. Perhaps the major development of the Cambrian was the advent of hard parts—protective shells, plates and skins. It was at this point, therefore, that the continuous fossil record began.

As in every age, advances were irregular. At the very outset of the Cambrian (*top panel*), a lowly type of sponge, the pleosponge, enjoyed an enormous short-term success, spreading across the sea floor in tangled profusion and building reefs along the continental shelves from pole to pole. Then sometime in the Mid-Cambrian all the pleosponges died; why, no one knows. Another group of prime importance were the brachiopods, or lampshells, which constitute nearly one third of all Cambrian fossils. Many other groups expanded more modestly: the durable and still-increasing mollusks, whose first fossil representatives were snails; the annelids or segmented worms; the echinoderms, represented by now-extinct carpoids and edrioasteroids; and the graptolites, colonial animals that faded away 200 million years later. By far the most successful Cambrian group were the arthropods. From the beginning of the period they peopled the seas with a variety of small shrimplike creatures—*Marrella*, *Hymenocaris* and *Tuzoia*. But incomparably the most prolific of all Cambrian arthropods were the trilobites, which in some ways resembled lobsters, in some crabs. Most were not more than three inches long; the giant trilobite, biggest of all Cambrian fossils, did not exceed 18 inches.

In the Ordovician period (*center panel*), which lasted from 425 to 360 million years ago, the climate continued mild and the waters of the earth rose higher, drowning the lands in the greatest floods of all time. Amid the warm Ordovician seas vast numbers of invertebrates spawned, increasing in size and diversity and in the complexity of their defensive armor. Before the period ended, members of every major group of animals except the lower worms wore shells. The first corals flourished, studding the nether seascapes with skeleton cities. The graptolites erected a variety of housing developments, some attached to rocks and seaweeds, some dangling from curious floats. Another group of colonial animals, bryozoa, built complex edifices branched and forked like the antlers of a moose. The first clams appeared and along with them their archenemy, the starfish. The trilobites also persisted, though their hegemony of the sea passed to the nautiloids, an order of mollusks related to the modern squid and octopus but clad in shells up to 15 feet long.

The Ordovician period slid quietly into the Silurian (360–325 million years ago). Around the globe brachiopods, bryozoa, corals, crinoids, sponges, clams and snails continued to thrive, maintaining their old lines and launching a few new ones (*bottom panel*). The graptolites and trilobites declined; the nautiloids continued to multiply their forms. But the most powerful dynasts of the Silurian waters were the sea scorpions, ranging in size from a few inches up to giants which sometimes attained a length of nine feet.

Paleontologists think that the first vertebrate fish originated in lakes and rivers and later came down to the sea. The most primitive of these were jawless, armored creatures which swam about with their mouths open, sifting microscopic organisms from the mud and water. One order, the anaspids, may have been ancestors of the modern lamprey; another, the heterostracans, stood probably closer to the main line of fish descent. The first true jawed fish appeared late in the Silurian and were represented by a single type; the acanthodians. Though only a few inches in length they were sharklike in appearance and probably predators. With their advent fish evolution was well on its way. As the Silurian period drew to a close, the drama of life shifted to the land.

MARRELLA   SPONGE   TRILOBITE
                  HYMENOCARIS   MARRELLA   PLEOSPONG
TRILOBITE   BURGESSIA   TRILOBITES BRACHIOPOD
                          TRILOBITE   PLEOSPONGES

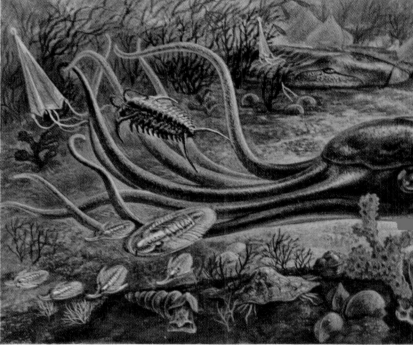

CONULARID   CONULARID GIANT TRILOBITE   SPONG
        TRILOBITE   GIANT NAUTILOID
           TRILOBITE   BRYOZOA
TRILOBITES   SNAIL   OPHIOCISTIOID   CLAMS

          ARCHAEOSTRACODS   SEA SCORPION
    SEA SCORPION GRAPTOLITE   CRINOID
TRILOBITES   COILED NAUTILOID   SPONGES   TRILOBITE
    OPHIOCISTIOID   TRILOBITE   CLAMS EARTHWORM CHAIN CORAL

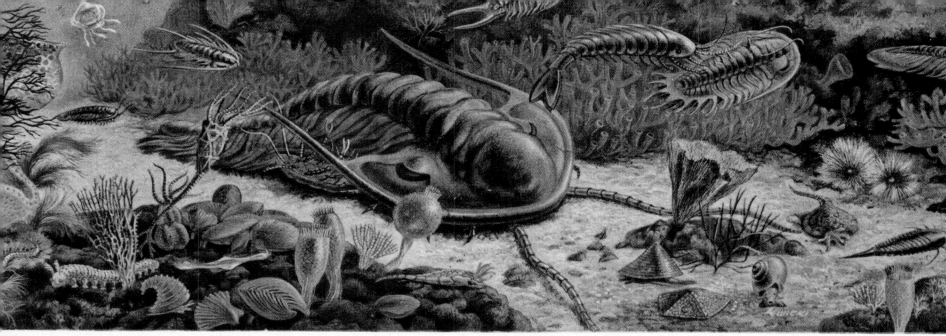

UZOIA   JELLYFISH   SPONGES TRILOBITE   SIDNEYIA   TRILOBITE   TRILOBITE

LEOSPONGE   TRILOBITE   CYSTOID   GIANT TRILOBITE EATING SIDNEYIA   GRAPTOLITE   CHOIA

ANNELID   GRAPTOLITE   CYSTOID ARROWWORM   GRAPTOLITE   GLASS SPONGE   BRACHIOPODS SNAIL   GRAPTOLITE   CARPOID   STRABOPS

AYSHEAIA   SNAIL   BRACHIOPODS   GLASS SPONGES   CARPOID   EDRIOASTEROID   SNAIL   GLASS SPONGE

RINOID   CYSTOID   GRAPTOLITE   CYSTOIDS CRINOID   SEA SCORPION   HORN CORALS

TOID   GIANT SNAIL   SPONGE   GRAPTOLITE   NAUTILOIDS   TRILOBITES

TRACODS SPONGE   EDRIOASTEROIDS STARFISH   TRILOBITE   CLAMS   OSTRACODS   HORN CORALS   CRINOID

RAPTOLITE BRACHIOPOD   BRACHIOPODS   BRITTLE STAR   STARFISH   GRAPTOLITE SNAIL   STARFISH   CYSTOID   SNAIL   BRYOZOA   CORAL

CRINOID   CRINOIDS   CRINOID   CRINOIDS HETEROSTRACANS   HETEROSTRACAN

BRYOZOA   GIANT SEA SCORPION   GRAPTOLITE   ANASPIDS   ACANTHODIAN

SPONGE GIANT BRACHIOPOD BRYOZOA   CYSTOID SPONGE   CRINOID   ANASPID   BLASTOID   COELOLEPID

OPHIOCISTIOID   CRINOID CORALS   SPONGE   KING CRAB   SNAIL   TRILOBITE

NEMATOPHYTON   PSILOPHYTON   DUISBERGIA   PSEUDOSPOROCHNUS
HORNEOPHYTON   RHYNIA   DREPANOPHYCUS   PROTOLEPIDODENDRON   DUISBERGIA
TAENIOCRADA   SCIADOPHYTON   SCORPION   MILLEPEDE   ASTEROXYLON   HYENIA

THE LAND IS CLOTHED IN GREEN

LATE in the Silurian period the internal forces that recurrently revise the contours of the land caused the earth's crust to buckle. New mountain ranges arose, and the waters of the inland seas slowly withdrew into the oceanic basins, leaving behind rich overlayers of organic marine sediments. Under such circumstances it was doubtless more than coincidence that at this moment of earth history, about 330 million years ago, the first *land* plants began to creep out of marshes and estuaries to lay green fingers upon the shore and thence spread swiftly across the earth's gray, cheerless face.

For perhaps a billion years the marine plants had drifted virtually unchanged in the primeval seas. Then astonishingly, in a space of 50 million years, after the late Silurian upheaval and during the Devonian period (325–280 million years ago), they evolved from simple seaweeds into great cone-bearing trees, carpeting the lowlands

with ferns and leafy plants, transfiguring the naked hills. The first emergence was probably on tidal marshland where seaweeds learned to anchor themselves and survive in air when the waters ebbed. Thence they advanced to higher, drier land, sending up aerial shoots to scatter their spores and thrusting branches down into the earth for water. Their greatest problem was a reproductive one. As in modern ferns, their spores did not produce identical plants but grew into tiny heart-shaped sheets called gametophytes, which clung to the damp earth. The gametophytes in turn produced spore bearers like their parents by manufacturing sperm and egg cells which could merge only in water. This dependence on water may have restricted early plants to moist lowlands until the evolution of the true seed (*diagrams below*).

One of the earliest terrestrial experiments was the giant seaweed-like *Nematophyton*, whose tube-filled trunk may have served to conduct water. The first authentic land plants form a complex called the psilophytes: *Taeniocrada, Sciadophyton, Horneophyton, Rhynia, Psilophyton, Asteroxylon, Duisbergia* and *Pseudosporochnus*. Some, like

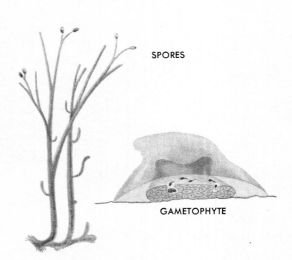

FIRST LAND PLANTS reproduced by alternate sexless and sexual generations. Sexless plant's spore generated gametophyte which made sperm and eggs. Sperm fertilized egg to produce a new sexless plant.

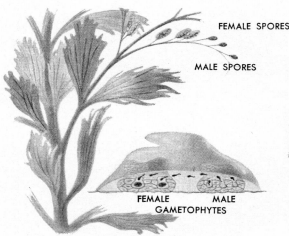

SEXUAL SPECIALIZATION of gametophytes for making only eggs or only sperm led sexless parent to develop different "male" and "female" spores for each. On wet ground, sperm swam to fertilize egg.

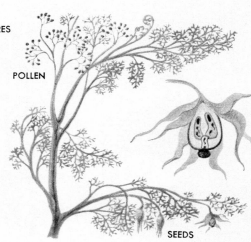

DEVELOPMENT OF SEED permitted reproduction without water, for the seed held "female" spore till it bore eggs, then drew in sperm from pollen, which was "male" spore adapted for alighting on seed.

PSEUDOSPOROCHNUS   ASTEROCALAMITES   ANEUROPHYTON   ARCHAEOSIGILLARIA   CALLIXYLON

LUNGFISHES   ENIGMOPHYTON   ARCHAEOPTERIS   SEED FERN

PROTOPTERIDIUM   BARRANDEINA   PSEUDOBORNIA **EUSTHENOPTERON**   **ICHTHYOSTEGA**   **SPIDER**

Taeniocrada and *Rhynia*, were primitive, without true leaves or roots. Others, like *Pseudosporochnus* and *Duisbergia*, grew seven and eight feet high and resembled small trees with swollen stems. The psilophytes are generally regarded as the progenitors of all modern terrestrial flora save for mosses and fungi.

Soon there appeared other lines which matured eventually into the major contemporary plant groups: the scouring rushes or horsetails (*Hyenia, Pseudobornia, Asterocalamites*); the ferns (*Protopteridium, Archaeopteris, Aneurophyton*); the lycopods, (*Drepanophycus, Protolepidodendron, Archaeosigillaria*), which later became the mightiest trees on earth and which man now burns in the form of coal; and finally, at the close of the Devonian, the cordaites, whose most splendid representative, *Callixylon*, often attained a height of 50 to 60 feet and was the precursor of the modern conifers.

The green mantling of the land in the Devonian period created a new domain of existence. So long as the continents lay bare, animal life was necessarily impounded in the sea. But with the unfoldment of new food supplies, certain humble creatures fled from the deadly competition of the marine world to the untenanted vistas of the land. The first were members of the resourceful arthropod line—scorpions, millepedes and spiders—probably descended from sea scorpions which had migrated to fresh water. (In captions above and on following pages, plants are named in light-face type, animals in dark-face type.)

Then, toward the end of the period, at least two groups of bony fish developed a respiratory system enabling them to absorb oxygen through the walls of their swim bladders; in short, they could breathe. Abiding as they did in fresh rain-fed waters subject to seasonal desiccation, one group, the lungfish, acquired the art of lying dormant in dried mud flats, breathing air. Their more active cousins, the crossopterygians (like *Eusthenopteron*), grew extraordinarily muscular fins, suggesting that in times of drought they dragged themselves along arid stream beds from pool to pool. From these air-breathing fish it was only a small step to *Ichthyostega*, the first amphibian, who carried a fishlike tail, but whose fins were no longer fins but feet.

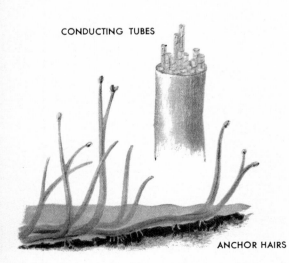

LEAFLESS STEMS marked the first plants which crept beneath the tidal marsh water or grew aloft to scatter spores. Crude tubes pumped water in their stems; tiny hairs attached them to the soil.

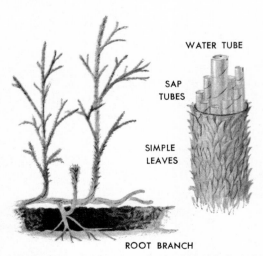

SIMPLE LEAVES to catch the sunlight clothed the stems of plants as they took to drier ground. Some of their branches reached down into the earth for water, and some tubes specialized to circulate sap.

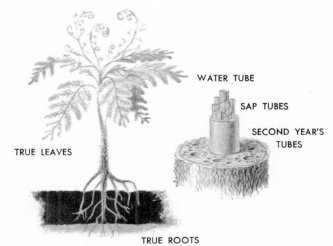

TRUE LEAVES formed when simple leaves fused and webbed branches together. Plants no longer crept but climbed sunward while true roots delved in soil. The thickened stems contained more tubes.

SIGILLARIA   LEPIDODENDRON   CORDAITES

ERYOPS   SEYMOURIA   LIMNOSCELIS   OPHIACODON   SPHENACODON   DIMETRODON

MEGANEURON   CALAMITES   VARANOSAURUS   ARAEOSCELIS

REPTILES INHERIT THE EARTH

UNOBTRUSIVELY, in the bogs and by the edge of running water in the dark places of the forest, the first amphibians clung to their small niche of existence. For a long time—perhaps 50 million years— nature seemingly favored them. Around most of the earth the climate was dank and benign. Swamps covered vast areas of the land, engendering in their choked waters all manner of scouring rushes, horsetails and ferns. Upon their moist margins many strange, soft-tissued trees grew swiftly and swiftly died. There were no flowers.

From this miasmic world of 250 million years ago certain legacies have survived. A great many of the earth's rich beds of coal were created from the rotted vegetation of the marshes and fens that stifled the lowlands from Greenland to Antarctica. The ancient trees that luxuriated there were principally of three kinds: *Sigillaria*, plumed with odd pompons of top foliage; *Lepidodendron*, which sometimes soared to a height of 130 feet on slender tapered trunks; and *Cordaites*, precursor of the modern conifers. It was in this beneficently

humid environment of the Mississippian and Pennsylvanian periods (280–230 million years ago) that insect life came into prolific being and began to swarm into the more than 800,000 species that infest man's domain today. Some developed into giants of their kind, like *Meganeuron*, a form of dragonfly with a wingspread of 29 inches.

But the principal drama of this sodden epoch was enacted by the sluggish amphibians, for it was from their first tentative footsteps in the Paleozoic mires that the great procession of terrestrial life—reptiles, birds and mammals—ultimately unwound. Like many eventually successful dynasties, the amphibians won no quick triumph. Their competitors for food were the fishes from which they sprang. And even those that learned to live on insects and land plants still returned to water to lay their eggs. Fat, slow-moving, they "pottered," as Thomas Huxley said, "with much belly and little leg, like Falstaff in his old age." Yet they prospered. Some grew to a length of 10 to 15 feet. Some of them, like aggressive *Eryops*, learned to live most of their lives on dry land.

This was a crucial adjustment. For as the peaceful Pennsylvanian period passed into the Permian (230–205 million years ago),

STEGOSAURUS
WILLIAMSONIA ARCHAEOPTERYX RHAMPHORHYNCHUS
BRONTOSAURUS
MATONIDIUM NEOCALAMITES

THE GREAT AGE OF DINOSAURS

FOR all the grotesque, gigantic forms the early Mesozoic era had unveiled, the golden age of dinosaurs still lay ahead. In the late Jurassic and Cretaceous periods the warm seas rose again, submerging much of Europe and almost half of North America. Corals spread 2,000 miles north of their present outposts. Figs and breadfruit grew in Greenland and palm trees in Alaska. And the cold-blooded dinosaurs lumbered far north and everywhere prospered.

In the lush swamps and stagnant waters, among the horsetails and the ferns, the saurischian herbivores grew into the hugest animals that ever trod the trembling earth. To undergird their enormous weight they had reverted to four legs, which evolved into pillars of monolithic solidity and strength, and sought surcease from the tug of gravity by spending much of their lives wallowing half submerged in shallow lakes and mires. The archetype of these lowland giants was *Brontosaurus* (from the Greek *bronto sauros* meaning "thunder lizard"). His prodigious body weighed about 30 tons and measured nearly 70 feet from nostrils to the extremity of his attenuated tail. His small head, scarcely more than a swelling at the end of his long serpentine neck, contained a small mouth with many weak, spoon-shaped teeth and, almost incidentally, a small weak brain, which probably did little more than work the jaws and filter such dim impressions as his limited senses received. His hind legs were operated by an oversized ganglion toward the base of his spinal cord; it was several times as big as his brain—a fact which inspired the aphorism that dinosaurs could reason best *a posteriori*.

While the saurischians of the swamplands were the largest of the dinosaurs, there appeared in the ornithischian dynasty some of the most bizarre creatures capricious nature ever designed. *Stegosaurus* was a ponderous, low-slung, humpbacked beast—10 tons in weight, 20 feet in length—which plodded awkwardly along on extraordinarily mismatched legs, carrying his inconsequential, pointed head close to the ground, bowed down by an apparently useless parapet of heavy, triangular plates running almost the entire length of his spine. His powerful hind limbs were controlled, like those of *Brontosaurus*, by a sacral ganglion some 20 times larger than his brain—which

FOLD OUT, DO NOT TEAR

WILLIAMSONIA

WIELANDIELLA   CYCADELLA   **CAMPTOSAURUS**   **ALLOSAURUS**   **COMPSOGNATHUS**

ARAUCARITES

ALLOSAURUS

CYCADEOIDEA   **ARCHAEOPTERYX**

modern snakes and lizards. From yet another, stemming from a highly active quadruped, *Cynognathus*, whose veins may have held the first incipiently warm blood, there later came the first mammals.

The main line of reptiles, however, derived from a smaller but far swifter and more agile order that had risen up on their hind legs. Their forelimbs had become arms, capable of grasping; their legs were sinewy and muscular, adapted to swift pursuit; their jaws held many sharp, needlelike teeth. Some such creature as *Saltoposuchus*, barely four feet long, nimble and predaceous, was the ancestor not only of modern birds and crocodiles—but more immediately of the largest and most fearsome land animals of all time—the dinosaurs (from the Greek *deinos sauros* meaning "terrible lizard").

Through the Jurassic to the end of the Cretaceous period 75 million years ago, the dinosaurs ruled the earth. On the ever warmer and damper plains of the hospitable continents they proliferated freely. Some grew to enormous size; some became vegetarians, others rapacious predators; some strode on two feet, others had reverted to four. They evolved early into two main orders: the saurischians (meaning "reptile hips") and ornithischians ("bird hips"). The latter

consisted for the most part of stupid, inoffensive herbivores, like *Camptosaurus*, whose flat blunt teeth hid behind a birdlike beak and whose brain was of birdlike dimensions. From the beginning the saurischians were dominant: their herbivores became the biggest land animals that ever lived, their carnivores the most dreadful. Among the earliest of the saurischian giants were the vegetarian plateosaurs, measuring as much as 20 feet from head to tip of tail. The first predators, however, were small, like *Podokesaurus* and *Compsognathus*— light, fleet-footed marauders that may have subsisted in part by stealing the big, tough-skinned eggs of their larger, lumbering relatives. But in time, as the millennia rolled by, the flesh-eating saurischians produced giants too.

Foremost of these and scourge of the late Jurassic plains and forests was *Allosaurus*, a ravening monster more than 30 feet long, armed with rows of savage, knifelike teeth and prehensile claws. Stalking across the antique landscapes in quest of living prey, *Allosaurus* was the unchallenged tyrant of his age. No large animal could oppose him. The small could but hide or flee. There was only one, perhaps, that felt no terror at his massive approach—*Archaeopteryx*, the first bird.

WALCHIA   LEPIDODENDRON   ARAUCARIOXYLON   **PLATEOSAURUS**
EDAPHOSAURUS   PALAEOCYCAS   **CYNOGNATHUS**   **PODOKESAURUS**
VOLTZIA   **SALTOPOSUCHUS**   MACROTAENIOPTERIS

revolutionary changes began to alter the face of the planet. Huge mountain ranges, the primeval Appalachians and the Urals, were uplifted. The inland waters receded, swamps evaporated, glaciers marched across the land and the climate underwent greater extremes of severity than at any period except the present. The soft pithy trees of the coal swamps surrendered to hardy conifers, cycads and cycadeoids. In these new circumstances the amphibian line degenerated, and many returned completely to the water. But meanwhile a few of them had learned a new way of life; they had dispensed with the transitional tadpole or larval stage through which most amphibians pass and had begun to lay eggs which could hatch on dry land: they had become reptiles. A small creature named *Seymouria* may have been the first reptile—or the last amphibian of his line.

More completely reptilian was *Limnoscelis,* typical of the group from which all higher forms of terrestrial fauna evolved. Despite the vicissitudes of the Permian period his cold-blooded tribe increased, for its members, no longer dependent on water, could wander where they would. An early and vigorous branch, the pelycosaurs, sired the ancestors of mammals. Although the earliest of these, *Varanosaurus*

and *Ophiacodon,* were doubtless fish-eaters like many of their amphibian forebears, the line later adjusted to other diets. *Sphenacodon* was probably a meat-eater. The giant finbacks, *Dimetrodon* and *Edaphosaurus,* for all their exterior resemblance, were carnivore and herbivore respectively—hunter and hunted. The function of their grotesque spinal crests has never been satisfactorily explained.

When the Permian period ended, it brought to a close the 300-million-year expanse of geologic time known as the Paleozoic era and ushered in the 130-million-year span of the Mesozoic. During the first two Mesozoic subdivisions, the Triassic (205–165 million years ago) and the Jurassic (165–135 million years ago), the climate grew slowly less severe. In the plant world true conifers (*Walchia, Araucarioxylon, Voltzia, Araucarites*) joined cycads (*Palaeocycas, Macrotaeniopteris*) and cycadeoids (*Wielandiella, Cycadella, Cycadeoidea, Williamsonia*) on the hillsides and plains. In the animal kingdom the reptiles differentiated swiftly into the many branches of their flourishing family tree. Among the first to develop were the turtles, which soon reached their present state of evolution and have come down through the ages virtually unchanged. Another branch gave rise to

FAN PALM

HORSETAILS

SCREW PINE
ANATOSAURUS   SASSAFRAS   LAUREL
              ANKYLOSAURUS

weighed 2½ ounces, about as much as a fox terrier's. Since *Stegosaurus* became extinct shortly after the end of the Jurassic, it would appear that his unique physical and mental endowments were ineffective against the saurischian meat-eaters.

For a time, early in the Cretaceous period (135–75 million years ago), the climate turned cool. Swamp life diminished and greater numbers of the herbivorous dinosaurs had to adapt to life on the uplands and open plains. As a consequence, later suborders of the ornithischian quadrupeds perfected better defensive equipment. Two at least evolved into walking fortresses, impregnable to the weapons of all but the greatest of the carnivores. One member of this armored corps of the Cretaceous plains was *Ankylosaurus*, a medium-sized dinosaur somewhat resembling a modern armadillo, whose entire body was encased in thick armor plates, lavishly spiked and studded, and whose tail—his only offensive weapon—terminated in a wicked bludgeon of solid bone. The culmination of defensive armament was attained in a family of horned dinosaurs; *Triceratops* sometimes attained a length of 20 feet and stood eight feet high at the hips. As his name implies, *Triceratops* carried three horns, projecting from a great flaring frill of

bone that helmeted his seven-foot skull. Like the modern rhinoceros, which he resembled superficially, *Triceratops* probably fought by charging his opponents head-down and impaling them on his sharp, stilettolike horns.

The ornithischian bipeds made equally strange adaptations, producing several types of semiaquatic, or "duck-billed," dinosaurs. By the late Cretaceous some of these had evolved into giants 25 feet long, like *Anatosaurus*, with flattened skulls and ducklike beaks suitable for cropping water plants and dredging in the mire of swamps for roots and perhaps mollusks. Their dental equipment was highly specialized. *Anatosaurus* contained in his horny mouth no less than 2,000 teeth, arranged in overlapping rows to form nearly solid pavements between which he ground his food into a pulp as between millstones. Another example of evolutionary specialization appeared in the saurischian *Struthiomimus*, an "ostrich dinosaur," whose long slender legs were obviously built for speed. Though birdlike in aspect, *Struthiomimus* was not one of the duckbills but a saurischian.

The apogee of dinosaur development was attained with the creation of *Tyrannosaurus rex*, the mightiest and most fearsome flesh-eater

that ever terrorized the land. A towering agent of destruction, endowed with gigantic strength and power, *Tyrannosaurus* spanned 50 feet from nose to tail and carried his terrible head 18 to 20 feet above the ground. His hind legs were superbly muscled, from his thick thighs down to his three-toed, cruelly taloned feet. His main weapon of attack was his murderous mouth which had a gape of incredible size and was armed with rows of six-inch, saberlike teeth. Though he feared no creature on earth, *Tyrannosaurus*' reign was relatively brief as evolution goes. He did not appear on the terrestrial scene until late in the Cretaceous, and he vanished with the rest of the dinosaurs when their death knell suddenly and mysteriously tolled.

During this epoch of explosive evolution while dinosaurs dominated the dry land, other members of the reptile kingdom were invading different domains of existence. One group took to the air, where they evolved along two main lines of development. *Archaeopteryx*, the first bird, was only one step removed from his reptile forebears; he had teeth and a long tail. But he also wore feathers, and it was this modification, perhaps, that enabled him to survive and beget the modern dynasty of birds. From related stock came the pterosaurs—

the toothy, long-jawed, leather-winged, featherless flying reptiles that reeled about in the Jurassic and Cretaceous skies. One of the earliest, *Rhamphorhynchus*, was scarcely larger than a crow. But they evolved swiftly, along with the terrestrial dinosaurs, until by the end of the Cretaceous period *Pteranodon*, a virtual living glider, had attained a wingspread of 27 feet.

An event of far greater ultimate significance, however, than any occurrence in the animal kingdom was the arrival on earth of the first flowering plants, or angiosperms. No one knows where they came from. But early in the Cretaceous period they began to compete aggressively with the ancient flora and, abetted by bees and other insects, became dominant by its close. As they strode across the uplands and through the swamps, the last of the great dinosaurs crushed under their heedless pads and claws such familiar shrubs as magnolias, dogwoods and sassafras, and moved among groves of ancestral oaks, laurels, willows, fan palms and palmettos. The advent of these plants, together with a new epoch of mountain-building and volcanism that profoundly altered the contours and climate of the land, proved a contingency of fateful import to all the animals of earth.

THE REPTILES RETURN TO THE SEA

DEEP within all creatures on earth there persist certain physiological and instinctual bonds attaching them to the waters from which life initially arose. None can exist without water; the elements of the sea linger in their very cells. And hardly a class of land animals has lived that at some time has not remitted some of its members to the ocean. Whales, walruses, sea lions, porpoises—all these are air-breathing mammals whose ancestors for some reason returned to the sea. From pole to pole waterfowl flourish as vigorously as terrestrial birds. Among the reptiles individual species began returning to the aquatic life not long after their immediate forebears had made the great transition from amphibious existence to the dry land.

While the vast dynasty of dinosaurs climbed slowly to ultimate dominance of the solid earth, several groups of reptiles established equal hegemony in the waters of the Mesozoic seas. Paramount among these were the ichthyosaurs, the plesiosaurs, the mosasaurs and the

KRONOSAURUS
ELASMOSAURUS
PTERANODON
ELASMOSAURUS
ICHTHYOSAUR AND YOUNG
PORTHEUS
SCHOOL OF AIPICHTHYS
BELEMNITES

giant sea turtles. Ranging around the world, they flourished in North America in the great inland sea that covered much of the central plains during the Cretaceous period. Their fossil remains have been found in abundance in the chalk beds of western Kansas. With them in perilous coexistence in those ancient waters there also dwelt such extinct anomalies as *Portheus*, a giant, 14-foot relative of the tarpon and herring; and *Hesperornis*, a primitive, wingless, toothed water-fowl, superficially resembling a loon.

Of these aboriginal sea monsters, only the giant sea turtles like

Archelon still survive. Why turtles were selected for survival on land and sea remains one of evolution's mysteries. For like their cousins, the dinosaurs of the land, the marine reptiles attained, before they died, fantastic heights of stature, strength and power.

Among the earliest reptiles to go back to the sea were the ichthyo-saurs, sometimes 25 feet long. The sports of the ocean, they were capable of rapid swimming and prodigious leaps into the air. More than any of the other marine reptiles they had adapted fully to ocean-going life: their limbs had grown small and finlike, their tails

SCHOOL OF BENTHESIKYMES   PTERANODON   ICHTHYORNIS   PTERANODON   ICHTHYORNIS
BRACHAUCHENIUS   TYLOSAURUS   ELASMOSAURUS   HESPERORNIS   HESPERORNIS
SAWFISH   SCHOOL OF HOPLOPTERYX   SCHOOL OF EURYPHOLIS
                                                                   ARCHELON   SHARK

RF ZALLINGER

large and forked. Unlike most reptiles they hatched their eggs internally and bore their young alive. Yet despite their aquatic adaptations, the ichthyosaurs were the first of the reptilian sea creatures to vanish from the earth.

The largest of the seagoing reptiles were the plesiosaurs, which ranged up to 50 feet in length. One type, including *Kronosaurus* and *Brachauchenius*, had long skulls and short necks; another, including *Elasmosaurus*, had small skulls and long necks. The plesiosaurs swam through the water with large flippers similar to a turtle's. Slow and ungainly, they were nonetheless fiercely efficient predators, swinging their heads almost 40 feet from side to side and seizing fish in their long, sharp teeth.

The ichthyosaurs and plesiosaurs shared their dominance of the late Mesozoic seas with a group of marine lizards called mosasaurs which were perhaps the most rapacious pirates of them all. One of the fiercest of them was *Tylosaurus*, who flourished in the teeming waters of Kansas, growing up to 25 feet in length. These giant sea lizards were late comers among the aquatic reptiles; they appeared in the latter part of the Cretaceous period and vanished as dramatically as they came.

The extinction of the dinosaurs of the land, the swimming reptiles of the sea and the flying reptiles of the air at the end of the Mesozoic era poses one of the deepest enigmas of evolution. Why should creatures so great and powerful, so well adapted to their spheres of existence, vanish almost simultaneously from the face of the earth? And of this great dynasty, why did only a few lines survive—the turtles, crocodiles, snakes and a few small lizards?

A classic theory finds an answer in climatic change. Throughout most of the Mesozoic era the planet enjoyed a warm climate with little seasonal change around the globe. But as the Mesozoic ended, mountain ranges were uplifted, marshes dried up, inland seas receded and land bridges arose. Thus warm ocean currents no longer circulated freely from pole to pole and wind systems were revised. Beneficent, unvarying temperatures gave way to blistering summers and frosty winters. Yet the reptiles had survived severe climatic changes in the past. And although the dinosaurs of the swamps might have succumbed to cold and aridity, there remains the mystery of why the aquatic reptiles did not migrate to equatorial waters and there continue their strains.

Many theorists believe that the evolution of plant life may have been a second major factor in the extinction of the dinosaurs. For it was in the Cretaceous period that flowering plants and hardwood forests overran the land and supplanted the ginkgoes, cycadeoids and numerous conifers of the previous period. Their swift success may have brought starvation to herbivorous dinosaurs which could not adjust to a change of diet. And as the herbivores starved, so did the carnivores. Yet, again, while providing a possible answer to the disappearance of the terrestrial reptiles, this theory offers no clue to the extinction of the monsters of the sea.

The only factor that has been adduced to explain the downfall of all the giant reptiles is the concept known as "racial senescence." According to this hypothesis the dinosaurs, aquatic reptiles and flying reptiles all died out because they had overspecialized—they had acquired exaggerated and bizarre forms which resisted modifications necessary to survival. Thus, in the case of *Stegosaurus* and *Triceratops*, the growth of bone and armor plate had become in the end an excrescence far surpassing the limits of utility and imposing an intolerable burden. Racial senescence, however, can hardly apply to the extinction of such superbly equipped animals as *Tyrannosaurus* and *Tylosaurus*. Still less does it explain why the turtles went on living after they had virtually completed their evolutionary development. Perhaps they survived by mere accident, perhaps by reason of their very primitiveness and lack of specialization.

Finally it has been suggested that the mammals, which emerged in the late Triassic and lived obscurely in the shadow of the dinosaurs for the next 90 million years, were responsible for the extinction of the giant reptiles. In the late Cretaceous they began to expand rapidly. Though small, they were active and often predatory, and some may have eaten the huge eggs which the dinosaurs laid and abandoned to the contingencies of weather and circumstance. Whether or not the mammals contributed significantly to the destruction of the dinosaur population is a question that cannot be answered in the light of present knowledge. The facts of evolutionary history suggest that their ascendancy was the result rather than the cause of the great reptiles' fall.

It is conventional to speak of any animal order that suffered extinction as an unsuccessful experiment of nature. And it is true that the dinosaurs, which began as small, agile creatures, grew so vast, so ponderous, that they expanded into decadence and doom. Yet the fact remains that they dominated the earth for more than 100 million years—a period at least 100 times as long as the entire existence of mankind—and so must be considered as among the most successful vertebrates that ever lived.

When they vanished their sovereignty passed to a class of animals small in body but endowed with the mental and physical vitality to meet the demands of the changing world. The mystery of this crucial transition may never be fully resolved. Science can only note a few glimmerings of light in the dark abyss of time and perhaps echo the words of Paul, "God hath chosen the weak things of the world to confound the things which are mighty."

THE AGE
OF MAMMALS

THE AGE OF MAMMALS

And God made the beast of the earth after his kind and cattle after their kind . . . and God saw that it was good. . . .

GENESIS 1:25

DURING 100 million years of the Mesozoic era when dinosaurs ruled the earth, a group of small and timorous creatures dwelt furtively amid the shadows of the swamplands and sought safety in the high branches of the softwood forests. Lowly in origin but unique in their endowments, they represented a new class of animals: the mammals, warm-blooded vertebrates that bore their young alive and gave them milk in infancy. Never numerous—they have brought to the modern world only 3,500 species as against 8,600 bird species and 800,000 species of insects—they now encompass the largest and most intelligent of all terrestrial fauna. Headed and transcended by *Homo sapiens*, their most creative and destructive protagonist, they are the dominant form of life on the planet Earth today.

Beholding the bewildering diversity of living things that populate the lands and waters of the world, man has uneasily recognized both his basic spiritual differences from other creatures and his kinship with them. Since the dawn of reason he has repeatedly defined and redefined himself both as a participant and spectator in the pageant of life. The Greeks saw man as a rational animal, set apart from the lower orders by the uniqueness of his intellectual faculties. In the Christian view man is both flesh and spirit. To the modern naturalist he is "*Homo faber*"—a tool-making animal. To the psychologist he is a talking animal, capable of feeling guilt. But to the evolutionist man is essentially a mammal with an oversized brain.

This specialized organ, seat of the peculiarly human attribute of reason, is a heritage from the ancient past, born of the uncompromising demands imposed on man's remote forebears in their fight for survival during the tyranny of the dinosaurs. Unlike the reptiles, which abandoned their young to circumstance, the mammals cared for their offspring in infancy, providing them with a period of education and experience. Those with the highest capacity for learning emerged best equipped for the struggle to survive. Hence, through natural selection, the mammalian brain enlarged rapidly—especially the cerebral hemispheres which are the centers of memory and intelligence. Moreover, unlike the dinosaurs, the mammals were endowed with heat control and an even body temperature and could resist climatic variations and sustain physical effort over longer periods of time. Activity, directed by intelligence, was the touchstone of mammalian success.

So for many millions of years the mammals lived in perilous coexistence with the dinosaurs. While their fossil record is scant, four groups of primitive mammals have been identified as early as the Jurassic period, 165 million years ago; all of these must have descended from ancestral forms which evolved from therapsid reptiles in the late Triassic. It was not until the Cretaceous period, however, that the mammalian line began to burgeon. And then, with what seems from our remote point of time incredible swiftness, the dinosaurs died and the shy and humble mammals came into a great inheritance—the entire face of the land.

The period of time since the mammals took over the earth is called the Cenozoic era. It is divided into seven epochs beginning with the Paleocene, 75 million years ago, and coming down to the Recent which is the epoch in which we now live. The story of the mammals during all these periods but the last, which we see around us, is depicted chronologically in the painting shown in sections on the following pages, as it has been deciphered from the bone beds of America's West. It differs from the other chapters of evolutionary history only in that it has not ended. The climax of the story—the ultimate fate of the mammals—lies in the unknowable void of the future.

DOMINANT ANIMALS of the Cenozoic era are shown above in chronological order (*bottom to top*) as they appeared epoch after epoch in successive strata of rock (*see chart at right*) representing the times in which they lived and died.

PART VI

From furtive creatures hiding in the gloom of ancient reptile-ridden forests evolved the vigorous and intelligent animals that dominate the earth today

GIGANTOCAMELUS

MEGACAMELUS

PROCAMELUS

POËBROTHERIUM

PROTYLOPUS

TETRACLAENODON

PLEISTOCENE
1 MILLION YEARS AGO

PLIOCENE
10 MILLION YEARS AGO

MIOCENE
30 MILLION YEARS AGO

OLIGOCENE
40 MILLION YEARS AGO

EOCENE
60 MILLION YEARS AGO

PALEOCENE
75 MILLION YEARS AGO

CAMEL'S PROGRESS as reconstructed (*above*) from skulls (*right*) found in superimposed layers of rock is traced through six epochs of Cenozoic time. Beginning with a primitive herbivore of the Paleocene (lowest stratum), camels continued to evolve in western America until they mysteriously died after the Pleistocene (dark brown ridges and valley at top). In the Old World camels have survived into the seventh Cenozoic epoch, the Recent, in which we live.

109

PSITTACOTHERIUM   PLANETETHERIUM   ALLIGATOR   PLANETETHERIU
PLESIADAPIS   BOA CONSTRICTOR   TAENIOLABIS   PRODIACODON   SOFT-SHELLED TURTLE

EARLY MORNING OF THE MAMMALS' REIGN

NEVER since the aquatic creatures first crawled from Devonian waters onto the margins of the land had the earth seemed so desolate of life as at the dawn of the Paleocene epoch. Of the mighty dynasty of reptiles only a few minor strains survived: alligators, turtles, and certain snakes and lizards. And the mammals that had clung to existence in the shadow of the dinosaurs were uniformly small and sequestered. Once again the land lay waiting for the leitmotiv of evolution—the recurring growth of large animals from small ones and specialized from primitive forms.

In western America, which is depicted in the painting above, the

shallow sea that had covered most of the great plains withdrew and the Rockies arose. The climate remained bland. Subtropical plants—figs, breadfruit, palmettos—bloomed across the wilderness. Onto the moist, warm expanses of low-lying lands, almost doubled in size by the recession of the inland waters, there deployed the small advance guard of the mammals, freed now by the death of the dinosaurs to descend from the trees, where most of them had lived, and seek new ways of life upon the ground.

Among the first of these were a few small insect-eaters, insignificant in stature but vastly important in the evolutionary story, for they were the basic stock from which all true mammals of the modern world would eventually evolve. Their unimpressive prototype was *Prodiacodon*, a primitive hedgehog; more specialized members of the

LOXOLOPHUS
PALAEORYCTES

TETRACLAENODON

PANTOLAMBDA

BARYLAMBDA
THYLACODON   MIOCLAENUS

same group included *Planetetherium*, a gliding animal, and shrew-like *Palaeoryctes*. With them came the herbivore, *Psittacotherium*, and two survivors from the Mesozoic, ungainly *Taeniolabis*, whose tribe died out in the next epoch, and the marsupial *Thylacodon*, whose progeny persists in the opossums.

As the Paleocene progressed there diverged from the original stock several lines of great future significance. Notable among these were the first primates, small arboreal, nocturnal animals like *Plesiadapis*, with bushy hair and a long tail. One of the first carnivores was *Loxolophus*, a small raccoonlike creature whose sharp-cusped teeth identify him unmistakably as an early flesh-eater only just beginning to relinquish the insectivorous habits of his forebears. The group of herbivores represented by *Tetraclaenodon* and *Mioclaenus*,

small horse-headed, cat-bodied creatures, was probably ancestral to the ungulates (hoofed animals) of today, though they still wore claws adapted to life in the trees. Later in the Paleocene there appeared an order of truly hoofed vegetarians known as amblypods, or "slow-footed ones," among them sheep-sized *Pantolambda* and larger *Barylambda*, which sometimes attained a length of eight feet. As with many orders that specialized quickly for a particular way of life, the amblypods were destined for extinction.

Although the immediate ancestors of modern mammalian lines did not emerge until a later epoch, by the close of the Paleocene the land once more teemed with life. The hospitable plains and lowlands were peopled with flourishing forms that ultimately would produce the most vigorous and efficient animals that ever trod the earth.

111

NOTHARCTUS   OXYAENA   PHENACODUS   CORYPHODON   PALAEOSYOPS

TETONIUS   PARAMYS   EOHIPPUS

AN EPOCH OF UNCERTAINTY

IN the 20 million years of the Eocene, nature indulged the evolving mammalian lines. The climate remained amicable. The upheaval that had reared the Rockies subsided and the patient rain began its quiet leveling. The lowlands lay carpeted in subtropical green. Upon them new orders appeared, the ancestral forms of most modern mammals.

At some interval early in the Eocene the continents of North and South America were sundered by rising waters. As a consequence several orders of primitive mammals thrived in isolation in the Southern Hemisphere while their kin died out in the north. Among the short-lived northerners were *Metacheiromys*, whose South American cousins survive today in the order of armadillos, anteaters and sloths, and the early primates—lemurs like *Notharctus* and tarsioids like *Tetonius*. Intermediate between lemurs and monkeys, the tarsioids were the first animals to develop close-set eyes, sharing a single field of vision and perceiving depth in the stereoscopic fashion that has since enabled man to examine his environment with unique understanding. In North America lemurs and tarsioids persisted to the end of the Eocene and then disappeared, leaving our country empty of primates until the immigration of *Homo sapiens* in recent times.

A native North American development was the expansion of the rodents. Small squirrelish forms like *Paramys* were prolific in the

Eocene and by its end they had begun to diverge into all the varied types that make rodents the most adaptable of contemporary mammals. Along with the rodents the descendants of the primitive Paleocene carnivores continued to specialize, producing catlike *Oxyaena*, doglike *Mesonyx* and weasellike *Tritemnodon*. The Paleocene ungulates also specialized, but less successfully, fabricating such ineffective creatures as *Phenacodus* and slow-footed *Coryphodon*. Still more grotesque were their distant relatives the uintatheres, which enlarged into the awkward giants *Eobasileus* and *Uintatherium*, the size of modern rhinos. Both died out near the end of the Eocene.

The extinction of the primitive herbivores may have been effected by the advent of modern ungulates. *Eohippus*, the first horse, stood no higher than a fox terrier, yet his slender legs and even teeth made him a far more felicitous form than his lumbering precursors. With *Eohippus* appeared his horselike cousins, the titanothere *Palaeosyops*, whose descendants would flourish in the next epoch as the largest animals on earth, and *Hyrachyus*, a forebear of modern rhinos.

Among the competing mammals of the Eocene there also stalked a giant from another domain, *Diatryma*, a huge running bird, seven feet high, with massive legs and a powerfully beaked head. *Diatryma*'s appearance in a world of small, inexpert mammals suggests that at this moment of evolutionary history the face of the earth may have been a battleground upon which two growing dynasties, the birds and mammals, were locked in an uncertain struggle for sovereignty.

HERD OF OREODON
ARCHAEOTHERIUM
BRONTOPS
RABBIT
MESOHIPPUS

A TIME OF TRIAL AND TRIUMPH

OF all the epochs of the Cenozoic era none brought greater events than the Oligocene. Within its span the earth assumed many of the aspects it wears today. In Europe the first folds of the Alps arched from the Mediterranean. Eastward the immense Himalayan paroxysm began to buckle the crust of Asia. And in the New World volcanoes spewed fire and ash over large areas of the Northwest. Meanwhile the climate grew cooler, and in the heartland of America the ancient subtropical forests began to retreat southward, surrendering their dominions to grasses, conifers and hardwood trees.

In the animal kingdom the Oligocene witnessed the fading away of most of the primitive mammals and the founding of the modern faunas. Of the earliest mammalian lines only a few lingered on, unchanged and unchanging through later epochs, as persisting reminders of the humble origins from which all contemporary creatures came —the opossums, hedgehogs, moles and shrews. The order of rodents enlarged rapidly, augmenting their numbers early in the epoch with the ranks of the beavers, gophers, rats and mice. Ahead of them raced their relatives, the rabbits, which had begun to multiply at the end of the Eocene and which have multiplied exuberantly ever since.

The protagonists of the new epoch, however, were larger animals. The giants of the Oligocene were the titanotheres, ponderous planteaters that had appeared in the previous epoch and then proceeded to evolve into *Brontops*, a hoofed and horned beast, 14 feet long,

PROTOCERAS   HOPLOPHONEUS   PROTAPIRUS   POËBROTHERIUM

HYAENODON   SUBHYRACODON   BOTHRIODON

with weak teeth and a brain the size of an orange. Of the primitive flesh-eaters only *Hyaenodon* and his close kin survived, but two great modern groups of carnivores had already begun to emerge: the dogs, specializing in pack pursuit, and the cats, specializing in solitary stalking. The latter were already notably represented by sabre-toothed *Hoplophoneus*, a powerful predator with two-inch fangs, sinewy loins and savage, retractile claws.

The hoofed vegetarians had earlier evolved along two major lines: odd-toed ungulates—horses, asses and zebras, rhinos and tapirs; and even-toed ungulates—cattle, sheep, goats, pigs, hippos, antelopes, camels, giraffes and deer. Within the former group the horse continued to evolve along undeviating lines. *Mesohippus*, the three-toed Oligocene horse, had longer legs and a straighter back than his tiny

Eocene forebear. Though he was still no larger than a collie, his brain had expanded swiftly, and it was doubtless his intelligence, combined with agility, that enabled him to survive. To the roll of his odd-toed relatives the Oligocene also added the first tapir, *Protapirus*, and one of the first true rhinoceroses, *Subhyracodon*. Concurrently the even-toed ungulates brought forth an unlovely species of giant pig, *Archaeotherium*; an amphibious swine, *Bothriodon*, ancestral perhaps to the hippos; a gregarious type of ruminant, *Oreodon*; a six-horned, deerlike cud-chewer, *Protoceras*; and an ancestral camel, *Poëbrotherium*. Thus as the Oligocene drew to its close the varied hosts of the herbivores and clans of the carnivores were already hastening down their diverse evolutionary corridors into the domains they occupy today. The outlines of the modern animal kingdom were clearly cast.

115

DICERATHERIUM

PROMERYCOCHOERUS   MERYCOCHOERUS

A PERIOD OF PLAINS-DWELLING

THE most momentous phenomenon of the Miocene, and indeed one of the great milestones in the history of life, was the sudden spreading of the grasses, which, having slumbered in the shade of the old subtropical forests, swiftly responded to the ever cooler, drier climate of the new epoch and seized vast areas of the land, creating the prairies, plains and veldts of the modern world. From their first harsh, stubbly blades there evolved in time the forage plants and cereals that have become the basic food supply of man and his domesticated animals. As the grasses spread across the flatlands of America the grazing mammals ranged in ever larger herds, and many forest dwellers emerged from the green shadows onto the golden sunlit plains.

Under these auspicious conditions both branches of the ungulates expanded rapidly. The Miocene horse, *Merychippus*, approached the last lap of his evolutionary course. He had now attained the stature of a modern pony, and his proportions were slim and graceful. His outer toes had grown smaller; his middle toe had evolved into the functional hoof of the contemporary horse. His teeth had developed high crowns and hard surfaces suitable for pulverizing prairie grass. By the end of the Miocene, *Merychippus* was thoroughly adapted to life on the open range. His odd-toed cousins, the rhinos and chalicotheres, however, were less successful. For a time, *Diceratherium*, a small but prolific rhinoceros of the Miocene, appeared to thrive, but in the next epoch he, along with all other rhinos, vanished from the American

TELEOCERAS   HERD OF PROCAMELUS   SPHENOPHALOS   SYNTHETOCERAS

AMEBELODON   PLIOHIPPUS   PLIOHIPPUS

EPIGAULUS   AGRIOTHERIUM   AMPHICYON   RABBIT

THE AGES OF GIANTS AND ICE

THE Pliocene, which ended one million years ago, was the autumn of the Cenozoic era, the last lenient epoch before the invasion of the cruel ice sheets from the north. Little by little the bite of the winds grew sharper. Over the wide prairies of North America the tall grasses surrendered to shorter, hardier herbage. In the Southwest the ancient, subtropical forests shriveled in the rain shadow of the newly reared coastal Sierra, and then vanished under desert sands. Northward, pine trees marched down the mountain slopes of the resurgent Rockies and young craggy Cascades, out across the high plateaus, driving the sequoias of earlier epochs from all but their present sanctuary in the California hills.

For the most part Pliocene life remained as rich and variegated as in the past, and the evolving mammals continued to increase in size. Even the small rodents prospered, begetting *Epigaulus*, who was notable not only as a giant among midgets but as the only member of his breed that ever grew horns. At the other end of the scale loomed *Teleoceras*, an immense amphibious rhino that had migrated from Asia during the Miocene and all but supplanted his indigenous American cousins. The second-generation mastodons had adjusted well to their new environment and produced several native genera, among them *Amebelodon*, a "shovel tusker," whose lower

FOLD OUT, DO NOT TEAR

PROCAMELUS   MERYCHYUS   ALTICAMELUS   GOMPHOTHERIUM   CRANIOCERAS   MERYCODUS

many branches—the weasels themselves, martens, fishers, wolverines, skunks and otters. Raccoons and bears appeared, both offshoots of the primal dogs. And on the wide plains, as on the veldts of Africa today, large cats like *Machairodus* stood silent in the shade of scattered groves or crept on their bellies through the long, rippling grass as they stalked their living quarry.

At some time in the middle of the Miocene there appeared a stranger from the far side of the world. *Gomphotherium* the mastodon had come out of Egypt. Ever since the late Eocene his tribe had been evolving by the Mediterranean and in the valley of the Nile. Sprung from primitive subungulate stock, they gradually increased in size. Their trunks and tusks grew longer. Then in the late Oligocene, impelled by some mysterious wanderlust, they made their exodus

from Africa and headed eastward on one of the greatest pilgrimages in the history of living things. Century after century, millennium after millennium, they stamped and trumpeted their way across southern Asia to the Pacific and then northward to the Arctic Sea. At the Bering Straits they found a land bridge temporarily emergent; they crossed it and entered the New World some 20 million years ago.

Thus at the end of the Miocene the plains of America teemed with life more abundant than ever flourished in the past, more luxuriant than ever would thrive again after the coming of man. The golden age of mammals would last for one more epoch only. For great changes were in store. Imperceptibly the climate of the earth was growing colder. Far to the north the ice caps were beginning to form. Soon their chill breath would be felt on the happy plains.

MOROPUS   MACHAIRODUS   HERD OF MERYCHIPPUS
MOROPUS   DINOHYUS   SYNDYOCERAS

plains. Still swifter extinction overtook the chalicothere *Moropus*, a weird caricature of a horse with primitive teeth and mismatched legs that terminated not in hoofs but claws.

Meanwhile the even-toed ungulates assumed numerical ascendancy over their odd-toed competitors. Three genera of ruminants, members of a now-extinct family known as oreodonts, flourished briefly but extravagantly and then died out. Of these *Promerycochoerus* and *Merycochoerus* were amphibious; the third, *Merychyus*, was a plains dweller. The pig complex produced a Miocene giant, *Dinohyus*, which, standing six feet high, almost as massive as a hippopotamus, was the largest of all nonamphibious swine. The camels put forth two models: *Procamelus*, a small but familiar looking prototype, slightly larger than a sheep; and *Alticamelus*, an outlandish sort of super-camel with

a neck as long as a giraffe's, adapted to an arboreal diet. Deerlike ruminants also tried several experiments. The line initiated in the preceding epoch by *Protoceras* continued in the Miocene with *Syndyoceras*, a long-nosed, overspecialized creature burdened with two sets of horns, one emerging from under his ears, the other sprouting from the bridge of his nose. A more successful conception was tiny *Merycodus*, who carried on his small head a handsome set of branching horns and who ultimately sired the family of American antelopes known as pronghorns. A Miocene forebear of true deer and giraffes was graceful *Cranioceras*.

As in other ages the affluence of herbivores brought opulence to the flesh-eaters who preyed upon them. Along the fringes of the forests and in the depths of the woods the weasel family diversified into

TERATORNIS

MASTODON
CASTOROIDES

WOOLLY MAMMOTH

TERATORNIS
MUSK OX

jaw extruded two long scooplike incisors ideally suited for dredging roots from soft earth. The canine-ursine line also essayed gigantism: *Agriotherium* was an enormous bear, fully four feet high at the shoulder; *Amphicyon* was a huge dog who doubtless dominated all other canine carnivores that harried the Pliocene plains. Among the hoofed animals appeared *Sphenophalos*, a sturdy pronghorn, and *Synthetoceras*, culmination of the *Protoceras* line and the closest facsimile of a unicorn that capricious nature ever contrived. The evolving horse meanwhile entered the homestretch with the advent of *Pliohippus*, the immediate and virtually full-grown forebear of *Equus*, the genus man exploits today.

The transition from Pliocene to Pleistocene marked one of the

great crises in the history of life. The stupendous ice sheets overlying Greenland, Siberia and northern Europe now began to thicken rapidly. And as they grew, accumulating and compacting the snows of innumerable winters, the waters of the oceans fell. The Isthmus of Panama rose again from the depths and the land bridge across the Bering Straits lay completely dry. Across these great transoceanic causeways the animals of three continents streamed in ever increasing numbers, intermingling, interbreeding, waging an internecine struggle to survive. An immediate consequence was the all but total extermination of the archaic herbivores and marsupials that had thrived in happy isolation in South America since the Paleocene.

During the first 100,000 years of the Pleistocene the ice sheets

crept ever southward, refrigerating a third of the earth's surface. Then they receded and temperate climates again prevailed. Four times in all, the continental glaciers crunched down from the north, and four times they withdrew. (The latest retreat, which began some 10,000 years ago, is still continuing today.) As they ground across the great plains, abrading the face of the land, carving valleys and creating new lakes and rivers, the animals responded with tremendous vitality, some of them growing to proportions greater than any terrestrial mammals ever attained before or since. Notable among them were *Castoroides*, a beaver the size of a small bear; *Canis dirus*, a six-foot wolf that ranged the continent from coast to coast; *Smilodon*, the saber-toothed tiger, larger and heavier than the tiger of today,

who dared to attack even the giant mastodons, and whose great jaws, capable of a 90° gape, were armed with six-inch fangs with which he stabbed his victims to death; and *Teratornis*, a carrion-eating cousin of the modern condor with a wingspread of 12 feet, the largest flying bird in the history of life. There were also giants among the ungulates —*Bison crassiocornis* and the durable musk ox which still persists in the Arctic today. The horse reached the climax of his evolutionary growth with *Equus*, only to die out in America at the end of the epoch. He did not return to the New World until the Spanish *conquistadores* imported his descendants from Europe a mere four centuries ago.

The mightiest of all the Pleistocene mammals were the mastodons and mammoths. The latter, recent arrivals from Asia, swiftly came to rule the American plains, diversifying into at least four species, of which one, the 10-foot-high woolly mammoth, ranged the top of the world, dwelling among the glaciers and dying among them in such numbers that half of the world's ivory stores have come from his imperishable tusks. Among the immigrants from south of the border there arrived three prodigies: *Boreostracon*, a giant glyptodont, offshoot of the armadillo line, visored and carapaced in armor plate from nose to tail; and the ground sloths *Mylodon* and *Megatherium*. The latter, one of the largest mammals that ever lived, weighed more than a modern elephant and, when he reared on his hind legs, lifted his witless head 20 feet above the ground.

Unfathomably these giants of the Pleistocene—the mammoths, mastodons, saber-tooths and sloths—died out as swiftly as the dinosaurs before them. As spring returned after the million-year-long winter, they vanished like ice statues in the sun, leaving the reaches of North America to the small animals and the bison. And so once again, as had occurred before in the changeful history of life on earth, vast multitudes of living creatures—whole species, genera, families—abruptly vanished from the face of the planet. All the largest and strongest animals of the Cenozoic era, representing the most splendid assemblage of mammals that ever existed before or since, disappeared from the temperate zones of both hemispheres. Only tropical Africa and Asia somehow escaped the wholesale extinctions.

The great dying of the late Pleistocene and early Recent epochs marked the most far-flung and radically destructive crisis in the entire history of the mammals. To the modern evolutionist it presents an enigma no less baffling than the great dying of the reptiles 75 million years before, and as in the earlier instance he can only suggest multiple causes—climatic changes, competition, failure to adapt. Yet many of the faunas that died out at the end of the Pleistocene had survived the equally drastic changes that had accompanied the transitions from glacial to interglacial ages. Competition has ever been a factor in the processes of life: the extinction of many local populations can be directly attributed to the invasions of their habitats by competing genera. As the last of the great ice sheets withdrew, primitive man, the most ruthless competitor of all, crossed Bering Straits into North America. Today his chipped-stone weapons are still occasionally excised from the bones of some great animal that survived the glaciers only to fall victim to his implacable hand.

Yet human rapacity provides only a fragmentary explanation, for the science of paleontology has proved beyond doubt that extinction has occurred time and again on a worldwide scale since the dawn of life. It is, indeed, one of the striking configurations of evolutionary history that in each age some group of animals has risen from obscure beginnings to a period of ascendancy, only to surrender its sway to another incipient and apparently unaggressive line. Thus the Cambrian period was dominated by the extinct trilobites, the Ordovician by the extinct giant nautiloids, the Silurian by the extinct sea scorpions, the Devonian by the fishes, the Pennsylvanian by the amphibians which survive today in only a few inconspicuous lines, and the entire vast span of the Mesozoic era by the extinct giant reptiles.

Evolutionists hesitate, therefore, to assign specific causes to specific extinctions, preferring rather to state simply that over great periods of time the physical environment changes and certain populations die off because for some reason they fail to adapt. The apparent suddenness and simultaneity of the great extinctions, moreover, may be an illusion created either by gaps in the chronicle of the rocks or by the immense perspectives of geologic time. Thus the great dying of the Pleistocene mammals was sudden only in a relative sense. It would appear that the extinctions occurred sporadically, spreading gradually from local centers, and were often as not partial, wiping out faunas in one place and leaving them untouched in another. The consequences of these incomplete extinctions are visible today in the spotty distribution of many animal populations—a phenomenon that long baffled zoologists. Tapirs, for example, now exist only in such

widely separated regions as Malaya and Central and South America, though they once flourished over vast areas of both hemispheres. And, more familiarly, elephants, rhinos, camels—these too represent vestiges of far greater populations, impounded today in habitats incomparably smaller than they occupied during the great days of the Pleistocene.

As in earlier ages, however, the vitality of animal life proved greater than the destructive power of whatever forces had combined to imperil it. At the moment the sheer mass of life on the planet stands close to an all-time high and, more significant, its diversity is greater than in any age prior to the dawn of the Cenozoic. For the major pattern of the evolutionary panorama is *divergence*, the tendency of life to differentiate, to become more variegated, to educe more and more forms and varieties of organisms ingeniously adapted to every conceivable habitat. It is true that divergence is not the only configuration woven in the long tapestry of life on earth. Around it lie other patterns: static lines of arrested development (like the unchanging opossum, oyster, rabbit and turtle); forms of *parallel* evolution, where allied groups follow independent avenues of development and arrive at similar results (as in the case of deer and antelope); and forms of *convergent* evolution, where utterly unrelated groups change slowly into near facsimiles of one another (as in the case of the reptile ichthyosaurs and the mammal porpoises). Nor are these necessarily rarities. Nature offers its players only a limited number of roles, of habitats and techniques for exploiting them; whenever a biological niche is temporarily vacated, it must in time be filled.

From the network of natural forces it is difficult to select a single strand representing a main line of progression, of advance to a propitious end. Yet, as the life saga has unfolded, it would appear that the factor most conducive to survival has been an increase in perception—the development of more efficient sense organs and more complex and sensitive nervous systems, capable of interpreting sensations and responding to them swiftly. From the beginning these attributes have constituted the great arsenal of the mammals. Pound for pound, brain for brain, the dinosaurs were by comparison with the mammals mere automatons. Indeed it is probable that the mammals may have survived and succeeded to hegemony of the earth not in spite of but by reason of their very weakness and obscurity, their smallness in a world dominated by giants, their nakedness in a world of armor plate—in particular, by their fear and sensitivity and awareness in a world of unperceiving, insensate, brainless brutes. And as the epochs of the Cenozoic flowed past, these priceless endowments were augmented in certain lines through the elaboration of nervous systems and enlargement of brains.

The culmination of the present evolutionary progression is man. Proud of his intellectual equipment and of his sense of immortality, man has often tended to underestimate his other legacies—to envisage himself as a puny, hairless, wingless, shivering, unarmored, slow-footed pygmy in an arena of superior physical specimens, and to attribute all conquests to his rational faculties. Actually *Homo sapiens* is a giant in the animal kingdom; only a handful of mammalian lines are larger, stronger, swifter. Of the more than one million species of animals on earth man is capable of killing all but a few without recourse to the weapons he ingeniously contrives for his own destruction. Yet it is true that man's supreme heritage is his brain—that mysterious and convoluted mass of soft tissue which enables him to perceive the world around him with unique acuity and respond to its stimuli with a subtlety and self-consciousness that sets him apart from all other living things. It invests him, moreover, with a power which no other creature ever possessed—the power to modify his environment, to govern and alter the very course of evolution for all the multifarious estates of life, including his own. Though a relative newcomer, an upstart on the planet Earth, man nevertheless stands alone in the complex of nature, the master of vast and incalculable forces, and arbiter of his own fate. For as Plato succinctly observed more than 2,000 years ago, "Mind is ever the ruler of the universe."

CREATURES
OF THE SEA

PART VII

CREATURES OF THE SEA

From its shimmering surface layers to the eternal darkness of its deeps the ocean holds a range of life from one-celled animals to mighty whales

For all that here on earth we dreadfull hold,
Be but as bugs to fearen babes withall,
Comparèd to the creatures in the seas entrall.
SPENSER, *Faerie Queene*

FROM the day when man first ventured on the surface of the seas he has feared not only the open fury of the winds and waves but even more profoundly the unseen hordes of creatures with which his fancy filled the secret depths. In the mythology and literature of every age great monsters inhabit the abyss, rising recurrently to drag their victims down to weedy caverns on the ocean floor.

Although the human imagination forever transcends nature, there are grounds for these persisting fantasies and fears. For the sea abides, of all realms of life, the least known, the least explored, the largest, the darkest. Dropping to depths of nearly six miles, it encompasses about 300 times the habitable space of land and fresh water areas combined. And most of it is a domain of everlasting night, black as Milton's sightless sphere—"O dark, dark, dark, amid the blaze of noon, Irrevocably dark . . ."

Hence man knows far less of the ocean's creatures than of the animals with which he shares the land. Yet the frontiers of marine biology have advanced in recent years and can provide some glimpses now not only of the populations that subsist in shallow waters, but of those that dwell below the glistening surface layers of light, in the canyons of the continental slopes and amid the oozes of the abyssal floor. And one can say that while Scylla and Leviathan lived only in legend, the most gigantic creatures that ever existed on earth wage war still in the oceanic deeps. With them too abide some of the loveliest forms the hand of nature ever wrought, sculptured with silvery grace and symmetry, tinted with iridescent jewellike hues, shining sometimes with magic luminescence in the night.

Since the sea is the ancestral home of all living things, the creatures that inhabit it embody an animate panorama of evolution from the dawn of existence. All of the main divisions (phyla) of the animal kingdom appear in the sea, as well as all of their component classes—save only amphibians, birds, insects and true spiders. From bacteria and protozoans up to the most highly evolved of aquatic organisms, true fish and marine mammals, the long procession of life unfolds in the sea with a clarity and detail that have no parallel among the faunas of the land. For the sea has many living fossils—animals for whom the ages have stood still. Eon after eon, jellyfish, corals, glass sponges, starfish, sand dollars, horseshoe crabs, clams and other forms have reproduced their kind, virtually untouched by the slow sorcery of time.

At the moment of earth history when the first plants and animals climbed from the seas onto the dry land, the invertebrates were lords of creation. Single-celled protozoans drifted in the surface waters. Jellyfish shimmered through the upper layers. Mollusks and arthropods ruled the sunless sea floor. Sluggish, even sedentary, many of these bottom dwellers had no need or ability to swim. And so the middle reaches of the open sea lay almost empty for millions of years. But in the lakes and rivers of the continents a new class of life was evolving—the fishes, which may have sprung from a special group of fresh-water invertebrates and learned to swim through the

necessity of escaping enemies and maintaining their position and balance in swift-running streams. Their contours became more streamlined, their fins more flexible; they developed movable jaws and specialized teeth suited to a predatory life. In time they branched into two subclasses: the cartilagenous fish, such as sharks, skates, rays, whose skeletons are made of cartilage rather than bone; and the bony fish, the dynasty of cod, herring, salmon, tuna, mackerel, bass and other true fish (teleosts) of the present day. Sometime in the late Devonian and Triassic periods the ancestral vertebrate fish came down to the sea, and finding the ability to swim a distinct advantage among the slow, crawling communities of the salt water, survived, thrived and improved their unique mode of locomotion. Today the teleosts, over 20,000 species strong, are the common fish of the sea.

Since the sea is a more homogeneous environment than the land, its creatures are generally more primitive, less diversified than those that emerged onto the harsh and variable reaches of the continental platforms. By and large they have not had to specialize, to adapt themselves to such contrasting habitats as deserts and swamps, jungles and grassy plains, nor to endure extreme climatic variations. Even in the tropics the temperature of the surface waters seldom exceeds 85°; in the polar regions it never falls much below 29°. Over more than three quarters of the ocean's surface the seasonal temperature variation is less than 5°; below 800 feet there is no seasonal change at all. The sea is lenient in other ways. Its populations have no lack of the essential component of all life—water—for they are constantly bathed in it, both externally and internally. Sea creatures absorb water directly into their systems, and along with it the dissolved gases necessary for life—oxygen and carbon dioxide—and the requisite amounts of salts and minerals necessary to growth.

Moreover the water in which aquatic creatures live sustains them against the relentless tug of gravity. Unlike land animals which require solid supports to undergird them in the thin medium of air, marine organisms in the denser medium of water have no need for heavy legs or hard internal frames. Sea plants have no trunks or rigid stems. The limbs of most sea animals are designed for swimming, digging or fighting rather than support. This is true even of the great whales, whose bones are spongy and filled with oil. Indeed a whale, though an air-breathing mammal, quickly dies if washed ashore, its lungs crushed by the weight of its own vast body.

Yet despite the homogeneity of the marine environment, its lack of impassable deserts and unscalable mountains, the sea too has its barriers: invisible boundaries of temperature, salinity, pressure and light. Most sea creatures, having no regulator systems like those of land animals designed to protect them against sudden and intense environmental changes, are extremely sensitive to slight variations in their watery medium. Thus temperature differences serve to confine marine life to certain regions of the sea. Many cold-water creatures of north and south latitudes are identical, yet differ sharply from tropical species that inhabit the seas between. Sudden shifts in ocean currents, bringing, for example, masses of warm water into regions occupied by cold-water creatures, may completely destroy existing populations within vast areas. In the same way a sudden change in salinity, caused perhaps by a heavy rainy season and the disgorging of flooded rivers

AMID CORAL SPIRES in a world of rippled sands and swaying plumes, monstrous and magnificent creatures glide through glimmering, blue-green water. Here a grouper, goggle-eyed and heavy-jowled, hangs lightly above the sunlit ocean floor. He is a member of that class of streamlined, neckless, water-breathing vertebrate animals called fish, the best known to man of all the many thousands of kinds of creatures that inhabit the far-flung dominions of the teeming sea.

THE CROWDED SEA teems with schools of fish, gliding like well-disciplined armies through the clear water. Some fish are solitary hunters like marlin, barracudas and sharks. But many more, like these Australian Caesios, locally but incorrectly called kingfish, travel together in great numbers, possibly for mutual protection, possibly in response to some deep instinct. The precision with which such schools swim in formation, twisting, diving, accelerating in unison with

into coastal waters, may decimate oyster beds and other inshore invertebrates. Pressure too draws horizontal boundaries between layers of the sea. Although some fish reveal an amazing ability to move from one pressure level to another without harm—and whales are capable of plunging to 3,000 feet or more—most sea creatures remain between certain self-imposed strata marking the upper and lower limits of their abode.

A more obdurate barrier is light—not because vision is the most important sense to the majority of marine organisms, but because light is indispensable to the aquatic plants that compose the basic food supply of the sea. All plants obtain their nourishment by converting inorganic substances—water, carbon dioxide and certain minerals and salts—into food. The process by which they do this, called photosynthesis, depends entirely on the energy of the sun. So in contrast to the land where sunlight bathes all but the deepest ravines and where all regions save the deserts and the poles are garbed in green, plants in the ocean are confined to the sunlit upper waters; none grows below 250 feet. The hidden mountains of the sea are more bleak than the high Himalayas, the great plains and valleys of

the ocean floor more barren than the sands of the Sahara. Nowhere beneath the waters is there vegetation comparable to the thick forests of the land. Marine plants are primitive, rootless, trunkless, generally small, and limited in kind. There are only a few seed plants—such as eel grass and surf grass. The rest consist of the seaweeds, of minute blue-green algae and of the single-celled plants called diatoms. The latter, though microscopic in size, reproduce faster than any terrestrial flora, often doubling in number every second day and in a year producing many tons per acre of open water. In spring and fall the surface of the sea turns yellow, brown and green as the diatoms bloom. Thriving in cold water, in regions of turbulence and upwelling where the rich organic nutrients of the ocean floor ride upward on deep currents, the diatoms lure hordes of sea creatures to their enormous pastures. Where the diatoms flourish, there too flourish the world's great fisheries—along the west coasts of North and South America, in the North Sea, off Portugal, Japan and Newfoundland.

And so the broad unbroken sea is a diversified domain, divided, like the land, into many provinces and precincts, each with its own populations and ways of life, separated one from another by unseen walls

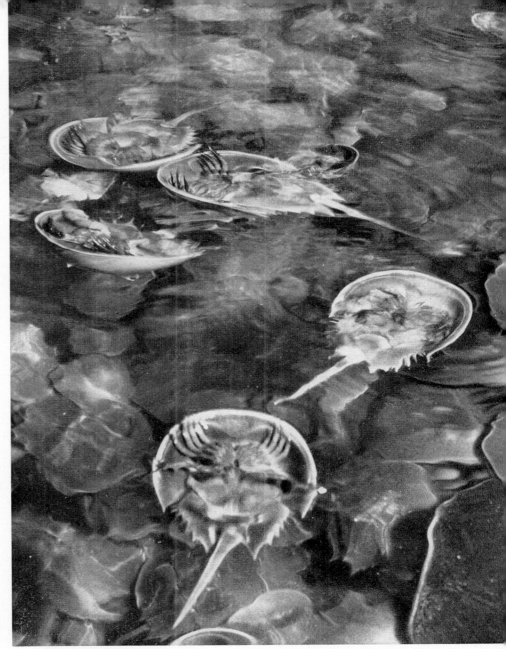

THE SUPPORTING SEA enables marine creatures to stay afloat with a minimum of effort. Here horseshoe crabs float on the surface on their backs using shells as boats, legs as oars. They can also swim right side up or crawl along the bottom.

THE FERTILE SEA provides hanging gardens of sea plants as pasturage for small creatures. Here a halfbeak skims under a patch of Sargassum in the Caribbean looking for prey. Its long lower jaw is designed for snatching food from below.

their leaders, never colliding. remains a mystery of nature comparable to that presented by the formation flying of birds. Whether they maneuver chiefly by sight, sound or response to the "backwash" of the lead fish, no one can now say.

of physical condition. From the perspective of marine biology the sea encompasses two great dominions of nature: the pelagic environment (open water) and the benthic environment (the bottom). And each of these in turn embraces several separate and distinct categories of life. Pelagic life is divided into plankton (floating creatures that have little power of locomotion and drift with the currents) and nekton (free-swimming creatures of all kinds). Benthic life exists all the way from the littoral benthos (the inshore bottom) downward to the abyssal benthos (the deep sea floor beyond the continental slopes). Though drowned in a common medium and interpenetrated by the ever-restless currents of the deep, each of these great domains of life is nevertheless a world of its own, shaped by disparate circumstance. There are no collective answers but many diverse ones to the questions addressed to the seas' creatures by the English poet, Leigh Hunt, a century ago:

> O scaly, slippery, wet, swift, staring wights,
> What is 't ye do? what life lead? eh, dull goggles?
> How do you vary your vile days and nights?
> How pass your Sundays?

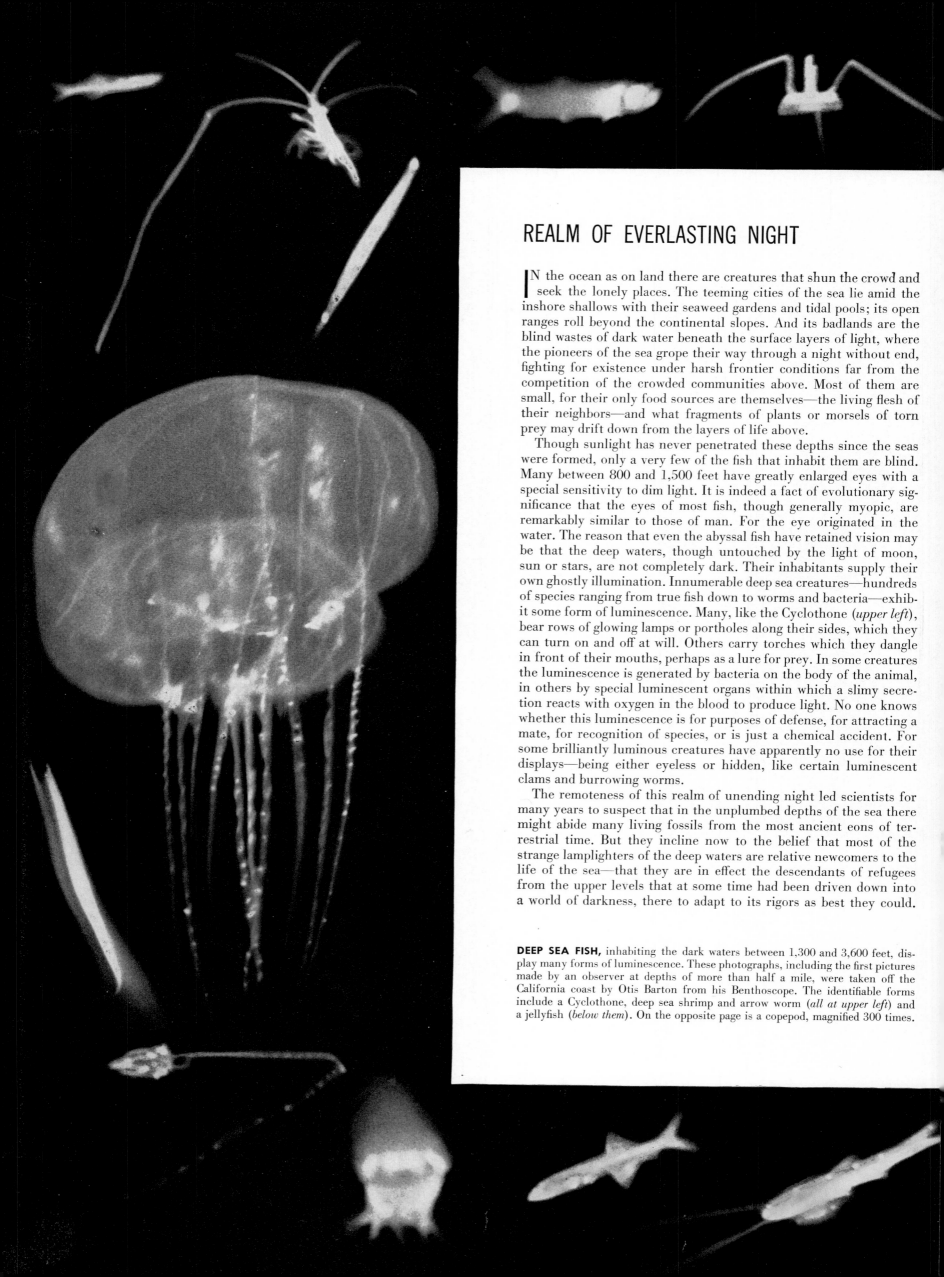

REALM OF EVERLASTING NIGHT

IN the ocean as on land there are creatures that shun the crowd and seek the lonely places. The teeming cities of the sea lie amid the inshore shallows with their seaweed gardens and tidal pools; its open ranges roll beyond the continental slopes. And its badlands are the blind wastes of dark water beneath the surface layers of light, where the pioneers of the sea grope their way through a night without end, fighting for existence under harsh frontier conditions far from the competition of the crowded communities above. Most of them are small, for their only food sources are themselves—the living flesh of their neighbors—and what fragments of plants or morsels of torn prey may drift down from the layers of life above.

Though sunlight has never penetrated these depths since the seas were formed, only a very few of the fish that inhabit them are blind. Many between 800 and 1,500 feet have greatly enlarged eyes with a special sensitivity to dim light. It is indeed a fact of evolutionary significance that the eyes of most fish, though generally myopic, are remarkably similar to those of man. For the eye originated in the water. The reason that even the abyssal fish have retained vision may be that the deep waters, though untouched by the light of moon, sun or stars, are not completely dark. Their inhabitants supply their own ghostly illumination. Innumerable deep sea creatures—hundreds of species ranging from true fish down to worms and bacteria—exhibit some form of luminescence. Many, like the Cyclothone (*upper left*), bear rows of glowing lamps or portholes along their sides, which they can turn on and off at will. Others carry torches which they dangle in front of their mouths, perhaps as a lure for prey. In some creatures the luminescence is generated by bacteria on the body of the animal, in others by special luminescent organs within which a slimy secretion reacts with oxygen in the blood to produce light. No one knows whether this luminescence is for purposes of defense, for attracting a mate, for recognition of species, or is just a chemical accident. For some brilliantly luminous creatures have apparently no use for their displays—being either eyeless or hidden, like certain luminescent clams and burrowing worms.

The remoteness of this realm of unending night led scientists for many years to suspect that in the unplumbed depths of the sea there might abide many living fossils from the most ancient eons of terrestrial time. But they incline now to the belief that most of the strange lamplighters of the deep waters are relative newcomers to the life of the sea—that they are in effect the descendants of refugees from the upper levels that at some time had been driven down into a world of darkness, there to adapt to its rigors as best they could.

DEEP SEA FISH, inhabiting the dark waters between 1,300 and 3,600 feet, display many forms of luminescence. These photographs, including the first pictures made by an observer at depths of more than half a mile, were taken off the California coast by Otis Barton from his Benthoscope. The identifiable forms include a Cyclothone, deep sea shrimp and arrow worm (*all at upper left*) and a jellyfish (*below them*). On the opposite page is a copepod, magnified 300 times.

FREE SWIMMERS OF THE OPEN SEA

UNLIKE bottom dwellers, fettered to the ocean floor, the free-swimming creatures of the sea move buoyantly through a three-dimensional world in which mobility, keen senses and protective coloration are the implements of survival. From the blue upper layers of the water to its lightless depths, ocean life varies in form, abundance and habit with its level in the many-storied sea.

The domain of open waters is the domain of vertebrate fish, though they share their sovereignty with some invertebrates, like the giant squid, and the mightiest of mammals, the whales. The aristocrats among them—the swiftest, strongest, handsomest—hunt near the surface where food is more abundant. Their speed kings are the blue marlin, capable of spurts up to 50 mph; the dolphin; and the dolphin's favorite prey, the sailfish; the

flying fish, which taxis at 35 mph and soars rather than flies through the air. Not much slower are the tuna and the oceanic bonito. Sharks, largest of all fish, are the wolves of the sea. A near kin of the shark is the harmless manta or devilfish, which may attain a weight of 3,000 pounds and, like a sailfish, often leaps from the water, falling back with a splash resounding for several miles.

Most of these surface-dwelling fish have been tinted by nature to blend with their glimmering environment. Since the long wavelengths of sunlight are absorbed in the upper 75 feet of water, the dominant undersea colors are green, blue and violet. These persist feebly to a depth of 2,000 feet in clear waters (like those shown from the surface to 4,000 feet in the composite painting below). Pelagic creatures inhabiting the upper stories of the sea tend to be bluish above and silver underneath. From about 600 to 1,500 feet, a twilight grayish zone, the fish are correspondingly light-hued—like the

silvery *Sternoptyx*, *Diretmus* and *Opisthoproctus*. Below, in the zone of utter blackness, animals display the brown and black shades of *Melanocetus* and *Photostomias*, though a few, such as the scarlet deep-sea prawns, astonishingly wear bright colors for reasons no one can guess. Indeed, the little that is known about creatures of the deep has been deduced from the occasional strange specimens brought up in the nets of marine biologists. (The curious forms shown below, strangely named from the lexicon of science, represent much of what man has seen of life in the lower levels of the sea.) But the fact that most deep-sea fish are also equipped with enormous gaping mouths and long, needlelike teeth is suggestive of the bitter struggle to survive in the blind depths where food is located by chance. One such fish, *Chiasmodon*, has a distensible stomach enabling it to swallow prey somewhat larger than itself. But the greatest battles of the oceanic deep are waged a quarter mile down by the sperm whale and its ancient prey, the giant squid.

BLUE MARLIN 10 FT.

FLYING FISH 9 IN.

DOLPHIN 4 FT.

SAILFISH 8 FT.

MANTA 20 FT.

SUNFISH 7 FT.

SEA COLANDER
PHYLLARIA DERMATODEA SEAWEED

SEA GRAPES

DOG WHELKS
PERIWINKLES

EDIBLE MUSSELS
PINK HEARTED HYDROIDS

SEA VASES

PURPLE STARFISH

REDBEARD SPONGE   OYSTER DRILLS
RIBBED MUSSELS   ROCK BARNACLES
                         IRISH MOSS

SEA ANEMONE, RETRACTED
SEA PORK

CORALLINE ALGAE
BLOOD STARFISH

MUSSEL SHELL

COMMON STARFISH
RAZOR CLAM SHELL

MOON SNAIL SHELL
BOAT SHELL

SUN STAR

FOLD OUT, DO NOT TEAR

DIRETMUS ARGENTEUS 2 IN.

HATCHET FISH 1 IN.

LAMPROTOXUS FLAGELLIBARBA 8 IN.

VIPERFISH 12 IN.

CHIASMODON NIGER 2 IN.

SNIPE EEL 2 FT.

EEL LARVA 4 IN.

ROOSTER FISH 15 FT.

LANTERN FISH 3 IN.

PLATYBERIX OPALESCENS 3 IN.

PHOTOSTOMIAS GUERNEI 7 IN.

MELANOCETUS JOHNSONI 2 IN.

PRAWNS 4 IN.

OPISTHOPROCTUS SOLEATUS 1 IN.

WHITE-TIPPED SHARK 7 FT.

BLUEFIN TUNA 7 FT.

SPERM WHALE 60 FT.

OCEANIC BONITO 2 FT.

GIANT SQUID 55 FT.

STERNOPTYX DIAPHANA 2 IN.

ROCKWEED   ROCKWEED

ROCK CRAB   SOFT CORAL

JINGLE SHELLS   SEA CUCUMBER

GREEN SEA URCHIN AND SHELL   GREEN CRAB   WHELK EGG CASE

SAND DOLLAR AND SHELL   SEA PEACHES   SEA ANEMONE, EXPANDED   SKATE EGG CAPSULE

MUD STAR   HERMIT CRAB IN BORROWED SHELL   PURPLE SEA URCHIN

BRITTLE STAR   BAY SCALLOP SHELL

KELP

SEA ANEMONE

BLUE CRAB

LADY CRAB

TORTOISE-SHELL LIMPETS

CLATHRIA DELICATA SPONGE
EYED FINGER SPONGE

YOUNG HORSESHOE CRAB

THE BOTTOM DWELLERS

AMID the weedy gardens of the inshore shallows, life flourishes as in no other region of the sea. Here upon the benthos, on the pallid sands and mud, a multitude of sluggish creatures subsists in a strange, slow-motion world where journeys are made in inches, and time brings imperceptible change. The very quality of existence seems more akin to the kingdom of plants than that of the swift, darting fish, and many benthic creatures resemble plants in outer aspect and have plantlike names: sea anemones, sea cucumbers, sea peaches, sea grapes. Yet they are animals—members of the vast empire of soft-bodied invertebrates, engineered by nature for life on the ocean floor.

Since many of these are fixed or sessile creatures, like the Clathria sponge and soft coral, their major problem of subsistence is to find available space for attachment. Virtually every rock or sunken object, every area of sand or mud, has its creeping, crawling or sedentary tenants. An old piling rapidly becomes an apartment house for barnacles, mussels, drills, sea vases, sponges and pink-hearted hydroids. Layers of snails exploit the shells of their fellows as anchorage. When a snail dies a hermit crab may move into its vacated shell and carry it around with him like a trailer home, often with an anemone free-loading on top. Even beneath the surface of the sand and silt there are many mansions—the mazes of sea worms, the holes of moon shells, the burrows of fiddler crabs which venture forth at low tide in quest of food, and the hideaways of razor clams which thrust up their siphons only when the tide is in.

The foundation on which the whole edifice of benthic life depends is the rich supply of minerals dissolved in the water and stored on the ocean floor. To most marine life calcium is a crucial element, but especially to soft-bodied benthic creatures whose hard outer coverings not only protect them against predators and the pounding of the surf, but also provide anchorage for the muscles with which they dig and crawl. Calcium compounds reinforce the leggings and pincers of crabs, and help to form the delicate swirls of whelk, periwinkle and other snail shells, the spines of the sea urchin, and the "razor" of the razor clam. In the tropics, where calcium is absorbed more readily than in cold water, one species of clam grows shells of great thickness, often weighing up to 500 pounds.

The bottom minerals are also important to the plant life which flourishes in the sea gardens of rock weed, kelp and Irish moss that adorn the coastal shelves. Like most plants, large seaweeds require anchorage—even the floating masses of seaweed in the Sargasso Sea may consist of shore forms that have been torn away and swept into the circular backwash of the Gulf Stream. Though rootless, many seaweeds anchor themselves to rocks or sand by threadlike "holdfasts" or flat disks, as shown by the sea colander and *Phyllaria*. If their anchorage is deep, they may put forth stems up to 100 feet long so that their main foliage can float in sunlight, buoyed up by little self-contained bulbs of gas. The largest of the seaweeds are the kelps, flat brown plants that anchor in rocky areas offshore, beyond the zone of crashing surf. Few marine animals browse directly on the larger seaweeds. (One that does is the sea hare.) Some smaller algae, however, which grow like a furry slime on rocks and other sunken objects, provide food for certain crabs and shrimps and many sharp-tongued snails.

135

SEA SQUIRTS often cluster in inch-high colonies over rocks and pilings where they feed by pumping water in and out of their digestive cavities through two body orifices. When alarmed they squirt water from both holes.

LAZY HUNTERS OF THE OCEAN FLOOR

FOR many creatures of the sea, the water in which they dwell provides more than a medium of residence and respiration. It is also a kind of soup, a rich chowder, filled with an abundance of food particles which they need only strain out and injest. In open water these particles consist of numberless small living animals and plants. On the bottom there is detritus—a kind of slime composed of decaying matter and the bacteria that break it down—as well as swarms of protozoans, tiny worms, larval forms and other small organisms. So whereas fish of the open sea expend their energies in a never-ending quest for food, most bottom dwellers live engulfed in food and have little more to do than open their mouths, if they have mouths.

Since locomotion is not necessary for a livelihood, many benthic creatures lead completely sedentary lives and simply wait for food to float past in the water with the moving tides and currents. Sponges and sea squirts anchor themselves to rocks or other solid objects and feed by pumping detritus-laden water in and out of their body apertures. Oysters and clams are also pumpers and spend their entire adult lives in beds. A few livelier organisms make somewhat more of an effort. Barnacles, for example, catch food particles in the bristles of their outstretched hairy legs which intermittently draw in the haul like seining nets. Sea cucumbers snuffle along the sea floor like vacuum cleaners, using their tentacles to shovel slime into their mouths. Their rate of movement is slow; some make 18 inches a day.

STINGING TENTACLES of a sea anemone paralyze a small fish. The spiral whitish bands around each tentacle contain many small poisoned "needles." When the prey has been immobilized, it is drawn into the mouth.

THE SEA ANEMONE looks like a flower but is actually a carnivorous three-inch animal capable of catching, killing and digesting relatively large prey. Its basal end is a slimy disk with which it clings to rocks or glides slowly across the sea floor.

THE FILE SHELL is the most active and alert of the bivalves. A colorful relative of the scallop, it has tentacles which are sensitive to both taste and touch. It feeds by straining water through its scarlet, sheetlike gills.

SERPENT STARS are carnivores and scavengers which crawl along the bottom, mouth downward, searching for mollusks and also feeding on slime. If a serpent star is cut in two, each half will regenerate a complete animal.

THE SEA URCHIN (*right*) has a voracious-looking mouth on its underside armed with five efficient "teeth" which are capable of crushing small mollusks, of cutting up sea lettuce (a seaweed) and of scraping algae off rocks.

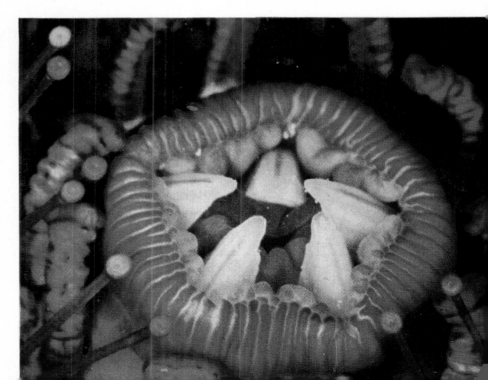

A BOXING SHRIMP fights off fishes that are larger than itself. Though only about one inch long and almost transparent, this delicate tropical creature pluckily rears up on its spindly hind legs at the first approach of danger and, raising its enlarged forearms, armed with strong pincers, fends off would-be predators with right and left jabs and uppercuts. Its long sensitive antennae and sensory hairs on its legs enable it to detect the approach of both danger and of food.

THE ARTS OF DEFENSE AND CAMOUFLAGE

TO the creatures that inhabit its unvaried waters, the open sea offers little sanctuary comparable to the woods and thickets of the land, little refuge or ambush other than occasional flotsam, a random fragment of floating kelp or Sargassum weed. And so, to survive in a world of bitter predators, each species has had to evolve its own weapons and defenses. To some, like the tuna, shark and barracuda, have gone the implements of sheer power—sharp teeth, swift reflexes, speed and strength. To others, slow-moving and apathetic, have gone shells or armor plate—as to the oyster, snail and clam.

Apart from these more familiar armaments, marine creatures have developed unique and highly specialized defenses of their own. Squid, octopi and some shrimp blind their enemies by discharging "ink" in the waters around them. The sting cells of jellyfish and anemones contain coiled, hollow darts which, when triggered, inject poison that paralyzes their attackers. Sting rays carry poisoned spines on their

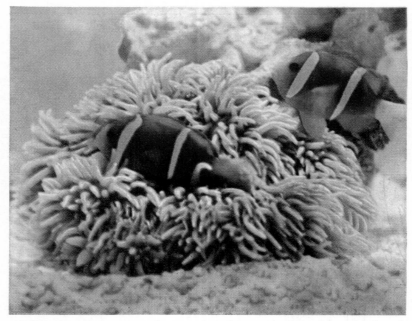

HIDING FISH lurk among the tentacles of a sea anemone. Mysteriously safe from the anemone's sting, these damselfish live in harmony with their dangerous host. They lure larger fish which the anemone kills. Then they share the feast.

A SQUIRTING SEA HARE defends itself by ejecting "ink." A species of mollusk, the sea hare gets its name from its long earlike "antennae." A related mollusk provided the "Tyrian purple" dye used by the ancient Phoenicians.

A SLASHING SAWFISH defends itself in combat with great flailing strokes of its serrated proboscis, which is equipped with two rows of 25 to 29 bony "teeth." No kin to the swordfish or marlin, the sawfish inhabits warm, shallow waters of the Atlantic and Pacific. It descends suddenly on a school of smaller fish, swimming into the midst of them and hacking them to pieces before they escape. Then at leisure it eats up the mangled victims that have fallen to the sea floor.

tails; other rays and some eels are equipped with electric organs capable of administering a severe shock. Sponges have minute spikes that lodge in the enemy. Most extraordinary of all is the diversionary tactic of certain sea cucumbers which, in a moment of extreme peril, eviscerate themselves and then, leaving their internal organs behind to distract the foe, slip away and grow new ones.

Many creatures that dwell upon the sand and among the eel grass and seaweed groves of the coastal shallows survive by imitating the forms and colors of their environment. Nowhere in nature has the art of camouflage been more highly developed than among these otherwise poorly defended animals. Flatfish and rockfish change color in accordance with the color of their background. Decorator crabs cement bits of seaweed over their shells and legs. The hermit crab, which has a tender rump, adorns it with discarded shells. Some sea urchins become covered with snails so they will look like a snail colony. There are, finally, certain relationships where a small animal attaches itself to a larger one for reasons of security—as in the case of the shark sucker and the shark, and the barnacles on the head of a whale.

A CAMOUFLAGED PIPEFISH poises vertically among blades of eelgrass off the California coast, hardly distinguishable from them in form, position and color. Its long snout is adapted to probing for the small crustaceans on which it feeds.

A BRISTLING BLOWFISH, denizen of coral seas, inflates itself with water, thus presenting too big a mouthful for most of its natural foes to swallow. At the same time it erects the forbidding-looking spines that normally lie flat on its body.

UNDULATING its entire body, a reef-dwelling moray eel, shown in repetitive flash photograph, advances somewhat as a snake wriggles on land. A moray is a true fish. Its suppleness enables it to slither into rock crannies in search of prey.

ARTS OF LOCOMOTION

UNLIKE land animals to whom the thin air offers little resistance, aquatic creatures must expend great stores of energy to force their way through the dense medium in which they dwell. And so the populations of the sea have evolved many techniques and aids to locomotion—streamlining, jet propulsion and varied rhythms of movement. Since the specific gravity, or density, of water is virtually the same as that of its inhabitants, they have little difficulty staying afloat. Most living things are composed principally of water, and this is especially true of aquatic life—a jellyfish, for example, is 96% water. Yet even the smallest of marine creatures are not entirely free from the tug of gravity, and in death the bones and shells of all, including the one-celled protozoans, sink into the oozes of the ocean floor.

For this reason many are endowed with special mechanisms to keep them suspended. Most fish have air sacs; others are honeycombed with oil deposits or swaddled in thick layers of fat. Not all creatures of the sea are fish, however, nor do all of them swim. Planktonic forms move but feebly and, for the most part, simply drift with the wandering currents, buoyed up by various flotation devices—such as long, branched feelers or side appendages. Bottom dwellers are for the most part either ambulatory—like crabs and lobsters which crawl on jointed legs, and like snails and anemones which glide on slimy feet—or sedentary—like oysters, sponges, barnacles and corals which simply anchor themselves to the ocean floor. The truly accomplished swimmers of the sea are fish and the marine mammals—whales, porpoises and seals.

Contrary to popular opinion, most fish do not swim with their side or back fins; or more precisely, their fins serve less as implements of propulsion than as stabilizers, ailerons, rudders and brakes. Their main propellant is body movement, augmented by pushing action from the tail or the extrusion of water from the gills. The movements range in degree from the complete undulation of the eel to the restricted action of the stiff, armored boxfish which can move only its tiny fins and tail. But with the majority of fish, body movement falls

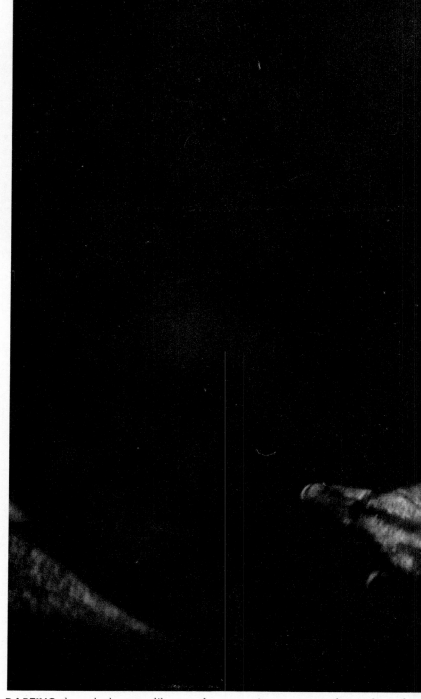

DARTING through the water like torpedoes, porpoises are among the acrobats of the sea. Speedy swimmers, they travel in spurts up to 25 mph, often leaping from the water in a sequence of graceful, arching bounds. Since they are air-breathing

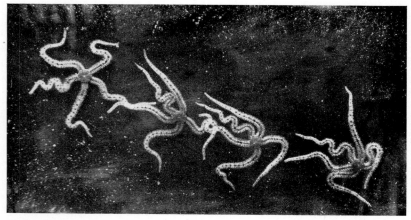

CREEPING, a Caribbean brittle star, shown in repetitive flash photograph, pulls itself along with its two anterior arms and shoves with the other three. It is far more agile and flexible than its sluggish, stiff-armed cousin, the common starfish.

JET-PROPELLED, an octopus is equipped with a thick muscular mantle which it fills with water. It then extrudes the water through a movable funnel which can be turned in any direction. On the bottom an octopus crawls on its tentacles.

mammals they must surface frequently, sucking in air through a blowhole situated on top of their heads, visible above in the porpoise which has just burst the surface. The holes close with amazing rapidity when they dive. Although porpoises have excellent eyesight, some scientists believe they gauge their distance from solid objects by emitting sonic and supersonic noises and mentally computing their position from the time of the echo, as bats do in the air.

JUMPING, a file shell escapes enemies by clapping its shells together like castanets. With every bang water is ejected, stirring up a small cloud of sand and debris and sometimes carrying the creature a few feet from its point of take-off.

WALKING, a West Indian batfish appears to move like a land animal. Its fins not only look like legs but support the batfish when it rests on the bottom, and enable it to walk on the ocean floor. In swimming, it uses its tail as a propellant.

AN EAGLE RAY flies like some great bird of prey through its world of water and a school of sheepshead, flapping its huge and winglike pectoral fins. A bottom feeder, the ray also uses its "wings" to agitate the sand in quest of mollusks. In a single night a ray may dig a ditch as wide as its 4-foot wingspread, a foot deep and 20 feet long. As it digs it scoops up clams and crushes them between its rows of flat teeth. It ranges in the Atlantic from tropical waters north to Cape Cod.

between these two extremes; a pivotal point, usually at the base of the skull, moves straight ahead while segments of the body fore and aft oscillate. Fish probably navigate partly by eyesight, partly by hearing, partly by tactile sense and partly by smell. Although they have no external ears, their auditory sense is highly developed, functioning by means of a lateral line or row of sound-receptor cells along the sides of their bodies which are connected in turn to the inner ear and the brain. They maintain equilibrium through small organs called statocysts. These are cavities lined with sensory hairs and containing some loose objects, like a bony accretion or grain of sand, which informs them, even in the utter blackness of the abyss, whether they are upright or upside down.

One of the mysteries of marine biology is the manner in which fish manage to sleep, for they have no eyelids and, like airplanes, must keep in motion to keep from falling. A few flat, benthic fish, notably flounders, soles, skates and rays, often lie down on the bottom mud and sands. Others wedge themselves in crevices for the night. Small pelagic types occasionally appear to bask among drifting seaweeds. But so far as the free swimmers of the open waters are concerned no one can say how they sleep, or indeed if they ever sleep at all.

A GREEN TURTLE uses its slender front flippers as oars, feathering them neatly in unison, and its rear limbs as steering apparatus and kickers. On dry land it moves ponderously and without grace, crawling slowly along the warm Atlantic beaches to which it must return periodically to lay eggs. Of all the marine reptiles of the Mesozoic era, the turtle tribe almost alone has survived to flourish in the present day. A few small sea snakes also persist in parts of the Pacific.

SEA SLUGS or nudibranchs, which are mollusks without shells, move about by sliding along on a muscular foot. They often crawl upside down while grazing on hydroids (*shown above*). If disturbed they lower themselves to the ocean floor at the end of an almost invisible thread of slime anchored to the hydroid, or, if in open water, to the surface film. Sea slugs nibble off the heads of hydroids, animals related to the coral polyp. The hydroids then grow new heads.

PLANKTON, the basic food store of the sea, encompasses an immense variety of small floating plants and animals. The more important specimens are shown here without regard to true scale. Most are microscopic, although the largest, the bell-like medusa at bottom of left-hand page, is two inches long. They include: a diatom (*straight yellow rod near center of right-hand page*); radiolarians and foraminifera (*small circular shells to left of diatom*); a dinoflagellate (*pick-shaped object in*

THE LUSH PASTURES OF THE SEA

OF all the categories of life in the sea the most far-flung and important is the diffuse aggregate of living things known as plankton. Spread across the oceans of earth, plankton is a floating community of both plants and animals concentrated in the surface waters. Most of them are small, even microscopic in size. But included also are slightly larger forms, tiny animals that feed on the single-celled organisms and spend their entire existence on the open waters, drifting whither the ocean currents impel them. The characteristic of plankton that sets it apart from other forms of oceanic life is that its powers of locomotion are too feeble to compete with the moving currents. Its name is from the Greek word *planktos*, meaning "wandering."

The importance of plankton to oceanic life is that it represents the prime food supply of the sea. For in the sea as on land the animal kingdom depends on the plant kingdom for food. Plants have the ability to convert simple inorganic substances into the complicated compounds like sugars, starches and proteins that provide nourishment and energy to animals. And so all life in the sea is dependent ultimately on the single-celled microscopic plants called diatoms, which constitute six tenths of planktonic material.

In addition to diatoms, plankton includes incomputable numbers of protozoans—one-celled animals like radiolarians and foraminifera,

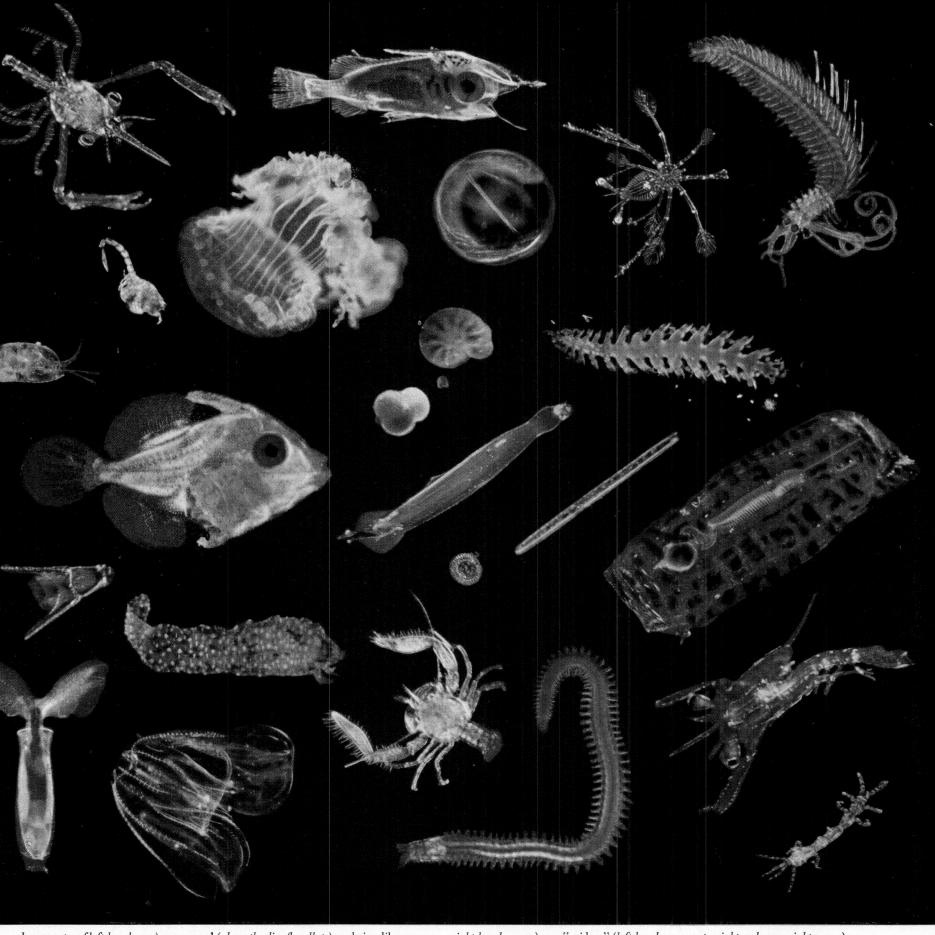

lower center of left-hand page); a copepod (*above the dinoflagellate*); a shrimplike my-
sid (*to right of copepod*); a "flying" snail (*top, center of left-hand page*); sea worms,
one with two egg sacs (*near upper left-hand corner*) and one with tentacles (*upper
right-hand corner*); sea "spiders" (*left-hand page, center right and upper right corner*);
young fishes (*right-hand page, left center and top center*); larvae of sea urchin (*V-
shaped object below fish*) and of spiny lobster (*next to tentacled worm at upper right*).

whose minute shells compose the oozes that blanket vast areas of the
ocean floor, and the equally prolific dinoflagellates, half plant, half
animal, whose transparent bodies give forth much of the ghostly
luminescence that enkindles the tropic seas by night. Along with
these, borne on the restless currents, ride numberless intermediate
forms—tiny arthropods, such as copepods and mysids; the larvae of
sea urchins, snails and lobsters; sea worms and sea "spiders"; and
many kinds of baby fish, together with a few larger floating forms such
as jellyfish and Portuguese men-of-war. All these, representing thousands of species of aquatic creatures, make up the world of plankton.

Although plankton does not include free-swimming adult fish,
some of its creatures move about within a small range. Each day at
dawn the planktonic animals descend to avoid the light of day; each
evening at dusk they rise again. Their daily vertical migration is
probably the source of one of the outstanding mysteries of oceanography—the so-called scattering layer of unidentified solid objects that
reflect sound echoes within a fluctuating range of 300 to 1,500 feet.
While some scientists attribute this phenomenon entirely to planktonic creatures, others think it may be caused by the dense hordes of
shrimp, squid and larger fish that graze upon them. Wherever the
teeming pastures of plankton luxuriate, all forms of marine life
abound. For plankton is the food factory of the sea, the start of the
endless food cycle that sustains all creatures of the open waters
from sardines and herring to the titan of the oceans, the blue whale.

THE ENDLESS CHAIN OF FOOD

SAVE for those small animals that graze on diatoms in the huge communities of plankton, virtually every free-swimming creature lives on the flesh of others smaller than itself and represents a meal for others larger than itself. It is estimated that 10 pounds of food are required to build one pound of the animal that eats it. Thus it would take 10,000 pounds of diatoms to make 1,000 pounds of copepods to make 100 pounds of herring to make 10 pounds of mackerel to make one pound of tuna to make 1/10th of a pound of man.

Since the open sea provides no repository or hiding place for food, each meal must be caught and eaten alive. And so the ocean's populations are involved in a never-ending cycle of eat and be eaten, pursuit and flight; each living creature in the sea is at once hunter and hunted, feeder and food, predator and prey. And when an animal dies or is torn asunder, its remains fall to the bottom where they are devoured by scavengers or decomposed by bacteria. Then they become detritus, either to be consumed again by detritus feeders or wafted aloft through upwellings to provide dissolved fertilizer for the diatoms on the surface waters. And so the food cycle of the sea is eternally renewed.

COPEPOD EATS DIATOMS. Despite their tiny size—from a pinhead to a quarter of an inch—copepods are among the world's most important food animals. For the food cycle of the sea begins with their consumption of microscopic diatoms.

HERRING EATS COPEPODS. Diatom-fed copepods constitute a favorite food of the baby herring which has sievelike "rakers" in its gills to sift them with. Examination of a herring's stomach once disclosed 60,895 copepods inside. The herring group, which includes sardines, shad, menhaden and alewives, is considered to be the most valuable of all fish groups because of its wide distribution and the abundance of food it supplies to other marine creatures and to man.

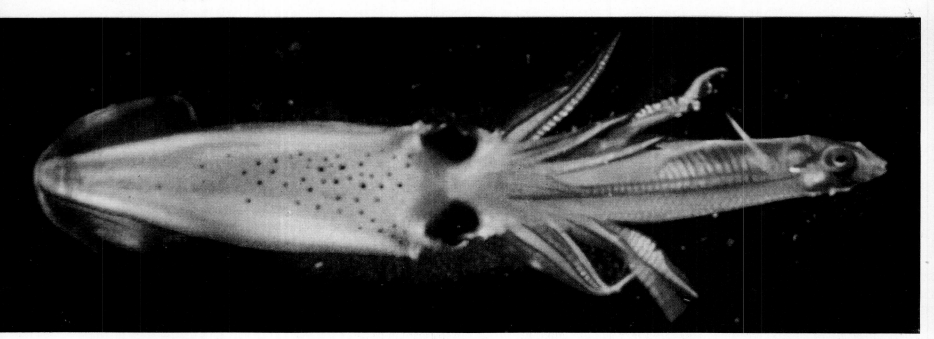

SQUID EATS HERRING. Varying in size from one inch to more than 50 feet, all squid are carnivorous and predacious, subsisting on fish, crustaceans and other mollusks. When a squid catches a fish in its tentacles, it draws the fish toward its mouth, which is equipped with a horny, parrotlike beak; then, holding its victim firmly, it bites out big chunks which it gulps down. The eyes and brains of squid and octopi are among the most highly developed in the marine world.

BASS EATS SQUID. An adult sea bass attains a length of about 18 inches and a weight of perhaps six pounds. Its consumption of the squid that ate the herring that ate the copepod that ate the diatoms marks the penultimate stage of this particular food cycle. The ultimate stage may be reached when the bass is caught and eaten by man. Or if the bass escapes predators and dies of other causes, its dead body will sink to the bottom and there be consumed by scavengers.

LIFE AND DEATH IN THE SEA

THE sea is at once a vast cradle and graveyard of life, a nursery where incalculable hosts of visible and invisible creatures procreate and abide and a battleground wherein the chances of survival may be but one against 10 million of violent death. In the transition from egg to adult each creature must run a gantlet of ever larger enemies whose pursuit never ends (*pictures at right*).

Those that escape being eaten may succumb to starvation, to parasites that invade their internal organs, or to immense catastrophes occasioned by storms, shifts in ocean currents or changes in the temperature or composition of the sea water. Recurrent "red tides" caused by an explosive increase of dinoflagellates, which consume vast quantities of oxygen and emit vast quantities of toxic wastes, from time to time annihilate fish life on a prodigious scale.

But if the sea is wasteful of life, it is also prodigal in its inception. The reproductive rate of marine creatures confounds the imagination of slow-breeding man. If every codfish egg laid in the sea ultimately grew into a surviving adult, in six years the Atlantic Ocean would be packed solid with cod. A female codfish may lay up to five million eggs at one time, an oyster 11 million, a sunfish 300 million. A spawning sea hare lays eggs at the rate of 41,000 per minute, producing perhaps 500 million in a single season. If each one matured and reproduced for four generations, the resulting mass of sea hares would occupy a space about six times the volume of the planet Earth.

The exigencies of existence in the sea are such, however, that the miracle of marine life consists not so much in the profusion of eggs as in the fact that any survive at all. Only a few sea creatures care for either their eggs or their young. One that does is the octopus: the female broods over her clusters of eggs, stroking them and fanning the water around them with her tentacles to assure proper circulation (*see picture below*). In most cases eggs are discharged freely into the water, there to drift with the currents or settle to the bottom and take their chances of escaping the numberless voracious predators, including their own parents, that wait to devour them. Yet the mechanisms of nature are so exquisitely adjusted that the average survival, for example, of only one oyster egg in half a billion is sufficient to preserve the balance between overpopulation and extinction of the species.

The development of an egg into a larva neither terminates the individual's hazards of survival nor greatly lessens its prospects of

IN SWIFT PURSUIT, a three-foot Caribbean octopus reaches for a blue crab which is its favorite article of diet. The crab first tries to bury itself in the sand, then darts away and temporarily escapes the octopus's lashing tentacles.

CAPTURED, the crab lies helpless in the octopus's grasp, already minus one joint which the octopus has torn off. If necessary, as with larger prey, the octopus might simply drop down and engulf the crab in its mantle like a tent.

GUARDING EGGS, a female octopus pulls boulders around herself to form a "nest" in Florida waters. The eggs hang like grape clusters at upper right, and the mother cleans them off periodically with suction cups on her tentacles.

DOOMED, the crab is drawn inexorably toward the octopus's mouth, which is equipped with a horny, pointed beak easily capable of crushing the crab's shell. But the octopus prefers to suck the crab's flesh slowly from its casing.

LINGERING OVER ITS REPAST, the octopus plucks the soft crabmeat from each joint with its beak while holding the crab with the powerful suction cups on its tentacles. At the end of two hours the crab is nothing but a hollow shell.

Reputedly dangerous to man, the octopus is actually a timid animal that flees at the approach of any swimmer. Various species range in diameter from one inch to almost 30 feet. All octopi have eight tentacles. Their relatives the squids have 10.

annihilation. For example, the eggs of one species of clam develop into free-swimming larvae one day following fertilization. After subsequent days of growth and development, a larva that has escaped being eaten settles finally to the ocean floor where, if currents have swept it over an uncrowded area of bottom, it may dig into the sand or mud and there ultimately mature into an adult clam. But it may also drop down onto the parental bed where the older population may be clustered thickly—perhaps several adult clams to every square foot of surface—all busily pumping sea water in and out of their double-barreled syphons. There the baby clam may be sucked into the syphons of some kinsman and cannibalistically consumed.

The development of sea creatures from egg to adulthood sometimes involves an interval of many years and the negotiation of many a sea mile from birthplace to final habitat. Many forms of both vertebrate and invertebrate life employ the restless currents to disperse and deploy the species. Some creatures cover tremendous distances during their early development. Perhaps the greatest of all instinctual migrations is that of the European eel. Each autumn, in response to some deep and mysterious urge, adult eels leave the fresh waters where they dwell and come down to the sea. Then, guided no one knows how, they find their way across almost 3,000 miles of the open Atlantic to their spawning grounds in the depths of the weed-strewn Sargasso Sea. It is here that their eggs are laid, and from here that the new-hatched eel larvae start their long journey home, sweeping with the great clockwise swirl of the Gulf Stream northward and eastward to the European shore. This immense journey takes the larvae three years. At its end, metamorphosed into elvers, they swim unerringly upstream into the rivers and lakes where they slowly develop into adult eels. About ten years later, reaching sexual maturity, they return to the sea, and head back to their remote Sargasso spawning grounds, there to reproduce and die. It is in these same far reaches of the sea that the American eels also engender their kind. Only for them the journey is shorter; the swing of the Gulf Stream carries the larvae back to the American coast in a matter of six months.

No less mysterious than the ability of eels to navigate their way across the uncharted ocean waste is the sensitivity of other fish to the rhythm of the tides. The success of their spawning depends on a delicate calculation of the phases of the moon and the advance of the tidal flood. Shortly after each full moon and each new moon between March and August hordes of silvery grunion appear in the surf off the California beaches. As the semimonthly high tide reaches its maximum and begins to ebb, the grunion ride ashore on the large waves. Glistening in the moonlight, they thrash around briefly on the wet sands, long enough for the female to extrude her eggs and the male to fertilize them. Then they fling themselves into an outgoing wave and are gone. Behind them, buried in the sand, the mass of fertilized eggs lies safe from the hammering of the surf, because the tide is on the ebb and not for about two weeks will the alignment of sun, moon and earth produce another tidal peak. So for a fortnight the eggs incubate in the warm sand. And then, when once again the waves break high on the beach, the eggs rupture, the baby fishlets emerge into the water and are borne out to sea on the breast of the outgoing tide.

And so it is not only by the extravagance of their reproductive processes but by such exquisite adaptations to the environment of the sea that marine life sustains itself in the face of infinite dangers and the unceasing, implacable, internecine wars of kind against kind. Yet there is another thread that binds together the tapestry of life in the sea. That is longevity. No one knows how long fish, if spared from predators, starvation or disease, can live. But the age of some fish, like that of trees, may be read from annual growth rings formed in their scales, and there is evidence that certain freshwater fish—carp, catfish, pike—may live 100 years. Of the age of oceanic fish little is known. But one of the most provocative theories of modern biologists investigating the complex mechanisms of life is that the process of aging is inextricably linked with the process of growth and begins only when growth comes to an end. In the case of man and all terrestrial animals, the organism undergoes a definite period of growth during which the protoplasm, the actual living cells, continually divide and do not age. But when certain fixed dimensions are attained, growth terminates and the process of deterioration or aging begins. Although this does not apply to trees which may live for thousands of years, adding outer growth year after year until they succumb to disease, fire or the ax of man, it probably holds true for most land animals, because the tug of gravity imposes an outside limit on the size of moving bodies. Only a few terrestrial creatures ever exceeded the dimensions of the elephant and they are now extinct. But beside the 140-ton whale, the five-ton elephant is a dwarf, for the support of weight is no problem in the sea.

Some biologists believe that for aquatic animals, liberated from the destructive power of gravity by the dense medium in which they dwell, growth, though it may slacken almost to cessation, never halts entirely. So long as they escape—or are protected—from the primitive dangers of the sea, fish may therefore continue to grow by simple enlargement year after year. And so long as they continue to grow, according to this theory, they do not grow old. For them there is no old age, only the violent death that lurks everywhere in the world of waters. From this profound paradox of the sea there may sometime emerge new answers to the ultimate mysteries of life and death—for it was in the sea that life and death began.

From the sea too may some day arise a solution to the eternal problem of human hunger. The luxuriance of marine life is such that, in the opinion of some biologists, the earth's waters can never be utterly fished out. Every year man lifts more than 27 million tons of fish from the oceans without perceptibly affecting the population of any species. But even should a day arrive when the great fish dynasties begin to wane, the fructiferous sea holds other untouched riches.

The world's greatest potential source of food lies in the globe-encircling meadows of plankton with their incomputable multitudes of living creatures. The algae that sustain the planktonic communities, most prolific of all plants on earth, may some day surrender to man the nourishment they contain. The hosts of crustaceans, tiny fish and other animals that graze upon them represent an almost inexhaustible future harvest. And so in the end, man may turn again to his original home, seeking sustenance in what the Elizabethan playwright, Thomas Dekker, described as "that great fishpond, the sea."

THE
CORAL REEF

PART VIII

THE CORAL REEF

Reared by tiny and primitive creatures, master builders of palaces under the sea,
its spires and grottoes encompass the most luxuriant domain of natural existence

> But here is only movement deep
> As breathing . . . the reef fish hover
> Dancing in their silver sleep
> Around their stone, enchanted tree.
>
> ARCHIBALD MacLEISH *The Reef Fisher*

AROUND the periphery of the great wandering sphere on which man rides down the trackless avenues of space there stand many edifices of nature—mountain ranges erected by paroxysms of the planetary crusts and sculpted by the slow, cold chisels of wind, frost and rain; canyons and gorges incised by running water and creeping ice; and oceanic deeps formed by inscrutable forces in the earth's hot core. The preceding portions of this book have described the great structural features of man's environment and the agencies that brought them into being. But in addition to the general land forms, the patterns of rock and water that shape the visible world, the earth encompasses many special areas of existence—windy plains, parched deserts, luxuriant forests. Of these none is more wonderful, none lovelier than the coral reef wrought not by blind physical agencies but by living creatures, diminutive in stature and primitive in form, yet master builders of the palaces of the sea.

Ever since European explorers began to rove the tropic oceans, the Western world has vaguely discerned the phantasmagoria of coral isles rising, palm-fringed and surf-ruffled, amid the blue desolation of the sea. As the centuries passed the image sharpened; new details emerged—of island necklaces ringing bright turquoise lagoons, and many an arched beach of pastel sands. Below the sun-spangled satin of the waters there loomed a fabulous world of living creatures, more prolific and colorful than any known to man, a magic glimmering realm of flowerlike animals, giant clams and gaudy fish with iridescent scales of gold and silver, ruby and emerald, glinting among the groves and grottoes of the coral gardens.

Until the last century, however, the nature of coral remained a mystery. Today it is generally known that the substance called coral —both the hard reef-building variety and the polished material used in the jewelry trade—is composed of the skeletons of innumerable small marine animals. Flourishing around the world in warm tropic waters, these tiny creatures are the creators of thousands of reefs, atolls and island festoons, including the Great Barrier Reef of Australia (*see next page*). No one knows precisely how much coral there is on earth, but it takes its place with the mineral substances of the planetary surface as one of the major architectural ingredients of the world in which man lives.

Owing to the blossomlike aspect of coral gardens, with their branching fronds, fans and clusters of infinitely variegated hues, corals were long mistaken for plants. Actually corals are members of the great phylum of the animal kingdom known as Coelenterata, which includes jellyfish, sea anemones and hydroids. An individual coral polyp consists of little more than a fleshy cylinder or tube, ridged inside with spokelike partitions. At the top is a mouth, bearded with tentacles, serving both as an inlet for food and an outlet for excreta, sperm and eggs; the other end, or pedal disk, is anchored to a limy cup which rests in turn on some solid object, generally the skeletons of dead ancestors. Voracious carnivores, corals feed on planktonic animals—young fish, tiny crustaceans, worms—which they catch and paralyze with their stinging tentacles. Save for a brief, free-swimming larval stage, corals lead completely sedentary lives; as soon as they settle down, they start secreting lime, and quickly invest themselves in cuplike armor into which they retract for protection. Some corals are solitary, but most forms, notably the reef-builders, are colonial creatures, joined physically in an immense variety of ramified structures which grow upward and outward by budding. As coral colonies grow, the feeding heads on the upper and outer fringes thrive at the expense of those beneath them, which slowly smother and die, leaving their empty skeletons as foundations for future progeny to build on. It is thus, by the never-ending labor of untold generations of small artisans, each in turn erecting its delicate castle, that the profuse coral islands, reefs and atolls of the earth's oceans have been reared.

Although coral grows in all the seas, the reef-builders exist only in shallow, sunlit, tropic waters—seldom more than 22° from the equator, and rarely at temperatures below 68°F. or at depths greater than 150 feet. Their requirements are rigorous. They must have clean water, for heavy mud and sediment quickly suffocate them. They must have sunlit water, for within the tissues of each coral polyp there exists a form of alga which, it is thought, provides oxygen and abets the excretory process of the coral, and which itself requires sunlight for photosynthesis. And finally they seem to demand restless, moving water, for only through the surge of waves and currents can sufficient oxygen and food be wafted within range of their tentacles—this explains why reefs are always best developed on their seaward side.

More than a century ago Charles Darwin observed that there appear to be three kinds of coral reefs: the fringing reef, which fans out from the edge of land in an almost solid shelf; the barrier reef, which is separated from land by a wide lagoon or channel, and the atoll, a coral ring enclosing a lagoon in the open sea. Since coral grows only in the bright surface layers of water, one of the mysteries of atolls and barrier reefs, whose seaward ramparts plunge to depths of thousands of feet, has been the nature of the foundations on which the original growth began. The best answer to this riddle was suggested by Darwin himself and is accepted with a few revisions today: *i.e.,* modern atolls and barrier reefs stand on a sunken basement of ancient fringing reefs that have been submerged either through the slow settling of the ocean floor or a rise in ocean levels. And as the land subsided, or the waters rose, the corals kept on growing upward toward the sun, outward toward the open sea, widening the distance between reef and shoreline, or, as in the case of atolls, until an entire island disappeared into the depths. Final confirmation of Darwin's submergence theory came only recently from Eniwetok atoll, where drills bit downward through layer after layer of antique coral. Finally from a depth of 4,000 feet they brought up a core of volcanic rock—vestige of a long-vanished island on whose drowned flanks corals began to build untold ages ago and continued to build, generation after generation, fighting ever upward through the encroaching waters, so that the living corals of Eniwitok today bestride the summit of a mighty unseen tower, at once a catacomb of countless creatures long since dead and a monument to the continuity of life.

THE REEF BUILDERS, living coral polyps, twinkle their tentacles in lucent Bahamian waters like a field of stars. It is only at night that a coral garden thus comes to bloom, for corals are nocturnal feeders. In the light of day they fold their tentacles and shrink back into their pale stone mansions. Enthroned in the middle of this coral colony is a familiar reef-dweller, a tubeworm, with its feathery gills partially expanded, waving in the clear water like a peacock fan.

TOWNSVILLE

HINCHINBROOK IS.

MACKAY

FLINDERS PASSAGE

BUNKER GROUP

CAPRICORN GROUP

WHITSUNDAY PASSAGE

SWAIN REEFS

N

South Pacific Ocean

THE WORLD'S BIGGEST CORAL REEF extends for 1,260 miles along the northeast coast of Australia from the Bunker Islands in the south (*left*) to the Murray Group near New Guinea in the north (*right*). The width of the channel or lagoon between the outer fringes of the reef and the mainland varies from about 100 miles in the vicinity of Swain Reefs to a minimum of seven miles. On the outer edges of the Great Barrier the coral walls fall away to depths as great as 8,000

THE GREAT BARRIER REEF
OF AUSTRALIA

ACROSS the tropics of both hemispheres coral structures stud the blue girdle of the encircling oceans. The mightiest of these and one of the supreme wonders of the natural world is the Great Barrier Reef, a stupendous rampart or submarine buttress, 1,260 miles long and 500 feet high, enclosing a watery domain of approximately 80,000

square miles off the northeastern coast of the Australian continent. Beside it the works of man are dwarfed; it is the greatest single edifice ever reared by living creatures on the face of the earth.

Owing to its remoteness—stretching as it does along subtropical and sparsely populated shores—relatively few people, even Australians, have ever laid eyes on this fabulous coral world. The pictures on these pages are therefore windows opening on one of the most extraordinary and little-known regions of the planet. An aerial observer, looking down on the Great Barrier Reef from a plane, would note that it is not a solid wall, but rather a complex construction in which all three major categories of coral reef (*below*) are represented. In the south, where the waters are cooler and therefore inimical

BARRIER-TYPE REEF is disclosed by surf crashing against its submerged coral cliffs. In this aerial photograph, looking south, the 600-foot-deep waters of the open sea appear at left, the shallow waters of the protected channel at right.

AN ATOLL in the Capricorn Group exhibits the characteristic ringlike configuration of coral structures that have grown upward from the shores of sunken islands. Set back from the Barrier's outer edge, the atoll stands in less than 200

LAND

CAIRNS

LOW IS.

TRINITY PASSAGE

COOK'S PASSAGE

CAPE YORK PENINSULA

TORRES STRAIT

PANDORA PASSAGE

MURRAY GROUP

NEW GUINEA

Coral Sea

feet. Inside, the waters of the great lagoon are shallow, seldom more than 120 feet deep, and dappled with numberless islands, atolls and uncharted coral outcroppings that render navigation hazardous. The islands close to the mainland

represent the peaks of drowned hills and mountains of a faulted or submerged coastal plain. The clustered isles of the reef are almost all of coral construction, most of them uninhabited save by a few pearl fishermen and lighthouse keepers.

to coral growth, the Barrier is fragmented, comprising a labyrinth of subsidiary reefs, patch reefs, islets, coral sand bars, atolls, sand dunes and shoals separated by many wide, navigable channels. But as it curves northward into warmer waters, the length of its component reefs increases and the channels between them diminish in number so that for the northernmost 500 miles it presents an almost unbroken parapet, rising like an underwater mountain chain from the depths of the sea.

Although many of the constituent units of the Great Barrier are submerged at high tide and some never rise above the surface at all, they effectively defend the inner lagoon from the violence of the ocean waves. Windward of the reef the waters are white with savage

surf beating at the outer ramparts, expending its fury against the hidden coral cliffs. To leeward, within the calm waters of the inner lagoon, often referred to as Australia's grand canal, coastal vessels cruise between Brisbane and Cape York, picking their way cautiously amid the coral flats and islands that divide the inshore waters into a maze of tortuous channels navigable only to experienced sailors. In wintertime antarctic whales enter the warm, still waters of the lagoon to bear their young.

At one time far in the geologic past the floor of this inland sea formed part of the Australian mainland, a flat coastal plain dotted here and there with hills and low mountains. Then, in response to the huge forces that recurrently re-form the crust of the planet, these

feet of water. From the windward side (*foreground*) surf foams over the parapet into the shallows of the central lagoon. Within the leeward arc in the distance, a small island has been formed of coral sand; on it stands a lonely lighthouse.

FRINGING REEFS skirt the flanks of volcanic islands in the northern Murray Group. Here the coral has built outward from solid rock shores. If the islands should sink, their fringed reefs could form an atoll like that in picture at left.

STAGHORN CORALS are among the most prolific and most beautiful architects of the Great Barrier Reef. Their name derives from the antlerlike arrangement of their branches. They flourish over reef flats everywhere but thrive best in sheltered waters. Slender, brittle as glass, staghorns are recurrently decimated by storms. Following typhoons, masses of their dead branches litter the weather side of reefs. Here a school of blue damsel fish wanders amid a staghorn grove.

marginal lands began to settle, leaving only the crests of the coastal hills protruding above the waters: the inshore islands visible today. The warm shallows favored the growth of coral, and slowly, at a rate of perhaps three feet per 1,000 years, the coral grew as the coastal plains and continental shelf subsided and the ocean levels rose.

In the building of the Great Barrier, however, the corals have not labored alone. Here, as in every reef, other agencies were and are continually at work. The skeletons of the builders themselves represent the main building blocks, the primary units of construction. But their interjacence is often loose and honeycombed with apertures which are filled with smaller units—tiny shells and other skeletal debris. Even so the structure might remain a loosely compacted mound of rubble, subject to disintegration by the pounding of waves, were it not for encrusting deposits of lime laid down by coralline algae. This mortar binds the reef together, filling the apertures between coral fragments and shells and cementing them into solid ramparts of coral rock.

By day and by night, while the coral polyps are fabricating their complex houses, other forces are relentlessly at work tearing them down. Foremost among the destroyers are the ocean waves, beating on the seaward walls, forever driven by the Southeast Trades. Recurring typhoons break up vast sections of reef, excising huge blocks of coral and tumbling them across the flats into the catch basins of the lagoon. Great havoc is also wrought by fresh water descending in torrential tropic downpours of rain, diluting the salt water in which polyps and other marine animals must live and converting the teeming community of the reef into a desolate coral graveyard. Beside these inanimate forces of destruction there are plant and animal enemies—sea urchins that rasp holes in the coral surface, boring mollusks and algae, and clams that wedge themselves into ever-deepening cavities. All these undermine the structure of a reef. And so, as in every domain of nature, growth and destruction, life and death are forever in conflict.

In this never-ending battle the forces of creation have been consistently victorious. Along the entire length of the Great Barrier the

STAR CORAL SKELETONS mesh together like cogwheels in a part of the Great Barrier Reef. Hard, unbranched star corals are among the most important reef builders. Below, standing empty, are pipelike houses built by organ coral polyps.

A HUGE CLAM is wedged among the living corals of the reef. Largest bivalves in the world, giant clams weigh up to 500 pounds and measure four feet across. Human swimmers sometimes drown when they step into open shells and are trapped.

PANDANUS TREES weave a dense fabric of roots and branches on an island of the Great Barrier Reef. One of the commonest of coral island trees, the pandanus offers both food and shelter to the human residents of the reef, who pound its pineapple-shaped fruit into a kind of dough and weave its strong, supple leaves into walls and thatches. Its stilt roots provide support in the shifting sands in which it grows. Its fallen leaves choke out all other plant life.

corals continue to build, consolidating their holdings and extending the reef area, wresting new dominions from the sea. In time it is possible that discontinuous units of the Barrier will fuse into a solid mass, for the living, tide-washed coral of today may become the coral island of tomorrow. As the skeletons of coral and other reef organisms disintegrate under the waves' attack, they crumble into sand, which washes down the slopes of fringing reefs and piles up in the leeward side of lagoons, forming beaches. In time the sands are cemented together with shells and coral fragments and harden into coral rock. The next phase is the addition of vegetation, which may be brought by bird droppings or driftwood containing the seeds of grass, shrubs or trees. Coconuts floating with the currents and the seedlings of mangrove trees travel over many a sea mile and wash ashore, still viable, and propagate their kind. When the seeds germinate and put down roots in the sand, it may remain only a matter of time until the former bleak and tide-drowned reef becomes one of the romantic "Summer isles of Eden lying in dark-purple spheres of sea."

Lovely as they loom from a distance, with their plumed crests and white encircling necklaces of surf and sand, coral islands do not invariably present in close proximity the aspect of enchanted gardens. For their vegetation is often unruly, consisting in part of unkempt mangrove swamps with weird, strangled trees wading in a sodden ooze of mud (*below*), and in drier sections of a tangled and nearly impenetrable jungle of pandanus trees (*left*), often interspersed with coconut palms, banyans, Tournefortia and papaw trees, ferns and ironwood. Since mangroves thrive only in salty, boggy terrain, they are seldom found on the windswept side of reefs but rather in the lee where drainage produces an accumulation of mud. Unsightly as they are, with their tangled network of aerial and stilt roots, mangroves perform an important role in island building. For their spreading roots tend to collect debris and sediment which in time consolidate a higher soil base suitable for other vegetation but, paradoxically, fatal to the tree that created it.

The most notable tenants of the Barrier Reef isles are birds. In certain months of the year incomputable multitudes of aquatic fowl dramatically appear out of the blue lonely wastes of the Pacific and converge on the Barrier islands to mate, build their nests and rear their young. Sometimes from a ship at sea one of these islands appears to be overhung by a black and menacing cloud. On closer approach the cloud resolves into galaxies of soaring, wheeling birds—noddy

SPINY SEA URCHINS thrive among the mangrove roots. Their movable spines protect them from predators. The round object in center is a brain coral.

A MANGROVE TREE rises from swampy waters of a Barrier Reef atoll. Growing in mud, the mangrove anchors itself on a tangled base of stilt roots rising high above the water and intertwined with aerial roots sent down from the branches.

URCHIN FISH lurk for protection among the sea urchin's upright spines, maintaining their vertical position by swift movements of their delicate fins.

159

NODDY TERNS congregate in vast numbers in the pisonia trees of the Barrier isles. Their nests are rough structures of leaves, seaweed and grass, cemented together with excrement. As many as 143 nests have been counted in a single tree.

A GREEN TURTLE digs a hole in the sand in preparation for egg-laying. First, using all four flippers, she digs until her shell is flush with the surface of the beach. Then with her rear flippers she excavates a deeper hole under her ovipositor.

terns (*left*), sooty terns (*below*), boobies and muttonbirds, or shearwaters. For most of the year these vast hosts of birds range the farflung islands of the South Seas. But in season some urgent instinct summons them back to the Great Barrier Reef. One island, scarcely three miles in circumference, has a seasonal bird population of more than a million. During the breeding season the birds appear never to sleep. By day they fly out over the waters in quest of the small fish and squid on which they subsist. By night they make love, fight and feed their young, accompanying their domestic activities with a wild cacophony of eerie shrieks and screeches, groans and moans that in the days of sailing ships gave rise to a legend that the islands were haunted by condemned souls in torment. Heron Island, in the Capricorn Group, a favorite of the muttonbirds, is honeycombed with their burrows. Michaelmas Cay, near Trinity Passage, a roost of the sooty terns, is drenched with their droppings and the sky above is continually obscured by their swift echelons.

The birds share their coral dominion with two other prolific populations: the soldier crabs and the giant green turtles. When the tide

SOOTY TERNS promenade the beach at Michaelmas Cay, a favorite breeding spot of aquatic birds. The entire island is one vast roost, teeming with terns, cluttered with nests, pervaded by the acrid odor of their innumerable droppings. Most

active of the many species of birds that inhabit the islands of the Great Barrier Reef, the sooty tern is also known as the wide-awake, for it is on the wing almost all day, searching the sea for small fish and squid, and during the breeding season

TURTLE EGGS emerge rapidly until 100 or more, each about the size of a ping-pong ball, have been laid. The mother turtle then covers them with sand. In a few weeks the young turtles hatch, head straight for the water and swim out to sea.

ebbs at night, the beaches come alive with ranks of tiny crabs out for food, swaying and turning like an army in maneuvers, then scattering to dig small burrows at the first gleam of dawn when their implacable enemies, the birds, take to wing. It is at night too that the giant green turtle comes ashore to spawn. Plodding up the beach in an undeviating line, struggling awkwardly over coral boulders instead of circling around them, the mother turtle climbs above the high-tide mark, digs a hole and lays her eggs (*above*). Then, covering them firmly and abandoning them to the contingencies of nature and circumstance, she returns to the water, leaving her unmistakable tracks upon the sands. A few weeks later, when the baby turtles hatch, they find themselves cast into a world of infinite peril. As they make their way instinctively down the open strand, the shadow of dark wings falls across them, and the rapacious claws and murderous beaks of the larger birds pluck them helpless from the earth, rending their tender shells. Those that escape this first aerial attack and reach the sanctuary of the surf are still not secure, for hungry fish lie waiting for them in the insatiable sea.

A SOOTY TERN CHICK stands forlornly on the beach, waiting for its parents to return from their daily hunting trip at sea. At this age the young tern wears speckled brown and white plumage. The adult has black on its back, white on its belly.

seems to be up all night, mating, fighting, scooping shallow nests in the sand or caring for its vociferous young. What little rest it gets probably consists of brief naps while perched on flotsam or strips of sand. Terns are monogamous, each male having but a single mate which during the breeding season lays but a single egg. However, so numerous are the eggs of the assembled sooty terns that the beaches of Michaelmas Cay are virtually covered with their white gleaming shells.

A CORAL RIDGE edges the outer barrier at Bikini atoll where the reef disappears beneath the white surf and falls away into the depths. The seaward margin is coated with encrustations of purplish algae that protect the coral from the waves. Its edge (*right*) is deeply grooved with surge channels, formed by irregular growth of the coral and sculptured by wave-erosion. Underwater the reef shelves into terraces, then drops steeply and finally slopes to the deep floor.

THE TEEMING UNDERWATER WORLD OF REEFS

THE preceding pages have described the structure, vegetation and animal populations of Australia's Great Barrier Reef. Beneath the surface of the water there lies another, far stranger, more exciting domain, and it is in this submarine realm that all the coral reefs of the world become as one. For although the Great Barrier Reef is the largest and most splendid of all the world's coral structures, its great size and unusual situation render it unique rather than typical. The other reefs of the sea are not only smaller but scattered, associated more with islands and the open sea. They rarely appear along the western coasts of continents, possibly because wind systems and currents combine there to produce upwellings of deep, cold water.

Wherever in the world they exist, however, all coral reefs reveal certain basic structures in common. And whatever type they may represent—atolls, barrier reefs or fringing reefs—their tide-exposed flats resemble crumbly fields of multicolored stones, mirrored in small pools in which many forms of vertebrate and invertebrate life abound. At the seaward edges of the flats broad algal ridges stand above the water (*above*), wrought by the pink algae that cover the underlying coral with a veneerlike glaze. Serrating the ridges of many reefs are innumerable surge channels through which the waves course and drain. At the outer edges of the ridges the coral cliffs drop away in slopes sometimes steeper than those found in most mountains of the land. It is at the dizzying brink of these enormous ramparts that the fantastic blue underwater realm of the reef begins (*opposite page*).

AN ANCHOR WORM uncoils in the shallows of a coral flat. Amazingly contractile, anchor worms can curl themselves up into small blobs or stretch into slender tubes several feet long. They dwell among rotting coral and empty shells.

A MARINE SNAIL glides along the bottom of a tidal pool. It propels itself by means of a broad, muscular foot and takes in water through its trunklike syphon. To eat it scrapes up food with a rasplike tongue at the tip of a proboscis.

THE SUBMARINE FORESTS of a coral reef luxuriate in clear blue light that filters down from the surface layers. Here, 25 feet down in Bahamian waters, coral trees and coral shrubs, coral spires and coral boulders loom on every side, and every type abounds: delicate, stone-hard staghorn corals branched like candelabra (*right center*), flexible sea whips and sea fans (*center*), round, corrugated brain corals (*upper left*), and encrusting cabbagelike Porites (*center foreground*).

KING CORAL, an Alcyonarian form, spreads its delicate branches above a school of butterfly fish in shoal waters of New Caledonia. The red coral of the jewel trade is a deep-water Mediterranean variety distantly related to this species.

STAGHORNS strain upward toward the surface off Nassau. At their base (*left to right*) are sea whips, an Alcyonarian type of coral; a trumpet fish, swimming vertically; and a sea fan. Below are chimney sponges of Harrington Sound, Bermuda.

IN A CORAL GLADE refulgent Bermudian reef fish poise jewellike above the exotic shrubs and blossoms of the shallow floor. At left a clump of purple sea rods point crooked fingers at the sun, partially screening the waving tentacles of an

ARTISANS OF THE REEF

LIKE riotous gardens congealed capriciously in stone, coral reefs bear many varieties of blooms, charmed frozen flowers of every shape and hue. Exquisite branching trees and shrubs, tapered spires and stems, fans and fronds sprout from the tide-bathed beds and borders of the sunlit flats and cling to the ledges of the seaward cliffs as alpine blossoms cling to the rock gardens of the land, staining the blue waters with their pure and profuse colors.

But in addition to flowerlike forms, many other structures diversify the underwater world of coral. There are corals that look like toadstools and corals that resemble the cortex of a human brain, corals that grow in tiers like apartment houses and hang in folds like draperies, corals that form caves and grottoes, and corals that sprawl in

anemone. In the right foreground a pink squirrel fish—so-called because it chatters like a squirrel—nuzzles a cluster of Alcyonarian corals, while an angel fish hovers overhead. Above the angel fish is a spotted chub. In the background a squad of sergeant-majors deploy in loose formation. At the extreme right is a blue-striped grunt, which gets its name because it grunts. Contrary to popular belief, many fish and invertebrates make noises; the sea is not a silent place.

strange, convoluted masses, lobed and puckered like fungus growths.

Only an expert can identify the hundreds of different species that abide in reefs, for their aspect often varies with circumstance. But in general the dominant reef-building corals, which usually have six smooth tentacles (or multiples of six), separate into two main categories: the delicate branching forms represented by the staghorn corals; and the solid, unbranched sturdier types such as the meandrine or yellow-green "brain" corals, the gray or bluish Goniopora and the yellow-brown Porites. Among these the fragile staghorn corals are incomparably the most beautiful. The tougher brain corals and Goniopora are usually round and boulderlike; Porites often assume the shape of domes or basins. Less important, but nevertheless common on most coral reefs are: the mushroom coral, a solitary polyp about the size of a dinner plate; Millepore corals, which form yellow bladelike encrustations on the surface of reefs; soft Alcyonarian corals which have eight fringed tentacles and with a few exceptions do not armor themselves in limy skeletons; and the so-called horny Alcyonarian corals which include the types commonly known as sea whips, sea rods and sea fans.

Among the permanent inhabitants of a coral reef are certain other fixed or sessile creatures such as burrowing mollusks, bryozoans (minute colonial sacklike animals with tentacles, superficially resembling corals in the shrublike form they assume), tunicates and sponges (below, left). Yet these are essentially tenants, not proprietors. The corals alone are the hosts, for they are the craftsmen that actually create the crenellated castles of the sea and embellish them with magic palettes. It is one of the deep paradoxes of nature that creatures so small and all but insensate, so lowly in the evolutionary scale, could be such supreme artists and sculptors, jewelsmiths whose "Rich and various gems inlay The unadorned bosom of the Deep."

165

PEACOCK WORMS, a variety of tubeworm, extend their gills to breathe. Their bodies are housed in limy or parchmentlike tubes which they build and anchor to coral or sand; only their heads protrude. Their gills both fulfill a respiratory function and serve to convey food particles down to their clawlike feelers and mouth by rippling movements of the fine hairs or "feathers" edging each gill. When alarmed they close their gills like parasols and retract into their tubes.

MULTICOLORED CREATURES gleam in the sunlit shallows along the Atlantic shores. Though flowerlike in appearance, all the objects shown here are animals save for the rockweed at top. The redbeard sponge (*left*) and the speckled sea pork (*center*) are sedentary. But around them crawl a few slow-moving transients: scarlet starfish, pink anemones (*right*) and a gray sea urchin. Widespread in range, these hardy invertebrates thrive in both tropic and temperate waters.

THE INVERTEBRATE VISITORS

OF all the enclaves of life in the sea, none is more populous per cubic foot, none more prolific, than the waters of a coral reef. Here nature creates with an exuberance manifested in no other precinct of the living world. And here, in particular, among the bright stone cities of the corals, the humble orders of invertebrates have come into their own, flourishing in these benign waters and producing giants of their kind—starfish a foot in diameter, anemones two feet across, seven-pound oysters and clams that weigh a quarter of a ton.

It is not only in numbers and dimension, however, that the invertebrates of a coral reef transcend others of their kind, but even more notably in the brilliance of their investiture. Species which elsewhere hide in drab and inconspicuous attire flaunt gorgeous raiment on the coral causeways of the reefs—enamelled, bright-striped cone shells and purple sea slugs with rippling gills. Starfish shine in sapphire and scarlet. The carapaces of tiny shrimps glow with many iridescent hues. Painted lobsters promenade in purple and green, orange and black, with spots on their backs and stripes down their legs. But of all the invertebrate dandies of the coral reef, none perhaps is handsomer, none more elegant than the shy and dainty tubeworm (*opposite page*).

A GIANT BLUE STARFISH basks on a coral flat. Common to Pacific reefs, the blue starfish ranges from 8 to 12 inches across. In feeding, a starfish extrudes its stomach through its mouth, envelops its prey and digests it outside its own body.

A DECORATOR CRAB makes use of a reef growth to camouflage itself—a piece of fire sponge, which it holds on with a pair of turned-up legs. Other decorator crabs grow plants on their backs, pruning them when they become too dense.

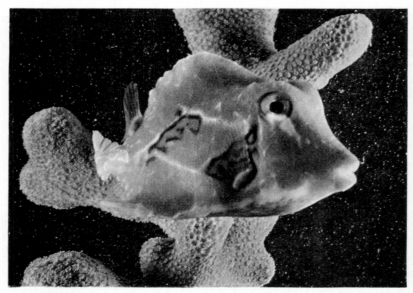

A **TRUNKFISH** moves stiffly past a coral tree. Unlike other fish which swim with undulating movements of their bodies, the trunkfish has a rigid torso. Lacking flexibility, it propels itself with rapid movements of its supple fins and tail.

THE VERTEBRATE VISITORS

BECAUSE of the profusion of life with which they abound, coral reefs have been called "oases in an aquatic desert." Around them stretch the sparse waters of the open ocean. But the lagoons and shallows, tidal pools and grottoes of a reef swarm not only with invertebrate life but with myriads of darting fish more varied than any in the sea. While in actual tonnage the reef populations are exceeded by those of the continental shelves, the warm tropic waters that embrace them engender a multiplicity of rare and exotic species.

Since the clear reef waters contain little plankton, however, they do not sustain the vast hordes of big edible fish that thrive in colder, nutrient-rich areas of the sea. The four main fish families of the reefs —butterflies, damsels, surgeons and wrasse—are able to subsist as vegetarians when living prey grows scarce. Another sizable family— the parrot fish—actually crunch and swallow coral rock in quest of the algal growths on which they subsist. One species of filefish grazes on the coral polyps. Other fish eat crustaceans and mollusks. Save for the ever-present predators—groupers, amberjacks and barracudas—most reef fish tend to be small and delicate. But like the invertebrates with which they share the coral world they are splendidly arrayed.

A **PARROT FISH** is unique among vertebrates of the reef in that it is able to eat and digest the hard encrustations of coral algae. For this purpose it is equipped with a horny beak and four molars, set deep in its throat, that act as a grinding mill.

A **LION FISH,** most rococo of reef dwellers, flutters lazily past a coral rock like some winged migrant from the flower gardens of the dry land. While other fish wear brighter colors, none is bedizened with such a frippery of frills and furbelows

as the lion fish with its fanlike, feathered, fringed dorsal and pectoral fins and dappled tail. For all its garish splendor, the lion fish is among the most dangerous of the coral reef's inhabitants. It is a cousin of the poisonous Pacific stonefish, deadliest of all marine creatures. Though its venom is less lethal, the lion fish can nevertheless inflict a painful wound on any creature that comes in contact with the sharp, virulent, erectile spines that ridge its handsome back.

A FROG FISH, camouflaged as an algae-covered coral rock, lies in wait for prey. From its head dangles a movable rod tipped with a fleshy tassel or lure. When smaller fish approach to investigate, they vanish in the angler's cavernous jaws.

FISH: FROG, CONCH AND SARGASSUM

FROM the standpoint of marine biology, a coral reef exists as a distinct domain of life, unique in its environment and populations, and differentiated from such other realms as the pelagic and benthic regions of the sea. Yet like all great divisions of the natural world, a coral reef too has its own manifold subdivisions, its small subsidiary provinces of sand and coral rock, deep and shallow water, each with its own habitual and proprietary incumbents.

Thus there are reef fish that choose to live in the lagoons and reef fish that prefer the open waters beyond the seaward walls. The silverside Atherion plays in the surf zone of the surge channels. The dwarf sea bass Pseudochromis lurks in the algae-covered edges of the coral cliffs. Blennies, gobies and snake eels haunt the coral flats, burrowing into loose sand and gravel and hiding there when the tide is out.

A CONCHFISH seeks security behind the shell of one of the numerous large conch mollusks that creep on coral sands. Among the most timorous of reef fish, it has pinkish, iridescent scales that blend perfectly with the inner lip of the conch.

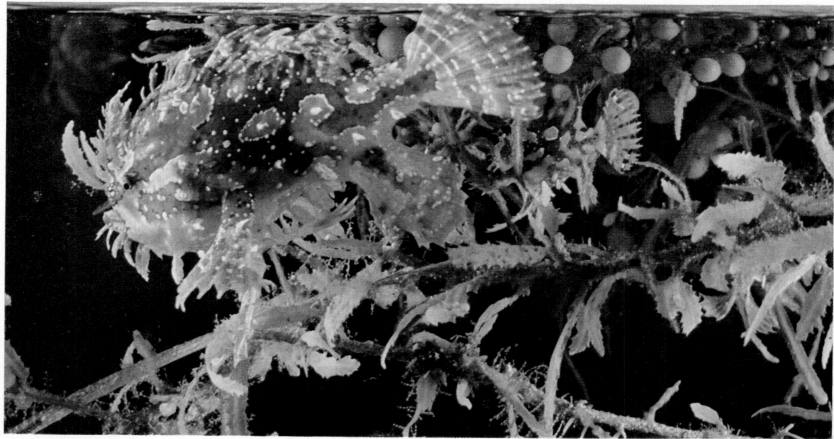

THE SARGASSUM FISH, one of the most voracious carnivores in the sea, is virtually indistinguishable from the floating seaweeds that drift in the Sargasso Sea and the reef waters of the Caribbean. From nose to tail it is embellished and upholstered with golden-brown tassels, knobs and striated ribbons that simulate the foliage and flotation bladders of the Sargassum weeds to which it clings with handlike fins and among whose tangled stalks it hunts its living prey.

A SCORPION FISH sprawls motionless on the bottom, resting on its winglike fins, waiting for one of the little sardines above it to blunder within range of its oversized mouth. Its body is embossed and embroidered with a filigree of fleshy protuberances that serve to camouflage it as a seaweed-bearded coral stone. But these dangling threads, whisps and tatting serve a double purpose, for they are also sensory organs that notify the scorpion fish of the approach of prey or enemies.

171

A BARRACUDA, one of the fiercest and most voracious of fish, is capable of attacking anything that moves in the water, including man. Ranging from two to eight feet in length, barracudas are swifter, craftier and more courageous than the dull, thick-bodied sharks which also prowl the coral seas. They often lie in wait, motionless, near rocks or coral heads, then suddenly dart out with the speed of a javelin to sever the flesh and bone of their terrified prey.

A STING RAY carries on its tail a venomous spike capable of producing paralysis. A bottom dweller, the ray, which camouflages itself with sand, uses its sting not for killing prey but only to defend itself against attack.

A MORAY EEL habitually lurks in crannies of coral reefs, waiting for its prey, and strikes savagely at human swimmers who come within range. Growing sometimes to eight feet in length, moray eels can cause serious injury.

A NEEDLEFISH is armed with beaklike jaws, studded with many fine teeth. Ranging in size from 15 inches to four feet, needlefish are no menace to divers, although they are among the most implacable destroyers of small fish.

A GIANT GROUPER is dangerous, not by disposition but because of its great size and carnivorous appetite. Some species attain a length of eight feet and a weight of 600 pounds and when hungry could engulf a boy in one bite.

The specialization of reef fish for particular habitats attains its apogee with those that exist in close relationships with other creatures, as, for example, the urchin fish which lives among the spines of the sea urchin, the damsel fish which hides among the tentacles of the sea anemone, and the tiny pearl fish, Carapus, which actually makes its home inside the body cavities of sea cucumbers.

Many reef fish have evolved unique physical features in adapting to their chosen ways of life. Thus a species of mullet which feeds in shoal waters has developed fleshy, fringed lips which serve to keep sand out of its mouth. The needlefish and certain other fish which hunt near the surface of the water have ridges over their eyes to shade them from the glaring sun. The flounders, which lie on their sides on sandy bottoms, are perfectly designed for their individual habitats; the mouth is situated on one side and, even more remarkable, one eye migrates in early life from the downward side to join the other on the upward side.

In the diversified and multicolored world of the coral reef the art of camouflage is more highly developed than in any other domain of nature. Scorpion, Sargassum and frog fishes blend perfectly with their baroque surroundings. Hogfish and groupers change color as they glide past variegated backgrounds. Butterfly fish wear eye-shaped patterns on their tails, possibly to confuse their attackers.

Some reef creatures are further equipped with poison. Among these are certain sea urchins and reef starfish, the sting ray, and the scorpion and lion fish whose poisonous spines cause temporary paralysis. Deadliest of all reef creatures, however, is the stonefish.

Upon its slimy, warty back stand 13 erectile spines, each needle-sharp and fed by a pair of venom glands containing a nerve poison for which there is no known antidote.

These virulent fish present the principal perils of coral reefs to man. Yet all are passive. The only other dangerous reef creatures are the active predators that steal in from the open waters—the shark, the barracuda, and an occasional giant grouper. Students of reef life do not agree, however, on the degree of aggressiveness of these carnivorous fish. All have been known to attack man and to cause injury or death. Yet some naturalists insist that a swimmer is safe so long as he remains under water where the fish can see him, and risks attack only when he splashes about on the surface like a school of frightened herring. Most authorities agree that, unless stimulated by blood in the water, sharks are relatively cautious; a swimmer can frighten them away by advancing toward them and making a noise. Barracudas, however, are utterly savage and without fear. Their monstrous mouths and knifelike teeth can slash an arm or leg to the bone. They are generally the fiercest pirates of the sea.

For the sea contains, insofar as modern man has been able to ascertain, no horned serpents or monsters of ancient myth. Apart from these hungrily predacious hunters and certain poisonous but completely unaggressive creatures the underwater cosmos of the coral reef contains few hazards. Year by year, as naturalists and amateur divers explore its skeleton stone cities, new wonders, new beauties are disclosed, evoking ever afresh the poet's words, "In chambers deep, Where waters sleep, What unknown treasures pave the floor!"

THE LAND
OF THE SUN

PART IX

THE LAND OF THE SUN

The desert's stark domain supports creatures bred to its harsh demands

> Geographers crowd in the edges of their maps parts of the world which they do not know about, adding notes in the margin to the effect that beyond this lies nothing but the sandy deserts full of wild beasts. . . .
>
> PLUTARCH, *Lives*

NO less compelling than man's age-old dread of the unknown is his irresistible impulse to patch the crevices in the facade of his knowledge with conjecture. And so from the dawn of exploration man has encouraged himself to believe that remote and uncharted terrain must be either too perilous or too worthless to know. Ancient geographers surrounded the known world with limitless wastes, infinite waters or an abyss. They peopled distant lands with barbarians, and supplied the deserts and the seas with magnificent monsters.

Today there are few blank areas remaining on the maps of the earth and they appear mostly in the Antarctic. Yet many misconceptions persist; among these one of the most stubborn overhangs the 10 million square miles of the planetary surface that consist of desert country. For although most of the earth's wastelands have been crossed and recrossed by explorers and scientists—and sometimes by casual tourists as well—popular fancy continues to envisage a desert as a cruel, inimical expanse of shifting sands, lifeless, rainless, sun-seared, bleak and hostile as the dusty craters of the moon. This picture, however, is a fragmentary representation, applicable to only a small portion of the earth's desert land. Less than 30% of the Sahara consists of sand dunes; only 2% of the deserts of North America are overspread with dunes. In most desert regions plants grow, animals prosper and some rain descends.

Although differing widely in climate and conformation, all deserts, wherever they exist—whether they are hot like those of central Australia or cold like the Gobi—share certain aspects in common. They are lands of the sky—an enormous, overpowering sky, crystalline, fiery blue, arching above vistas of seemingly infinite space. Beneath its implacable glare the colors of the earth efface themselves; the world appears painted in pastel hues—soft tans, gray-greens and dull, muted reds. The mantle of green vegetation that softens the face of the land in gentler climes is sparse, worn and threadbare, and the geometry of the planet's crust is clearly disclosed. Hills and mountains stand forth bold and austere, naked in the clean, transparent air. Dry riverbeds furrow the eroded hills, crease the desert flats and vanish in the cracked mud of empty lakes, miles from the seas to which other rivers lead. From time to time swift winds race across the open plain, driving yellow clouds of dust aloft into the clean sky. By day the great ineluctable fact of the desert is the sun. By night it is the purple bowl of the heavens, sequined with innumerable stars.

Authorities do not agree on the precise geographical boundaries which delineate the deserts of the earth—where, for example, a

SAND DUNES ROLLING TO REMOTE HORIZONS EPITOMIZE THE DESERT TO THE

semiarid region ends and a desert begins. Meteorologists have long cited as deserts those regions where evaporation exceeds precipitation. Botanists envisage them as regions of widely spaced and peculiarly specialized vegetation. And geologists describe them in terms of land forms, erosion cycles and interior drainage systems. A common rule of thumb defines them as areas with an annual rainfall of less than 10 inches. For all the arguing over definition, the outstanding attribute of all deserts is dryness. And from this one basic quality stem all the other characteristics—botanical, zoological, geological —that make deserts what they are.

Although the word desert means, literally, a deserted or uninhabited place, the connotation is misleading. For the deserts have their populations—not the savage beasts of ancient superstition, but instead a host of small, burrowing creatures many of which are uniquely endowed with an ability to go through life without drinking water. And along with these unusual animals dwell similarly specialized

MIND OF MAN. BUT THOUGH THEY COMPOSE A CLASSIC SCENE, DUNES COVER BUT A FRACTION OF THE EARTH'S ARID LANDS. THESE STAND IN THE SONORAN DESERT

plants, sparse and stunted but nevertheless dappling the pale wilderness with patches of silver-green. Unlike the grimly competing flora that struggles for light and root space in the moist valleys and lowlands of the rain-washed regions of the globe, these desert plants are widely dispersed, as in a park, with generous footpaths in between. Many bear thorns and other defenses. Many have tiny leaves or no leaves at all. Yet they are plants and they are green and they flourish in the parched desert soil.

Contrary to popular opinion, the desert, though dry, is not completely dry. Some rain falls from time to time, though it is so meager, irregular and undependable that permanent lakes and streams cannot exist. (Rivers like the Nile or Colorado may flow through a desert, creating a narrow oasis along its banks, but their waters always spring from sources beyond the desert area.) Occasionally, however, a sudden downpour will fill the dried drainage systems of the desert with rushing torrents that roar down the parched canyons for perhaps

an hour or two and then sink without trace into the insatiable earth.

Although in most of the world's deserts the relative humidity is extremely low throughout the year, as in every domain of nature there are paradoxes. The coastal deserts of South America and Africa, for example, are "fog deserts"; they have high humidity, clouds and mists, but virtually no rain. The Sahara, on the other hand, shows a cloud cover of only 10% during the winter and less than 4% from June to October. As a corollary, deserts are the hottest places on earth. The highest temperature ever officially recorded was taken in the Sahara at Azizia, Libya: 136° in the shade. The U.S. record is not much lower: 134° at Death Valley, Calif. Yet, owing to their low humidity, deserts are subject to great ranges of temperature, both diurnally and seasonally. Such middle latitude deserts as the Gobi and Takla Makan of central Asia experience both scorching summers and freezing winters, with blizzards and wild subzero winds out of the Siberian wastes to the north.

The deserts that stipple the visage of the planet today did not exist always. Most of them evolved concurrently with the uplifting of the earth's highest mountain ranges during the last 15 million years. Today they form a distinct pattern, girdling the globe in two great belts above and below the equator in latitudes approximately 15° to 40° north and south (*see map, right*). Their distribution on the earth's surface reflects the physical factors that created them. Many complex agencies contribute to the formation of a desert, and it is seldom that the pattern of their interweaving is repeated. One feature common to most deserts is their location in the western portions of continents wherever warm, dry, descending air dissipates the cloud cover and allows more sunlight to reach and heat the land. Another obvious but inadequate factor is the rain-shadow effect of mountain ranges. It is evident that just as some of the rainiest regions of the earth lie on the windward side of mountains, so some of its most arid areas are situated in their lee. Yet mountain barriers alone cannot explain the intensely dry coastal deserts of Chile and Peru. Here the factor of ocean currents becomes important, for when cold currents parallel a coast, an anomalous combination of fog and aridity may be produced. In this case the Peru Current, which flows northward from the Antarctic, cools breezes from the Pacific, causing condensation and creating a heavy fog. And when the chilled and misty air reaches the land, it is warmed and its moisture capacity is thereby increased; and so, though the fog blows inland, it dissipates rapidly and seldom resolves into rain. The city of Lima, for example, has an annual rainfall of two inches, though it is often enshrouded in melancholy mists. And the adjacent Atacama Desert, with a precipitation average of less than .5 inch per year, is the driest desert in the world—though it lies only a few miles from the sea.

Virtually all these factors affect America's Sonoran Desert whose various aspects are illustrated in this essay as archetypal of the deserts of the world. Coastal ranges of California and Mexico shadow its inland reaches from rain-bearing winds from the Pacific. The cold California Current influences its coastal sections, creating typical fog-desert conditions along the narrow peninsula of Baja California. Its interior is bathed by dry, descending air. Though smaller by far, the Sonoran Desert presents a compact analogue of the great Sahara. In some respects it is peculiarly American. But its elemental land forms —its bald, eroded mountains, its desert flats, alluvial fans and restless dunes, its parched riverbeds and waterless lakes—are features of the greater desert world.

From above, by day, the golden sun glares down with the same unblinking eye that scans the haunted wastes of Asia. By night the Milky Way streams across the firmament and the stars burn with the same intensity that bemused Alexandrian astronomers 2,000 years ago. In every direction across its vast, flat and clean expanses there flow glassy rivers of pellucid space. Everywhere—as in the harsh Gobi Desert, the sandy wastes of the Empty Quarter of Saudi Arabia, and the scorched gibber plains of Australia—everywhere

. . . The desert-circle spreads,
Like the round ocean, girdled with the sky.

NORTH AMERICA'S DESERTS are situated in the western portion of the U.S. and the northern part of Mexico, mostly in rugged country where high coastal ranges effectively shadow their depressed basins from moisture-laden winds from the sea. Although geographers recognize four separate deserts in this generally arid region, their boundaries are not everywhere distinct. This map focuses on the heart of the Sonoran Desert which covers a total area of about 120,000 square

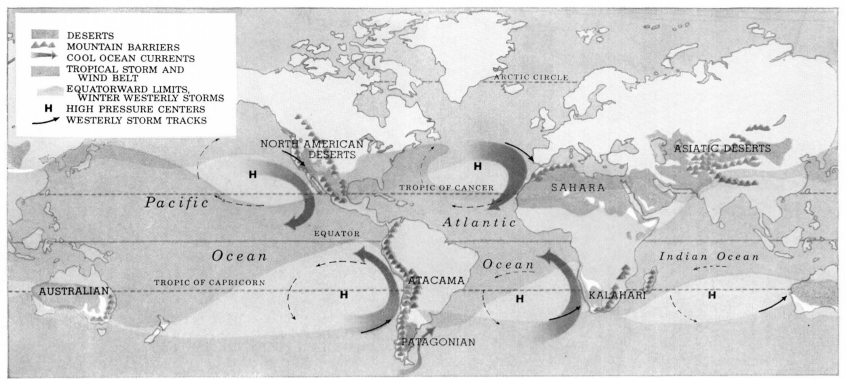

DESERTS OF THE WORLD are deployed in two globe-girdling bands, north and south of the equator. They lie generally between the moist mid-latitude westerlies and the equatorial rainy belt. Often they occur in the west of continents where dry winds, circling offshore highs, sweep parallel to the shore, creating mist over cold currents but carrying little rain inland. The Asiatic deserts are exceptions. They are caused by sheer distance from the sea and by encircling mountains.

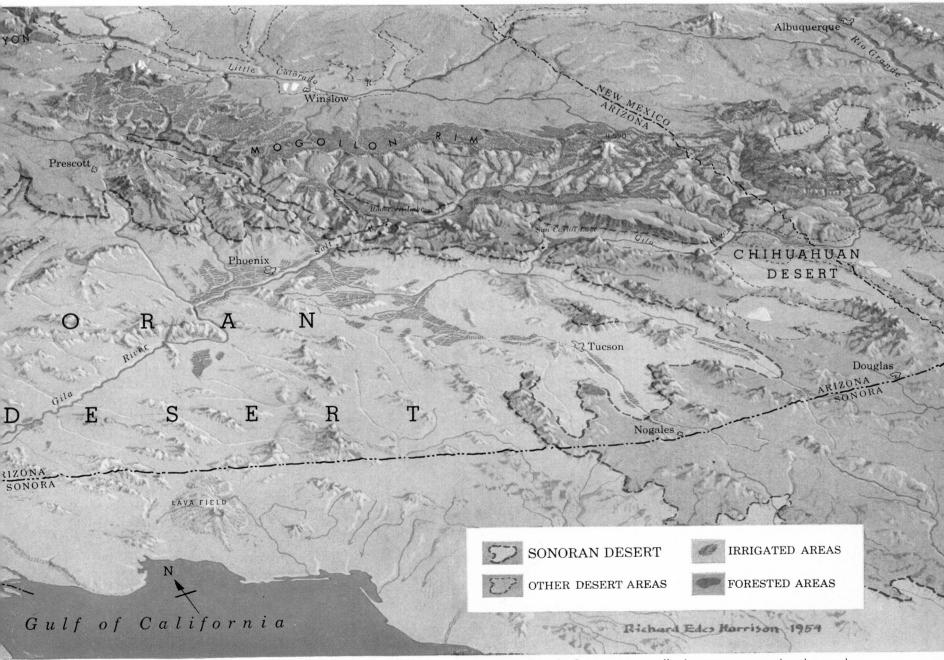

miles in those sections of the U.S. and Mexico surrounding the Gulf of California. Also visible are the Mojave Desert, a western extension of the Chihuahuan Desert (*right*) and a bit of the Great Basin Desert of Nevada to the north (*top left*). Of the four the Sonoran is generally the most extreme, though a weather station at Death Valley holds the U.S. records for high temperature and minimum precipitation. The average July temperature at Death Valley is 102° in the shade.

THE DESERT COUNTENANCE

IN the desert, more than anywhere on earth, the architecture of the planet's surface stands revealed. Here no obscuring mask of green conceals the craggy contours of the earth's tormented crust. The creased and furrowed faces of the mountains rise abruptly from the naked flats. The arid beds of evanescent streams are walled by steep banks and sheer cliffs. The floors of empty lakes are intricate mosaics wrought in mud, seamed and fissured by the thirsty sun.

Paradoxically the architect and sculptor of the harsh desert landscape is running water. Sparse and infrequent though they are, desert rains descend with torrential violence, creating wild streams which rush down the barren flanks of mountains, unhindered by trees or soil, and bite deeply into the rock, carving it into sharp, angular forms. And as they erode they transport and deposit sediment, piling it up at the foot of the mountains in gently sloping bajadas or alluvial fans. Thence they spread out across the desert flats, cutting their own drainage channels. Sometimes, when the underlying rock is soft, they dissect the land into an intricate maze of narrow canyons and knife-edge ridges known as badlands (*left, below*).

But unlike the streams of humid lands they seldom reach the sea. For the drainage pattern of desert regions is an internal one, distinctive to deserts the world over. The dry washes which in the U.S. are called canyons or arroyos are known as *wadis* in the Sahara, *sai* in the Gobi Desert, and *laagtes* in the Kalahari of South Africa. The swift flood waters that pour briefly down their scorched beds end up eventually in closed basins where they form temporary lakes or playas. Some playas remain moist, with water tables only a foot or two below the surface or even with a shallow brackish layer of water above the floor. But more often the ephemeral floods seep into the parched earth and disappear, leaving a surface that quickly anneals and cracks in the hot sun (*left, above*). Few plants can grow on these dry lakes for their floors are cement-hard and laden with salts. But around their edges a few green rings of saltbush and mesquite subsist, merging gradually into the bur sage and creosote bushes of the surrounding desert flats.

Usually no more than one fifth of the vast, level expanse of the desert flats is covered with vegetation. For the rest, there are only vistas of mingled sand and gravel, or naked rock. Where sands are exposed to persistent winds, dunes may form and march across the landscape in endless, shifting ranks. More widespread than dunes are areas where coarse fragments of rocks have been laid down by water and planed by winds, leaving a desert "pavement" neatly fitted as though by man. In the Sahara and other arid regions of the ancient world, though not in North America, broad stretches of the underlying bedrock called *hammadas* lie exposed to the sky.

Here and there, amid the most forbidding of desert wastelands, an occasional emerald oasis glistens in the wilderness as a reminder of the persistence of life. For underground water may sometimes emerge at the toe of alluvial fans or seep to the surface in isolated pockets and basins; and wherever fresh water exists, plants will grow.

A DRY LAKE, called a playa, lies in the bottom of a valley in the Sonoran Desert. The flat, cracked floors of playas are familiar features of desert landscapes. Below: the Borrego badlands reveal the intricate sculpture of violent desert rains.

AN OASIS flourishes around a snow-fed stream in a canyon of Mt. San Jacinto on the western border of the Sonoran Desert. Any green or fertile place in the desert is an oasis, whatever the source of water. Thus the flood plains of the Nile and Colorado rivers are vast oases, and so are arid areas irrigated by man. Here fresh water has engendered a handsome stand of desert fan palms. Equally common in American oases are cottonwoods, desert willows, rushes and tules.

A KANGAROO RAT leaps to evade the strikes of a hungry king snake. Like most desert carnivores the king snake requires moist-fleshed prey to fulfill his water needs. The little kangaroo rat can subsist on dry seeds alone.

ANIMALS OF THE WATERLESS WORLD

SINCE water is the basis of life, composing the greater part of the tissues of all living things, the crucial problem of desert animals is to survive in a world where sources of flowing water are rare. And since man's inexorable necessity is to absorb large quantities of water at frequent intervals, he can scarcely comprehend that many creatures of the desert pass their entire lives without a single drop.

Uncompromising as it is, the desert has not eliminated life but only those forms unable to withstand its desiccating effects. No moist-skinned, water-loving animals can exist there. Few large animals are found: the giants of the North American desert are the deer, the coyote and the bobcat. Since desert country is open, it holds more swift-footed, running and leaping creatures than the tangled forests. Its populations are largely nocturnal, silent, filled with reticence and ruled by stealth. Yet they are not emaciated. Having adapted to their austere environment, they are as healthy as animals anywhere on earth.

The secret of their adjustment lies in a combination of behavior and physiology. None could survive if, like mad dogs and Englishmen, they went out in the midday sun; many would die in a matter of minutes. So most of them pass the burning hours asleep in cool, humid burrows underneath the ground, emerging to hunt only by night. The surface of the sun-baked desert averages around 150°, but 18 inches down the temperature is only 60°.

While most desert animals will drink water if confronted with it, for many of them the opportunity never comes. Yet all living things must have water or expire. The herbivores find it in desert plants. The carnivores slake their thirst with the flesh and blood of living prey. One of the most remarkable adjustments, however, has been made by the tiny kangaroo rat (*above*), who not only lives without drinking but subsists on a diet of dry seeds containing but 5% of free water. Like other animals he has the ability to manufacture water in his body by the metabolic conversion of carbohydrates. But he is notable for the parsimony with which he conserves his small supply by every possible means, expending only minuscule amounts in his excreta and through evaporation from his respiratory tract.

Given these endowments, man might be the most successful of desert animals, for he can subject himself to sustained activity in temperatures that would kill other creatures. But his very capacity for this is the consequence of his delicate heat-regulating system. Man's body is a water-cooled engine. In extreme heat he may lose as much as a quart an hour by perspiration. Without water he could live only two or three days at a temperature of 100°. At 120° he might not last a day.

DESERT MULE DEER convene by night at a water hole. Most creatures of the desert drink when water is at hand, but for many it is a luxury rather than a need. Whether deer are drawn to oases for water or for their vegetation is not known.

PECCARY grub in the damp mud at the base of a spiny chola. The only native American wild pig, the peccary (known in the Southwest as javelina) has omnivorous tastes and a hearty appetite: it will eat anything from snakes to cactus.

A PACK RAT makes a meal of prickly pear. Like most cactus plants the prickly pear is extremely succulent: 90% of its weight consists of water. For such vegetarians of the desert as the pack rat it effectively resolves all water problems.

A BOBCAT devours a ground squirrel which provides him with both food and ➝ drink. A versatile beast, the bobcat ranges from coast to coast. At home in both swamps and woodlands, he has adapted himself to the desert environment.

A **WIND-SHEARED BUSH** in San Gorgonio Pass attests to the abrasive power of the desert wind. Blowing up the hill from right to left with steady force, the wind has pruned the shrub in line with the contours of the rock that shelters it.

CUTTING WIND AND SAVAGE SUN

ALTHOUGH the living things of the desert dwell in a relatively uniform and unchanging climate, wind and sun occasionally subject them to rigorous extremes. The clear and lucent air that overhangs the desert like a skylight of the purest glass is sullied from time to time by clouds of dust and sand. Trammeled by no thick stands of trees, winds ride unbridled across the barren flats. With them rides the fierce sand, blasting objects in its path. The finer particles of dust spiral aloft, diffusing in opaque clouds that dim the sun until the caprice of the winds sets them down on other landscapes far away.

The desert air is often troubled too on windless days by the influence of the sun. Heated by the blaze of noon, the atmospheric layer closest to the ground may form a refracting layer that bends light waves from above, producing inverse images and reflecting the blue ocean of the sky. From this effect originates the mirage—blue lakes and rivers shimmering in the arid wilderness, where the very absence of water has brought into being a unique domain of life (*next pages*).

A **WATER MIRAGE** (*below*) shimmers above a dry lake in Mexico. This common type of mirage is caused by a thin layer of hot air near the ground on which the sky is reflected. Here vegetation appears to be reflected in turn upon the "lake."

A DUST STORM (*above*) sweeps across the Arizona desert, filling the air with billowing clouds of choking particles. With little vegetation to slow its course, the desert wind can lift dust aloft until the sun is darkened. Dust storms differ from sandstorms, whose heavier particles move across the desert in a low cloud or carpet with a clearly defined upper boundary. Dust, however, is so fine that a strong wind can waft it thousands of feet into the air, hundreds of miles away.

CHUCKWALLA
SPOTTED SKUNK
PACK RAT
COLLARED LIZARD
GILA MONSTER
WHITE-FOOTED MOUSE
ANTELOPE GROUND SQUIRREL
CACTUS WREN
JACK RABBIT
LECONTE'S THRASHER
BULL SNAK[E]

J. R. WILSON

THE DESERT BY DAY

AS dawn breaks over the desert flats, the golden embers of the stars grow cold and the sky begins to glimmer with pale internal light. Now the animal populations are on the move, now is the time for the changing of the watch. The last hunters of the night come home and vanish into their burrows. The diurnal animals begin to stir, poking their noses forth to sniff the air of morning.

The sun climbs higher, and by 9 a.m. the day's activities are under way. It is this particular hour on a bright May morning in the Sonoran Desert that the painting on these pages reveals, encompassing in a single panorama life above and below the ground and illustrating two kinds of desert terrain — a bajada slope (*left*) with its

coarse soil and plant cover of giant saguaros, yellow-green paloverde trees, flame-tipped deerhorn chollas, barrel cactus, teddybear cactus and prickly pears; and a desert flat (*right*) with its finer soil and mottling of green creosote bushes and bur sage.

In the desert, as everywhere, the first creatures to arise are the birds. High temperatures are fatal to them and they must feed either early in the morning or late in the afternoon. During the heat of midday they must seek shade. Some make their homes inside the thick, moisture-laden columns of the giant saguaros. The cactus wren establishes its fortress among the fierce, impregnable spines of the cholla. Some birds fly long distances in quest of springs or pools. But most of them, like Leconte's thrasher and Gambel's quail, fulfill their needs with berries, seeds, insects and spiders. Predaceous birds obtain sufficient moisture from the bodies of their prey. The turkey vulture

RING-TAILED CAT
CHUCKWALLA
PACK RAT
ANTELOPE GROUND SQUIRREL
HORNED OWL
BULL SNAKE
SPOTTED SKUNK
DESERT TORTOISE

THE DESERT BY NIGHT

BY evening the unending battles of hunter and hunted are raging underneath the heedless stars. Snug in their secret strongholds, the creatures of the day lie sleeping—the chuckwalla in his rock crevice, the squirrel, tortoise and iguana in their burrows, the horned lizard beneath a shallow coverlet of sand. The bull snake occupies the home of some hapless rodent—with the rodent inside its belly. Meanwhile above them the desert flats shimmer with the silent shadows of the protagonists of the night, ever hungry, ever alert, darting in swift pursuit and flight.

In the grim food chain of the desert nearly every creature represents a meal for others larger than itself. As in the sea and every realm of nature, the great devour the small. At the bottom of the hierarchy stand the rodents, whose enemies lurk everywhere. They provide food for all—mammals, reptiles, birds. Yet they too must eat, and so they walk forth into the night's infinite dangers. The pack rat, having dined on cactus, mesquite leaves and prickly pear, proceeds with his obsessive occupation—adding litter to his nest—cactus pads, sticks, stones, rubbish of every description. Oblivious of his fate he goes about his business like the fanatical collector that he is. His cousin, the white-footed mouse, also lives dangerously, for though he can subsist on vegetation, he owns a fondness for insects and spiders and sometimes risks his life to get them. A more distant relative, the kangaroo rat, has somewhat better habits. He too is a hoarder and spends much time sifting the soil for seeds which he carries to his ample, underground abode. But he is extremely agile, capable of leaping high in the air; he has a trick, too, of kicking sand into the eyes of would-be assassins. Yet the kangaroo rat is a tasty morsel, enjoyed

FOLD OUT, DO NOT TEAR

bull snake and the tortoise. By and large the mammals remain inactive during the day. The jack rabbit may appear in early morning but often as not will seek the shade of a jojoba bush when the heat becomes intense. Only the playful ground squirrels and the peccary—native wild pigs—may still be active as the sun climbs toward the zenith. For the others the approach of noon is the signal for siesta, a time to take refuge in their burrows or in the shelter of rocks and shrubs. Noon and early afternoon are silent hours—the desert appears an empty wasteland, devoid of motion and of life. Toward evening, when the ferocity of the sun has waned, the creatures of the day emerge again for one last feeding before night falls.

Meanwhile, all day long, another entire population has lain dormant, sleeping away the intolerable bright hours. Some of its members, like the spotted skunk and the poisonous Gila monster, slumber

in rock cavities. The pack rat enjoys security in his shallow trench overlain with cactus pads, plant litter and other movable debris. The coyote, which has few enemies save man, dozes in the shade of a creosote bush. The badger suns himself in the mouth of his capacious burrow. The sidewinder rattlesnake coils himself in a flattened pad, sometimes—if the heat is not too great—in the open sand. But there are also many less audacious creatures underneath the ground—the kangaroo rat, the white-footed mouse, the pocket mouse, and the shy kit fox, asleep in their subterranean chambers. As daylight dies, surrendering its colors to silver dusk, the first of these nocturnal animals awake and stretch themselves. Emerging from their hiding places, they meet the rear guard of the day, withdrawing from their darkening hunting grounds. It is at this transitional hour of fading twilight, spreading starlight, that the desert comes most alive.

PECCARY

DESERT TORTOISE

BADGER   SIDEWINDER   COYOTE

POCKET MOUSE   DESERT IGUANA

circles ceaselessly in the flaming sky, scanning the desert for the morsel of carrion that will provide its dinner. On the ground the swift road-runner sprints across the flats, topknot bobbing, tail rampant, in hot pursuit of juicy snakes and lizards. And among the branches of a creosote bush the shrike impales his living prey upon a twig and leaves it there for future reference.

The lizards are by and large diurnal animals, though cold-blooded and extremely sensitive to heat. Even the beady-eyed chuckwalla, which reputedly suns itself on rocks too hot for man to touch, can stand only a few minutes' exposure before retreating to his cool crevice in the rocks. Like other desert populations the lizards display a wide diversity of habit and ways of life. The chuckwalla is a vegetarian, especially addicted to flower buds and blossoms. The collared lizard is not only carnivorous but cannibalistic. The horned

lizard (often misnamed horned toad) loves ants and spends long happy hours squatting next to anthills, lapping up the occupants as they appear. In the matter of defense lizards are equally diversified. The gridiron-tailed lizard relies on speed, running on his hind legs like a miniature dinosaur, and making as much as 15 miles per hour —high speed for a lizard but not quite fast enough to escape the road-runner's rapacious beak. The chuckwalla's curious defense when in peril is to squeeze himself into a crevice in the rocks and inflate himself with air, thus making it impossible to pull him out— unless he is punctured first. The desert iguana has a more spectacular talent; when seized from behind he sheds his tail and, leaving it behind to fascinate the foe, he escapes and grows a new one.

Apart from the birds and lizards the desert animals are generally nocturnal (*following pages*). Two notable reptilian exceptions are the

COYOTE   JACK RABBIT   GILA MONSTER
DIAMONDBACK RATTLESNAKE   WHITE-FOOTED MOUSE   KANGAROO RAT   SIDEWINDER
                                                                            DESERT IGUANA

by virtually every carnivore on the desert flats. His close kin, the pocket mouse, another seed collector, is almost equally in demand.

Less vulnerable than the mice, but still a fugitive, is the black-tailed jack rabbit, a lean and lanky sprinter capable of bursts of speed up to 45 mph and leaps as long as 15 feet. Essentially a vegetarian, fond of succulent plants and the bark of shrubs, the jack is active day and night, for his appetite is large. Intermediate in the food chain is the spotted skunk—at once predator and prey. Omnivorous, his diet includes cactus fruits, crickets, grasshoppers and at times carrion. But he is also a flesh-eater, a fancier of mice and baby rabbits. Livelier and smaller than his cousin, the familiar striped skunk, he possesses the same chemical armament, plus a psychological weapon —a trick of standing on his hands in moments of peril or excitement to confuse his enemies. He has a number of foes, among them the horned owl, a nocturnal bird of prey whose soft plumage renders its

flight completely noiseless as it swoops down upon an unsuspecting victim with cruel talons outspread.

Certain poisonous reptiles also haunt the flats by night. One of the few nocturnal lizards is the Gila monster, which, along with a related Mexican species, shares the distinction of being the only venomous lizard in the world. Docile and slow-moving, the Gila monster does not bite unless provoked. Its favorite food consists of quail eggs, young rabbits and ground squirrels. Vastly more dangerous and aggressive are the desert rattlesnakes: the diamondback, an irritable predator, averaging about 3½ feet in length, which comes forth at night in quest of rodents, birds and rabbits; and the sidewinder, a smaller but no less active reptile with a unique method of locomotion that carries it broadside across the sands.

The aristocrats of the desert night are the larger mammals. Perhaps the most curious of these is the shrewd and handsome ring-tailed cat.

POCKET MOUSE **KIT FOX** **BOBCAT** **BADGER**

Agile, inquisitive, strictly nocturnal, he spends his days in the rocky foothills and appears on the desert floor late at night. His favorite food is pack rat; indeed he seldom is found where pack rats are not present. Equally single-minded, the shy and dainty kit fox is the special connoisseur of kangaroo rats, preferring them above all other prey. Diminutive, scarcely larger than a house cat, the kit fox can run for short distances at incredible speed and succumbs to few antagonists. One of these is the bobcat, a sly hunter and ferocious fighter that dwells in the rugged canyons and ledge country by day, descending only at night to prowl the desert flats. He has few enemies to fear. Another confident and relatively independent hunter is the badger, whose specialty is digging. Endowed with powerful front feet and long, sharp claws, he lives boldly in open places where he can best practice his profession of excavating the homes of ground-dwelling, diurnal rodents. The best known of desert animals, and monarch of the flats,

however, is the handsome, lean coyote, whose lonely howls resound at dusk across the darkening sands. A versatile hunter, he can stalk and dig with equal success. Though a carnivore by preference, the coyote will not turn up his nose at carrion, cactus or mesquite beans.

And so at night the starlit flats become a murmurous battleground of innumerable small, secret tragedies and triumphs known only to the principals for whom the outcome means a sated belly or sudden death. Gradually, as the stars fade, the animals dissolve from the scene. One of the last to retire is the little western bat who through the long, dark hours has fluttered above the flats, hunting moths and other insects of the night. Then, as the bright banners of dawn unfurl across the sky and the white blossoms of the night-blooming cereus end their brief interlude of fragrant life, he folds his leathern wings and crawls into some narrow crevice in the rocks to slumber away the day. By then the birds of morning are already on the wing.

A SUMMER THUNDERSTORM expends its fury on the Arizona desert, lashing the cactus-covered flats with wind, water and hail. Such savage downpours occur mainly in the midsummer months when seasonal changes in wind and pressure

systems bring moist tongues of air in from the Gulf of Mexico. Some of these reach southern Arizona where low pressure centers tend to form over the desert as a consequence of the intense heating of the land. Crossing the hot sands, the

A PILLAR OF RAIN slants out of a thunderhead in the distance. It is at the base of such dense rain columns that deluges like that shown in the picture at top occur. Summer rain will soon bring leaves to the naked ocotillo in the foreground.

WHEN THE RAINS COME

THERE is no place on earth so arid that it has never felt the touch of rain. For the skies are open and from time to time errant storm clouds wheel around the barriers reared by mountain ranges, pressure systems and the seas and pour their waters onto unaccustomed lands. In general desert rains originate from two seasonal sources: cyclonic storms borne by the westerlies in winter and local thunderstorms in summer. Yet they are so capricious that in one place none will fall for years on end; others may receive a year's supply in one swift deluge. Frequently evaporation is so rapid that raindrops dissipate in the upper air and never reach the ground. Since desert storms are often local, moistening a few square miles at most, regional averages are meaningless. The whole Sahara, for example, is said to average a little under five inches annually. Yet at the outpost of Dakhla no rain fell for 11 years.

When they arrive, the desert rains often descend in brief but torrential downpours. As they hit the bone-dry ground, the baked surface at first sheds them as indifferently as asphalt paving. The accumulating waters may then run off in sheets across the sun-baked flats or pour through deep canyons in savage, turbulent cataracts. Supercharged with mud, sweeping debris before them, they rush furiously down the steeply graded washes, tearing, destroying, eroding until, captured by myriad minute pores in the soil, they seep into the ground or find their way ultimately to some waiting playa. A few hours later nothing will remain but damp mud, cracking in the desert sun.

lower portions of the moist air masses are warmed and spiral upward, creating towering thunderheads which occasionally explode in violent paroxysms of lightning and rain. During such downpours the water descends in nearly solid sheets, and hailstones frozen in the upper storys of the thunderhead bombard the desert flats with an icy barrage. In wintertime rains come to the desert principally from the Pacific Ocean, and though less violent are more general and prolonged.

A FLASH FLOOD covers the central wash channel of a bajada slope with sheets of turbulent, muddy water. Desert drainage is so swift that the run-off from tributary rivulets can produce a wild, rampaging torrent in less than half an hour.

A DAY LATER the same wash channel shown in the photograph at left appears virtually dry, save for a few random patches of still-damp mud. Baked by the hot sun's rays, it will soon look as desiccated as the flats of the surrounding desert.

SAGUARO BLOSSOMS appear atop the ordinarily bald summits of the giant cactus during the month of May, capping its spiny stalks incongruously with delicate, waxy blooms. Arizona recognizes the saguaro blossom as its state flower.

HEDGEHOG CACTUS BLOSSOMS adorn the squat, foot-high, branched cactus on which they grow. Brightening the rocky ledges of the Arizona desert, the hedgehog's vivid blooms are forerunners of its thin-fleshed, juicy, edible fruit.

MARIPOSA LILIES touch the flats with tongues of flame. Among the loveliest of Southwestern flowers, the Mariposa lily is a root perennial. Its bulb remains alive in time of drought, while the plant dies back, blooming again only after rain.

'AND THE DESERT SHALL . . . BLOSSOM'

FOR all their brevity and violence, the desert rains do not invariably vanish without effect. The year-round desert plants have ways of utilizing sudden downpours. Many of the cacti have spreading root systems that are able to absorb quantities of water in a single rainstorm and thick, expansible stems that can store it for many arid months. Other plants, like the paloverde, conserve water by resorting to minute leaves in order to reduce the amount lost from their surfaces by transpiration. Still others, like the ocotillo, survive prolonged dry spells by shedding their leaves entirely, or like the brittlebush, by letting whole branches die back, while keeping their roots alive. It is thus that the permanent plant inhabitants of the desert withstand their harsh environment, immune to circumstance and the fickleness of rain.

But the desert has other equally remarkable plants, which once or twice during the year dramatically revise the austere scene. These are the ephemerals or flowering annuals which recurrently, following the breaking of a bitter drought, burst into bloom and carpet the pale desert valleys with varicolored blossoms. At such times the desert miraculously revives. Insects proliferate; toads and other moisture-loving creatures emerge from estivation. Unlike the cacti and other drought-resistant plants, the ephemerals lie dormant through the dry periods of the calendar. Then astonishingly, after a freshening rain, they germinate, flower and bear seeds—all in six to eight weeks. These short-lived ephemerals are among the most prolific of desert plants, representing almost half of the vegetation of the Sonoran region. Swift to blossom, swift to die, they paint the landscape briefly with bright, magic colors, fulfilling for a time the ancient prophecy, "And the desert shall rejoice, and blossom as the rose."

BARREL CACTUS BLOSSOMS encircle the bristly stem of their parent plant like a coronet. The tough, springy spines of this well-known cactus were used by Indians for fishhooks. The blooms usually appear during March and April.

SPRING REVEILLE of rains makes the desert sands come alive with color. During the dry season seeds of flowering annuals lie dormant. Quickened by the kiss of rain, they swiftly germinate and flower, transfiguring the somber landscape with their gaudy pigments. Here in the Coachella Valley the wan green of the perennials is spangled with the yellow buttons of desert dandelions, the white cups of evening primroses and the purple clusters of fragrant sand verbena.

Although the deserts of the earth, covering about 19% of the planetary land surface, sustain only 5% of its population, their desolate horizons encompass far more than the apparently valueless wastelands that offend man's eye. Under their shifting scarves of sunseared sand and soil lie many of the earth's richest resources—the diamonds of Africa's Namib Desert and the oil of Arabia and Iran. The vast nitrate deposits of Chile's Atacama Desert and the borax of the Mojave owe their very existence to lack of rainfall. For nitrate, gypsum, borax and other valuable salts are water-soluble substances that would be leached out and borne away to the sea in regions of more abundant precipitation and exterior drainage.

Long before man ever uncovered these hidden riches, however, he wrested some food from the desert soil by regulating the limited water supplies at hand. The Egyptians were among the first to develop the art of watering the desert, for the periodic flooding of the Nile, alternating with long periods of drought, suggested the control of water flow by dikes, canals and dams. Other ancient civilizations also practiced desert irrigation. The Tigris and Euphrates supplied water to the Sumerians, Babylonians and Assyrians. The Indus River supported an early culture in India. Indeed it is thought that agriculture first flourished in irrigated regions, like these river floodplains whose open tracts were easier to cultivate than the tangled forests and stubbly grasslands of more favorable climes. Desert soils, though deficient in humus, are often rich in other plant foods; and the perennial sunshine may engender two or three crops a year. Some of the richest farmland in the world lies in the irrigated Imperial Valley of the Sonoran Desert.

In many ways man has conquered the desert. He has punctured its parched surface with oil wells and mines, spanned it with roads and flown above it in planes. Yet, like the oceans and lofty mountain ranges of the earth, the desert remains among the great barriers of the planet's surface, dividing mankind and repelling human encroachments. Though here and there man has occupied its scattered green oases, he has barely dotted the vast antipathetic expanses that roll to the empty horizons, as they have for centuries, mile after burning mile, barren, implacable, a "sea-like, pathless, limitless waste."

THE ARCTIC
BARRENS

PART X
THE ARCTIC BARRENS

A frozen desert ringing the polar sea, the tundra quickens in the summer sun

Here where the fires of Phoebus touch the chariots of the Pole,
In the luminous night the wheel of the sun burns with a flame
Continuous, and the emulous night brings in the clear day. . . .
RUFIUS FESTUS AVIENUS, *Descriptio orbis terrarum*

FAR in the north where the fabric of the forest frays, unraveling in a fringe of ragged brush, the land opens upon a bleak and barren plain. Here, dramatically, the horizon recedes into the immense distance and the sky arches hugely above an interminable expanse of frozen prairie. This is the tundra—the arctic desert which rings the Northern Hemisphere below the polar sea.

Of all realms on earth only the Antarctic is less known, less accessible. For although the edges of the tundra have often felt the step of man, its interior remains, as it has through history, remote, invulnerable, maleficent. To civilizations of the past the Arctic was only dimly discernible. Save for the Icelandic sagas there is little in literature about the Far North and, until recent times, even less in history. A Greek explorer, Pytheas of Massalia, reputedly sailed up the coast of Norway in 325 B.C. until he attained a region where the sun hung long and late above the red horizon. Though his own accounts were lost, his voyage was celebrated by many writers, most notably by the Latin poet Avienus 700 years later. Sometime in the Ninth Century, Iceland was settled by the Norsemen, and during the four years between 982 and 986 Eric the Red explored Greenland and founded a colony there. Although the later voyages of Henry Hudson and other explorers in search of a northwest passage awakened interest in the geography of the north, it was only in the last century that the outlines of the polar landscape took shape in any detail. It was not until April 6, 1909 that man—in the persons of Commander Robert Peary, U.S.N., his Negro companion, Matthew Henson, and four Eskimos—reached the North Pole.

Although popular fancy tends to equate the arctic and antarctic regions, they differ enormously in many respects. The South Pole is situated on a continent surrounded by water, the North Pole in a sea surrounded by the land of the tundra. Owing to its great mass and high elevation the Antarctic has the most savage climate on earth; in the frozen reaches below 60° south latitude no human beings live nor any trees nor land animals larger than insects. By contrast the Arctic is vastly more benign. Between 60° north latitude and the North Pole there are millions of human inhabitants; tall forests flourish and animal life abounds. In summer most of its land areas enjoy temperate and even warm weather. Snow melts, plants bloom, birds flock from the south. Even the arctic sea never freezes solidly; its ice floes, though 10 to 100 feet thick, circle the Pole in slow, incessant motion.

Unlike the Antarctic, which lies still in the relentless grip of a glacial age, the Arctic is not a homogeneous region, but contains within itself two distinct climatic zones. One is the polar region proper which

UNDER A BROODING SPRING SKY A COMPANY OF CARIBOU FILES ACROSS A FROZEN

embraces those parts of the polar sea, Greenland and a number of other partly glaciated islands where snow and ice never vanish; the other is the tundra, where for two or three months out of 12 the face of the land turns green. The word tundra is of Lapp or Finnish origin, but it has passed into many other languages with many shadings of meaning. In its widest international sense it defines the enormous reaches of bleak, treeless plains encircling the earth between the polar sea and the world tree line, overlying most of northern Canada, Siberia, Russia, the Scandinavian countries, parts of Alaska and the islands above the northern continental coasts. It exists only in the north; there is no tundra in the Antarctic.

Although here and there its flat countenance is wrinkled with occasional mountains and rivers, as in Siberia, or pocked by bleak fields of frost-shattered rock, gravel or sand, as in Canada, for the most part the tundra rolls away, mile after empty mile, featureless

LAKE IN THE CANADIAN TUNDRA. IN THE DISTANCE—LEVEL, DESOLATE, TREELESS—THE ENORMOUS BARREN LANDS REACH NORTHWARD TO THE SHORES OF THE ARCTIC SEA

and undifferentiated save for the innumerable lakes and ponds that blue-spangle its monotonous expanse. Although the tundra covers more than one-twentieth of the earth's surface, it is largely unexplored and uninhabited. In Canada, for example, the barren lands cover approximately 400,000 square miles of a great triangle sprawling between the Mackenzie River, Hudson Bay and the shores of the Arctic Ocean. It was in the approximate center of this huge wilderness that a LIFE expedition, which had been flown in, encamped many weeks under the most rigorous circumstances to obtain photographs for these pages.

The flatness of the tundra is partly the consequence of the titanic glaciation of the Pleistocene epoch when the great ice sheets freighted the earth. For tens of thousands of years their enormous mass, up to two miles thick, lay upon the tundra regions, scouring the tops of hills and ridges, planing away all angles, grinding and abrading the face of

the land. Now, across most of the tundra, a mound a few hundred feet high may loom like a mountain peak, visible 20 miles away. It is only when the sun hovers close on the horizon that its level rays suddenly define with highlight and shadow the faint profile of the arctic plain.

The distinctive feature of the tundra and, indeed, its architect and sculptor is permafrost, the name given by geologists to permanently frozen ground. Yet the congealing frost that solidifies the soil to depths of hundreds of feet is not completely permanent. Each summer the topmost few inches thaw, permitting the growth of arctic vegetation. It is this limited thaw that gives the tundra its special character. It does not penetrate deep enough to encourage the roots of trees, save for a few stunted, specialized forms. Nor does it go deep enough to permit efficient surface drainage. Hence most of the rain and snow that descends is trapped in numberless lakes and

THE TREE LINE, where the northern forests end and the arctic plain begins, is defined by the snow-clad evergreens edging the northern shore of Canada's Great Bear Lake. Within a few poleward miles the crowded trees thin, then vanish.

THE BARREN GROUND of the open tundra, grooved by the passage of glaciers and pocked with countless ponds, stretches vast and dreary under a pallid sun. Little vegetation appears on its bleak surface and there is no sign of animal life.

ponds which form in every small depression and cover half of the tundra surface. Since the permafrost holds the land in a relentless grasp, hardening the soil almost to the solidity of stone, erosion by wind and water is reduced to a minimum and the few rivers that crease the tundra meander to the polar sea between flat and shallow banks. The southernmost extension of continuous permafrost—the so-called permafrost line—marks the lower limit of the tundra and the approximate upper limit of the world's forests. It is here that the Arctic begins and ends. Although circumpolar, the permafrost line is extremely irregular, dipping far south in certain regions, such as the shores of Hudson Bay, and veering 1,500 miles to the north, high above the Arctic Circle, in the western portions of Canada and much of Siberia.

For nine months of the year the heart of the mainland tundra lies in the long clutch of winter. Day by day from September onward, the sun settles lower and lower toward the horizon, and the nights grow ever longer. Lakes and ponds vanish under sheaths of ice, and flowing waters are stilled. The first snows come early, and though generally light, quickly cover the barrens, softening land forms and converting all the world into an infinite, unvarying monochrome. On days of overcast the white land and the white sky seem to blend into an endless void. North of the Arctic Circle the sun drops below the horizon in early December and then the great cold descends and the skies shimmer and glow with the ghostly fires of the aurora borealis. Not until mid-January—and even later in higher latitudes—does the sun return briefly, casting pale rays across the frozen earth but presaging no spring for many a month.

Toward the end of May, when the sun once more circles the horizon day and night, the snows melt and the ice on rivers and lakes breaks up noisily, casting weirdly shaped blocks on the muddy shores. Yet this early spring does not at once alleviate the dreary desolation of the arctic desert. For now the melt waters collect in dank pools, drowning lichen and moss. Low clouds mass and curtains of mist enshroud the sullen land. It is not till the middle of June that the arctic plants begin to stain the sodden earth with living color. Then swiftly, miraculously, warmed and nourished by the constant sun, flowers appear—forget-me-nots, lupins, poppies—bejeweling and transfiguring the landscape. The muddy shores of lakes and streams become bright with gold and green. Birds arrive from the south and loud insects fill the air.

From May to July there is no darkness. On quiet afternoons, great cumulus clouds mass overhead, battlement on battlement, towering above the flat earth. At night, when the rose-pink sun poises briefly below the rim of the horizon, the sky remains suffused with life-breathing light. It is in this brief interlude of summer that the tundra comes fully alive. Hundreds of species of arctic plants spread across the bogs and muskeg marshes, transforming drab straw-colored expanses of brittle stalks and desiccated moss into lush carpets of green. But the green soon turns to red and yellow, for the first bleak breath of autumn comes out of the north before August ends. By late September the land again is white.

Though sections of the tundra have been inhabited by aborigines for thousands of years, to the eyes of civilized man its principal quality is loneliness. From time to time strings of caribou wander across the central wastes. Here and there musk oxen or solitary bear appear. In summer there are birds and incomputable hordes of mosquitoes. For most of the year, however, the tundra stands as an ultimate wilderness, empty and austere. Yet for some men who have known it the tundra has its fascination—the enchantment of open space and sky, of untouched nature and untrodden land. And to a few who call it home the tundra sometimes appears a place of beauty. A Caribou Indian once remarked to a priest who had been trying to convey to him an idea of the Christian heaven: "My father, you have told me that heaven is very beautiful. Is it more beautiful than the country of the musk ox in summer, when sometimes the wind blows over the lakes, and sometimes the water is blue and the loons cry very often? That is beautiful, and if heaven is still more beautiful, my heart will be glad, and I shall be content to rest there till I am very old."

AN ICE-GIRT HEADLAND rises above the grinding, wind-blown floes of the arctic ➤ sea on the western edge of the Melville Peninsula. Now, in early August, the grass grows green on the sun-warmed summits of these thousand-foot-high hills.

A WINDING STREAM meanders in broad curves across the tundra's level plain, missing rather than joining the lakes along its way. This is the Thelon River, largest in the Canadian barrens.

STORM RIDGES of frost-shattered, sea-strewn rock ornament the raised beaches of Southampton Island. The successive ridges were formed as the land, freed of its vast ice load, rose out of the sea.

STUNTED BIRCHES rising white and frozen from the snows of Abisko, in Swedish Lapland, reveal the inhibiting effect of the bitter northern climate on even the sturdiest of vegetation. These trees, the only kind that grow in the Abisko hills, mark the beginning of alpine tundra—the sparsely forested wastelands characteristic of the high altitudes. The arctic tundra, where the climate is generally too cruel to support even such hardy dwarfs as these, lies 800 miles farther north.

LAKE BREAKUP marks the height of spring in the far north. In the big lakes melt water sometimes spreads over the ice, completely drowning it until, thawed at the edges, the whole ice pan breaks from the shore and floats to the surface.

THE CLIMATE OF THE TUNDRA

NO place on earth experiences such vast annual extremes of weather as the arctic tundra. In winter it is colder than the ice-packed arctic sea, colder than the North Pole itself. For the oceans tend to warm the polar area, while the more southerly land masses lie refrigerated in winter beneath their shields of snow and ice. Although the temperature never drops below −62° F. in the arctic ice pack, a weather station on the fringe of the Canadian tundra once recorded a low of −82° F., and comparable temperatures have been reported in the tundra bordering Hudson Bay. The lowest temperature ever known on earth, −93.6° F., was recorded at Verkhoyansk below the southern edge of the Siberian tundra, 1,500 miles from the North Pole. In summer, however, the arctic tundra basks in the rays of the ever-present sun. Temperatures of 50° are normal and days of 60° and 70° not uncommon. A record high of 100° was once reported at Fort Yukon.

By contrast again with the bitter Antarctic, the arctic tundra is one of the least stormy regions on earth. During the winter it is overhung with a semipermanent high-pressure air mass, characterized by still, dry air. Since daily variations in temperature are slight, owing to the scant hours of sun in winter and its continual effect in summer, the tundra seldom experiences the fluctuating air movements that engender changes in weather. Strong winds are infrequent. (The average for the Canadian tundra is 6 mph.) It is principally in spring and fall that storms descend. Even so, total precipitation for the tundra averages only 11 inches a year—less than in certain desert areas. Warm-weather rains account for most of this; the annual snowfall in the Canadian barrens is less than the equivalent of two inches of water.

It is a paradox of the tundra that it combines innumerable lakes, marshes and bogs with an arid climate. Yet these sodden wastelands are created largely by the poor drainage imposed by the permafrost beneath the surface. Today, as world temperatures rise, the permafrost appears to be retreating by a few hundred feet a year. If it disappears entirely, permitting drainage, while rain and snowfall remain the same, the tundra may someday become the greatest desert on earth.

CANDLED ICE, formed when melting ice is reconstituted into vertical crystals or "candles," lies 10 feet up on the shore of a lake where it was driven by the relentless thrust of the entire massive ice pan moving ponderously down wind.

SPRING TORRENTS, swollen with the run-off water of melting snow, course wildly across the tundra during breakup, emptying into the sea and the larger lakes. Lacking any permanent water source, they disappear completely in summer.

MUSK OXEN feed on the purple saxifrage of Cornwallis Island. When danger threatens, these animals stand shoulder to shoulder in a protective line to defend themselves and the young of the herd.

A WIDE LAND FOR WANDERING

LIKE all harsh, uncompromising lands the tundra shapes the habits of its animal inhabitants. Some are by disposition solitary while others seek the company of their kind. Yet, singly or in groups, the creatures of the tundra must wander ceaselessly across the barren plains in quest of food. Bound together by mutual necessity and common impulse, companies of caribou, musk oxen, arctic hares and ptarmigan punctuate the solitude of the wilderness.

Of all the tundra residents the most conspicuous are the caribou, or arctic deer. Unlike the domesticated European reindeer (from which they are virtually indistinguishable), the caribou are continually on the move. Traveling in extended ranks or files, they follow a generally predictable migratory pattern, seldom diverging from a chosen route even when pursued by wolves or goaded by the fierce flies that harry them unendurably in the summer months. Their migrations are influenced in part by the exigency of finding new forage grounds and in part by the reproductive instinct.

Each spring before the first thaws dissolve the surface snows the caribou emerge from the forests where they have wintered and head out across the tundra, with cows and yearlings leading the way and the bulls straggling several days behind. Ever northward across the greening tundra, across rivers and lakes, sometimes to the shores of the polar sea, the cows press on until in the farthest of the tundra's ranges they halt at last and drop their calves. Perhaps a fortnight later when the calves are strong enough to travel, the herd turns about, and now with the cows in the wake of the bulls, they start slowly back toward the forests in the south. Late in the summer the sexes intermingle and travel in mixed herds. The rut occurs just north of the tree line in late October or early November and lasts about two weeks. Then, leaving the snowbound tundra, they re-enter their winter sanctuary in the woods.

The only other large gregarious mammal of the tundra is the musk ox. Where the caribou population of the Canadian tundra is estimated at about 750,000, the musk ox seems to have been reduced in numbers. Today there are only a few hundred left on the mainland, with perhaps another 35,000 scattered along the coasts of Greenland and some of the arctic islands. They are extinct in Europe and Asia. Unlike the caribou which ranges restlessly over many thousands of square miles, the musk ox tends to stay at home, often passing his entire life in a radius of a hundred miles. In some ways he is better equipped than the caribou for existence on the open tundra. His dietary demands are as simple and he has the same ability to forage underneath the snow. But his thick coat defends him against the cold of winter and the ferocious flies of summer; his agility, heavy horns, and defensive tactics render him immune to wolves. Placid, unaggressive and highly edible, the musk ox has had one implacable enemy: man.

ROCK PTARMIGAN, conspicuous in their winter plumage against a snowless countryside, feast on cranberries near the shore of Hudson Bay. During the bitterest months of the winter these ground-dwelling birds travel to the nearest

ARCTIC DEER move slowly across the tundra, a press of dun bodies under a forest of clubbed antlers. These are bucks and does traveling together. They are part of a herd of 4,000 animals on Richards Island in the Mackenzie Delta.

shrubbery—usually along river banks—seeking shelter in this meager cover from the occasional high winds that sweep the frozen prairie. In spring they return to the open lands, brown-feathered and black-barred, to nest on the bare ground. Protected by their summer coloration, the nesting birds are almost indistinguishable from the drab hummocks among which they sit and thus survive despite the hawks which circle overhead and the lean foxes that prowl the barrens.

ARCTIC HARES, more gregarious than their southern cousins, scamper away in an orderly pack across the rocky soil of Hare Point on Ellesmere Island. The hares of the southern tundra change color in spring, as do the ptarmigan and other arctic creatures. But the hares of the far north remain white the year round since snow is on the ground most of the year. Present everywhere in the Arctic but nowhere common, they are efficient foragers, reaching a weight of 14 pounds.

A GIANT FROST HEAVE, called a pingo, rises 330 feet from the floor of an old lake bed in the Mackenzie Delta. Its dark outer covering of earth is mantled with lichens and other vegetation, but its exposed core consists of solid blue ice.

A LAYER OF GROUND ICE, two feet thick, lies sandwiched between a cover of grassy vegetation and a base of silty clay. Exposed by the erosion of spring freshets, this layer may have been formed when a pond froze and was then buried.

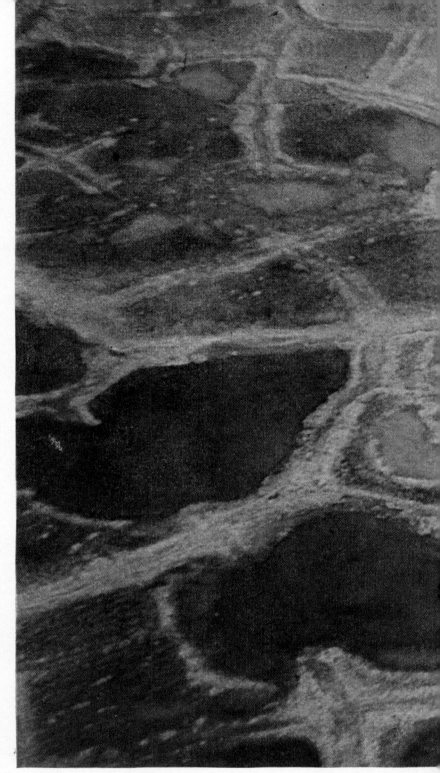

A PATTERN OF POLYGONS decorates the land surface near Pitt Point, Alaska. These regular geometric forms are created by the action of ground frost and are common throughout all tundra regions. In the same way that the exposed mud of

FIGURES IN THE EARTH

THE physical features of the tundra seem to exist in two dimensions. There are no great heights or depths, no geological panorama of mountains being uplifted or valleys carved. For untold years the underlying permafrost has helped to preserve from the ravages of erosion the gentle contours of the tundra. Yet bland and immutable as its visage appears to be, the tundra has its lineaments which alter year by year. For the permafrost and winter cold that prevent deep, basic changes serve also to effect a great variety of minor changes in the few upper inches of the surface soil which annually are liberated from the shackles of the ice. Here there is ceaseless activity. A result is the curious tundra phenomenon known as "patterned ground."

The patterns formed may take the shape of circles, polygons or stripes, clearly outlined by ranks of stones, lines of vegetation or grooves in the surface of the soil. Of many theories advanced to account for these figures in the earth, one of the most generally accepted points to the process called multigelation: the periodic expansion and contraction of the soil during repeated freezes and thaws. Patches of fine silt and clay absorb more moisture than coarser soils. When the ground freezes, these finer materials, containing more water, undergo greater expansion; and the coarser materials—gravel and stones

a drained lake bed is cracked into patterned plaques by the drying action of the sun, so the tundra soil is dissected by the shrinking action of intense arctic cold. These polygons measure 30 to 50 feet in width. Eventually, as the angular structures continue to evolve, each of them will develop a raised center. Shown here in mid-July, the polygons are bright with summer vegetation and checkered with patches of shallow standing water, trapped in the forms by the raised edges.

—are thrust radially outward in all directions. At the next thaw the finer materials contract again, adhering together, while the stones and gravel remain where they were placed by the freezing action. This process, repeated season after season, eventually results in a sorting of soil materials wherein the stones are relegated to the outer rim of an ever-expanding circular figure ranging from a few inches to 30 feet in diameter.

But many other factors are at work shaping the geometry of the tundra surface, and its figures have many variants. Often polygons are formed. And often the circles and polygons are outlined by grooves instead of stones, which may remain distributed haphazardly in the central area; these are known as "nonsorted" patterns. On slopes the slow downhill creep of unfrozen soil over permafrost acts as a leveling agent on the tundra's land forms and sometimes elongates circles and polygons into vertical stripes. Vast areas of exposed bedrock are recurrently shattered and dissected by frost action. Here and there huge slabs have been heaved upward in a vertical position like the mysterious monoliths of Stonehenge. Elsewhere small columns of frozen soil, furred with vegetation, rise abruptly from the tundra floor. Most spectacular of all are the giant volcanolike mounds called pingos (*above, left*) erected by the tremendous pressures that occur when layers of unfrozen material are squeezed between a frozen top layer and the permafrost basement and erupt finally to the surface.

A MEADOW OF MOUNDS, stone strewn and barren, stretches along the stark coast of Cornwallis Island. These irregular shapes are immature polygons, about six feet across, their boundaries accentuated by the erosion of running water.

MUSK OX

ARCTIC HARE

ARCTIC WOLF

LIFE IN WINTER AND SUMMER

FROM any one perspective the tundra sprawls between curved horizons like a forsaken void of nature, vacant of movement and of life. In the desolate vistas of the arctic plain solitary creatures are lost to view. Yet this impression of utter emptiness is illusive. The painting on these six pages discloses the procession of living things that pause on a segment of the Canadian tundra landscape as the

arctic year unfolds. Even in winter, when lakes are frozen and the land lies blanketed in snow, a few hardy creatures stir on the inhospitable wastes. In the bright, warm months hordes of summer visitors sweep up from the south and the muskeg marshes shimmer with the wings of many migratory birds.

Unscarred by roads or railways or by human habitation, the tundra provides a vast natural habitat for the arctic animals that have adapted themselves to its exigencies and made it their special domain. Here in the Thelon Game Sanctuary of the Canadian Northwest

WHISTLING SWAN   HERRING GULLS   SANDHILL CRANE   OLD-SQUAW DUCKS   RED-BREASTED MERGANS
GROUND SQUIRREL

predacious, wheels the long-tailed jaeger, enemy of gull and tern.

By July the arctic poppy and arctic cotton are in full flower, the sunlight never ends, and the cheeks of the ground squirrel are fat with seeds. The surface of the waters ripples in the wake of many ducks. The silent land is silent no longer, for from every lake and riverbank resounds the *Woo-hoo Woo-hoo Woo-hoo* of the whistling swans, the deep, rolling, trumpetlike *Kroooo* of the sandhill crane, and the strange honking call of the Lesser Canada goose. Now in mid-summer innumerable eggs hatch in innumerable secret nests; the

young birds stretch their wings; and the sturdiest among them, like the rough-legged hawks, prepare for their first solo flight.

At this time the caribou return from their remote fawning grounds with their weeks-old calves. Footsore from their long journey across the barrens, they walk slowly with an ambling gait, cropping the summer growth of lichens, mosses and grasses as they march. Their coats are thin and fly-bitten for this is the shedding season and the season of the scourge of flies. Throughout the unending day they are driven to madness by the numberless needles of the voracious warble fly

FOLD OUT, DO NOT TEAR

LONG-TAILED JAEGER
SEMIPALMATED PLOVER GOLDEN PLOVER   NORTHERN PHALAROPE
SNOW BUNTING

CARIBOU HERD

CARIBOU SKULL

touch with color the level riverbanks, the land begins to stir. Scarcely have the snows melted when inconceivable swarms of mosquitoes rise from the sodden muskeg swamps and infest the air. Now the long strings of caribous, out of their forests, come mushing across the barrens on their seasonal pilgrimage to the northern fawning grounds. And with them trots the red fox, an occasional wanderer onto the tundra, who also has wintered in the woods.

But the great change begins with the arrival of the birds—first the ptarmigan, or arctic grouse, from nearby winter quarters. Staking out their nesting grounds, the female settles down to hatch a family while the male stands guard, strutting about with fierce but harmless arrogance. Soon afterward the true migrants arrive, many of them from warm lands far away. Among these is the northern phalarope, who has flown thousands of miles from the South Atlantic to nest and rear his young beside the tundra lakes. Snow buntings flutter across the barrens like the petals of white spring blossoms, and the shores of ponds and rivers are brightly flecked with plovers, standing at attention in their golden summer livery. Overhead, patient and

WILLOW PTARMIGAN, MALE AND FEMALE

ROCK PTARMIGAN

SNOWY OWL

ARCTIC FOX

RED FOX

Territories—a wilderness hundreds of miles from the nearest Eskimo and Indian communities—virtually all the animals of the arctic prairies convene and flourish. Here the musk ox finds refuge from the depredations of man.

In late winter—which lingers in the Thelon till the end of May—the barrens are still mottled with snow. At this season the warm woolly coat of the musk ox is thickest and the arctic hare and arctic fox still go forth camouflaged in winter uniforms of white. Next month the musk ox will shed his overcoat and fox and hare will don their summer suits of brown and gray. The white arctic wolf, however, wears his white the year around, as does the snowy owl. For herbivore and carnivore alike the winter is a desperate time when forage plants lie buried under drifted snow and living prey is scarce and difficult to find in the sourceless twilight of the arctic night. It is for this reason, perhaps, that the arctic wolf is fiercer than his woodland cousins, and that the cunning arctic fox prudently disposes caches of food for emergency consumption.

As the sun climbs higher and the willow buds and dryas begin to

BARREN-GROUND CARIBOU   LESSER CANADA GEESE

which assails them mercilessly and lays its eggs in their hides. The many-pointed antlers of the bulls are nearly full grown—after the autumn rut they will be shed. The cows, whose antlers are less intricately branched, are four to five months out of phase with the bulls in antler shedding.

As autumn dyes the arctic plains with red and gold the lemming senses the approach of winter and expands the elaborate straw-lined burrow in which it will take shelter from the winter cold. A circumpolar tenant of the tundra, the lemming is best known for the legend

of its periodic impulse to mass suicide. It is true that the lemming has a tendency to emigrate from its habitat when the local population exceeds the means of support. But its suicidal reputation probably derives from recorded instances of wholesale drownings when entire bands have been swept away by outgoing tides while attempting to swim across fjords or inlets of the sea. Most lemmings, however, die between the jaws of foxes and weasels, or in the talons of hawks and owls, for all of whom they represent a favored article of diet. It has been noted that a drop in the lemming population is often followed

YOUNG ROUGH-LEGGED HAWKS

COLLARED LEMMING

BARREN-GROUND GRIZZLY
ARCTIC GRAYLING

by a corresponding drop in yearly fox fur yields from the barren lands.

In this season the barren-ground grizzly bear, mightiest animal of the tundra, stalks hungrily across the russet plains. For all his fierce appearance he is not a threat to caribou or any of the larger mammals, but confines his predations largely to rodents like the ground squirrel whose private root caches he likes to raid. Essentially a vegetarian, he appears indifferent to such delicacies as the arctic grayling, even when one leaps from the water before his eyes. For the most part he fills his belly with a variety of arctic plants—masu root, licorice root,

berries—and occasionally when times are hard he will even down a few tufts of grass.

Gradually as the days of autumn wane, the sounds and movement of the summer fade with the fading sun. The last straggling platoons of caribou disappear over the southern horizon. The final echelons of geese pass overhead, knifing the air in clean formation, and the skies echo for the last time their lonely parting cry. Then silence descends upon the barren grounds. Soon the white snowflakes will fall and the tundra again will sleep in the immense solitude of the arctic night.

MARSH FLEABANE, a golden hemispherical cluster of many heads on a single erect stalk, is a flowering tundra plant that is able to grow only in wet, marshy muskeg of the southern arctic plains.

THE FLOWERING TUNDRA

SAVE for the rock deserts that scar its vast expanse the tundra is carpeted continuously with plants. Even at the top of Greenland, 400 miles from the Pole, dozens of varieties of flowering plants and ferns come to bloom each spring. The Canadian tundra supports innumerable species ranging from primitive mosses and lichens up to ground birch, willow, flowering shrubs and heather. All are uniquely adapted to arctic existence and will not survive in a temperate clime.

It is not so much the cold that gives the arctic plants their distinctive character as the short growing season and the arid climate. For nine months of the year its waters are locked away in ice. Its acid, badly drained soil is chill and sour, inhibiting root absorption. And so, like desert plants, the vegetation of the tundra is especially equipped for living in a harsh environment; it is generally stunted and compact, with spreading root systems and small tough leaves. Rather than depend on seeds, many tundra plants reproduce asexually by adventitious budding. Although their rate of growth is slow, their seasonal processes are rapid. Bathed in perpetual daylight, they awake from winter dormancy and come to bloom in three or four swift weeks. Before the last snowdrifts have disappeared, the melancholy barrens are aglow with the bright pigments of the arctic flowers.

WHITE HEATHER BELLS transform the late winter lifelessness of the dwarf-shrub heath for a few weeks in spring. Heather occupies land depressions, where snow provides a protective winter cover.

FIREWEED, sometimes called the broad-leaved willow herb, is the largest, most flamboyant of the barren-land flowers and is found growing in large patches, usually on dry, exposed sand or gravel, in nearly all the arctic lands of the world.

ARCTIC COTTON GRASS annually produces these silky white spheres that rise upward on slender reedlike stems from shallow fresh-water pools to present a lush, subtropical appearance against the surrounding frost-sculptured rock.

BEARBERRY LEAVES, bright red against the green of alpine cranberry, relieve the gray granite outcroppings of the Hudson Bay coast during fall. These luxuriant berry plants grow in thick mats in dry poor soil in the southern Arctic.

"TÊTES DE FEMMES," small grass-covered hummocks of frozen earth, are often found in densely vegetated marshes in the north. These hummocks are probably formed by frost upheaval and are protected from the sun's heat by grasses.

CORAL-LIKE LICHENS proliferate in the drier parts of the frozen earth and are among the most important food plants of the foraging caribou which must search out new grazing areas when these slow-growing primitive plants are depleted.

LICHEN RING, spreading outward across the rock on which it grows, is formed by a sequence of death and rebirth. Each year the outer edge awakens from dormancy and spreads across the rock, while the center slowly dies and falls away.

THE LOWLY LICHENS

ALL across the barrens and in the uttermost reaches of the High Arctic the humble lichens—flat, rootless plants—cling to existence in areas where no higher forms will grow. Halted only by the barrier of perpetual snow, they thrive everywhere on earth, but they are especially suited to arctic life by virtue of their capacity to withstand cold and drought and to subsist on naked rock. Among the more primitive living things, they are usually the first members of a plant community to appear in barren ground, and as they propagate they provide an initial foothold for higher forms of vegetation.

The lichens' ability to live on rock derives from their dual nature. For lichens are composite entities, made up of two separate and dissimilar organisms, an alga and a fungus, united in an inextricable partnership. The fungus produces acids that disintegrate the rock, supplying necessary minerals to the alga; in return the alga supplies organic materials to the fungus which would die without them.

It is in great measure due to the lichens that the tundra wears its continuous plant cover. For they grow in the bleakest areas, carpeting whole landscapes to the exclusion of other plants. Many lichens are edible, most notably Cladonia, or reindeer moss, which provides the caribou with an important food source in the leanest times of year.

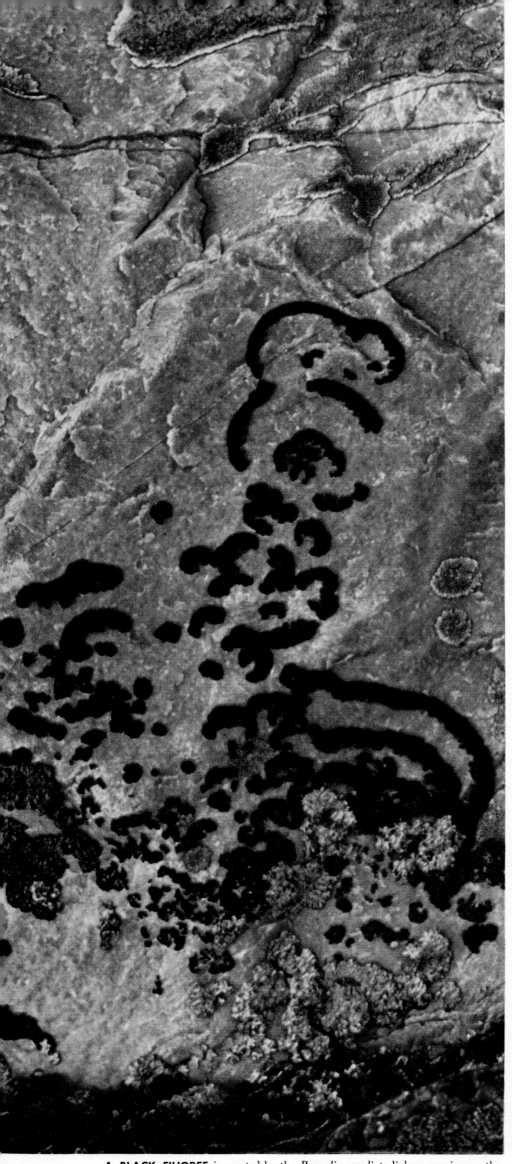

A BLACK FILIGREE is created by the *Parmelia sorediata* lichen growing on the smooth face of a glacier-borne boulder. The normally pink stone, here photographed just after sundown, has taken on an unearthly luminous purple hue.

ORANGE LICHEN, the brightest in the Arctic, displays its strident colors on tundra rocks. Like all lichens this species (*Caloplaca elegans*) thrives on nitrogen and grows mostly on the sides of rocks where owls and hawks habitually perch.

THE SPRING TUNDRA, seen here in the warm light of a June morning, is enlivened by the touches of color that brighten the barrens during the fleeting weeks between the passing of one winter and the coming of the next. Jagged boulders, fractured by frost, are richly adorned in blazing lichens. Last year's dry grass gleams golden in the crevices, while the melt water on a thawing lake reflects the pale blue sky. The chalk-white skull of a caribou bleaches under the vernal sun.

IN an overcrowded and tumultuous world where all the friendly, comfortable lands have long since been appropriated, the tundra looms on the northern horizon as an ultimate frontier. The eye of man has always rested covetously on open land, however inhospitable its surface aspect. Today the people of every national domain that impinges on the Arctic are scrutinizing the tundra with a new and inquisitive regard.

The peripheral lands of the Arctic are owned and administered by proprietary nations, specifically the six countries whose coasts encircle the polar sea. Of these barren dominions, 37% belong to Canada, 28% to the Soviet Union, 28% to Denmark, 6% to the U.S. and 1% to Norway and Iceland. The wealth of the tundra is both animal and mineral. For centuries the flesh and hides of caribou and reindeer and the pelts of smaller fur-bearing animals have provided an economic mainstay to Indians, Eskimos, Lapps and other aborigines of the Far North. In the last 100 years civilized man, probing successfully beneath the desolate barrens, has uncovered immense riches in gold and platinum, as well as many of the baser metals.

Although some sheep are raised in parts of Greenland and Iceland, the principal domestic animal of the tundra is the reindeer. To those dependent on it, the reindeer provides not only a source of meat but of milk, clothing, transportation and a variety of by-products such as furniture, mattresses, gelatin, felt, suede and glue. In the Russian and Scandinavian tundras, reindeer husbandry is a major industry. Although heavy slaughter during the war years reduced their numbers, the reindeer population of the Eurasian tundra is estimated today at about two million. On the North American continent, however, reindeer herding has not been consistently successful. The explorer, Vilhjalmur Stefansson, has long urged the domestication of caribou as a means of increasing the subsistence levels of the Eskimo inhabitants of the Alaskan and Canadian tundras. But the temperament of the American arctic natives inclines them more to the hunter's existence than that of the herdsman. And even though a few small herds of semi-domesticated reindeer were imported into Alaska half a century ago and multiplied for a while, their numbers have since been sadly depleted through mismanagement, and they have failed to divert the Eskimos from their nomadic way of life.

The fur trade has been the principal business of the Canadian tundra for nearly three centuries, ever since the Hudson's Bay company received its charter from Charles II. In the great barren lands lying between Hudson Bay and the Mackenzie River the unit of currency was the pelt of the white arctic fox, and it was through this medium that Indians and Eskimos purchased the products of civilization.

Today, however, the major focus of interest in all the tundra regions of the world is directed upon their still unexplored mineral resources. Although certain deposits—Swedish iron from the great mine at Kiruna, Russian nickel and copper from Noril'sk, and gold from Alaska—have been exploited for many years, new resources are constantly being discovered. Mining first surpassed the fur trade as the major industry of the Canadian tundra in 1939. Today miners and prospectors are streaming out upon the barren lands in every country in quest of new mineral reserves. Gold, copper, lead, asbestos, beryllium, lithium, coal, oil and tin have been found in remote parts of the North American tundra. More important than any of these, the recent discovery and exploitation of tremendous iron deposits on the edge of the Quebec tundra indicate the presence of ore reserves equal to any now known on earth.

The most dramatic development of recent years, however, has been the enormous, unspecified increase of production in the uranium deposits at Port Radium, on the shore of Great Bear Lake on the western edge of the Canadian tundra. Radium-bearing ores were first discovered there in 1930; by the end of 1933 a milling plant and refinery were in steady production. When nuclear fission became a possibility in 1939, the mine was enlarged and deepened. Today Canada stands (with the Belgian Congo) as one of the two foremost producers of uranium in the world.

For all these past achievements and promises of future rewards, the tundra still holds on its expanses only widely scattered communities, many of them inhabited by but a handful of people. The difficulties of living on the tundra derive no less from its rigorous climate than from the problem of transportation. The Mackenzie River and the great waterways of the Siberian tundra provide north-and-south transport during the summer months. But the wilderness of lakes and bogs that stretches between these widely spaced rivers for countless miles renders east-and-west ground traffic virtually impossible, save to the dog teams that traverse them in winter.

Little by little, however, the airplane is opening up the arctic desert. It is the airplane too that has directed upon it a new and serious kind of attention. In the embattled world of today the tundra regions, facing each other across the ice packs of the polar sea, now constitute the closest frontiers between the Soviet Union and the democracies of the West. For this reason the bleak and malevolent barren lands are dotted with air bases, meteorological stations and military installations extending to the farthest reaches of the arctic islands. For this reason, if for no other, man now, more ardently than ever before, "woos . . . the frozen bosom of the North."

THE
RAIN FOREST

PART XI

THE RAIN FOREST

Its ever-green mantle of noble trees, blanketing the moist tropic lowlands, holds a richer array of plant and animal life than any land area on earth

> . . . where highest woods impenetrable
> to star or sunlight, spread their umbrage broad.
> MILTON, *Paradise Lost*

MILLIONS of years ago, before the advent of the ice ages, the earth basked in never-ending summer and its lands lay mantled almost to the poles beneath a forest cover of eternal green. Unlike the needled evergreens of temperate woods today, those antique trees bore broad leaves and bright exotic blooms. The forest they composed unfurled magnificently to north and south from its heartland on the equator. On the equator it still stands today, reduced in area but revealing still the splendor and luxuriance it has worn for untold eons of time. This is the true forest primeval—the rain forest.

Accustomed to the marching seasons—to the buds of spring, the full leaf of summer and autumn's dying fires—modern man tends to think of his changing woodlands as normal and to regard tropical vegetation as somehow excessive and bizarre. This is understandable, for civilization and literature have flourished principally in temperate regions where the varying moods of the year are most pronounced. Yet in the ebb and flow of terrestrial life, oaks and maples, pines and hemlocks are comparatively recent immigrants to the temperate latitudes they now adorn. In the morning of their existence, they constituted only the ragged upper fringe of the earth's forest cover. But with the approach of the great ice ages, the primal rain forests shrank slowly southward, retreating ever deeper into the tropics, while the hardier conifers and deciduous trees pursued them from the cool lands to the north. Today, ever-green rain forest still blankets millions of square miles of moist equatorial lowlands, covering more than a tenth of the planet's total land surface and nearly half of the total forest areas of earth.

In popular fancy the tropical rain forest is envisaged as a stifling labyrinth of strangled, impenetrable undergrowth, creepers, vines and rotting vegetation through which man must hack his way inch by inch, by tortuous inch. But this is the jungle or "bush" of adventure stories—a limited concept that applies best to areas of secondary growth where virgin forest has been despoiled. In true rain forest the spreading canopy of treetops, interwoven layer on green layer, filters the sun's rays, creating below a dim and murky twilight that overcasts the forest floor and thus suppresses all but a scattered undergrowth of shrubs and saplings. In the dark roomy aisles between the straight, unbranching boles of the high trees the ground is relatively open, covered with only a thin carpet of leaves that flutter down in a slow, gentle, never-ending fall the year around. Here and there the pervading gloom is traversed by descending shafts of sunlight that have somehow penetrated the intricate fabric of the sheltering canopy and, coming to rest, gold-fleck the forest floor.

One of the unique characteristics of the rain forest is that most of its vegetation is treelike in size and woody in character. Plant families which are represented in cooler regions by insignificant ground herbs here attain enormous stature—"violets" bigger than apple trees, "myrtles" with thigh-thick woody stems, "roses" 150 feet high. The forest is taller than most temperate zone woods, averaging 110 to 120 feet in height with occasional trees sometimes soaring to 200 feet. Leaves are large and leathery, dark green in color. Everywhere,

interspersed among the pillars of the trees, dangle the sinewy cables of lianas and other climbing plants, sometimes taut as the lines of a sailing vessel, sometimes festooned like Christmas tinsel or looped like lariats.

Owing to the predominance of woody plants and the general uniformity of their dark foliage, the rain forest presents a somber and even monotonous visage which is unvaried by seasonal change. Yet for all its apparent homogeneity, it comprises an extraordinarily complex domain of life, richer in plant and animal species than any other community in nature—save perhaps the sea. Where temperate woods may embrace a few dozen varieties of trees at most, a square mile of rain forest encompasses two or three hundred—counting only those with trunks more than a foot in diameter. Its smaller trees and woody shrubs are equally multifarious, as are the animal tenants who inhabit every tier of the leafy edifice from its shadowed floor to the green mansions of the sunlit upper terraces.

The opulence of forest life has evolved through the seasonless operation of a warm, wet climate, shaping its creations imperceptibly through eons of geologic time. In the extreme tropics there are no winters or springs, only perpetual midsummer. The uniformly high mean temperature varies within a range of only about 5° between January and July, and averages about 80° the year around. But as the sun passes overhead on its annual round trip between Cancer and Capricorn it leaves in its track in each latitude masses of heated air which rise, cool and wring out their water content in rain. In regions from about 3° to 10° north and south of the equator there are two rainy seasons a year, alternating with two seasons which are relatively dry. Even in the so-called dry seasons three to four inches of rain may descend monthly, out of an annual mean of perhaps 90 inches.

During the season of rains wild avalanches of water recurrently descend in thunderous cloudbursts which may disgorge 30 inches of water in as many days. At such periods the forest roof drips almost continually, even under fair skies. Beneath it the atmosphere is charged with moisture and the forest corridors lie dank and sweltering. By day the canopy of treetops, excluding wind and sun, retards evaporation; by night, like a giant greenhouse, it imprisons the heat of day. Under such conditions plant life proliferates with incredible luxuriance. New leaves compete riotously to fill each sunlit chink in the tangled canopy; in cut-over clearings bamboos may shoot upward at the rate of a foot a day.

The rain forest weaves a green belt around the midriff of the earth, investing all equatorial land areas save those where irregularities of the planetary profile oppose it. Where mountains lift their shoulders skyward into cool realms of perpetual mist and cloud, the forest cover dwindles into a curious elfin wood of giant ferns and gnarled, stunted trees, bearded with moss. Elsewhere complicated air and ocean currents combine to desiccate the land and create deserts or tropical deciduous forests. And wherever man has ravaged the land the forest has given way to squat, smothered thickets of secondary growth. The last major centers of undisturbed primeval rain forest on the face of the earth lie in West Africa, Indonesia and adjacent areas, and South America. A few scattered stands also survive in northeastern Australia, southwestern India, Central America and some Caribbean and Pacific

IN THE HEART OF THE FOREST a shallow stream tunnels its way through luxuriant walls of swamp vegetation. Here, in the dry season, the current flows gently, spanned by a broken branch to which there clings a bromeliad, one of the many air plants that flourish in the soilless crannies of fallen logs and living trees.

THE MISTS OF MORNING curl upward from the canopy as the sudden heat of sunrise warms the forest's dew-drenched foliage. Here, 125 feet above the ground, the changing humors of the day are clearly manifest; and soon, as the sun ascends towards the zenith, the humidity will drop sharply and all vapors vanish. But underneath the roof of trees the shadowed forest corridors lie steeped in moisture from dawn to dusk, insulated from the drying agencies of wind and sun.

A SMALL SAVANNAH mottles the forest mantle with a pattern of white sand and scrub. Across it runs a gallery forest whose trees loom high in the distance, their crowns bedecked with flowers, their roots lodged in damp earth beside a brook.

IN SODDEN HOLLOWS where soaked earth and stagnant water have stunted the forest cover, palm bogs put forth a tangle of rank, thin-stemmed undergrowth. Below: a gallery creek runs red with tannin from leaves on its moist margins.

islands. Of the three great rain forests, the largest and richest is the South American hylaea (from the Greek *hule*, meaning wood) which covers more than a million square miles of the Amazon and Guiana river valleys from the Mato Grosso of Brazil to the Caribbean coast. It was here, in the deep forest of Dutch Guiana, that a LIFE expedition made the photographs and paintings for "The Rain Forest."

From the air the hylaea appears as a limitless and undifferentiated ocean of treetops, an immense green sea surging to the round horizons. On the ground, however, there is bewildering variety. The land rolls gently between choked, twilit creeks. Small plateaus of open sand or rock occasionally punctuate the forest cover. Amid innumerable swamps strange distorted trees perch on bulbous pediments, and in bogs arching palms shadow the leaf-stained water. At intervals the forest canopy is severed by slow rivers; on their banks the walls of vegetation loom massively above the water, filigreed with traceries of countless vines.

The complexity of the hylaea is so great that botanists consider it not one but many forests, differing from each other through local peculiarities of topography or soil. It thus embraces "dry rain forests" on sandy hills, "swamp forests" in flooded vales, "montane rain forests" on fog-shrouded mountain slopes, and "gallery forests" by the shores of streams that flow through dry savannah lands. "Climax" or completely nonseasonal rain forest at its peak development flourishes only in sheltered, well-drained lowlands where precipitation is never less than four inches in any month of the year. In certain otherwise favorable areas where the rainfall does decline below this mark, trees may look little different but tend to shed their leaves and put forth blossoms less evenly the year around: these are called "ever-green seasonal rain forests." Throughout the hylaea any of these components may stand in confusing proximity with others. Thus the single square mile in which the pictures for this chapter were made contains not only the most magnificent "ever-green seasonal rain forest" but also a heathlike savannah (*above*) and a cluttered palm bog of stagnant pools and rank undergrowth (*upper right*).

To the eye of man the hylaea appears as majestic and overpowering in its way as a soaring range of mountains or the sea. In even a narrow segment, like that depicted in the painting on the following pages, the splendor of its pillared, overarching trees is never to be forgotten. The first European to glimpse America's primeval rain forest was Christopher Columbus, when he sighted the green-robed island of Hispaniola from his flagship in 1492. Profoundly moved by what he saw, Columbus later wrote: "Its lands . . . are most beautiful . . . and filled with trees of a thousand kinds and tall, and they seem to touch the sky. And I am told that they never lose their foliage, as I can understand, for I saw them as green and as lovely as they are in Spain in May, and some of them were flowering, some bearing fruit, and some in another stage, according to their nature . . . in the month of November there where I went."

THE FOREST PROFILE

THE painting on the preceding pages reveals the grandeur and lovely disarray of an actual 60-foot-wide section of rain forest in Dutch Guiana. Unlike temperate woods with their clearly defined layers of vegetation—ground herbs, shrubs and trees—the rain forest presents a complex and bewildering facade. Here forests mount on forests like clouds on clouds. High above the lowly ground layers of herbs and shrubs, the crowns of the trees themselves form three or more superposed stories, creating "as the ranks ascend shade above shade, a woody theater of stateliest view."

Amid the confusion of leaves and climbing plants, the observer on the ground is a prisoner, for the rain forest is a many-storied mansion whose architecture can only with difficulty be discerned. The diagrams below define the vast dimensions of the forest and dissect these chaotic masses of verdure into their three component strata of trees: 1) sparse, narrow-crowned young trees up to 60 feet high that struggle for life in the perpetual gloom beneath the canopy; 2) taller, sturdier trees from 60 to 120 feet high whose round, competitive crowns interweave to form the canopy itself; and 3) the giants, ranging from 120 to 200 or more feet high, whose crowns have burst through the canopy into the sunny upper air and thus bask like tropic islands above a green sea. Each layer, like the varying layers of the ocean itself, receives a different amount of sunlight and harbors its own unique community of plant and animal life.

Though ever present, the three strata of trees are never clearly defined, for the forest is continually growing. Immature trees everywhere build balconies and mezzanines between the stories. The crowns of saplings belonging to giant species may interlock temporarily with trees of a lower stratum. Here the canopy may be continuous and close woven, elsewhere torn and threadbare. Curiously, for all its multiplicity of kind, the rain forest exhibits striking conformities of color, leaf shape, bark texture and other characteristics. This anomaly may be explained by the forest's enormous antiquity. Embosomed in the same environment for over a hundred million years, its component families have made similar adaptations and developed along similar lines. As these lines converged, they arrived ultimately at the same life forms, which have persisted through millennia of geologic time. The broad-leafed ever-green trees of the rain forest—"those green-robed senators of mighty woods"—are cut in the archetypal pattern from which all other forms of flowering plants have probably derived.

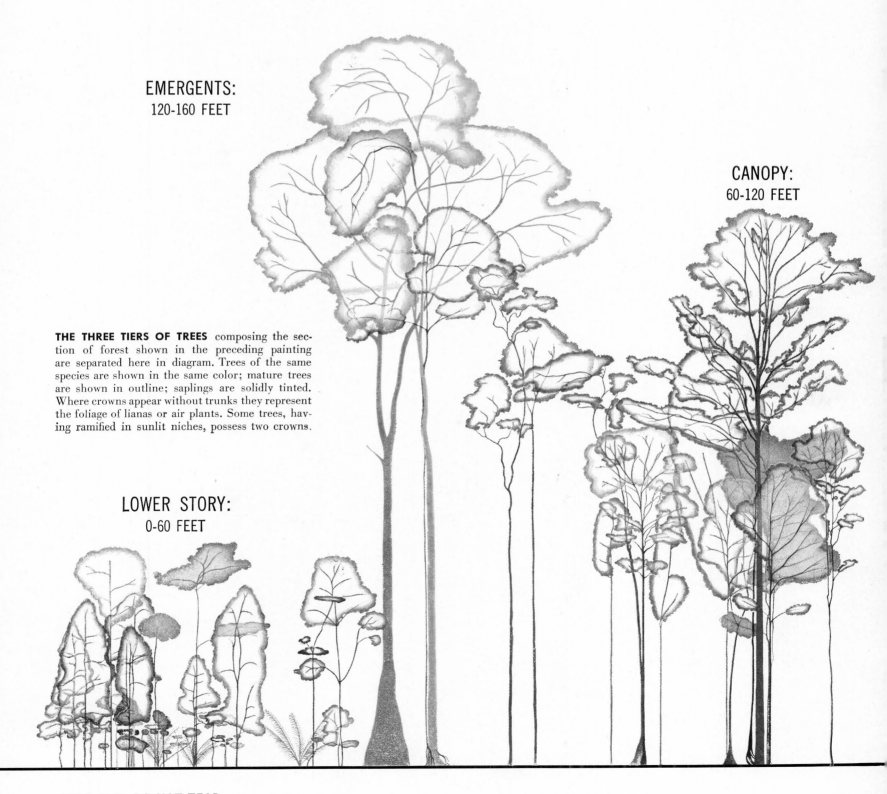

EMERGENTS:
120-160 FEET

CANOPY:
60-120 FEET

THE THREE TIERS OF TREES composing the section of forest shown in the preceding painting are separated here in diagram. Trees of the same species are shown in the same color; mature trees are shown in outline; saplings are solidly tinted. Where crowns appear without trunks they represent the foliage of lianas or air plants. Some trees, having ramified in sunlit niches, possess two crowns.

LOWER STORY:
0-60 FEET

FOLD OUT, DO NOT TEAR

GUIANA PARTRIDGE   COMMON OPOSSUM   COCK OF THE ROCK   CURASSOWS   PHILANDER OPOSSUM   FLINT-BILLED WOODPECKE
                       SUN BITTERN   CAYENNE GUAN   QUICA   JAGUAR   PECCARIES   YAGUAR
MATAMATA TURTLE   GIANT OTTER   ANACONDA   WATER OPOSSUM   TAPIR   BOA CONSTRICTOR   TEGU LIZARD
                                    CRAB-EATING RACCOON   SURINAM TOAD   NEOTROPICAL TOAD   PACA   TOAD   MARMOS

CREATURES OF THE SHADE

IN the green-gold hush of noon, the colonnades of the rain forest stand silent, immobile, apparently empty of life. From neither the dappled floor nor the leafy cloudland overhead comes evidence of the populations that inhabit every level of the forest's towering domain. Only at dawn and dusk when the hunters of night and day walk abroad together do multitudinous voices betray the profusion of the hylaea's living things. Furtive, seldom seen, the diverse animals assembled in this painting are the basement dwellers, the creatures of the shade.

The oldest of all forest mammals are the marsupial opossums, which here alone in the world have multiplied their species. Along with their common cousin, the familiar opossum of North America, they number among their flourishing tribe the web-footed water opossum, the nimble philander, the predaceous quica, and the wee, cowering, timorous *Marmosa*. Dynasties only slightly less venerable produced the lumbering anteater, whose swift tongue is the terror of termites; the giant armadillo with plated carapace; and two robust relatives of the guinea pig, the paca and agouti. The largest animals of the forest are of newer lineage: the shy, solitary tapir, a long-nosed cousin of the rhinoceros who emigrated from the north about a million years ago;

RED BROCKET DEER   TINAMOU   GIANT ANTEATER   PUMA   PIGEONS   MARGAY
QUADRILLE WREN   GECKO   CRIBO SNAKE   BUSH DOG   TRUMPETER   AGOUTI
OOD RAIL   MARBLED TREE LIZARD   YELLOW-LIPPED TREE SNAKE   GIANT ARMADILLO   BUSHMASTER   TAYRA   LIANA SNAKE
OAD-BANDED ARMADILLO   NINE-BANDED ARMADILLO   FER-DE-LANCE   BUSH SPIDER   JUNGLE RUNNER   BUSH TORTOISE

and his only dangerous adversaries, the puma and jaguar—the latter a versatile hunter who prowls the treetops as sure-footedly as he does the forest floor. Smaller predators include two other tree-climbing cats, the graceful margay and the bird-eating yaguarundi; and a grinning, ferocious four-foot weasel, the tayra.

The real aborigines of the rain forest, older by far than any mammal and even than the forest itself, are cold-blooded animals, reptiles and amphibians, whose ancient lines colonized the dank lowlands in Paleozoic times. Today the hylaea is still the abode of turtles, tortoises, toads and legions of lizards from the tiny gecko up. Here too flourish some of the world's most formidable serpents: the 25-foot aquatic anaconda and its terrestrial counterpart, the boa constrictor; and the deadly bushmaster and fer-de-lance. With the reptiles flourish their Mesozoic offshoots, the birds, shimmering in the upper stories and filling the forest aisles with their innumerable cries. Many of them never ascend out of the basement. Indeed a few large species—partridges, curassows, trumpeters and tinamous—are heavy flyers, garbed solemnly for permanent life in the shadows. As manifest as any of these, and outnumbering all other classes a millionfold, are the true dominants of the forest—the insects and spiders—numberless as the leaves of the canopy—attending to invisible pursuits in every fissure and cranny from the cellar floor to the topmost twigs of the tallest tree.

DEAD LEAVES, shed evenly the year round, lightly carpet the forest floor. As fast as they fall from the green boughs above they are decomposed by the action of creeping molds, fungi and bacteria, and entombed in softly falling rainwater.

THE FOREST FLOOR

IN the sunless world at the foot of the great trees, the life of the forest has all its ends and its beginnings. It is here that tiny saplings at the threshold of existence expose their first tentative shoots to the green half-light. And here ultimately descend the crown leaves of the proudest forest giants. Day by day around the cycle of the seasons they float down and lie where they fall.

By contrast with the prodigality of foliage in the upper stories and the magnificence of the forest as a whole, the leaf litter on the forest floor is thin, the underlying soil impoverished. The explanation of this paradox lies in the speed with which the agents of decay do their work. For decomposition keeps pace with the rain of dead leaves from above, while the feeding roots take up the products of decomposition as quickly as they dissolve into the earth. Hence at any and all times most of the nutrients are locked in the living vegetation. And so the richest of all forests springs from soil so poor that when cleared of trees it will seldom support crops for more than a single season.

No less remarkable than the nutritive cycle is the reproductive device by which some of the rain forest trees have adjusted to existence in their special domain of nature. This is the curious process known as cauliflory: the production of flowers on main trunk and branches. This blossoming of the bark, according to botanists, is less an expression of vegetable exuberance than an adaptation to a world where wind-pollinated plants can only hazardously survive. In the breathless cloisters of the forest the work of the wind is done by myriads of insects which transport the vivifying pollen from blossom to blossom. By bearing their flowers low, cauliflorous plants make them accessible to a special world of crawling and low-flying pollinators that never climb far above the forest floor.

"DRIP TIPS," which facilitate the runoff of rain water after torrential storms, characterize most leaves in the lower strata of the forest's foliage. The particularly pronounced tips shown here terminate the leaves of a *Bactris* palm.

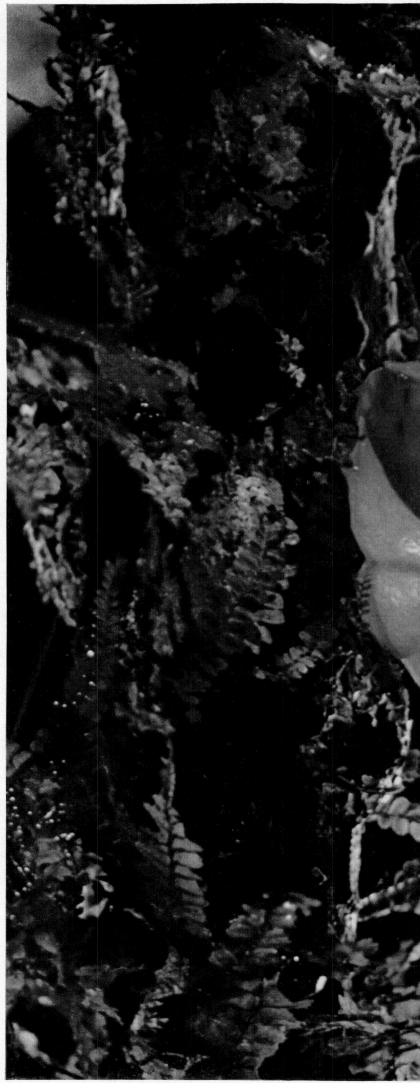

BURSTING THROUGH THE BARK of its parent trunk, an exotic cauliflorous fruit displays its rich-hued ripeness in the forest gloom. The waxy "petals" surrounding its pale blue berry impart to it a curiously flowerlike appearance.

A TREE SEED, engineered for aerial transport by its upholstery of fluff, lies amid the leaf litter on the forest floor. It is only a few exposed trees and climbing plants of the upper story that rely on the wind to disperse their seeds.

FRUITS OF THE FOREST, spiny bush grapes, nestle near the foot of their parent stem. Growing just above the floor, the blossoms of the bush grape, like those of most other cauliflorous plants, attract low-flying and crawling insects.

BUTTRESS ROOTS of an *Andira* tree compose a ponderous pedestal rising to a height of 12 feet, spreading over a diameter of 80. In contrast with this noble superstructure, the underground root system is astonishingly shallow. Common throughout the rain forest, buttress roots assume many varied and fantastic forms. Some slope gently to the ground, while others ascend so steeply that their tops are lost to sight in the leaves of the lower stories. Some have knife-sharp

THE FOUNDATIONS

LIKE the pillars of some immemorial temple, the clean, unbroken trunks of the trees often rest on massive pedestals. Along the naves of the forest their lines soar upward, severely vertical, uncluttered by traceries of twigs and branches such as obscure the northern woods. But nature has adorned their bases with a variety of ornament. Trees large and small rise from elaborate root structures that rear above the ground, grotesquely shoring up their giant burdens.

What purpose these strange root formations serve or what processes of natural selection brought them into being, botanists cannot definitely now say. Characteristic mostly of smaller trees, stilt roots (*below, right*) emerge from the trunk at intervals up to ten feet above the ground, turn downward and, entering the soil, ramify into multiple rootlets. In flood forests and mangrove swamps they evidently raise the base of the tree trunk above high-water mark, but why they should occur also in normal, well-drained areas remains a mystery.

Far commoner are buttresses (*above*)—flat, triangular plates surrounding the lower girth of trunks just above ground level—which

← DANGLING ROOTS OF AN AIR PLANT DRAW WATER FROM A GALLERY CREEK

A STRANGLER FIG encases a "host" tree in a sheath which grew from small dangling roots when the young fig was an air plant. The strangled tree still shows through its fatal jacket. Below: stilt roots raise a palm above high-water mark.

edges, others snake out in sinuous curves, dividing and subdividing repeatedly. Finally there are those which arch above the ground, leaving a clear space beneath their span so that they resemble the flying buttresses of Gothic cathedrals.

are produced by secondary growth along the upper surfaces of shallow lateral roots and sometimes span as much as a quarter acre. One theory relates their existence to the forest's shallow humus, which rarely extends more than three to four inches below the surface of the ground. As a consequence, few rain forest trees have tap roots, and even the giants among them exhibit superficial root systems. Buttresses may therefore assist the tree to withstand stresses due to wind or gravity. Yet they do not always occur where they would seem to be most needed. They seldom appear on trees outside the tropics and are, on the whole, more abundant in sheltered lowlands than in windy situations. A variety of other hypotheses relate their existence to light and humidity, to the conduction of nutrients in their trunks, and to the nature, texture and aeration of the soil. But no theory is entirely satisfactory.

For all their aspect of strength and solidity, buttresses cannot prevent many of the forest's loftiest trees from crashing daily to the ground as seeping water undermines their foundations and sudden gales blast their crowns. When they topple they bring inferior trees down with them, cutting a swath of havoc in the green. Prostrate, they reveal the inadequate foundations on which they climbed so high.

ACROBATS OF THE CANOPY

DOWN the ages incomputable numbers of animals, the hunted and the hunters, have made the trees their sanctuary—some temporarily, some for longer intervals, and a few permanently. Today no habitat on earth harbors so many arboreal creatures as the rain forest, no rain forest so many as the American hylaea.

Here abide the greatest acrobats on earth. The monkeys of the Old World, agile as they are, cannot hang by their tails. It is only the monkeys of America that possess this skill. Nor are primates the only residents thus endowed; for a prehensile tail, owned elsewhere only by the familiar opossum, is the common property of such unrelated hylaeans as the coonlike kinkajou, a porcupine and two arboreal anteaters. At dawn and dusk the illusive aerial spaces of the canopy assume the aspect of a carnival tent where, to the jeers and imprecations of many gaudy birds, the leaping acrobats of the middle branches mount their death-defying show—"mountebank angels," the naturalist W. H. Hudson called them, "living their fantastic lives far above earth in a halfway heaven of their own."

The American monkeys are called ceboids, after *Cebus*, the familiar capuchin or organ-grinder's monkey. But their unique group also includes marmosets, owl monkeys, sakis, spider monkeys, squirrel monkeys, howler monkeys and a few other genera. Among these the star gymnast is the skinny, intelligent spider monkey. Hanging head down like a trapeze artist from the loop of a liana, he may suddenly give a short swing, launch himself into space and, soaring outward and downward across a 50-foot void of air, lightly catch a bough on which he spied a shining berry. No owl monkey or saki can match his leap, for their arms are shorter, their tails untalented. The marmosets, smallest of the tribe, tough, noisy hoodlums that travel in gangs, are also capable of leaps into space, but their landings are rough: smack against a tree trunk with arms and legs spread wide.

The arenas of the canopy are also thoroughfares for competent hunters who walk sedately among the branches without hazarding dignity or health in reckless leaps. Among these are members of the raccoon family—the kinkajou, who uses his prehensile tail mostly when something good is out of reach; and the coati, who frequently descends to the ground for fishing trips and other forays and diversions. Here too with leisurely gait amble two relatives of the giant anteater—the golden-brown tamandua and the silky anteater. Of the climbing cats the most adept is the dainty ocelot, though the jaguar, yaguarundi and margay occasionally join him in the upper stories.

At the other end of the food chain, the only undeviating vegetarians within the canopy are the coendou, a porcupine with prehensile tail; frolicsome squirrels like the pigmy, *Sciurillus;* and the two-toed and three-toed sloths. The latter are also the slowest and dullest of eye, ear and wit. Hanging upside down with their powerful, clawed hands, they move slowly among the branches, munching leaves. So low-geared is the sloth's nervous system that usually lethal doses of some snake venoms will not affect him, nor can the most appalling injuries inflicted by his enemies, the eagles and jaguars, awake him from his lethargy. Utterly defenseless, unable to fight or flee, the sloth's only protection is camouflage. For this purpose his long hair is encrusted with a green alga that resembles lichen or moss. When asleep in thick foliage, his head tucked slothfully between his legs, he is virtually invisible.

In the tents of the canopy even the reptiles perform feats of grace and daring. The tiny, chameleonlike ho-ko-bee lizard not only leaps prodigiously but lands upside down on the underside of branches far above his head, clinging by means of adhesive pads on his feet. The iguana, a specialist in high diving, will plunge as much as 80 feet from an overhanging limb into a shallow pool below. The green tree boa and the venomous little parakeet snake softly rustle after prey to the very extremities of the tiniest twigs, while the heavier rainbow boa coils his six-foot length around a branch and hangs in ambush, waiting for arboreal rodents and opossums.

Amid the carnival and carnage, the birds provide bright color and loud music—the cotinga and his relatives, the red chatterer and red-cheeked woodpecker; the flamboyant parrots and macaws; thick-billed toucans and toucanets; flycatchers and giant orioles called oropendulas. Here in the stadia of the trees these birds live out their lives, seldom venturing into the shadows below or the eagle-haunted upper air.

RED CHATTERER   MACAWS
    OROPENDULA   WHITE-FACED SAKI   WHITE-FACED SAKI
MOTMOT   OWL MONKEYS   KINKAJOU
   SILKY ANTEATER   KINKAJOU

MANDUA TOUCANET   PARROT   COENDOU   OCELOT
   RED-BACKED SAKI   MACAWS   COATI SPIDER MONKEYS   SPIDER MONKEYS
-KO-BEE LIZARD   IGUANA   SULPHUR-THROATED TOUCAN   TOUCANET GREEN BOA TWO-TOED SLOTH PIGMY SQUIRREL THREE-TOED SLOTH
   TREE LIZARD   PARAKEET SNAKE   BLACK MIDAS MARMOSET   COTINGA   CRESTED FLYCATCHER   RAINBOW BOA

235

A LIANA dangles in knotted loops and loose spirals. Climbing plants like Monkey Ladder (*above*) often clamber into saplings and ride them as they grow.

THE ROOF OF THE FOREST, seen here through a leafy window in the dome of a 160-foot emergent tree, rolls away like a sea of green, foam-flecked with flowers. In the distance another giant emergent tree that has broken through the canopy towers above its neighbors and sprawls out under the sun. The

THE HANGING GARDENS

ATOP the canopy, far above the twilit crypts and shadowy arcades, the countenance of the forest is transfigured. Bathed in warm light, the rolling uplands of leaves create an enchanted parkland whose green domes are garlanded the year around with flowers that exhale perfumes constantly in the sweet mobile air. Not all the blossoms in these hidden gardens spring from the crowns of the trees themselves. Many stem from independent plants whose impulse toward light has placed them by strange mechanisms in the pinnacles of the forest.

One such group embraces the climbing plants, or lianas. Akin in habit to ivy, clematis, woodbine and other climbers of temperate woodlands, the lianas of the forest achieve astonishing dimensions, developing woody stems as much as two feet thick or 500 feet long, and competing vigorously with the trees themselves for light and space. Their fantastic forms festoon the forest with gigantic loops, spirals and arabesques. Aloft, they braid their stems from branch to branch, from crown to crown, closing the canopy, filling every empty leaf space, and weaving their own fabric into the vaulted roof so

PENDANT IN THE SHADE, a liana flower hangs below the canopy, accessible to butterflies and bees which never ascend above the roof. Suspending blossoms on long stalks is a device common to many rain forest trees and climbing plants.

crowns of *Vochysia* trees bristle on every hand with sprays of yellow blossoms, and the lookout tree itself is filled with the delicate, purple-hearted white trumpets and subtle scent of the basket liana (*left*). The large, rounded, deep green leaves in the right foreground belong to an enormous air plant.

AN AIR TREE 35 feet high grows among smaller air plants on the limb of a tree 120 feet above the ground. Its long thin roots dangle to the soil below.

inextricably that even if a tree is severed at the base it often cannot fall. Inured to shade in early life, lianas are essentially sun-lovers; quickened by its rays they bejewel the tree crowns with many blooms.

Even stranger than the lianas are the epiphytes, or air plants—a large group including orchids, cacti, aroids, bromeliads, lichens and mosses—which flower on high in the trees without benefit of ordinary soil. Attaching themselves to fissures and crannies in the branches of trees and lianas, most put forth a fine meshwork of roots which collect dust and plant debris and in time create a soil of their own; the roots of many harbor ants which augment the process by excretion and death. Since water is also a problem, epiphytes are adapted, like desert plants, to sustain periods of drought by quick absorption and careful conservation. Many develop rosettes of overlapping leaves which catch and hold water and incidentally serve as breeding places for mosquitoes, frogs and swarms of tiny invertebrates. Others send dangling roots down through the canopy until they can take nourishment directly from the earth itself, whereupon they may grow into large and burdensome trees atop the trees that cradled them. A few become stranglers, fabricating their own massive trunks around their supporting trees until they smother them completely and they die.

UPLIFTED TO THE SUN, the pink blossoms of another liana bloom in the well-lighted reaches of the treetops where they attract the gaudy butterflies of the roof. Delicately scented themselves, their stalks when broken smell of garlic.

PAVILIONS IN THE SKY

THE frontier regions of every realm of nature inevitably attract the adventurer, the vagabond and the marauder. And so it is with the hylaea, where only the most athletic and audacious climbers dare to scale the vertiginous scaffoldings of the highest treetops in the border zone between forest and sky. Here they not only expose themselves to every perversity of wind and weather, but to fierce aerial pirates that patrol the tropic skies: owls, eagles, falcons and hawks. By day the high-climbing animals usually remain safely below the canopy; it is mostly at night that they mount aloft to gather the nuts and fleshy fruits that flourish on the heights.

Most notable of the high perch artists are the squirrel monkeys, capuchins and red howlers. Of these, only the squirrel monkey lacks a prehensile tail; yet, agile and assured, he stands recklessly erect in places where squirrels themselves will not venture. A lover of heights, he seldom descends from his eminences, save to sleep or seek shelter from storms. The capuchins are less sensitive to rain—and, indeed, to any of life's adversities. So strong in body are they, so undiscriminating in diet, so insatiable in mating that they have succeeded numerically beyond all other South American monkeys.

The hylaea's most conspicuous primate, however, is the seldom seen but compellingly obtrusive red howler. Endowed by nature with a grotesque, humanoid face with a full, pointed beard, the howler's supreme attribute is his voice. Rendered fortissimo, the song of the howler is composed of the most electrifying, ear-splitting and blood-chilling series of animal sounds ever produced on earth. Perhaps the best description of a howler concert was set down by W. H. Hudson, in his famous novel of the rain forest, *Green Mansions:* "All at once, close to me sounded a cry, rising at the end to a shriek so loud, piercing and unearthly in character that the blood seemed to freeze in my veins. . . . It may give some faint conception of the tremendous power and awful character of the sound thus produced by their combined voices when I say that this animal—miscalled 'howler'— would out-roar the mightiest lion that ever woke the echoes of an African wilderness."

The howler's unparalleled vocal powers derive from an anatomical peculiarity: a hollow bone at the base of his tongue, specially shaped and enlarged into an apple-sized sound chamber that amplifies his vocal vibrations to incredible volume. How many choristers generally participate in a howler cantata is a matter of uncertainty, for it is performed from curtained stages, and in captivity howlers will not speak with full voice, but pine away wretchedly and soon die. In the forest their howls can be heard for miles and sound like a full choir in complex atonal harmony—yet many zoologists say only one or two voices are involved. The burden of their concert is clearer, for first one group, then another takes it up and hurls it back and forth across the forest roof, each proclaiming in menacing tones the extent of their territories. From late afternoon through the night, the challenges are made and answered intermittently, but towards sunup they rise in volume and blend into a continuous cacophony of snarls.

As the sky reddens in the east the last wails die away and a new series of sounds issues from the green belfries of the roof. Now, the monkeys are subjected to much irritable scolding from early-rising, bad-tempered parrots and macaws, umbrella birds, doves and toucanets. There is need for haste. For at any moment a drifting shadow may darken the green tapestry below. Then suddenly, silently, the tyrant of the treetops will descend from the sky—the cruel-taloned harpy eagle, with three-foot wings outspread. When he plummets, the eagle seldom misses his prey, whether a leaping monkey which he grasps in mid-air and bears off screaming, or a stupid sloth which he tears away limb by limb from the branch to which it soundlessly, stubbornly clings. Meanwhile overhead soars the feathered jackal of the skies, the huge king vulture.

The time of danger is now at hand, and amid the encircling mists of morning the monkeys clamber down to their shadowed playgrounds and dormitories in the canopy below, leaving the watchtowers of the forest to the birds. During the long, hot day, cloud swifts and other migrants wing past on their journeys to distant lands. Parrots and toucans parade their bright-painted feathers. And the tiny humming bird, *Chrysolampis mosquitus*, poises on invisible wings above a nectar-filled flower that has opened its tiny trumpet to the sun.

KING VULTURE	DOVE	DOVE
SQUIRREL MONKEY		CAPUCHIN MONKEY
CAPUCHIN MONKEY	GECKO	SQUIRREL MONKEYS

CLOUD SWIFTS   SQUIRREL MONKEY   PARROTS   MACAW   RED HOWLER MONKEY

HARPY EAGLE   UMBRELLA BIRD   MACAW   RED HOWLER MONKEY   MACAW

TOUCANET   POMPADOUR CHATTERER   RED HOWLER MONKEY   HUMMING BIRD   RED HOWLER MONKEYS

TREEHOPPERS and their white larvae feed on young red leaves while stinging ants stand guard. The treehoppers secrete a substance called "honey dew" which the ants lap up. In return the ants protect them from predatory insects.

WORKERS AND WASTERS

FROM the attic of the forest to its secret mazes beneath the floor the insects swarm in illimitable hordes. Their species alone are counted in hundreds of thousands; their disguises defy classification. In their arcane world mimicry attains its apogee: here leaves may hop, bits of bark may crawl, flowers may fly, butterflies may wear the garb of wasps, and caterpillars the sinister livery of spiders.

In the cycle of forest life insects play a dual role—as agents of destruction and regeneration, as wasters and workers. Most plants depend on bees and other insects for pollination. Conversely, innumerable trees are riddled by termites and beetle grubs; incalculable masses of foliage are destroyed by grasshoppers and leaf-cutting ants. Most dramatic of the insect populations are the army ants whose blindly marching legions ravage the forest floor of all life unable to flee them, and the huge *Morpho* butterflies whose iridescent wings shine like stained glass in the sun-touched galleries aloft.

A SUNNY-HUED BUTTERFLY (*Heliconius phyllis*) lights momentarily in a clearing on the forest floor, relying on his gaudy colors to warn birds that his taste is bitter. In general a roof-dweller, he sometimes descends in sunny glades where trees have fallen or skims above the surface of slow creeks.

A KATYDID perches on a branch like a growing leaf. The strangest feature of the katydid's perfect camouflage is that its two wings, artfully veined

BRIGHT AND VENOMOUS, A SIX-INCH CATERPILLAR SWARMS DOWN A STEM TO GORGE ITSELF ON LEAVES. CONTACT WITH ITS POISONED SPINES CAN MAKE A MAN ILL FOR DAYS

and blotched as if with blight, curve in opposite directions, cupping downward on one side and up on the other, yet somehow sustaining it in flight.

AN IRIDESCENT BUTTERFLY (*Morpho adonis*) spreads the five-inch span of its glittering sapphire wings. Ordinarily it flits languidly among the highest treetops, feeding on nectar. The large wings of morphos are often frayed in passing through foliage or in combat with other members of their species.

A FUNGUS FOREST half an inch high springs into being when tiny toadstools arise from rain-moist leaves. The main filamentous mass of the fungus *Marasmius* spreads beneath the litter; the toadstools are its reproductive shoots. Each one has, under its umbrella-shaped head, a number of slits or gills lined with spores. When ripe the microscopic spores are shot off by the millions and float away into the air. Most never germinate, but a few survive and beget new fungi.

THE FOREST GRAVEYARD

FOR many hours after a tropical storm, raindrops trickle down, leaf by leaf, through the close-spun layers of the canopy and fall to the forest floor. Lighting on humus and leaf litter, on fallen limbs and rotting logs, they abet the processes of decomposition and decay. As though to signalize this charnel work, tiny, brightly painted toadstools rise and stud the forest aisles with their small monuments.

Abstractly flowerlike in shape and pigmentation, each is the short-lived reproductive shoot of some fungus whose invisible root filaments are prying apart the tissues and sucking up the goodness of some dead or dying organism on which it lives. Some are molds so tiny that their presence is manifested only by a blotch of color on the surface across which they creep; others are minute mushroom shapes lifted a few millimeters in the air by delicate stalks rooted on a fallen leaf or twig; still others spread gross platters two feet or more in diameter across the bark of fallen trees. Fungi, however, are

A LEANING DOME two inches high is reared by the gill fungus *Lepiota*. Like the monument of some elfin cult, it flourishes throughout the tropics.

A MOSSY NEST built by termites out of chewed wood wraps a burl around a sapling's trunk. By eating wood, termites help fungi clear up debris.

VERMILION PARASOLS of gill fungus *Mycena* are edible mushrooms, despite their poisonous color. Unlike most fungus shoots, they live for months.

A BRIMMING BOWL of the cup fungus *Cookeina*, half an inch across, perches beside a rotting log. In structure this fungus is the antithesis of gill fungi, for it contains its spores in capsules on its upper surface. At maturity the spores are fired upward by hydraulic action and scattered like bird shot in the air. In time the disintegrating agencies of fungus and water convert the log and nearby leaf litter into humus which continually washes down into the soil.

not the only agents of decomposition in the rain forest. Collaborating with them in the never-ending chore of cleaning up the forest refuse are bacteria, protozoa, worms and various insects—most notably the termites, or white ants, which devour wood and swiftly riddle every wind-thrown bough or splintered stump that litters the forest floor.

Even the stoutest log of glass-hard wood may be converted in a few years by their voracious jaws into a spongy shell scarred with the claw marks of every perching bird. And while the termites and fungi tunnel the tissues of fallen trees, bacteria are at work, rapidly transforming wood into humus, and humus into nitrogen compounds, carbon dioxide and mineral matter. So, in time, all living things from the tallest tree to the smallest bird—gauzy leaf and woody limb, spent flower and errant seed, beetle corpse and butterfly wing—return to the earth in death, dissolved in the gentle dripping of the filtered rain.

As in every liturgy of nature, themes of death and decay are succeeded by those of regeneration. Over every wound opened by the fall of a giant tree, by fire or winds or the depredations of man, the forest ultimately repairs its scars. But the process of healing is slow and complex. As soon as a gash is torn in the forest cover, sunlight floods in, exciting a vigorous outburst of swift-growing invaders—first ephemerals, herbaceous weeds, grasses and scrambling sedges; later, shrubs, climbers and small trees, all glorying in the golden sun. In a few incredible weeks the ground is colonized with dense tangles of undergrowth. Then larger trees appear, soft-tissued, light-loving, mounting with astonishing eagerness toward the sky—often 24 feet in two years. Meanwhile the spread of the native trees is immobilized by the blinding barrier of the sun, for their saplings require shade; exposed to the glaring sunlight they are stillborn or quickly choke in the convolutions of the intruding vegetation.

Yet the triumph of the intruders is evanescent. Dependent on the sun, they carry the seeds of their own destruction. Fighting for light, they weave a new canopy that sheds an ever-thicker, ever-darker shade. Their offspring, light-demanding, die in the shadow of their progenitors, leaving space for the shade-tolerant saplings of the primary trees to move slowly back into their original domain. How long these processes require depends on the breach in the forest roof. Small trees which do not bring down others in their death throes may regenerate their kind in a decade. But the toppling of giants in swaths of broad destruction may inflict wounds that persist for a century and even longer. Devastation by such cataclysms as fire following drought may alter the forest mosaic forever.

Until relatively recent times man exercised little effect on the rain forest, for it was largely uninhabited save by hunting aborigines who knew little of agriculture. Today the forest fabric has been disturbed by Western civilization, by the demolition of vast tracts of forest for rubber, coffee and cocoa plantations and their subsequent abandonment and replacement by secondary growth. Even more destructive has been the spread of subsistence agriculture among the native populations. Throughout the hylaea, not only on the fringes and along the riverbanks but deep in the green heart of the forest, native tribesmen raze patches of timber, burn the fallen trees and plant such crops as cassava, maize, yams, bananas and hill rice. At once the character of the soil is changed. The glaring sun destroys the humus. The torrential rains, beating down in full fury, erode the naked surface layers. After a season or two the impoverished plot is abandoned and the chaos of secondary growth overruns the maimed earth.

Throughout extensive areas of the tropics the stately primeval forest has given way to scrub, savannah and the jumble of secondary growth. Just as the virgin forests of Europe and North America were laid low by man's improvidence, so those of the tropics are now vanishing—only their destruction may be encompassed in decades instead of centuries. A few authorities hold that, except for government reserves, the earth's great rain forests may vanish within a generation. The economic loss will be incalculable, for the primary rain forests are rich sources of timber (mahogany, teak) and such by-products as resins, gums, cellulose, camphor and rattans. No one, indeed, can compute their resources, for of the thousands of species that compose the forest cover, there are only a few whose properties have been studied with a view to commercial use.

Most important of all, the primeval rain forest is a reservoir of genetic diversity, a dynamic center of evolution whence the rest of the world's plant life has been continually enriched with new forms. Inevitably the destruction of the rain forest would alter the future course of botanical evolution. If specimens of the plant communities of the primeval rain forest are to persevere for future generations, extensive reserves must be defended from the acquisitive hand of man, whose ruthless ax would expose them to the ravages of sun and rain. For it is man, not nature, who in the final analysis is the agent of "the destruction that wasteth at noonday."

THE WOODS
OF HOME

PART XII
THE WOODS OF HOME

Loveliest of nature's realms, the leafy forests of earth's temperate zones are the product of climatic extremes that control the cycle of the seasons

The same leaves over and over again!	Before the leaves can mount again	They must be pierced by flowers and put
They fall from giving shade above	To fill the trees with another shade,	Beneath the feet of dancing flowers.
To make one texture of faded brown	They must go down past things coming up.	However it is in some other world
And fit the earth like a leather glove.	They must go down into the dark decayed.	I know that this is the way in ours.

ROBERT FROST, *In Hardwood Groves*

ALTHOUGH man has colonized the planet from its white polar regions to the hot midriff of the equator, he has clustered most thickly in those middle latitudes where the vagrant sun annually contrives the miracle of the seasons. It is here, in the so-called temperate regions, with their stimulating inconstancy of temperature, their alternation of summer languor and winter bite, that he has flourished most vigorously and evolved his most intricate societies. And it is here that nature has fashioned the loveliest of earth's adornments—the ever-changing woodlands whose yearly cycle of death and renascence has evoked the wonder and gratitude of mankind since the first savage minstrel sang the first hymn to spring.

Paradoxically, the temperate zones are not truly temperate at all. In deep winter they are recurrently gripped by cold almost as bitter as the breath of the Arctic; in deep summer they experience heat almost as intense as the shimmering fervors of the tropics. Hence all living things that have their abode within these middle latitudes must adapt themselves to antipodal climatic extremes. In the same way that the towering, forever green trees of the tropical rain forest are products of unending summer, and the spiny, water-hoarding flora of the desert are creations of a parched and thirsty domain, so the well-loved woods that grace our homeland hills and valleys represent a response to the excesses of a fickle climate. It is the annual rise and fall of the temperature that induces the bursting buds of spring, the lush leaf of summer, the gold and scarlet foliage of fall and winter's barren boughs.

The greatest environmental threat that these temperate zone woods must face is the physiological drought of winter, when freezing temperatures transmute water into ice, thus rendering it unavailable for use. To protect themselves in this hostile season they hibernate: they shed their leaves and enter a period of dormancy that endures until returning spring. Trees and plants that have developed this mechanism are called "deciduous"—from the Latin verb *decidere*, meaning "to fall off." During the summer they demand huge quantities of water for their broad leaf surfaces constantly lose moisture which is evaporated directly from the living cells. Stripped of their leaves, however, deciduous trees become as impervious to drought as any desert cactus. Growth and assimilation virtually cease. The thick armor of bark on their trunks and boughs, the tough scales that envelop each bud provide immunity to desiccating winter winds.

Almost all deciduous forests on earth lie in the Northern Hemisphere. South of the equator the continental land masses taper off into the sea at the latitudes where proper climatic conditions might prevail. But in the north three great bands of forest braid a green necklace around the globe. One reaches from the British Isles across Europe to western Asia. Another mantles portions of China, Korea and Japan. But the largest and richest deciduous forest in the world grows in the eastern U.S. Bounded on the north by the dark evergreens of Canada and on the south by the subtropic vegetation of the Gulf states, the forest realm rolls westward to the wide prairies of the continental heartland. Here the frontier between deciduous forest and grassland (the two dominant forms of vegetation in the U.S.) is limned by rain. Grasslands flourish where rainfall averages 10–30 inches a year; deciduous forests require more than 30 inches.

To the eye of urban man, who may casually agree with Vergil that "the woods please us above all things," the green arcades of a leafy forest seem undiversified; one woodland glade looks much like any other. Yet in actuality the forest is a complex domain within which the botanist distinguishes many plant communities. Thus, although the chief components of the American forest are the oak, maple, beech, basswood, hickory, ash and elm, their relationships vary from place to place. The western edges of the forest are dominated by an oak-hickory association. Along the Canadian border deciduous, coniferous and mixed forests alternate in a zone where northern and southern species continually strive for supremacy. These patterns within the overall tapestry were woven by events in prehistoric times—by climatic changes, the uplifting of mountain ranges and the advance and retreat of glaciers. Then came man, with fire and ax.

Today farms and secondary growth occupy most of the realm once blanketed by the mightiest deciduous forest in the world. Out of 400,000 square miles of primeval woods that greeted the incredulous eyes of the first Europeans, only 1,600 square miles now remain in unspoiled state. One such tract survives barely 50 miles from New York City on the rolling piedmont of New Jersey. It is known as Mettler's Woods, and it is this small (65 acres) but truly virgin forest that the pictures on the following pages disclose. The trees and plant life it harbors represent an unbroken succession dating back to the end of the ice ages when deciduous trees reconquered the land in the wake of the last glacier. Its preservation in primeval state derives from the fact that one family has maintained continuous ownership since 1701, consistently refusing, generation after generation, to allow it to be cut for timber, cleared for farming or scarred by fire.

As in every forest, the green colonnades of Mettler's Woods ascend in several tiers or galleries to the forest roof. The canopy trees, which average 75 feet in height, are the oaks and hickories, reinforced here and there with an occasional beech, sugar maple or ash. Midway between the upper canopy and the forest floor extends a complete understory of flowering dogwood, which in spring suffuses the forest aisles with hovering clouds of white bloom. Far below lies the shrub layer, ruled by maple-leafed viburnum, interspersed with spicebush, black haw and arrowwood. Clinging to the floor, stippling the red-brown soil with changing colors, are the woodland herbs— May apple, spring beauty, violet, anemone and a bright galaxy of others. On these four stages the pageantry of the seasons is annually revealed—a recurring miracle that moved the 18th Century English poet James Thomson to declare in his "A Hymn on the Seasons":

These, as they change, Almighty Father, these
Are but the varied God. The rolling year
Is full of Thee. . . .

IN APRIL ON THE FOREST FLOOR the never-ending sequence of the seasons unfolds as the new plants arise from the faded leaf litter of the vanished year. The small violet and the sturdy green skunk cabbage, spangled now with shining drops of rain, annually brighten the procession of spring. As the months advance these dead leaves will slowly disintegrate and return again to the soil. By the middle of May the floor of the woods will be freshly overlaid with varicolored blooms.

THE RUSH OF SPRING

IN the still depths of the woods the tides of spring rise from the forest floor, quietly at first, then quickening, gathering tempo, surging among the layered branches, mounting through the shrubs and dogwood till they engulf at last the promontories of the greatest oaks. Late in March, as the frost dissolves in the obdurate soil, the little ground herbs stir, for they must flower before the closing of the canopy deprives them of the sun. Long before the fading of the final snows, the green fingers of the skunk cabbage have thrust upward through the streamside mud. The buds of the May apple and the spring beauty arise from the matted leaf litter, along with the first shoots of the demure violets.

Meanwhile secret changes are taking place within the hearts of trees. The warming of air and ground sucks streams of sweet sap upward to the buds, wrapped in snug protective scales. In response the tiny leaflets within each bud begin to grow, forcing the scales to part, revealing the glint of green and gold. By mid-April the cherry wears clusters of white flowers on every striped branch, the spicebush veils the moist places with a yellow mist, and the red maple is hung with ruby blooms.

As April yields to May, spring comes with a rush, flooding the earth with waves of flowers, Swiftly the forest floor is carpeted with tassels of Solomon's seal, yellow bellwort and wild geranium. Overhead the dogwood blossoms white-feather the gold-flecked air. Here and there white bouquets of viburnum begin to gleam against the fresh new green of its leaves.

Finally the trees take up the cry of spring. The leaves of the sugar maples, the cherries and the beeches swell rapidly, and the long hairy catkins of the red oaks litter the ground. The candlelike buds on the hickory boughs explode in an emerald burst. By the middle of May the grand period of growth is at its peak. And now, as the laggard oaks, last to extend their leaves, weave the missing patterns of the canopy, summer stands quietly at the edge of the woods.

THE MONARCH OAK rises tall and straight to the budding canopy of spring. Aloft, its branches intertwine with those of a neighboring beech (*left*) and a black gum (*right*). On the following pages this same oak is shown in other seasons.

IN A SUN-FLECKED GLADE OF METTLER'S WOODS, OPENED BY THE HURRICANE OF 1950, BLOSSOMS OF FLOWERING DOGWOOD GLEAM WHITE AGAINST THE CLEAR YELLOW-GREEN

A FIVE-DAY-OLD FAWN struggles to its feet in a leafy retreat where its spotted coat blends perfectly with the dappled sunlight. Their camouflage and lack of scent protect fawns from predators during the month before they begin to wander.

A BABY SKUNK investigates a fallen log. Born in late April or early May, usually six or eight to a family, young skunks are playful as kittens. Unlike other mammals which disperse in the fall, skunks stay together as a family for a full year.

A PAIR OF BABY RACCOONS frolic beside the stream. Although raccoons are normally nocturnal animals, during the springtime mother raccoons often bring their babies out of their hollow tree home to play in the sunshine. By June they will be weaned; then they will begin to accompany their mother on her nightly hunting trips, learning how to catch frogs and fish, find turtle eggs, dig for earthworms and pull rotten logs apart in quest of insects and tasty grubs.

FOLD OUT, DO NOT TEAR

THE MAY APPLE blankets the forest floor throughout the spring. Its hidden white flowers come to bloom in the first weeks of May and are all but spent by June. During the summer its large yellow fruit ripens among the withered leaves.

THE JACK-IN-THE-PULPIT, a relative of the skunk cabbage, is a sturdy evangelist of early spring. It bears a number of tiny flowers on a club-shaped spadix (the jack) which is hooded by a green-and-purple, striped spathe (the pulpit).

CHANGING ANGLES OF SUNLIGHT FROM LEFT TO RIGHT. THE GREEN CARPET OF THE FOREST FLOOR IS COMPOSED OF MAY APPLE LEAVES. THE BIG TREE AT LEFT IS A BLACK OAK

THE SKUNK CABBAGE, earliest sign of spring, spreads its bold green leaves amidst the streamside mud. Even in the wintertime their initial spears sometimes probe tentatively upward through the snow or pierce the thin ice film beside the woodland brook. In March their streaked, purplish hoods unfold to reveal a spadix covered with tiny flowers that lure insects for pollination. After the flowers come the large, foul-smelling leaves which have given the plant its name.

OF THE STILL UNFOLDING LEAVES OF THE LARGER TREES. THIS WOODLAND SCENE, TAKEN WITH A ROTATING CAMERA, COVERS AN ARC OF 160°, THUS ACCOUNTING FOR THE

MOURNING DOVE   GRAY SQUIRREL   DOWNY WOODPECKER

BLACK RACER   GRAY FOX

DEER MOUSE   RED FOX CUBS

OPOSSUM   CROW   CHIPMUNK

RED-BACKED SALAMANDER   BOX TURTLE   RING-NECKED SNAKE   RED FOX   RACCOON AND YOUNG

MOLE   WOOD FROG   FOWLER'S TOA

THE FOREST DWELLERS

FOR the many shy animals that inhabit the woods, spring is a time of domestic enterprise. Awakening in their underground dormitories, the hibernators come forth lean and irritable, complaining of their empty bellies. The furry mammals discard their winter coats for light summer wear, and most of them become involved at once in obstetrical matters. In the trees the male birds, parading fine feathers and demonstrating their vocal range, swagger about trying to make a favorable impression. "All the veneration of Spring," Emerson observed, "connects itself with love. . . .

Since the clearing of the eastern forests many animals have learned to combine the shelter of woodlands with the diverse food supply of open fields and farms. Predators, like the foxes red and gray, hunt in the fields by night, returning to cover in the daylight hours. At dusk an entire raccoon family may descend from its tree house in quest of mice, frogs or insects. The striped skunk and opossum are also night rangers. Gentle, unaggressive, the skunk walks abroad secure in his weapon of liquid musk; his principal enemies are man and the horned owl. The omnivorous opossum will eat anything from snakes to nuts. The most bloodthirsty hunters of the woods are the weasel and the tiny shrew. The latter will attack prey larger than itself and can eat its own weight in flesh every day.

At the other terminus of the food spectrum stand the vegetarians and the hunted. Largest of these, and largest animal in the woods, is

FLYING SQUIRREL				WHITE-TAILED DEER		SCARLET TANAGER
	WEASEL		BLACK-CAPPED CHICKADEE	CARDINALS	GARTER SNAKE	
	TOWHEE	SHORT-TAILED SHREW	FAWNS	SONG SPARROW AND NEST		WOODCHUCK
	STRIPED SKUNK		BLACK-AND-WHITE WARBLER		COTTONTAIL RABBIT AND YOUNG	

the white-tailed deer. The cottontail rabbit survives by proliferation, as does the deer mouse which breeds throughout the summer. The stodgy woodchuck dwells snugly in a fortified burrow, while the mole passes virtually his entire life underground. The arboreal rodents find sanctuary in the trees, though the chipmunk is a ground feeder and the so-called flying squirrel cannot really fly, but merely glides, supported by a membrane between his legs. The alert, provident gray squirrel, once nearly exterminated by wholesale slaughter and the destruction of nut forests, has again increased his numbers.

Most secretive of the forest dwellers are the reptiles: the box turtle, the garter snake, the ring-necked snake and the speedy, carnivorous black racer. Among amphibians the red-backed salamander is unusual in laying its eggs on land. The wood frog and Fowler's toad are water breeders. During the mating season they serenade their loved ones with distinctive voices, the frog in a cadenza of sharp "chucks," the toad in a penetrating monotone.

Of all the populations of the forest by far the most conspicuous are the birds. Among the year-round residents of Mettler's Woods are the handsome cardinal, the rowdy crow, the downy woodpecker and the black-capped chickadee. One of the first migrants to arrive each year is the sweet-voiced song sparrow, who generally shows up in April, soon followed by the mourning dove making melancholy moan, the towhee, the black-and-white warbler and the scarlet tanager, gaudiest of summer birds. By June the galleries of the forest echo with their liquid notes, and in innumerable hidden nests lie the delicately tinted eggs within whose fragile shells new life begins to stir.

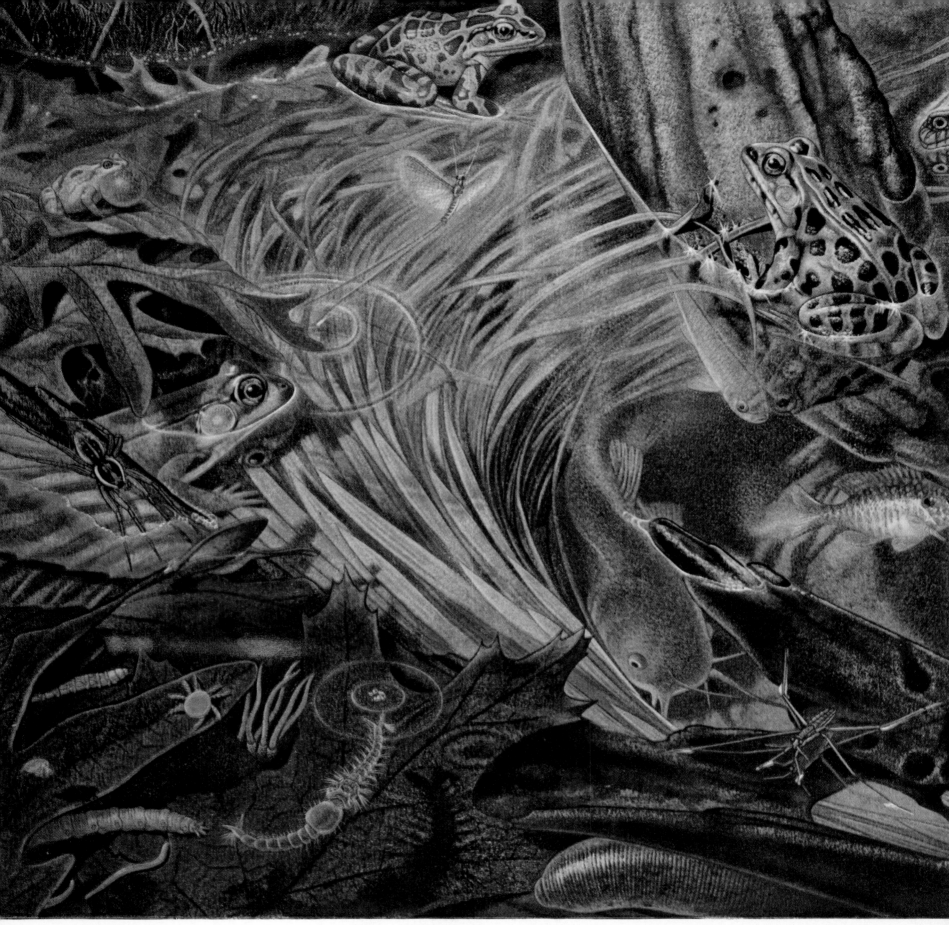

SPRING PEEPER
FISHER SPIDER   GREEN FROG   PICKEREL FROG
HORSEFLY LARVA   WATER MITE TUBIFEX WORMS   MOSQUITO LARVA   MAY FLY   SHINER   LEOPARD FROG
WATER FLEA   CRANE FLY LARVA   BULLHEAD   SUNFISH
ROUNDWORMS (NEMATODES)   PHANTOM LARVA   WATER STRIDER
                                                                                                 HORSE LEECH

THE WOODLAND STREAM

IN THE low places of the forest small watercourses sometimes thread their way beneath the boughs, creating a subsidiary province of life within the greater woodland domain. Such is the case in Mettler's Woods where a narrow rivulet called Spooky Brook flows quietly between shallow banks. Vanishing in summer, leaving only a wrinkle of mud behind, it overflows its margins each spring, flooding the land on either side and offering hospitality to a multitude of water-loving creatures. Fish and reptiles then move upstream from the river below. Choirs of frogs convene and shake the air with nightly oratorios. Aquatic insects pirouette upon the silvery surface.

The overlords of the stream are the larger vertebrates, of whom the undisputed autocrat is the irascible snapping turtle, biggest of fresh water turtles (up to 40 pounds). Attended by his two smaller cousins, the musk turtle and the mud turtle, he lurks half hidden on the bottom, ready to bite viciously at any edible morsel that wanders past his horny beak. The only other reptile in the stream is the harmless water snake which skims the surface at night in quest of small prey. Although many amphibians live on land in adulthood, most of them return to water each spring to breed and practice part singing. Top tenor of the frog glee club is the spring peeper, who turns up in March and whose throat, when he sings, inflates like bubble gum. In mid-April he is reinforced by the resonant baritones of the leopard frog and spotted pickerel frog, and by the green frog's bull-fiddle bass. Their silent

WATER SNAKE   DAMSEL FLIES

            PICKEREL   WHIRLIGIG BEETLE

FAIRY SHRIMP   POND SNAIL   SNAPPING TURTLE   BACK SWIMMER   MUD TURTLE

FINGERNAIL CLAM   HAIRWORMS   PREDACEOUS DIVING BEETLE   MUSK TURTLE

      ASELLUS   SCUD   TWO-LINED SALAMANDER   WORM LEECH

relative, the two-lined salamander, is more aquatic than the frogs, spending most of his life in the water.

The largest of the transient fish is the pickerel who, from his ambush in floating leaves, recurrently rushes forth to gulp a tiny jeweled sunfish or a silvery shiner. The whiskered catfish or bullhead prowls the stream bed by night, feeding on insect larvae, snails and fairy shrimp. Among the permanent residents of the stream many, like the pond snail, the leeches and the fingernail clam, survive the summer drought and winter cold by burying themselves in the mud. Other bottom lovers include the *Tubifex*, aquatic counterpart of the common earthworm, and the primitive hairworms and nematodes.

Although all adult insects breathe air, many of them lay their eggs in water. So the green channels of the stream glimmer in spring with the translucent wings of the short-lived May fly and of damsel flies mating in mid-air. The surface is etched with the rippled tracks of the long-legged water strider, the dizzy whirligig beetle, the back swimmer and a tiny crustacean, the water flea. On the muddy bottom the scud and *Asellus* scavenge for organic debris, and the predaceous diving beetle stalks his quarry, carrying his oxygen supply in a tiny bubble underneath his wing covers. Just below the surface, mosquito larvae float head downward, breathing air through short tubes and falling victim occasionally to a mobile phantom larva which swallows them whole. Under leaves at the edge of the stream, horsefly and crane fly larvae slowly mature. Here too, among the lush streamside plants, two members of the arachnid class, the big-eyed fisher spider and the small but brilliant water mite, hunt their living prey.

255

IN EARLY JUNE the final niches of the leafy canopy are sealed, admitting only intermittent shafts of sunlight to gild the trunks of the great trees. The white oak pictured here is the same tree that appears on the third page of this chapter.

THE FULLNESS OF SUMMER

WITH the closing of the canopy the splendor of summer descends upon the woods. The sounds and movements of spring surrender to stillness and the green serenity of full leaf and long shadow. From time to time brusque thunderstorms rend the afternoons, but mostly the boughs hang motionless, scattering motes of sunlight on the forest floor. The voices of the birds are muted save at the hours of dawn and dusk. Every transept of the woods is imbued with the rapture of fulfillment, of growth completed and work done.

By early June the turbulence of blossoms has abated. Although the flowered embroidery of the spring carpet has faded, a few shade-tolerant plants continue to blossom in the twilit arcades. Throughout July and August fitful glints reveal the pale lamps of the enchanter's nightshade, white clusters of pokeweed and the orange blooms of touch-me-not. In these tranquil weeks the trees settle down to quiet preparation for the year to come. Fruits ripen, and trunks and branches thicken in girth. The process of photosynthesis, by which plants convert inorganic materials into starches and sugars, begins with the first unfolding of new leaves and reaches its peak in May. As summer wears on, the nutrients manufactured by the leaves are stored away in twigs, trunks and roots to provide energy for the burst of growth next spring. Winter buds appear on the beeches in May, and on the maple, elm and ash in June.

But summer is not totally a time of triumph and abundance. For in the sultry silences of noon and night's breathless blackness, forces of destruction begin their quiet work. "There is something of summer in the hum of insects," wrote Landor. Now on a billion pendant leaves voracious mouths bite lacy filigrees. Gall blisters disfigure the oak, beetles infest the elm. And with the scourge of insects comes the ruthless summer drought, searing and scything the foliage. Long before the nights grow cool the canopy begins to thin, admitting with the intense starlight premonitions of the brevity of life.

THE GLOW OF SUMMER pervades the heart of the forest on a windy day. At the foot of the oaks and dogwoods the leaves of the spicebush and viburnum tremble in the warm breeze, while overhead the treetops glitter in dancing light.

SUMMER DROUGHT diminishes the flow of water in the shallow brook (*above*) that winds through Mettler's Woods. Along its banks the gay green leaves of the skunk cabbages are still bright. But by mid-July they will have shriveled and died.

A BOX TURTLE (*right*) paddles lazily in a tiny pool refilled by unusual August rains. Because small woodland streams often dry up by mid-July and seldom flow again till fall, many aquatic creatures burrow into the mud as they do in winter.

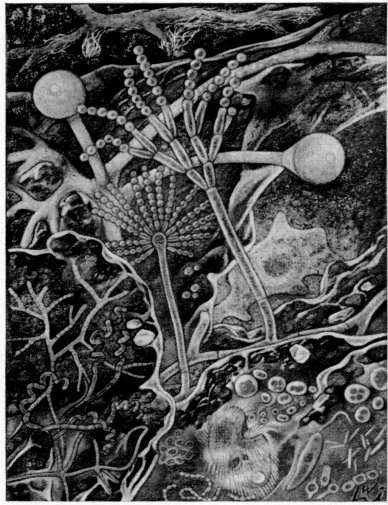

AGENTS OF DECAY are the fungi and other soil organisms. White fungus filaments interlace in the ground with strands of moldlike actinomycetes (*lower left*) and various bacteria, protozoans and green algae (*lower right*).

THE LIVING SOIL

DEEP in summer the byways of the woods are silent, sunk in golden calm. Yet all about, invisible hordes of living things abound in numbers inconceivable to man. These are the populations of the forest floor, of leaf litter and rotting logs, the lovers of decay. Devouring blighted and broken vegetation, riddling the sapless heartwood of fallen trees, they labor side by side with fungi and bacteria (*above*) in the never-ending processes of decomposition and rehabilitation of the soil.

Prime agents in this work are the termites, which tunnel tirelessly into every fallen tree to devour the dead wood that provides their whole food supply. The wood roach passes its entire life beneath the bark of rotting trees eating wood. The acrobat ant and the agile springtail both nest under bark. Other scavengers of the forest floor include the sow bug, mite, grouse locust, snail, slugs, nematodes and millepedes. Most important to soil structure are the earthworms whose underground operations help aerate and mix the soil, expediting drainage and root growth. Besides the excavators a number of flying insects hover close to the floor, among them the blue butterfly, moth fly, syrphus fly, crane fly and fungus gnat. Many, like the greenhead fly, firefly and fire-colored beetle, lay their eggs in the soil, so that when the larvae hatch they become temporary residents of the underworld. Of these transients the most chronic is the cicada, which lingers below ground 17 years in maturation from nymph to adult.

As in every habitat of nature the presence of life draws predators. The assassins of this blind cosmos are the brilliant tiger beetle, the burrowing worm snake and the prowling ground snake, the grass spider, pseudoscorpion, tick and centipede. Some of these assist too in the task of tunneling the litter and soil. The work these varied creatures begin is abetted by the fungi, whose ghostly filaments penetrate the ravaged tissues of leaves and logs, and by invisible bacteria which feed on complex substances untouched by larger scavengers and thus complete the mechanisms of decay.

TERMITES
    SYRPHUS FLY
CENTIPEDE
    LAND SNAIL
SOW BUG
    TICK
SLUG
    GROUSE LOCUST

CENTIPEDES   BLUES   SLUG   CENTIPEDE   FUNGUS GNAT

FIRE-COLORED BEETLE LARVA   WOOD ROACH   CRANE FLY   FIREFLY LARVA

EENHEAD FLY LARVA   WORM SNAKE   MILLEPEDE   TIGER BEETLE   GRASS SPIDER

MILLEPEDE   PSEUDOSCORPION   SPRINGTAIL   EARTHWORM

E   17-YEAR CICADA NYMPH   NEMATODE   GROUND SNAKE   ACROBAT ANT   MOTH FLY

CARPENTER ANTS   **UNDERWING MOTH**   **WOOD NYMPH**   **LACE BUG**
STINK BUG   **FIERY SEARCHER BEETLE**   **SPHINX CATERPILLAR WITH PARASITIC COCOONS**   **EASTERN TENT CATERPILLARS**
SWALLOWTAIL CHRYSALIS   **SADDLEBACK CATERPILLAR**   **POLYPHEMUS CATERPILLAR**   **POTTER WASP**

THE WINGED WOODS

HOVERING in the canopy, flitting among the shrubs and underbrush, incomputable myriads of insects claim the woods as their domain. In the temperate forest, as on the tundra and in the tropics, they outnumber all other visible forms of life, challenging by sheer proliferation man's boasted dominance on earth. Even in open country, exposed to the buffeting of winds, they threaten his ascendancy, devouring his crops, infecting his livestock, puncturing his skin. In the sheltered woods they reign supreme.

From forest floor to oak crown insects feast on green abundance.

High in the treetops the lace bug and the plant-hopper attack the undersides of leaves, sucking their juices and causing them to shrivel and die. Farther down carpenter ants invade weak places in the bark and tunnel extensive galleries. Tree borer eggs are laid in holes cut in the bark, whence the larvae spread and infest all parts of the afflicted tree. Far more destructive, the cottony maple scale and oyster-shell scale—legless, wingless insects that remain rooted to the same branch throughout their entire lives—often cover whole trees, eventually killing them and infesting all others in the vicinity. Even those plaintive minstrels of the summer night, the snowy tree cricket and the katydid, leaf eaters both, also wreak their share of damage.

The moths and butterflies, with powdered wings, engender supreme

COTTONY MAPLE SCALE

OYSTER-SHELL SCALE   LUNA MOTH

THALESSA FLY   KATYDID

GOLDEN-EYED LACEWING   PLANT-HOPPER

TREE BORER   MARBLED SPIDER   SNOWY TREE CRICKET

HICKORY HORNED DEVIL

agents of destruction. Although the pale green luna moth, loveliest of insects, never eats in its brief life on the wing, its caterpillar feeds on deciduous trees, as do those of the brown-cloaked underwing moth, the polyphemus moth and the swallowtail butterfly. The poison-spined saddleback caterpillar dines on oak and cherry leaves, and the hickory horned devil on the foliage of hickories and gums. The larvae of the wood nymph browse on grass. For wholesale devastation, however, none exceeds the Eastern tent caterpillars which come swarming from their silken canopies in spring and, streaming to the tops and terminal twigs of trees, defoliate huge areas of woodland.

But nature provides controls and balances: for every leaf eater there is a carnivore. The fiery searcher beetle nightly stalks the trees in quest of grubs. The potter wasp stings cankerworms and then imprisons them, alive but paralyzed, in neat clay jars as food for its young. The larvae of the thalessa fly devour the living larvae of the saw fly. The braconid wasp lays its eggs under the skin of the sphinx caterpillar; when the larvae hatch they bore their way out and spin cocoons on the doomed sphinx's back. The stink bug preys on pupae, puncturing cocoons with its sharp beak and sucking their vital juices. The marbled spider traps all kinds of insects in her web. And the delicate golden-eyed lacewing begets as its larva one of the fiercest killers in the insect world, the aphis lion, which ruthlessly hunts and gorges insatiably on plant lice, mites and scales. Through such internecine wars the green canopy of the woods is preserved from annihilation.

IN OCTOBER the canopy opens in a blaze of glory as autumn's frosty nights shear the painted leaves. Last to fall, the leaves of the oak—this is the same one shown previously—linger amid the gold and scarlet of beech and black gum.

THE FIRES OF AUTUMN

IN mid-September, as the sun dips toward the south and shadows lengthen, a sense of vague disquiet overhangs the woods. The soft-dying days are still bland, but there is melancholy in the slanting lights of afternoon, and in the evenings streamers of mist gather above the stream bed. Outwardly the woods appear unchanged, yet throughout their quiet chambers all life seems poised, entranced, upon the brink of some immense but unforeseeable event.

All summer long the trees have continued to manufacture green chlorophyll. Now, for mysterious reasons, long before the first frost, the chlorophyll supply begins to fail and the pure emerald of the foliage fades, giving way to red and yellow pigments. One by one the trees turn, partly through the addition of dyes, partly through the unmasking of colors that were always there. Slowly at first, then swiftly during the brilliant days of October, the blaze of autumn races through the woods, enkindling the scarlet conflagration of the maples and transfiguring the beeches and hickories in aureoles of golden fire. Each leaf prepares to fall by forming at the base of its stem a separation layer of thin-walled cells so fragile that they will part at the touch of a breeze or raindrop. A few at a time, then in fluttering myriads, the leaves detach themselves and spin like snowflakes down to the bright mosaic on the forest floor.

During these golden days in the evening of the year the forest animals prepare for the austere times ahead by growing winter coats and putting on fat. The squirrels and chipmunks store thousands of nuts and acorns in their underground granaries. The last migratory birds arrow southward and all insect voices are stilled. By November the forest floor is littered deep in rustling russet leaves. The hickories, elms and maples stand naked, and only the stubborn oaks retain a tattered shawl. It is a time of raw winds and dull skies, when the woods seem drained of light and without color or form. On certain nights the fingers of the frost reach down and touch the ground with rime.

A RACCOON prepares for winter by feasting on luscious insects from a fallen log. Irregular in their habits, raccoons do not hibernate, but when food gets scarce they take prolonged naps, living on stores of fat accumulated in the fall.

AN OPOSSUM peers lazily from its hideaway at the base of a tree. Like the raccoon its only preparation for winter is overeating during autumn. Females especially may remain in their tree homes for weeks at a time in bad weather.

A GRAY FOX, wearing his luxuriant winter coat complete with handsome brush, searches amid the leaf litter for nuts and berries. Normally carnivorous, foxes take advantage of autumn's fruiting season but return to hunting in deep winter.

A POTPOURRI OF AUTUMN LEAVES emblazons the floor of the forest in October. Drifted from the branches overhead, they lie where they have fallen against the crumbling fragments of a rotting hickory log. Conspicuous among them are the faded rose leaves of the maple, the red parallel-ribbed leaves of the flowering dogwood and the tawny leaves of the sassafras. A twig of fragrant spice-bush, with yellow-brown leaves, sprawls across the bright litter at upper right.

THE NAKED SKY of winter stares down through barren boughs that once supported the woodland canopy of leaves. Now stripped of all its vestments, the white oak stands in snow, shielded by its thick bark against the dry winter winds.

THE SLEEP OF WINTER

IN the dark of the year the stripped branches of the trees etch steely patterns against the sky. By day the pallid sun burns thinly, by night the cold stars pierce the skeleton boughs. The forest is sunk in silence so deep as to suggest all life has fled. Yet here and there its tokens persist. Even in deep winter warm airs recurrently breathe from the south and awaken the hardier plants to brief periods of growth. Then the withered sedges put forth shoots and mosses disclose patches of green.

All winter long there are footprints in the snow. The weasel and the fox venture forth in even the coldest weather, wandering farther afield as food grows ever scarcer. The rabbit, raccoon and skunk emerge on milder days, and the squirrel is housebound only by ice on trees. The winter birds are doubly active, combating cold by eating more. The chickadees, woodpeckers and nuthatches flit among the branches, probing the bark for insect eggs and larvae; the gregarious crows convene in solemn conclave every night to roost. Of all the mammals in the woods only the chipmunk and the woodchuck hibernate, curled in their snug burrows. But the cold-blooded reptiles and amphibians must sleep the winter through. The snakes and toads slumber under leaf litter or fallen logs; the frogs and turtles are buried in mud near the frozen stream. Insects in every phase lie dormant in the fissures of trees, burrowed in the soil or sealed in their silken cocoons.

Winter's deathlike countenance is thus but the mask of sleep. Everywhere beneath the hard soil and under the bark of trees, in innumerable dens, tunnels and secret chambers, there is life—in the form of seeds, eggs, cocoons, buds, sleeping animals and dormant roots, each holding locked within itself the forces of rebirth. Long before spring, while the translucent ice still clings to the edge of the stream, the active animals of the woods—the foxes, raccoon and skunk— choose their mates and breed, sensing in the blind roots of instinct that their young will thus be born into a world of gentle fruitfulness.

AFTER A JANUARY STORM THE WOODS LIE BLANKETED BENEATH A PROTECTIVE COAT

OF SNOW, WHICH HAS HEAPED A SOFT DRIFT AGAINST THE TRUNK OF THE WHITE OAK IN THE FOREGROUND AND FROSTED THE BRANCHES OF THE FALLEN TREE ON THE RIGHT

SEASON after season, century after century, the unending sequence of events in the temperate woodlands is recapitulated with magical precision. For all their proximity, these annual occurrences embody mysteries no less profound than those that enshroud the remoter domains of nature. Scientists have only begun to explore the complex mechanisms underlying such phenomena as the staining of the leaves in autumn and the migration of birds. Although the behavior patterns of animals and the growth of plants the world over are conditioned by many environmental factors—temperature, rainfall, winds—the temperate forests are especially influenced by one element: the changing length of the day. The agency called photoperiodism—the response of living things to the ratio of light and darkness in the day—appears to regulate such varied affairs as the reproductive cycles of animals and birds, their regular changes of fur and plumage, and the variant flowering of long-day plants (blooming only in summer) and short-day plants (blooming only in spring or fall).

Above and beyond these brief, visible cycles, there are longer pulsations of nature that govern the entire course of life in a given domain. Within this larger perspective Mettler's Woods stands as a "climax" forest community, which means that it has approached a state of equilibrium with its environment, perpetuating itself year after year essentially without change, secure against the invasions of all other forest types that might seek to displace it. But intermittently tropical storms roar up out of the Caribbean and, sweeping inland, shake the crowns of the great trees. In the autumn of 1950 one such storm felled scattered trees within the woods and thereby prepared the way for a greater threat that confronts the forest today. Until this occasion the Mettler family had allowed toppled trees to lie where they fell, there to decompose and replenish the soil. But the 1950 damage was so severe that the present owner, Thomas Mettler, asked a lumber company to salvage the fallen trees. Long covetous of the virgin timber, the company offered Mr. Mettler $85,000 for the entire tract. Reluctant to sell, the owner hesitated both for reasons of family tradition and because for the last two decades the science departments of nearby Rutgers University had utilized the woods as an outdoor laboratory. As a consequence, the Citizens Scientific and Historical Committee for the Preservation of Mettler's Woods was formed in New Brunswick, N.J. to buy the land and place it under the trusteeship of Rutgers. Mr. Mettler announced that he would sell the woods to the committee for $75,000. To date only $46,000 has been raised.

In view of the existing threat the question has arisen as to how long nature might take to recreate Mettler's Woods were they now despoiled and converted to cropland. A recent Rutgers study has forecast the probable sequence of events. In the first year following the abandonment of the broken soil, the open spaces will be invaded by weed plants, chiefly ragweed and evening primrose, along with other native annuals and nonindigenous flora. In the second year the first perennial herbs will establish themselves, choking out the annuals, and goldenrod will assume a dominance it will maintain for 15 years. In the fifth year the various herbs will reach their peak; wild aster will join the goldenrod as a dominant. Now the woody plants—bayberry, dogwood, viburnum and cherry seedlings—begin to take over. Red cedars crowd in; they will rule the land for the next six decades. In the 10th year the cedars will be more than three feet high. In the 15th year they will be eight feet high, intermixed with elm, red maple and apple seedlings. At this phase the woods will present an open, parklike aspect, with many small trees rising above the goldenrod, dewberry, sedges, asters and the omnipresent poison ivy.

Sixty years or more after the clearing of the land the red cedars will have reached their climax. But this is a time of transition. For among the crowding cedars the first seedlings of the original dominants are again struggling upward toward the light. The stage is set now for the long and gradual transformation of the ravaged land into a new deciduous forest. More than six decades have passed since oak and hickories last flourished here. The long delay in their reappearance derives from the fact that their seeds are not wind-disseminated but transported by squirrels and chipmunks which seldom venture far from the sanctuary of standing trees. Another four decades must elapse before the oaks and hickories can wrest dominance from the cedars and another 100 years after that before they become firmly re-established. Yet even this total interval of two centuries is but a prelude. For another 200 years must pass before the growing trees attain the stature of the giants that stand in Mettler's Woods today. No less than four full centuries are required for the creation of a climax forest of this kind. It is for such considerations that the scientists at Rutgers and other lovers of great trees are seeking now to preserve this unique vestige of the mighty forest that once blanketed vast areas of the continent. In their efforts lies more than an aversion to destroying an irreplaceable heritage of scientific and historical value. Since man's esthetic sense first awakened to the beauty of his natural environment, he has found solace and serenity in the calm cloisters of shady woods. In ancient Greece the oak was the tree of Zeus. Today, when modern man seeks escape from the stresses of his industrial civilization he still turns for sanctuary to the shade of tall trees, for as Wordsworth wrote:

> One impulse from a vernal wood
> May teach you more of man,
> Of moral evil and of good
> Than all the sages can.

THE STARRY
UNIVERSE

PART XIII

THE STARRY UNIVERSE

Beyond our planet with its rich domains of life lies a sea of space jeweled with galaxies and robed in mysteries man has yet to fathom

> Let there be lights in the firmament of the heaven
> to divide the day from the night; and let them be
> for signs, and for seasons, and for days, and years.
> GENESIS 1:14

STEADFASTLY through the ages men of science have sought to strip nature of its disguises and lay bare the hidden order that underlies the diversity of the visible world. Their quest has taken them to the depths of the sea and the highest fringes of the atmosphere, to deserts, jungles and the frozen lands that engird the terrestrial poles. With the slow enlargement of human knowledge, man's perspectives of space and time have correspondingly expanded. He has learned to count himself as one in the endless succession of living things that have populated the surface of the Earth since life appeared. And he has reluctantly recognized his dependency on the system of nature in which he stands—his ineluctable need for air, water and sunlight and for all the substances he must exploit to assuage his implacable hungers.

In no realm of science has new understanding so operated to disclose man's humbling situation in the natural world as in the advance of astronomy. Here he orients himself not merely with respect to the small planet on which he rides, but in relation to the outer universe. However strong his conviction that he is overlord of Earth, his self-image shrinks to insignificance when he lifts his eyes to the star-strewn vault of night and contemplates the dark and fathomless depths of space within which his petty domain is less than a grain of sand. This revelation was slow in coming and not easy to accept; it has always been man's nature to envisage himself at the center of the universe. Nor is this surprising, for until the insights and implements of modern science evolved, he could not penetrate deep into the void or discern his actual circumstance. From where he stands on the apparently stationary pedestal of Earth, the sun and moon regularly wheel westward from horizon to horizon, and the whole nocturnal sky seems like a great rotating bowl, carrying with it the bright diamonds of the fixed stars. It is only natural that during most of his existence, man has believed his Earth to be static, a solidly anchored object in a world of moving lights.

One of the paradoxes of science is that ancient astronomers, for all their misapprehensions, were able to chart the movements of celestial bodies with precision, and to employ their observations for utilitarian ends. Their first function was timekeeping; for all measurements of time come from the sky and are actually measurements in space; for instance, what we call an hour is simply an arc of 15° in the apparent daily rotation of the celestial sphere. As early as 3,000 B.C. the Egyptians evolved a calendar dividing the year into 12 months and 365 days. The Chinese kept records of eclipses from the 12th Century B.C. and of comets from the Seventh Century. It was in Greece, however, that certain men of genius, assisted by the new science of geometry but handicapped by lack of instruments, made some inspired deductions about the world they saw around them. Pythagoras and his followers inferred that the Earth, for all its seeming flatness, was a sphere. Aristarchus not only postulated that the Earth revolves around the sun but, first of all men, understood the difference in size and distance between the sun and moon and the remoteness of the fixed stars. These incredible insights surrendered, however, to the teaching of Claudius Ptolemy (about 150 A.D.) whose major work, the *Almagest*, the standard textbook of astronomy for the next 1,400 years, placed the Earth at the center of the universe, with the sun revolving around it.

The Ptolemaic system was still the accepted one in 1512, when the brilliant Pole, Nicholas Copernicus, began the 30 years of study that persuaded him that the Earth is a "wanderer," revolving like other planets in a circular orbit around the sun. It remained for Johannes Kepler in the following century to find that the planets travel in elliptical orbits and for Sir Isaac Newton to formulate the physical laws that define why they behave as they do. Soon after the invention of the telescope about 1600, Galileo discovered many of the major features of the solar system—the mountains of the moon, the phases of Venus, the satellites of Jupiter, and sunspots. As the centuries passed and telescopes improved, astronomers probed deeper into space, and slowly there dawned a sense of the immensity of the cosmos and the profusion of its quenchless fires. From their facts and theories they developed specific concepts of the universe which make possible such detailed paintings as those on the following pages.

On a clear night some 5,000 stars can be seen from the Earth with the naked eye. But a small telescope discloses over two million and the great Palomar telescope sucks in the light of billions. Yet for all their spangled myriads the distances between them are so vast that on another scale they might be envisaged as lonely lightships, a million miles apart, floating in an empty sea. The nearest to Earth, save the sun, is the multiple star Alpha Centauri, 4.4 light years away. (A light year is the distance light travels in a year, or roughly six trillion miles. The sun is only eight light minutes away.) Betelgeuse, the giant red star in the shoulder of Orion, is 300 light years away. The light from Rigel, the blue giant in Orion's knee, takes 540 years to reach our eyes.

Yet even these stars are close neighbors, and their distances are inches in the cosmic scale. It is only in recent decades that the terrifying dimensions and complexity of the universe have been dimly discerned. We know now that our solar system is actually but an infinitesimal unit on the outer rim of the great galaxy of stars that compose the Milky Way. And in turn the Milky Way, which once was thought to constitute the entire universe, is but one unit in a cluster of galaxies linked by gravitation and wheeling together through space. Yet it is not merely the size of the universe that dismays the cosmologist when he approaches the frontiers of vision two billion light years, or 12,000,000,000,000,000,000,000 terrestrial miles, away. For here he encounters enigmas that warn him not to assume—as man tends to do—that he can apply the evidence of his narrow experience on his earthly domain to the deeps of space and time. There is reason to believe that all his systems of measurement break down when he tries to fit them to the exterior vistas of the cosmos. And there is doubt that his ordinary notions of geometry and form, derived from his limited senses, can be used to understand a universe in which space may have no bounds. Staring into the void, he faces concepts like infinity and eternity, where science and imagination stand together on the brink of darkness, and he can perhaps but echo the words of the philosopher Schiller, "The universe is a thought of God."

AN ECLIPSE OF THE SUN, most awesome of celestial phenomena, briefly darkens the morning sky near St. Paul, Minn. on June 30, 1954. The sun, as seen in this multiple exposure photograph, rises as a golden crescent (*left*), partly covered by the moon. Its face dwindles as the moon moves on, then disappears and, for a few moments, only its flaring corona is visible. Gradually, in ever widening crescents, the sun soars into view again behind the silhouette of a tree.

THE RINGS OF SATURN gleam against the star-flecked sky of early dawn. They are seen here from a point high in the planet's atmosphere, 11,000 miles above its sheath of everlasting ice, 28,000 miles above its rocky core. The dense clouds of ammonia that perpetually enshroud Saturn cast their shadow on the rings at right. Although Saturn's three concentric rings rotate in a circle 171,000 miles across, they are only a few inches thick. They are composed of a swarm of gritty

THE WASTES OF MERCURY shimmer beneath the baleful eye of the sun, which glares down hot and white, undimmed by atmosphere or fall of night. Here on the perpetually sunlit side, the solar disk appears two to three times as large as it does from the more distant Earth. Windless, waterless, airless, the Mercurian landscape is diversified only by occasional craters gouged by meteoric bombardment, and jagged mountains and cliffs formed during the initial solidification of the planet.

NEIGHBORS IN NEARBY SPACE

THE first watchers of the sky, beside the Euphrates and the Nile, noticed that five bright stars changed their positions swiftly from night to night, drifting among the constellations in apparently capricious paths. The Greeks named them planetai, the wanderers. Today we know that they are not true stars, burning in distant space, but merely cold companions of the sun, like the Earth, shining by reflected light. We know too that in addition to the five visible to the naked eye, three others may be seen by telescope. Because of their kinship to Earth, man has often wondered if any of these neighboring worlds might support life comparable to his own.

All answers to this question rest on a basic postulate of science: the principle of the uniformity of nature, which asserts that the elements found on Earth persist throughout the universe and obey the same physical laws. For this reason the possibility of life on the five outer planets must be ruled out. They are far too cold; their surface temperatures range from $-170°$ F. on Jupiter to $-380°$ on distant Pluto. All save Pluto are heavily enshrouded in dense clouds of poisonous gases. Neither do the two inner planets offer any friendlier abode. Airless Mercury turns one face perpetually toward the sun. On this side the temperature reaches $670°$; on the other the temperature is near absolute zero $(-460°)$. Venus lies mantled beneath dense clouds containing much carbon dioxide, a gas whose insulating properties are such that the surface temperature of the planet may approximate that of boiling water.

Of all the planets, only Mars remains a possible domain of life. Although its maximum temperature barely reaches $50°$, seasonal color changes analogous to those of Earth can be observed over large areas. All one can say is that conditions on Mars are such as to render possible the growth of primitive vegetation. If higher forms of life exist elsewhere than on Earth, they must be found outside the solar system, in the starry fields of the Milky Way or the distant galaxies beyond.

snowballs, each a tiny satellite. The middle ring, largest and brightest of the three, is 16,000 miles wide and separated from the outer by a 2,000-mile gap. The outer ring and the translucent inner ring are each about 10,000 miles wide.

THE DESERTS OF MARS, studded with crescent dunes, are swept by dust storms that rise recurrently in the thin air. Lighted by the small disk of the remote sun, the Martian sky is relatively cloudless, the Martian land relatively arid. Yet seasonal changes are reflected by the burgeoning of green areas in spring and summer. The rounded reddish rocks in the foreground have been eroded by rapid temperature changes, resulting in a flaking-off of exterior irregularities.

THE HARMONY OF THE SPHERES

ROM the platform of the seemingly motionless Earth, the planets appear to move across the heavens within a narrow belt which the ancients called the zodiac. Today we know that the avenue of the zodiac is the flat plane of an enormous disk-shaped system in which our Earth and all the planets are forever imprisoned by gravitation, destined to revolve around our central star, the sun, so long as they exist. Infinitely complex, our solar system encompasses not only the nine planets, which are shown in true scale at right, but also 31 moons or smaller satellites of the planets, 30,000 asteroids or minor planets, thousands of comets, and incomputable numbers of meteors which burn their way into the Earth's atmosphere every day.

For all its complexity, the solar system also reveals an order and harmony that has ever impressed scientists contemplating the laws that govern the motions of the skies. The pictures at the bottom of this page show the orbits of the outer and inner planets, ranging from the vast sweep of distant Pluto, 3,670,000,000 miles from the sun, down to Mercury, 36 million miles away. The planets revolve in elliptical orbits, varying their distances and velocities—moving fastest when closest to the sun, more slowly when farther away. Their movements are governed by a delicate balance between their inertia (*i.e.*, their tendency to keep moving in a straight line) and the gravitational pull of the sun. It is this tenuous equilibrium that keeps them from flying away into space on the one hand or falling into the flaming mass of the sun on the other. The same laws rule the comets: as they reach the outer ends of their elongated orbits the gravitational tug of the sun slows their speed and pulls them back; as they reach the inner ends of their orbits their inertia and increasing speed impel them past the sun rather than into it.

To Earth-bound man the dimensions of the solar system seem stupendous. He himself lives 93 million miles from the sun. His small planet has a diameter of 7,900 miles, less than one tenth that of massive Jupiter and less than one hundredth that of the sun. In terms of volume it would take 1,300,000 building blocks the size of the Earth to make one sun—and the sun is but an average-size star. If the sun were imagined as a ball six inches in diameter, Earth would then be about 55 feet away and Pluto would be about half a mile away—but the nearest stars would be about 3,000 miles away. And even these are near neighbors in the vastness of the Milky Way.

THE NINE PLANETS and their 31 satellites are shown here in scale above the flaming rim of the enormous sun. On the solar horizon immense plumed prominences feather upward into space; below rages the wild solar atmosphere of

A. Petruccelli

intricate than the motions of the planets themselves. Saturn has, in addition to its rings of fine particles, nine satellites, one of which, Titan, is larger than our moon. The three outermost planets were discovered in recent times—Uranus accidentally in 1781; Neptune in 1846 after a deliberate search inspired by evidences of perturbations in the movement of Uranus; and small, distant Pluto in 1930. Astronomers are fairly certain the roster of the planets is complete.

which is calculated to return in four million years. The picture above depicts the orbits of the inner planets, Mercury and Venus (*both yellow*), Earth (*white*), Mars (*yellow*) and, shown again for comparison, Jupiter (*green*). Between Jupiter and Mars lies a belt of more than 30,000 asteroids (*purple bands*), the largest of which, Ceres (*purple line*), is only 480 miles in diameter. Encke's comet (*red*) has the smallest orbit and shortest period (3.3 years) of any comet known.

incandescent hydrogen. From left to right the planets march in the order of their orbital proximity to the sun. At the far left floats tiny Mercury and bright, cloud-veiled Venus. Next comes Earth, unique in the possession of a single moon so large that together they can be considered twin planets, and reddish Mars, escorted by two tiny satellites. Banded Jupiter, mightiest of the planets, is accompanied by a flock of 12 satellites whose motions around the planet are more

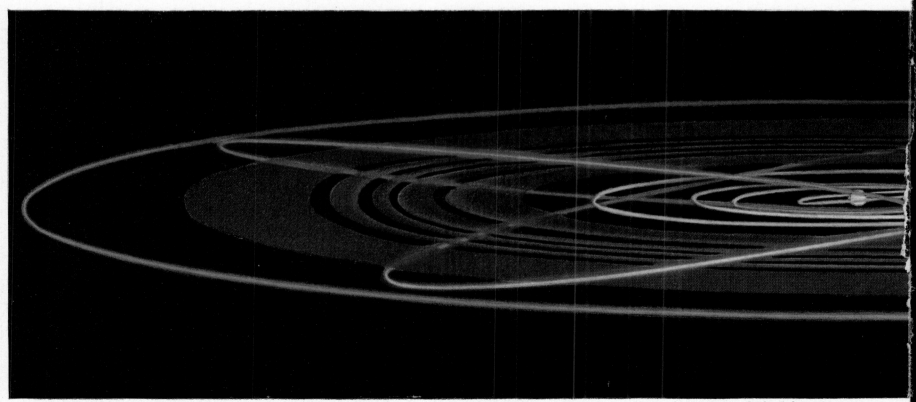

THE ORBITS OF THE PLANETS are shown here in two diagrams at left and above. At left are the orbits of the five outer planets (*green*) and the orbits of two comets (*red*). From the smallest circle outward the orbits shown are those of Jupiter, Saturn, Uranus, Neptune and Pluto, whose orbit is tilted off the main plane. Of the two comet orbits, the lower one is that of Halley's comet which reappears about every 77 years. The long slender orbit is that of Comet 1910*a*,

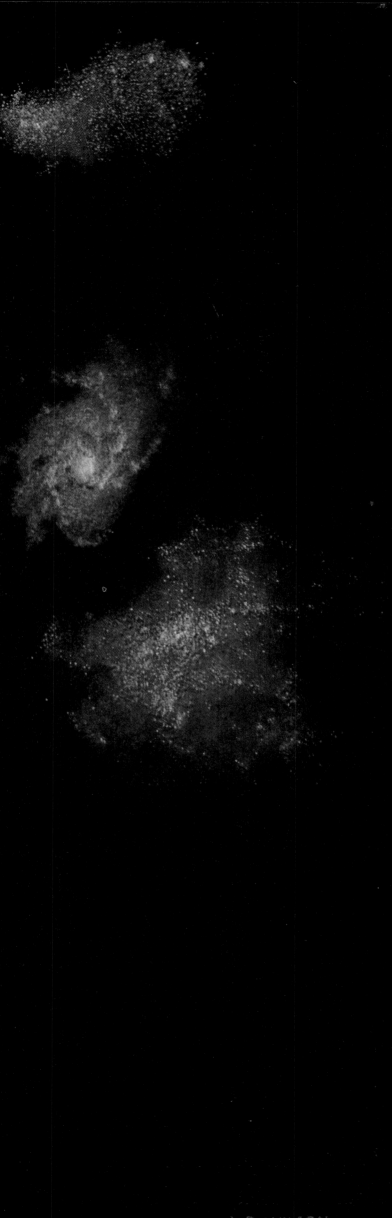

THE MILKY WAY AND ITS COMPANIONS

"LIKE a great ring of pure and endless light," the Milky Way girdles the heavens from pole to pole. Throughout the ages its pearly luminescence and intimations of fathomless distance have provoked the awe and imagination of man. It was not until recent times, however, that the Milky Way came to be recognized for what it is: a mighty river of suns, star fields, clusters and clouds composing the visible part of the galaxy in which our solar system moves. The difficulty in envisaging the architecture of the Milky Way is that we are *inside* it. Yet in the last century astronomers have broken through the confining perspective of Earth and ascertained that what we see of the Milky Way is actually the interior arc of a stupendous lens-shaped aggregation of stars similar to the galaxies of outer space. From the Earth, situated some 30,000 light years from the center of our galaxy, we can discern only a fraction of the billions of stars it contains, only a segment of its overall diameter of 100,000 light years.

Most of the matter in our galaxy—stars, dark clouds of gas and dust—lies within the main disk of the Milky Way and its spiral arms. The galaxy rotates, completing one revolution every 200 million years and carrying Earth and sun with it at a velocity of about 600,000 miles an hour. In its flight through space the great disk is accompanied by an outer swarm of globular clusters, each containing hundreds of thousands of stars, each revolving at random around the center of the galaxy. Together, the Milky Way and its aureole of globular clusters makes up what astronomers refer to as The Galaxy.

In the stupendous perspectives of the cosmos, however, our galaxy is but one member of a still larger cosmic aggregate, called the Local Group, which includes 17 or more systems held by gravitational force within a radius of 1.5 million light years. Near one end of this vast supersystem rides the glowing wheel of the Milky Way, at the other end the great spiral of its sister galaxy, Andromeda.

In the painting at left the Local Group is shown as it might be viewed by an observer 684,000 light years from the sun, looking down the long axis of the group toward Andromeda in the remote void. The nearest star systems are the two Magellanic Clouds, strange formless galaxies which attend the Milky Way as satellites. Between them, but farther away, whirls the fiery pinwheel of a small galaxy known simply as NGC 598. Distant Andromeda burns in the dark abyss of space, adorned like the Milky Way with globular clusters and accompanied by lesser satellite galaxies.

In addition to the systems shown here, the Local Group also embraces six small elliptical galaxies, possessing no spiral arms and little dust or gas, four structureless veils of stars like the Magellanic Clouds, and perhaps three distant spirals, sparsely distributed through the immense void. Remote as they are, they are nevertheless united by the mysterious force of gravitation and revolve around an unknown center somewhere between Andromeda and the Milky Way.

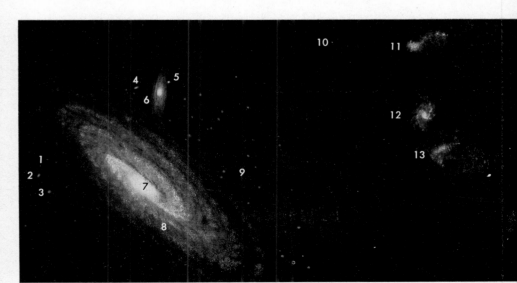

KEY TO THE GALAXIES in the painting at left is given above. Most galaxies are identified by numbers and the letters NGC, standing for New General Catalog, the astronomer's guidebook of outer space. The objects shown here are: 1—NGC 278; 2—NGC 147; 3—NGC 185; 4—NGC 205; 5—NGC 221; 6—Andromeda; 7—main disk of the Milky Way; 8—the sun; 9—globular clusters; 10—NGC 404; 11—Small Magellanic Cloud; 12—NGC 598; 13—Large Magellanic Cloud.

J. P. WILSON
R. Garland

TWO COLLIDING GALAXIES pass through each other at some trackless crossroad in space. Despite the apparent density of the galaxies, the stars within them never collide, for they are separated by trillions of miles. But the voluminous gas clouds accompanying them clash and fall behind, glowing red with the heat of molecular impacts. Such galactic collisions, though rare, explain the existence of spiral galaxies that are swept clean of gas like the upper arms of the two above.

THE GALAXIES OF OUTER SPACE

AS the eye of the telescope peers outward, past the familiar constellations, past the more distant star clouds and clusters of the Milky Way, it discovers an ever increasing number of hazy luminous patches suspended like cobwebs in the void. These are the outer galaxies, the so-called "island universes," each composed of billions of stars but so deeply sunk in the abyss of space that the light by which they disclose themselves required millions of years to traverse the distance to the Earth. Within the bowl of the Big Dipper alone, a rectangle enclosing only 1/2000th of the whole sky, faint glimmers of enfeebled light reveal a cluster of more than 300 galaxies. By comparison, our Local Group, with its 17 members, is a dwarf cluster. In general the galaxies of outer space tend to congregate into communities of about 500—into galaxies of galaxies—united by gravitation, sometimes interpenetrating one another in their huge wanderings, like those on the opposite page.

Astronomers estimate that about one trillion galaxies lie within range of our largest telescopes. Three main categories are recognized: elliptical galaxies, representing 17% of those catalogued; spirals, comprising 80%; and irregulars, composing 3%. Because they rotate at various speeds the ellipticals range from perfectly symmetrical spheres to flattened saucer-shaped disks. For the same reason, the spirals range from the tightly coiled (*above right*) through the more loosely coiled like the Milky Way (*right, center*) to wide-open pinwheels with small nuclei and arms thrown out by the centrifugal force of rapid rotation. Most spirals have round centers, but about 30% of them are "barred spirals" with elongated nuclei like the one below. The third main group of galaxies, the irregulars, are like the Magellanic Clouds formless, without nuclei or systematic rotational movement.

A few modern astronomers try to fit the various types of galaxies into an evolutionary sequence, suggesting that the turbulent irregular galaxies are newborn systems that will form into fast-spinning spirals, and then in time evolve into slower-moving ellipticals. But most astronomers insist that all galaxies are of about the same age. They assert that the various types of galaxies were shaped by their various rotational speeds at creation and that these speeds determined how much of their primordial matter should coalesce into stars and how much should continue to drift freely in clouds of gas and smoke.

A TIGHTLY COILED SPIRAL, NGC 4594 in Virgo, is viewed here through the Mount Palomar telescope so that the obscuring masses of gas and dust in its spiral arms form a dark belt around the equator of its huge, glowing nucleus.

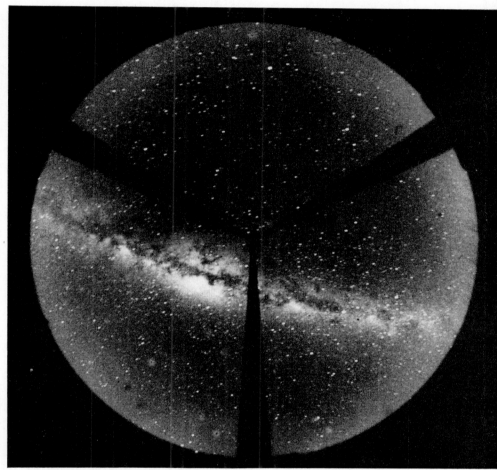

OUR OWN GALAXY, photographed with a red filter, shows a structure like that of galaxies in outer space. The nucleus is at the center, below the point where the camera's plate mountings meet. The spiral arms taper off to left and right.

A BARRED SPIRAL, so called for the characteristically elongated nucleus of its type, rotates like a fiery pinwheel in the constellation Eridanus, trailing its loosely coiled arms widely in space, where they finally attenuate in the void.

AN ELLIPTICAL GALAXY in the Andromeda group glows in space, 1.7 million light years from Earth. An ellipse in profile, it is actually a flattened sphere. The large individual stars around it are in the Milky Way, 100 to 100,000 times closer.

GLOWING STRANDS OF A GAS CLOUD IN CYGNUS FILIGREE THE SKY. THEY PASS BEHIND THE BRIGHT STAR AT CENTER, WHICH IS BLURRED BY LONG PHOTOGRAPHIC EXPOSURE

THE COSMIC CLOUDS

OF all the mysteries of the universe the darkest surround the inchoate masses of matter that drift in space as clouds of gas and dust. Floating between the stars in the arms of all spirals and large areas of irregular galaxies, this material reveals itself either by catching the light of adjacent stars, as in the fine-spun nebula above, or by obscuring it behind opaque shrouds, as in the formation shown on the opposite page. Its density is so inconceivably low—16 atoms per cubic inch—that it surpasses the most perfect vacuums that can be produced on earth. Yet in some regions these diffuse clouds are so vast that they equal in mass the total substance of the adjacent stars.

The cosmic clouds are significant because they are the raw material of creation. Some five billion years ago, according to present theory, our galaxy consisted of a stupendous mass of swirling hydrogen gas rotating invisibly in starless space. As the cloud spun, turbulence developed and eddies formed, and within the eddies gravitational force began to weld particles into ever greater bodies. Then as the enlarging masses felt the squeeze of gravitation their internal temperatures rose. Eventually, in the hot centers of each mass, atomic nuclei began to react; hydrogen changed to helium (as in the H-bomb), and so lit up the first stars. In this way the Milky Way and all other galaxies are thought to have formed. Among the immense dim clouds that can be seen hanging in the depths of the sky, astronomers believe the same slow processes of stellar creation may still be going on.

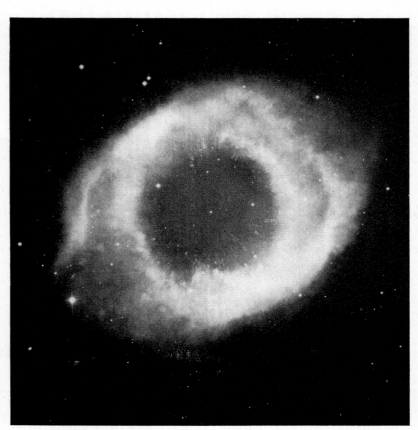

A COSMIC "SMOKE RING" surrounds a faint star in Aquarius. Actually what appears to be a ring is a shell of gas which absorbs the light of the star and re-emits it. Like any hollow, translucent sphere it appears denser around the edges.

A STELLAR EXPLOSION which occurred in 1054 A.D., according to the records of Chinese astronomers, left the gas cloud known as the Crab Nebula. Today the cloud is still expanding at 684 miles per second; its diameter is 3¼ light years.

CLOUDS OF GAS AND DUST 4,000 light years away spin turbulent configurations in the constellation Monoceros. At the top of the picture, gray scarves of gas are excited to luminosity by the big bright star with a halo in the background.

Below, a dark promontory of intruding opaque matter points upward from the abyss of space. The other stars in the picture are all much closer to earth; the distortion of their images is a diffraction effect originating inside the telescope.

SPIRAL ARMS on the rim of Andromeda, twin sister of our Milky Way, shine with the brilliance of many young blue stars of Population I (*top, opposite page*). This section of the galaxy, 1/30 of the total, is about 11,000 light years across.

A GLOBULAR CLUSTER hovering above the main disk of the Milky Way contains a million tightly packed stars of Population II, all of them old and in varying stages of evolution. The cluster is about 245 light years in diameter.

THE LIFE AND DEATH OF STARS

TO the naked eye the stars glitter like silver sequins, spangling the black fabric of the sky without dimension or identity, fixed pinpoints, infinitely remote. It is only through the sorcery of the telescope and spectroscope that their splendor and diversity emerge; for then their colors shine forth, transmuting them from faint sparks into brilliant jewels—rubies, diamonds, sapphires—aglow with every wavelength of the visible spectrum. Since stars are incandescent objects, their colors derive from their temperatures. Thus red stars like Antares and Aldebaran are relatively cool, with surface temperatures in the vicinity of about 6,000°F. Yellow stars like the sun are hotter by thousands of degrees. And the most intense ultraviolet stars are hottest of all, with temperatures ranging up to 100,000°.

In their unending effort to extract order from the apparent chaos of the skies, astronomers have uncovered certain striking relationships that link the color and size of stars with their age and location in galactic structures. Thus they divide all the stars of the heavens into two great categories. Population I consists of stars that exist in the arms of spiral galaxies and in irregular galaxies like the Magellanic Clouds. Population II consists of stars found in the nuclei of spiral galaxies, in elliptical galaxies and, classically, in globular clusters. This division is based not only on distribution in the universe, but on stellar types, for the two populations embrace markedly different kinds of stars. The biggest, brightest stars in Population I are blue giants, which cause the regions they inhabit—like the spiral arms of our own Milky Way—to glow with a soft, luminous blue radiance. The biggest, brightest stars of Population II are red giants, which impart to their environs a characteristic warm and ruddy light.

In addition to their brilliant luminaries both groups contain myriads of fainter stars of many colors and types. The family ties that unite the stars of Population I are simple, and it was these that astronomers discovered first. For in this category the relationship between color and size is a straightforward one: the smaller stars are red and cool; the bigger ones, blue and hot. Until a few decades ago astronomers believed that this rule—the bigger, the hotter—applied to all stars save for a few unaccountable freaks. Then as telescopes reached farther into the void—into the remote globular clusters and the still more distant outer galaxies—whole aberrant populations were disclosed. Here the giants were not blue and hot, but red and cool; and the smallest stars were either extremely hot or extremely cool—never of intermediate temperatures. Here too were curious pulsating stars that periodically fluctuated in color and size, and strange white dwarfs.

It was not until the development of modern nuclear physics, however, that these anomalies could be explained. With an understanding of the thermonuclear processes that control the burning of stars, astronomers realized that the different types of stars they discerned represented different stages in stellar evolution. Thus Population I stars, with their straightforward relationship of temperature to size, are simply stars that have not changed since their birth; they represent only the first stage of stellar evolution. Population II represents later stages. In general, the life cycle of a star unfolds as follows: 1) Until it has used up 15% of its hydrogen, it burns steadily without substantially changing character. Its rate of combustion depends on the amount of matter it contains—*i.e.*, massive stars burn more rapidly than small ones. 2) After a star has used up 15% of its hydrogen it starts to evolve. Now it expends its fuel wastefully, consuming the remaining 85% in the same time it took to burn the first 15%. It cools and expands, swelling and bloating to 50 or 100 times its original size. In this stage it becomes a red giant or supergiant as much as eight billion times more voluminous than the sun. 3) When it has used up 60% of its hydrogen, its internal pressure begins to fall; its bloated exterior starts to cave in. As it contracts, complicated atomic reactions come into play, and the star becomes unstable. Then, depending on circumstances, it may go through a phase as a pulsating star, or explode as a nova, before it collapses finally into an extinct white dwarf, glowing only by the feeble heat of slow compression.

This theoretical biography may be complicated if a star finds itself in close conjunction with another star, as is the case with the components of the double system, RW Persei, shown in the painting at right. Not all stars, moreover, run the entire course of stellar

A DOUBLE STAR, RW Persei casts overlapping two-toned shadows across the lifeless landscape of a hypothetical planet. One member of the strangely mated pair is a large, dim, orange-colored star; the other is a much smaller, brighter blue star, spectacularly engirdled by a ring of incandescent hydrogen. So closely associated are these stellar twins that they share a common envelope of gas within which they rotate one about the other in a period of about two weeks.

283

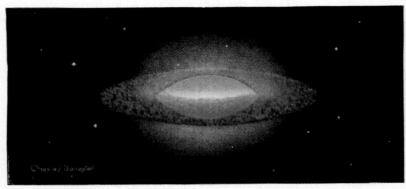

PURPLE PLEIONE, a star of the familiar Pleiades cluster, rotates so rapidly that it has flattened into a flying saucer and hurled forth a dark red ring of hydrogen. Where the excited gas crosses Pleione's equator, it obscures her violet light.

existence in the same length of time. Whereas the most massive stars may expend their energy and die in 10 million years, smaller, fainter stars may persist for 50 billion years.

The reason that Population II stars reveal such a variety of evolutionary types is that the globular clusters and elliptical galaxies in which they abide are devoid of dust and gas from which new stars can form. They have evolved in isolation, unreplenished since their creation; hence their aging individuals—varying in life expectancy according to their varying mass—illustrate advanced phases of stellar development. The stars of Population I undergo somewhat similar evolutionary processes, but *in toto* they appear to change little because their special environments, in spiral arms and irregular galaxies, contain quantities of dust and gas out of which new blue giants continually arise to replace those that burn out. It is for this reason that the Milky Way still sparkles with blue primordial brilliance. Inexorably, however, as the cosmic clouds are exhausted and the blue giants extinguished, it too will grow fainter and yellower. Even now it encompasses vastly more small red and yellow stars than blue giants. But its future is still long. Another 50 billion years may pass before the last faint, slow-burning star undergoes its final collapse and flickers out, leaving the galaxy to everlasting night.

Of all the myriad stars in the galaxy a few, like our sun, wheel through space alone. More than three quarters, however, belong to gravitational alliances of one sort or another, ranging from double or triple stars to populous stellar clusters revolving around common centers of gravity. In the most closely coupled of these systems, stars which have been deformed by forces of mutual attraction often rotate on their axes and circle their companions so rapidly that they hurl their outer gases into space and engird themselves in fiery rings or spirals like the ones shown on these pages. Paradoxically their loss of substance tends to prolong rather than diminish the life span of such stars, for as they dwindle they burn ever more slowly, husbanding their remaining fuel with increased economy. Their rapid rotation, stirring interior and outer layers together, enables them to burn evenly throughout their existence without suffering the violent pulsations and explosions to which single stars are subject in old age.

The first multiple star to be discovered was Mizar, situated at the bend of the Big Dipper's handle, two of whose components can be distinguished with the naked eye. The giant blue Dog Star, Sirius, has a white-dwarf companion, the Pup, which is not much larger than our planet, but whose substance is of such fantastic density that one cubic inch of it would weigh several tons on earth. Greatest of all double stars is Epsilon Aurigae, consisting of a yellow supergiant 250 times the size of the sun, and its still more stupendous companion, a cool, dark star with a diameter 3,000 times that of the sun. With less than one millionth of the sun's density, this giant among giants is so diffuse and cool that it emits no visible light. Its existence and properties are known only because it eclipses its companion once every 27 years. In addition to such double stars, many stars are linked in larger combinations. The familiar North Star, Polaris, for example, is actually three stars; Castor is six. The twinning and tripling of stars may result from various causes. A current theory suggests that most double and multiple systems were created from interacting eddies and countereddies in the primordial gas cloud out of which our galaxy condensed.

AN EXPANDING SPIRAL of glowing hydrogen, deep red against the empty sky above some bleak, imaginary planet, encircles the revolving star-couple known as Beta Lyrae. Ejected by centrifugal force from the rapidly spinning equator

of the larger blue star, the luminous gas is caught by the smaller yellow star which retains some of it in a band around its own equator and flings the rest outward to dissipate eventually in space. Because it is consuming its fuel extravagantly, the great blue star is likely to burn out relatively soon unless its rate of combustion is reduced as it surrenders mass to its yellow mate. A celestial freak, Beta Lyrae is the only twin star known to have a spiral envelope.

A. Petruccelli

THE VISIBLE UNIVERSE extends outward in all directions to a distance of two billion light years. In this conception each of the small balls represents millions of galaxies which are receding from each other and from our Local Group of galaxies (*center*) as the universe expands. Each has two positions connected by lines: an inner one where it emitted the light we see now and an outer one where it actually is now. In its visible position it is shown in a multicolored disk, for it is traveling so fast that its light crowds up in short blue waves in front of it and trails out in long red waves behind it. The speed of receding galaxies is computed by this reddening of the light. The innermost of the three large spheres above shows how far astronomers can measure the reddening (.8 billion light years). The second sphere indicates the limits of telescopic perception a decade ago (about 1.4 billion light years). The outer sphere indicates the present telescopic horizon (two billion light years) where the most distant galaxies are perhaps fleeing outward at speeds of more than 120,000 miles per second.

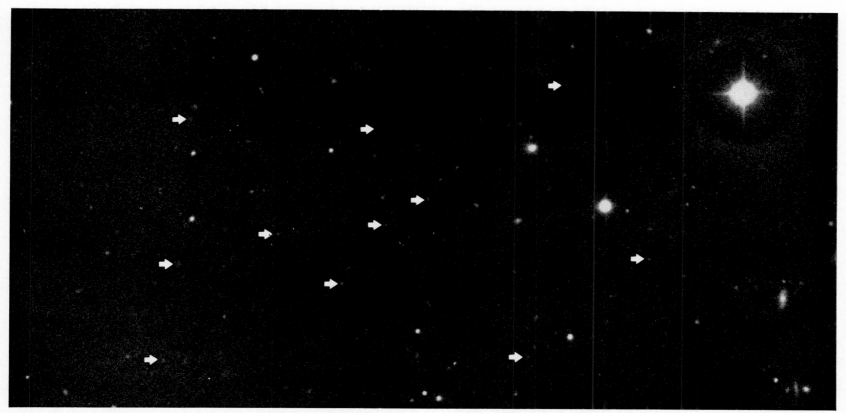

THE FARTHEST GALAXIES man can see are indicated by arrows in this photograph taken with Palomar's great telescope. Their light, which took two billion years to reach Earth, was so enfeebled that an exposure of one hour was required. The brighter objects are nearer galaxies and faint stars within the Milky Way.

THE EXPANDING UNIVERSE

THE history of astronomy has been a record of receding horizons. In the beginning the recession was slow; many centuries passed between the dim age when man believed that the sky—"this majestical roof fretted with golden fire"—hovered only a few miles above the earth and the dawn of his apprehension of cosmic distances. Indeed it was not until the beginning of our century that the focus of astronomy shifted from planets to stars. Only within the last 25 years has it comprehended the galaxies of outer space.

The astronomer most responsible for this change in perspective was the late Edwin Hubble of the Mount Wilson Observatory, who in 1924 published photographs proving once and for all that the far, hazy patches of light which astronomers had called nebulae and believed to be inchoate masses of gas and dust were actually huge systems of stars like the Milky Way. Thereafter he devoted himself to studying the galaxies, measuring their distances, charting their distribution in space and, most important, analyzing their movements. The curious feature of these movements was that they did not seem to be random, like the aimless drifting of molecules in a gas, but highly systematic: each distant galaxy appeared to be rushing away from our galaxy at a velocity directly proportional to its distance; that is, the greater the distance, the greater the speed. Hubble and his associate, Milton L. Humason, proceeded to work out the ratio, and in 1929 published an equation destined to be of supreme importance in cosmology and known today as the Hubble-Humason Law. It reads: $V_m = 38r$. In the shorthand of science V_m stands for the velocity of the receding galaxies in miles per second, and "r" expresses the present distance from Earth in units of one million light years. Hence a galaxy one hundred million light years away is found moving at a speed of 38x100 or 3,800 miles per second; galaxies one billion light years away flee outward at 38x1,000 or 38,000 miles per second, about one fifth the speed of light.

The universe thus appears to be expanding about us in all directions. Yet this does not mean that modern astronomy has reverted to the old anthropocentric picture of the cosmos; it does not imply that our Earth stands at the center of the universe any more than it does at the center of the solar system, Milky Way or Local Group. If one thinks of the universe as a balloon covered with inelastic spots representing galaxies, then as the balloon inflates each spot must recede from every other spot. Or to take another analogy, one can envisage the universe as a giant cloud of rarefied gas in which each individual galaxy is an individual molecule. If the cloud expands uniformly, each molecule doubles its distance from every other molecule in a given interval of time. And so, if sensate observers exist in the galaxies that we see hurrying away from us, they also see us hurrying away from them—at velocities proportional to distance.

Evidence for this flight of the galaxies derives from an analysis of the light they emit. Broken down by a spectroscope, the light of a far galaxy produces the same pattern of bright and dark bands as light from a stationary source. But each band is systematically moved toward the red or long-wavelength end of the spectrum. The distance of this shift across the spectrum is directly proportional to the speed of a galaxy's recession. Known as the "red shift," this effect may be compared to the familiar change in the sound emitted by a moving source as it advances and recedes. Anyone who has paused by a railroad crossing has noticed that the sound of a locomotive whistle appears higher in pitch as the train approaches and lower as it moves away. The reason for this is that the wavelengths of sound emitted by the approaching whistle are compressed and shortened by the forward motion of the source, which thus raises its pitch. As the train passes, they stretch out and lengthen in its wake, lowering the pitch of the sound. In the same way, light waves from an approaching source are compressed toward the blue or short-wavelength end of the spectrum, while those from a receding source stretch out toward the red or long-wavelength end—hence the deduction that the galaxies of outer space are receding. Since there are other factors that may redden celestial objects in a different way, some skeptics have sought opposing explanations for the red shift. Yet one by one their objections have been vitiated and today it is the almost unanimous view that the outrush of the galaxies is no illusion but an actual phenomenon of the mysterious universe.

The concept of an expanding space, however, has presented cosmological problems of enormous subtlety. For example, when an astronomer looks outward in space he looks backward in time. The dim, distant galaxies whose antique light swims to our vision through two billion years of terrestrial time do not actually exist where we see them now. The light by which we discern their images started its immense journey when life on earth was barely stirring in the primordial seas. While it has come to us, they have traveled another one and one-third billion light years farther away. It is thus that in any conception of the universe space and time become inseparable and cosmologists speak of a space-time continuum—which means that to describe the position of a galaxy one must fix it not only in three dimensions of space but also in one of time. In this sense the universe is four-dimensional, and the fourth dimension is time.

The cosmologist cannot therefore think of the universe as here and now in the way that one can think of New York City or the Earth as here and now. For every object in the heavens has two positions: 1) where we see it, and 2) where it is. Even in the case of the nearest star, Alpha Centauri, we cannot say that we see it "now," for its light takes a little over four years to reach our eyes. So what we actually see is the ghost of a star that was shining back in 1951. Whether or not it is still shining in 1955 we cannot know until 1959. The situation becomes vastly more complicated, however, in the case of the flying galaxies, not only because of their immense distance but because of their incredible velocities.

If one assumes that all the galaxies we see today have been traveling outward through eons of cosmic time in the same relative directions and at the same relative velocities—the farthest galaxies most swiftly, the nearer ones at lesser rates of speed—the startling corollary emerges that all started from the same place at the same time. Calculations made from present measurements of their rate of recession indicate that their cosmic journey began about five billion years ago. The extraordinary fact about this figure is that it coincides with recent findings as to the probable age of radioactive substances found in the Earth's crust, and the age of the oldest stars derived from modern theories of stellar evolution. All the clues of science point to a time of creation when the cosmic fires were ignited and the vast pageant of the present universe brought into being. And this time was five billion years ago.

Since the phenomenon of the expanding universe was discovered many hypotheses have been put forth to explain it. One of the first was proposed by the Belgian cosmologist Abbé LeMaître who suggested that the recession of the galaxies was initiated by a stupendous explosion—the blowing up of a single primordial super-atom whose fleeing fragments we still perceive. A variation of this theme has been developed more recently by Dr. George Gamow, of George Washington University. At some time prior to five billion years ago, according to Gamow, the universe was in a state of contraction which lasted until all matter and radiation were squeezed together in an inferno of elementary particles of incredible mass and density. Gamow calls this contracted state of matter *ylem*—an archaic English word meaning the primordial, elemental substance of all things. Its temperature raged in the billions of degrees. There were no elements in such heat, no atoms—only free atomic particles in a state of chaotic agitation. Directly following the climactic moment of supreme contraction, the cosmic mass began to expand. Light and other electromagnetic radiation flew outward into space. The temperature fell. When it had dropped to one billion degrees, the particles cohered and atoms were formed. As the primordial vapor surged outward and cooled, turbulence and gravitation shaped it into eddies from which galaxies and clusters of galaxies evolved. They were dark at first, but gradually, out of the swirling clouds, stars condensed and shone across the void.

In opposition to Gamow's theory a British school of cosmology has recently proposed a "steady state" universe. In essence it holds that the universe was not created with a bang—that indeed it had no beginning as such—and that creation is a continuous process. Throughout space, according to this theory, matter is continually being formed and condensing into galaxies in the intergalactic voids created by expansion. Yet this picture is less acceptable than Gamow's. In recent years observational evidence has been adduced in support of the postulate that all the galaxies were created at the same time. Astronomers have noted that the remotest elliptical galaxies are far redder than nearer ones, and that their intensity of color cannot be explained by the red shift. It can be accounted for only if they contain bigger and brighter red stars than the nearer galaxies—in short, red supergiants. But we see the outer elliptical galaxies by the light they emitted one or two billion years ago and the inner galaxies by the light they emitted a few million years ago. So we are seeing the nearer galaxies at a far more advanced age. Since supergiant red stars evolve and burn out quickly they have already vanished from the old inner galaxies but still burn in the young outer galaxies. The difference in their colors is precisely what one would expect were outer and inner galaxies created at the same time.

Profound as the problems of the expanding universe are when one looks back in time, enigmas no less deep arise in any attempt to guess what lies beyond the reaches of telescopic vision. It is here that cosmology leaves behind the ordinary realm of human experience. In trying to separate appearance from reality it has invaded domains of abstraction whose concepts stand utterly removed from the visible, tangible world perceived by man's senses. For example, would greater and greater telescopes disclose wider oceans of space and new myriads of galaxies, hurtling outward at ever greater speeds? The question leads to one of the great paradoxes of cosmology. For the galaxies we can see two billion light years away are traveling at two-thirds the speed of light. If mightier telescopes extended man's vision to two and a half billion light years he would then be in range, according to the Hubble-Humason Law, of galaxies whose speed equals that of light. But would he see them? For if they are rushing away from him at the speed of light, then by Newtonian physics the light they emit would never get back to Earth. At this point, the astronomer has to abandon simple logic and introduce the subtler rationalizations of Einstein's theory of relativity.

Although the laws of classical physics apply to all situations of man's ordinary experience, they break down in the realm of great velocities such as prevail within the atom and on the outer fringes of space. The underlying premise of relativity holds that all motion is relative and can be measured only with respect to some specific point of reference. But how is one to do this in a universe where everything is in motion? The earth has one speed relative to the sun, another relative to the Milky Way, and countless others relative to the systems of outer space. How, for example, can an observer in one galaxy, who sees another galaxy receding at 10,000 miles a second, know which of the two is moving faster? All he can ascertain is their combined rate of recession.

Early astronomers presupposed that space could be regarded as an immovable frame of reference in which the "true," or absolute, motion of the stars could be defined. This conviction was strengthened by physicists who postulated that space must be filled with an invisible substance called "ether," which carried light waves as water propagates the waves of the sea. In 1887 two American physicists, Michelson and Morley, performed a classic experiment designed to prove the existence of the ether. They reasoned that if the Earth moves like a ship through a motionless sea of ether, then the speed of a light ray must be retarded by the ether slipstream if it is projected in the direction of the Earth's movement through the ether, and accelerated if projected in the opposite direction. Their instrument, called an interferometer, was so delicate it could detect a variation of even a fraction of a mile per second in the enormous velocity of light (186,282 mps). But it found that the motion of the Earth did not affect the velocity of light regardless of direction. With one stroke the Michelson-Morley experiment demolished the ether and split scientific thought for the next quarter century.

In 1905 when Einstein was 26 years old he published the Special Theory of Relativity which opened a new world of physical science. He rejected the ether theory and with it the idea of space as a fixed framework within which it is possible to distinguish "true" from relative motion. The one indisputable result of the Michelson-Morley experiment, he pointed out, was its proof that the velocity of light is unaffected by the motion of Earth. He took this as a revelation of universal law. If the velocity of light is constant with respect to Earth, he argued, it must be constant with respect to any galaxy in the universe. So it is impossible to discover the "true" velocity of any galaxy by using light as a yardstick, for the speed of light will always be measured at 186,282 mps despite the motion of the source or the motion of the receiver. And since it cannot be increased by the motion of either source or receiver, he concluded, the velocity of light must be a governing constant of the universe which nature forbids any moving body to exceed.

From these premises Einstein formulated a series of equations that have become an integral part of modern physics and cosmology. Specifically, his equations make all measurements of distance and time vary with the velocity of the observer. For example, we may see two galaxies on opposite sides of the Earth, each one moving away from us at two-thirds the speed of light. Do they then see each other moving away at four-thirds the speed of light, as the simple addition of velocities would assert? According to relativity, observers in both galaxies would measure time and distance differently from observers here on Earth and would compute their combined velocities at somewhat less than that of light.

Strange as its concepts appear to the layman, relativity has been

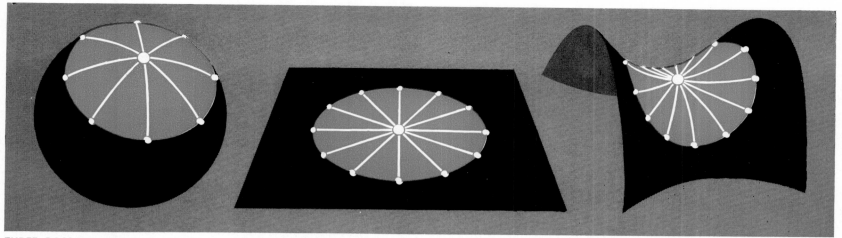

THREE POSSIBLE KINDS OF SPACE, "positively" curved (*left*), uncurved (*middle*) and "negatively" curved (*right*), are illustrated by the sphere, plane and saddle-shaped surface above. Colored sections represent the visible universe, with far galaxies (*white balls*) at the edge and Earth at center. On each surface light travels by the shortest available route (*white lines*): great circles on the sphere, straight lines on the plane and various curves on the saddle (*see below*).

repeatedly validated by observation and experiment. In cosmology the principle of the constant velocity of light has been confirmed by studies of double stars which show that the light from an approaching star in these revolving systems reaches Earth at the same speed as that from a receding star. But relativity also warns the cosmologist never to forget that his observations are limited by his situation in the universe, and that he can never be certain of what he measures in the vast drowned depths of space and time.

With these warnings in mind, modern cosmology has attempted warily to speculate on the possible size and architecture of the universe. Special Relativity plus the Hubble-Humason Law suggest that its radius cannot be greater than five billion light years, for: 1) The universe apparently began to expand five billion years ago; 2) The outermost galaxies have been flying into space since then at a constant velocity close to the speed of light; 3) Relativity asserts that no moving object can exceed the speed of light. Hence the swiftest galaxies can have traveled, at the most, a little less than five billion light years since creation. Since our observations encompass but two-thirds of that distance, we can only assume that the invisible galaxies are there, and that their farthest outrushing echelons mark the present limits of the universe.

The human mind recoils from the notion of a universe that somewhere terminates, just as it falters at the opposite concept of a space that never ends. We tend to think of space, however, in the familiar images of our experience—or, in the terms of Euclid's plane geometry, where a straight line is the shortest distance between two points and the area of a circle is always πr^2. But in the immensity of the cosmos where so many of our familiar terrestrial concepts fail, it may be that our simple Euclidean geometry is delusive too. Just as many believed till recently that his Earth was flat, perhaps we now are misled by our short perspectives into believing that the space of the universe must be like the space we see in our immediate neighborhood. Ultimately man discovered the curvature of the Earth —by observation and deduction. By analogous techniques cosmologists are now endeavoring to discover whether or not the space of the universe is curved.

Here again the first clues were provided by Einstein when, in 1915, he proposed his General Theory of Relativity, putting forth a new concept of gravitation. Instead of treating gravity as a "force," as Newton had, Einstein pointed out that the space around any celestial body represents a gravitational field akin to the magnetic field around a magnet. He concluded further that the presence of any gravitating body must warp or bend the region of space in which it lies, and hence that light rays passing through a gravitational field must travel not in straight lines but in curves. Four years later during an eclipse of the sun astronomers confirmed his theory by establishing that starlight passing through the gravitational field of the darkened sun was deflected precisely as Einstein had forecast.

Since the triumphant validation of Einstein's prediction concerning the bending of light, theorists have been speculating as to the curvature of the universe as a whole. They foresee three main possibilities: 1) The universe is Euclidean—it has no curvature and within it a straight line is the shortest distance between two points; 2) It has

positive curvature—within it the shortest distance between two points is a closed curve, like the great circles that form the meridians of longitude on the surface of the Earth; 3) It has negative curvature— analogous to a saddle-shaped surface and within it the shortest distance between two points is some type of open curve such as a parabola or hyperbola. The expectation of the cosmologist is that he will be able to choose among these possibilities by counting and analyzing the apportionment of the galaxies in space. At present, according to the most recent observations, the greatest likelihood is that space either curves negatively or not at all.

These concepts, though difficult to envisage, are inextricably entwined with the phenomenon of expansion and with the ancient philosophical debate as to whether space is infinite or finite. If it is Euclidean, it is by definition infinite. If it is negatively curved, it must also be infinite for its outer reaches would then curve away from each other indefinitely. But if it has positive curvature, it would then have the strange property of being at once finite and boundless, like the surface of our Earth which, though finite, has no boundaries.

At this present interval in the march of human knowledge, cosmology thus finds itself drawn ever farther from the familiar world of sensory impressions. Its theorists are constantly tormented by uncertainty as to the choice of their concepts, and beset by doubts as to the accuracy of their interpretations. The whole phantasmagoria of the outrushing galaxies and expanding space so assails the imagination as to make even cosmologists question the intricate framework of observation and deductive reasoning on which it rests. And yet there appears no other way to explain the faint glimmers of light which the great telescopes receive, and the undeniable reddening of that light which the spectrographs disclose.

Less than a century ago scientists felt confident that little remained for them to do but perfect more accurate systems of measurement. There seemed to be no process of nature that could not be described in terms of mechanical laws and accurately defined by Newton's beautiful equations. And the conviction grew that, given the immediate position and velocity of every particle in the universe, its past and future could be perfectly revealed. The events that shattered this assumption were the development of relativity and the swift advance of atomic science. For all the tremendous insights that modern physics has provided in its separate realms, it has also added to the enigma of man's existence, introducing new paradox, uncertainty, duality into his vision of the world he inhabits.

Today we can no longer distinguish clearly among the old entities by which the universe used to be described. In the new science it has become clear that mass and energy are the same thing. And similarly space and time grow indistinguishable in the vast, veiled depths of the outer cosmos. Handicapped by his inadequate conceptions, confined in the prison house of his senses, man can only grope through the twilight that dims both of his ultimate horizons—on the one hand the inscrutable universe of the elementary particles, on the other the illimitable universe of space and time. Whether he will ever penetrate them more deeply is a question that can be answered only with hope, not assurance. For in the words of Paul, "We know in part, and we prophesy in part. . . . Now we see through a glass, darkly."

LIST OF ILLUSTRATIONS

Pictures on each page are listed from left to right and from top to bottom. Photographic listings are followed by the name of the photographer or agency in parentheses.

293

BIBLIOGRAPHY

I THE EARTH IS BORN

BALDWIN, RALPH B., *The Face of the Moon*. Chicago: University of Chicago Press, 1949.

FISHER, CLYDE and MARIAN LOCKWOOD, *Astronomy*. New York: John Wiley, 1940.

GAMOW, GEORGE, *Biography of the Earth*. New York: Viking, 1948.

———, *The Birth and Death of the Sun*. New York: Viking, 1949.

HYNEK, J. A. (ed.), *Astrophysics*. New York: McGraw-Hill, 1951.

JEANS, SIR JAMES, *The Growth of Physical Science*. London: Cambridge University Press, 1951.

———, *The Mysterious Universe*. New York: Macmillan, 1947.

JEFFREYS, HAROLD, *The Earth*. London: Cambridge University Press, 1952.

KUIPER, GERARD P. (ed.), *The Earth as a Planet*. Vol. II of *The Solar System*. Chicago: University of Chicago Press, 1954.

RUSSELL, HENRY NORRIS, *The Solar System and Its Origin*. New York: Macmillan, 1935.

SHAPLEY, HARLOW, *Flights from Chaos*. New York: Whittlesey House, 1930.

UREY, HAROLD C., *The Planets*. New Haven: Yale University Press, 1952.

II THE MIRACLE OF THE SEA

BIGELOW, HENRY B. and W. T. EDMONDSON, *Wind Waves at Sea, Breakers and Surf*. Washington, D.C.: U.S. Navy, Hydrographic Office, 1947. (Publication No. 602).

BOUVIER, E. L., *Crustacés décapodes*. Vol. L of *Résultats des Campagnes scientifiques du Prince de Monaco*, ed. by Jules Richard. Monaco: Imprimerie de Monaco, 1917.

———, *Pycnogonides*. Vol. LI, *Ibid.*

CARSOLA, ALFRED J. and ROBERT S. DIETZ, "Submarine Geology of Two Flat-Topped Northeast Pacific Seamounts." *American Journal of Science*, Vol. 250, pp. 481–97; July, 1952.

CARSON, RACHEL L., *The Sea Around Us*. New York: Oxford University Press, 1951.

CLEMENS, W. A. and G. V. WILBY, *Fishes of the Pacific Coast of Canada*. Ottawa: Fisheries Research Board of Canada, 1946. (Bulletin No. 68).

COKER, ROBERT ERWIN, *This Great and Wide Sea*. Chapel Hill: University of North Carolina Press, 1947.

COLMAN, JOHN S., *The Sea and Its Mysteries*. New York: Norton, 1950.

DIETZ, ROBERT S., "The Pacific Floor." *Scientific American*, Vol. 186, No. 4; April, 1952.

DIETZ, ROBERT S. and HENRY W. MENARD, "Origin of Abrupt Change in Slope at Continental Shelf Margin." *Bulletin of the American Association of Petroleum Geologists*, Vol. 35, No. 9; September, 1951.

ERICSON, D. B., MAURICE EWING and BRUCE C. HEEZEN, "Deep-Sea Sands and Submarine Canyons." *Bulletin of The Geological Society of America*, Vol. 62, pp. 961–65; November, 1951.

FUGLISTER, F. C., "Multiple Currents in the Gulf Stream System." *Tellus*, Vol. 3, No. 4; November, 1951.

GOLDBERG, EDWARD D., "Marine Geochemistry I. Chemical Scavengers of the Sea." *The Journal of Geology*, Vol. 62, No. 3; May, 1954.

———, "Origin and Chemical Composition of the Oceans." *Scalacs*, Vol. VI, No. 8; November, 1951.

GOODE, GEORGE BROWN and TARLETON H. BEAN, *Oceanic Icthyology*. 2 Vols. Washington, D.C.: Smithsonian Institution, 1895. (Special Bulletin No. 2).

HEEZEN, BRUCE C., MAURICE EWING and D. B. ERICSON, "Submarine Topography in the North Atlantic." *Bulletin of The Geological Society of America*, Vol. 62, pp. 1407–17; December, 1951.

ISELIN, C. O'D., "Preliminary Report on Long-Period Variations in the Transport of the Gulf Stream System." *Papers in Physical Oceanography and Meteorology*, Vol. VIII, No. 1; July, 1940. Published by Massachusetts Institute of Technology and Woods Hole Oceanographic Institution.

JOHNSON, MYRTLE E. and HARRY JAMES SNOOK, *Seashore Animals of the Pacific Coast*. New York: Macmillan, 1927.

KUENEN, PH. H., *Marine Geology*. New York: John Wiley, 1950.

MARMER, HARRY AARON, *The Tide*. New York: D. Appleton and Co., 1926.

MENARD, HENRY W. and ROBERT S. DIETZ, "Mendocino Submarine Escarpment." *The Journal of Geology*, Vol. 60, No. 3; May, 1952.

———, "Submarine Geology of the Gulf of Alaska." *Bulletin of The Geological Society of America*, Vol. 62, pp. 1263–85; October, 1951.

MILNE-EDWARDS, A. and E. L. BOUVIER, *Crustacés décapodes*. From *Expéditions Scientifiques du Travailleur et du Talisman*, ed. by A. Milne-Edwards. Paris: Masson, 1900.

MUNK, WALTER H., *Wave Action on Structures*. New York: American Institute of Mining and Metallurgical Engineers, March, 1948. (Technical Publication No. 2322).

SHEPARD, FRANCIS P., *Submarine Geology*. New York: Harper, 1948.

STETSON, HENRY C., "The Sediments and Stratigraphy of the East Coast Continental Margin: Georges Bank to Norfolk Canyon." *Papers in Physical Oceanography and Meteorology*, Vol. XI, No. 2; August, 1949. Published by Massachusetts Institute of Technology and Woods Hole Oceanographic Institution.

STOMMEL, HENRY, "The Gulf Stream." *The Scientific Monthly*, Vol. LXX, No. 4; April, 1950.

SVEDRUP, H. U., MARTIN W. JOHNSON and RICHARD H. FLEMING, *The Oceans*. New York: Prentice-Hall, 1942.

III THE FACE OF THE LAND

CALIFORNIA INSTITUTE OF TECHNOLOGY, "Earthquakes." *Research Bulletin No. 21*; October, 1952.

DUNBAR, CARL O., *Historical Geology*. New York: John Wiley, 1949.

ENGELN, O. D. VON, *Geomorphology*. New York: Macmillan, 1949.

ENGELN, O. D. VON and KENNETH E. CASTER, *Geology*. New York: McGraw-Hill, 1952.

GILLULY, JAMES, "Distribution of Mountain Building in Geologic Time." *Bulletin of The Geological Society of America*, Vol. 60, No. 4; April, 1949.

GILLULY, JAMES, AARON C. WATERS and A. O. WOODFORD, *Principles of Geology*. San Francisco: W. H. Freeman and Company, 1952.

HAYNES, JACK ELLIS, *Haynes Guide, Yellowstone National Park*. Bozeman, Mont.: Haynes Studios Inc., 1952.

KAY, MARSHALL, *North American Geosynclines*. New York: The Geological Society of America, 1951. (Memoir 48).

KING, PHILIP B. and ARTHUR STUPKA, "The Great Smoky Mountains—Their Geology and Natural History." *The Scientific Monthly*, Vol. LXXI, No. 1; July, 1950.

LOBECK, ARMIN KOHL, *Geomorphology*. New York: McGraw-Hill, 1939.

LONGWELL, CHESTER R., ADOLPH KNOPF and RICHARD F. FLINT, *A Textbook of Geology. Part I: Physical Geology*. New York: John Wiley, 1939.

MARMER, H. A., "Sea Level Changes along the Coasts of the United States in Recent Years." *Transactions of the American Geophysical Union*, Vol. 30–32, pp. 201–204.

SCHULZ, PAUL E., *Geology of Lassen's Landscape*. Mineral, Calif.: Lassen Volcanic National Park, 1952.

U.S. DEPARTMENT OF THE INTERIOR, NATIONAL PARK SERVICE, *Lassen Volcanic National Park: Leaflet No. 1, Lily Pond* and *Leaflet No. 2, Bumpass Hell*.

WEGEMANN, CARROLL H., *A Guide to the Geology of Rocky Mountain National Park*. Washington, D.C.: U.S. Department of the Interior, National Park Service, 1944.

IV THE CANOPY OF AIR

BLAIR, THOMAS ARTHUR, *Climatology*. New York: Prentice-Hall, 1942.

BOTLEY, CICELY MARY, *The Air and Its Mysteries*. New York: D. Appleton-Century, 1940.

BROOKS, C. E. P., *Climate Through the Ages*. New York: McGraw-Hill, 1949.

DOBSON, G. M. B., "Ozone in the Earth's Atmosphere." *Endeavor*, October, 1952.

FINCH, VERNOR C. and GLENN T. TREWARTHA, *Physical Elements of Geography*. New York: McGraw-Hill, 1949.

GUNN, ROSS, "The Electricity of Rain and Thunderstorms." *Terrestrial Magnetism and Atmospheric Electricity*, Vol. 40, No. 1; March, 1935.

HAURWITZ, BERNHARD and J. M. AUSTIN, *Climatology*. New York: McGraw-Hill, 1944.

HOOD, PETER, *The Atmosphere*. London: Geoffrey Cumberlege, 1952.

HULBURT, E. O., "Physical Characteristics of the Upper Atmosphere of the Earth." From *Physics and Medicine of the Upper Atmosphere*, ed. by C. S. White and O. O. Benson Jr. Albuquerque: University of New Mexico Press, 1952.

HUMPHREYS, W. J., *Ways of the Weather*. Lancaster, Pa.: Jaques Cattell Press, 1942.

HUTCHINSON, G. EVELYN, "The Biochemistry of the Terrestrial Atmosphere." From *The Earth as a Planet*, Vol. II of *The Solar System*, ed. by Gerard P. Kuiper. Chicago: University of Chicago Press, 1954.

KAPLAN, JOSEPH, "The Earth's Atmosphere." *American Scientist*, Vol. 41, No. 1; January, 1953.

KUIPER, GERARD P. (ed.), *The Atmospheres of the Earth and Planets*. Chicago: University of Chicago Press, 1952.

MALONE, THOMAS F. (ed.), *Compendium of Meteorology*. Boston: American Meteorological Society, 1951.

NAMIAS, JEROME, "The Jet Stream." *Scientific American*, Vol. 187, No. 4; October, 1952.

RANKAMA, KALERVO and TH. G. SAHAMA, *Geochemistry*. Chicago: University of Chicago Press, 1950.

RUBEY, WILLIAM W., "Geologic History of Sea Water." *Bulletin of The Geological Society of America*, Vol. 62, No. 9; September, 1951.

SARTON, GEORGE, *A History of Science*. Cambridge: Harvard University Press, 1952.

SLOANE, ERIC, *Eric Sloane's Weather Book*. New York: Duell, Sloan and Pearce, 1952.

STÖRMER, CARL, "Problems of the Northern Lights." *The American-Scandinavian Review*, Vol. XII, No. 10; October, 1924.

TALMAN, CHARLES FITZHUGH, *The Realm of the Air*. Indianapolis: Bobbs-Merrill, 1931.

U.S. DEPARTMENT OF AGRICULTURE, *Climate and Man*. (Yearbook of Agriculture, 1941).

WILLET, HURD CURTIS, *Descriptive Meteorology*. New York: Academic Press, 1944.

WOLF, ABRAHAM, *A History of Science, Technology, and Philosophy in the 16th and 17th Centuries*. London: Allen & Unwin, 1950.

V THE PAGEANT OF LIFE
VI THE AGE OF MAMMALS

ANDREWS, HENRY NATHANIEL, JR., *Ancient Plants and the World They Lived In*. Ithaca: Comstock Publishing Co., 1947.

ARNOLD, CHESTER A., *An Introduction to Paleobotany*. New York: McGraw-Hill, 1947.

BLUM, HAROLD F., *Time's Arrow and Evolution*. Princeton: Princeton University Press, 1951.

BUCHSBAUM, RALPH, *Animals Without Backbones*. Chicago: University of Chicago Press, 1948.

CAIN, STANLEY A., *Foundations of Plant Geography*. New York: Harper, 1944.

CLARKE, JOHN M. and RUDOLF RUEDEMANN, *The Eurypterida of New York*. Albany: New York State Museum, 1912. (Memoir 14).

COLBERT, EDWIN H., *The Dinosaur Book*. New York: McGraw-Hill, 1951.

COOPER, G. ARTHUR, "Brachiopod Ecology and Paleoecology." *Report of the Committee on Paleoecology, 1936–37*. Washington, D.C.: National Research Council.

DARWIN, CHARLES, *The Origin of Species* and *The Descent of Man*. New York: The Modern Library.

FLOWER, ROUSSEAU H., "Studies of Paleozoic Nautiloidea, I–VII." *Bulletins of American Paleontology*, Vol. 28, No. 109; August 10, 1943.

GIBBS, R. DARNLEY, *Botany*. Philadelphia: Blakiston, 1950.

GREGORY, WILLIAM KING, *Evolution Emerging*. 2 Vols. New York: Macmillan, 1951.

HIRMER, MAX, *Handbuch der Paläobotanik*. München: R. Oldenbourg, 1927.

HUTCHINSON, G. EVELYN, "Restudy of some Burgess Shale Fossils." *Proceedings of the U.S. National Museum*, Vol. 78, Article 11; 1931.

HYMAN, LIBBIE H., *The Invertebrates*. 3 Vols. New York: McGraw-Hill, 1940–51.

KALMUS, H., *Genetics*. Harmondsworth: Penguin Books, 1952.

KNIGHT, J. BROOKES, "Paleozoic Gastropod Genotypes." New York: Geological Society of America, 1941. (*Special Papers*, No. 32).

MOORE, RAYMOND CECIL., *Introduction to Historical Geology*. New York: McGraw-Hill, 1949.

RAYMOND, PERCY E., "Pre-Cambrian Life." *Bulletin of The Geological Society of America*, Vol. 46, pp. 375–92, 1935.

———, *Prehistoric Life*. Cambridge: Harvard University Press, 1939.

ROMER, ALFRED SHERWOOD, *Man and the Vertebrates*. Chicago: University of Chicago Press, 1941.

———, *Vertebrate Paleontology*. Chicago: University of Chicago Press, 1945.

SCOTT, WILLIAM BERRYMAN, *A History of Land Mammals in the Western Hemisphere*. New York: Macmillan, 1913.

SEWARD, ALBERT CHARLES, *Plant Life Through the Ages*. New York: Macmillan, 1931.

SHROCK, ROBERT R. and WILLIAM H. TWENHOFEL, *Principles of Invertebrate Paleontology*. New York: McGraw-Hill, 1953.

SIMPSON, GEORGE GAYLORD, *Life of the Past*. New Haven: Yale University Press, 1953.

———, *The Meaning of Evolution*. New Haven: Yale University Press, 1949.

STORER, TRACY I., *General Zoology*. New York: McGraw-Hill, 1943.

WALCOTT, CHARLES DOOLITTLE, *Fossil Medusae*. Washington, D.C.: U.S. Department of the Interior, 1898. (Monographs of the U.S. Geological Survey, Vol. XXX).

ZITTEL, KARL A. (ed.), *Handbuch der Palaeontologie*. 5 Vols. München: R. Oldenbourg, 1876–93.

VII CREATURES OF THE SEA

BEEBE, WILLIAM, *Half Mile Down*. New York: Duell, Sloan and Pearce, 1951.

———, *The Arcturus Adventure*. New York: Putnam, 1926.

BREDER, CHARLES M., JR., *Field Book of Marine Fishes of the Atlantic Coast*. New York: Putnam, 1948.

HESSE, RICHARD, W. C. ALLEE and KARL P. SCHMIDT, *Ecological Animal Geography*. New York: John Wiley, 1951.

HUBBS, CARL L., "Nature's Own Seaplanes." *Smithsonian Report for 1933*, pp. 333–48.

LA MONTE, FRANCESCA, *North American Game Fishes*. New York: Doubleday, 1945.

MACGINITIE, G. E. and NETTIE, *Natural History of Marine Animals*. New York: McGraw-Hill, 1949.

MURRAY, SIR JOHN and JOHAN HJORT, *The Depths of the Ocean*. London: Macmillan, 1912.

RICKETTS, EDWARD F. and JACK CALVIN, *Between Pacific Tides*. Stanford: Stanford University Press, 1939.

ROULE, LOUIS, *Fishes and Their Ways of Life*. Translated from the French by Conrad Elphinstone. New York: Norton, 1935.

SCHULTZ, LEONARD P. with EDITH M. STERN, *The Ways of Fishes*. New York: Van Nostrand, 1948.

WALKER, BOYD W., "A Guide to the Grunion." *California Fish and Game*, Vol. 38, No. 3; July, 1952.

ZOBELL, CLAUDE E., "Bacterial Activities and the Origin of Oil." *World Oil*, Vol. 130, pp. 128–38; June, 1950.

———, "The Occurrence of Bacteria in the Deep Sea and their Significance for Animal Life," XIV International Zoological Congress. Copenhagen: 1953.

VIII THE CORAL REEF

British Museum, *Great Barrier Reef Expedition*, 1928–29, Vol. I.

HICKSON, SYDNEY JOHN, *An Introduction to the Study of Recent Corals*. Manchester: University of Manchester, 1924.

LADD, H. S. and J. I. TRACEY JR., "Coral Reefs in Colour." *The Geographical Magazine*; January, 1951.

ROUGHLEY, THEODORE CLEVELAND, *Wonders of the Great Barrier Reef*. New York: Anglobooks, 1952.

WHITLEY, G. P., *Poisonous and Harmful Fishes*. Melbourne: Council for Scientific and Industrial Research, 1943. (Bulletin No. 159).

YONGE, CHARLES MAURICE, *A Year on the Great Barrier Reef*. London: Putnam, 1930.

———, "The Form of Coral Reefs." *Endeavor*; July, 1951.

IX THE LAND OF THE SUN

ADOLPH, E. F. and ASSOCIATES, *Physiology of Man in the Desert*. New York: Interscience, 1947.

BAGNOLD, RALPH ALGER, *The Physics of Blown Sand and Desert Dunes*. New York: Morrow.

BENSON, LYMAN, *The Cacti of Arizona*. Tucson: University of Arizona Press, 1950.

BENSON, LYMAN and ROBERT A. DARROW, *A Manual of Southwestern Desert Trees and Shrubs*. Tucson: University of Arizona Press, 1945.

BOGERT, C. M., "Reptiles Under the Sun." *Natural History*, Vol. XLIV, No. 1; June, 1939.

BUXTON, P. A., *Animal Life in Deserts*. New York: Longmans, Green, 1923.

CANNON, WILLIAM AUSTIN, *Root Habits of Desert Plants*. Washington, D.C.: Carnegie Institution of Washington, 1911.

DILL, DAVID BRUCE, *Life, Heat, and Altitude*. Cambridge: Harvard University Press, 1938.

DITMARS, RAYMOND, *The Reptiles of North America*. New York: Doubleday, Doran, 1936.

JAEGER, EDMUND C., *Denizens of the Desert*. Boston: Houghton Mifflin, 1922.

———, *Desert Wild Flowers*. Stanford: Stanford University Press, 1950.

———, *Our Desert Neighbors*. Stanford: Stanford University Press, 1950.

———, *The California Deserts*. Stanford: Stanford University Press, 1948.

KEARNEY, THOMAS H. and ROBERT H. PEEBLES, *Arizona Flora*. Berkeley: University of California Press, 1951.

KENDREW, W. G., *The Climates of the Continents*. New York: Oxford University Press, 1942.

SCHMIDT-NIELSEN, BODIL and KNUT, "A Complete Account of the Water Metabolism in Kangaroo Rats and an Experimental Verification." *Journal of Cellular and Comparative Physiology*, Vol. 38, No. 2; October, 1951.

———, "The Water Economy of Desert Mammals." *The Scientific Monthly*, Vol. LXIX, No. 3; September, 1949.

———, "Water Conservation in Desert Rodents." *Journal of Cellular and Comparative Physiology*, Vol. 32, No. 3; December, 1948.

———, "Water Metabolism of Desert Mammals." *Physiological Reviews*, Vol. 32, No. 2; April, 1952.

SHREVE, FORREST, *Vegetation of the Sonoran Desert*. Vol. I of *Vegetation and Flora of the Sonoran Desert*. Washington, D.C.: Carnegie Institution of Washington, 1951.

X THE ARCTIC BARRENS

ARCTIC INSTITUTE OF NORTH AMERICA. *Arctic Bibliography*. 3 Vols. Washington, D.C.: U.S. Department of Defense, 1953.

BAILEY, ALFRED MARSHALL, *Birds of Arctic Alaska*. Denver: Colorado Museum of Natural History, 1948.

BAIRD, P. D. and J. LEWIS ROBINSON, "A Brief History of Exploration and Research in the Canadian Eastern Arctic." *Canadian Geographical Journal*, Vol. 30, No. 3; March, 1945.

BANFIELD, A. W. F., *The Barren-Ground Caribou*. (Mimeograph release from the Department of Resources and Development, Northern Administration and Lands Branch, Ottawa. 1951).

BERG, LEV S., *Natural Regions of the U.S.S.R.* Translated from the Russian by Olga Adler Titelbaum. New York: Macmillan, 1950.

BIRD, J. BRIAN, *Southampton Island*. Ottawa: Department of Mines and Technical Surveys, Geographical Branch, 1953. (Memoir 1).

BLACK, ROBERT F., "Permafrost—A Review." *Transactions of the New York Academy of Sciences*, Series 2, Vol. 15, No. 5; March, 1953.

CHRISTIAN, EDGAR, *Unflinching*. New York: Funk & Wagnalls, 1938.

CLARKE, C. H. D., *A Biological Investigation of the Thelon Game Sanctuary*. Ottawa: National Museum of Canada, 1940. (Bulletin No. 96).

DANSEREAU, PIERRE, "Biogeography of the Land and the Inland Waters." From *Geography of the Northlands*, ed. by George H. T. Kimble and Dorothy Good. New York: John Wiley, 1955.

DE PONCINS, GONTRAN, *Kabloona*. In collaboration with Lewis Galantière. New York: Reynal & Hitchcock, 1941.

FLINT, RICHARD FOSTER, *Glacial Geology and the Pleistocene Epoch*. New York: John Wiley, 1947.

HANBURY, DAVID T., *Sport and Travel in the Northland of Canada*. London: Edward Arnold, 1904.

HAVILAND, MAUD DORIA, *Forest, Steppe, & Tundra*. London: Cambridge University Press, 1926.

LLOYD, TREVOR, J. LEWIS ROBINSON and JOHN WEAVER, *Geography of the Polar Regions*. (To be published by McGraw-Hill, New York).

MIROV, NICHOLAS TIHO, *Geography of Russia*. New York: John Wiley, 1951.

MULLER, SIEMON WILLIAM, *Permafrost*. Ann Arbor: J. W. Edwards, 1947.

NORDENSKJÖLD, OTTO and LUDWIG MECKING, *The Geography of the Polar Regions*. New York: American Geographical Society, 1928.

PIKE, WARBURTON, *The Barren Ground of Northern Canada*. London: Macmillan, 1892.

POLUNIN, NICHOLAS, *Botany of the Canadian Eastern Arctic*. Parts I, II, and III. Ottawa: National Museum of Canada, 1940, 1947 and 1948. (Bulletins Nos. 92, 97 and 104).

PORSILD, A. E., "Plant Life in the Arctic." *Canadian Geographical Journal*; March 1951.

PUTNAM, DONALD F. (ed.), *Canadian Regions*. New York: Crowell, 1952.

ROBINSON, J. LEWIS, *The Canadian Arctic*. Ottawa: Department of Mines and Technical Surveys, Geographical Branch, 1952. (Information Bulletin No. 2).

———, "Weather and Climate of the Northwest Territories." *Canadian Geographical Journal*, Vol. 32, No. 3; March, 1946.

ROBINSON, M. J. and J. LEWIS ROBINSON, "Fur Protection in the Northwest Territories." *Canadian Geographical Journal*, Vol. 32, No. 1; January, 1946.

SCOTT, PETER M., *Wild Geese and Eskimos*. New York: Scribner's, 1952.

SETON, ERNEST THOMPSON, *The Arctic Prairies*. New York: International Universities Press, 1943.

———, *Lives of Game Animals*. 4 Vols. Boston: Branford, 1953.

STEFANSSON, VILHJALMUR (ed.), *Encyclopaedia Arctica*. Unpublished material available on microfilm through the Office of Naval Research, Washington, D.C.

———, *The Friendly Arctic*. New York: Macmillan, 1943.

———, *Ultima Thule*. New York: Macmillan, 1940.

SUTTON, GEORGE MIKSCH, *The Exploration of Southampton Island, Hudson Bay*. Vol. XII of *Memoirs of the Carnegie Museum*. Pittsburgh: Carnegie Institute, 1932–36.

TAVERNER, PERCY ALGERNON, *Birds of Canada*. Toronto: Musson Book Co., 1947.

TREWARTHA, GLENN THOMAS, *An Introduction to Weather and Climate*. New York: McGraw-Hill, 1937.

WASHBURN, A. L., *Reconnaissance Geology of Portions of Victoria Island and Adjacent Regions Arctic Canada*. New York: The Geological Society of America, 1947. (Memoir No. 22).

———, "Patterned Ground." *Revue Canadienne de Géographie*, Vol. IV, No. 3–4; July-October, 1950.

XI THE RAIN FOREST

BEEBE, CHARLES WILLIAM, G. INNESS HARTLEY and PAUL HOWES, *Tropical Wild Life of British Guiana*. New York: New York Zoological Society, 1917.

BOND, J., *Check-list of Birds of the West Indies*. Philadelphia: Academy of Natural Sciences, 1950.

CABRERA, ANGEL and JOSÉ YEPES, *Mamíferos Sudamericanos*. Buenos Aires: Gotelli, 1940.

HINGSTON, R. W. G., *A Naturalist in the Guiana Forest*. New York: Longmans, Green, 1932.

KERNER, ANTON VON MARILAUN and F. W. OLIVER, *The Natural History of Plants*. 2 Vols. London: Gresham, 1904.

RICHARDS, PAUL WESCOTT, *The Tropical Rain Forest*. London: Cambridge University Press, 1952.

SCHIMPER, A. F. W., *Plant Geography*. Translated from the German by William R. Fisher. London: Oxford University Press, 1903.

STURGIS, BERTHA BEMENT, *Field Book of Birds of the Panama Canal Zone*. New York: Putnam, 1928.

XII THE WOODS OF HOME

ANTHONY, H. E., *Field Book of North American Mammals*. New York: Putnam, 1928.

ALLEE, W. C., ALFRED E. EMERSON, ORLANDO PARK, THOMAS PARK and KARL P. SCHMIDT, *Principles of Animal Ecology*. Philadelphia: Saunders, 1949.

BARD, GILY E., "Mettler's Woods." *The Garden Journal of the New York Botanical Garden*, Vol. 4, No. 4; July-August, 1954.

———, "Secondary Succession on the Piedmont of New Jersey." *Ecological Monographs*, Vol. 22, No. 3, July, 1952.

BIRCH, L. C. and D. P. CLARK, "Forest Soil as an Ecological Community." *The Quarterly Review of Biology*, Vol. 28, No. 1; March, 1953.

BRAUN, E. LUCY, *Deciduous Forest of Eastern North America*. Philadelphia: Blakiston, 1950.

BUELL, MURRAY F., HELEN F. BUELL and JOHN A. SMALL, "Fire in the History of Mettler's Woods." *Bulletin of the Torrey Botanical Club*, Vol. 81, No. 3; May, 1954.

CAHALANE, VICTOR H., *Mammals of North America*. New York: Macmillan, 1947.

COLLINGWOOD, G. H. and WARREN D. BRUSH, *Knowing Your Trees*. Washington, D.C.: The American Forestry Association, 1947.

ESSIG, E. O., *College Entomology*. New York: Macmillan, 1942.

FERNALD, MERRITT LYNDON, *Gray's Manual of Botany*. New York: American Book Co., 1950.

GERTSCH, WILLIS J., *American Spiders*. New York: Van Nostrand, 1949.

JACOT, ARTHUR PAUL, "The Fauna of the Soil." *The Quarterly Review of Biology*, Vol. 15, No. 1; March, 1940.

MORGAN, ANN HAVEN, *Field Book of Ponds and Streams*. New York: Putnam, 1930.

———, *Field Book of Animals in Winter*. New York: Putnam, 1939.

MORRIS, PERCY A., *They Hop and Crawl*. New York: Ronald Press, 1945.

ODUM, EUGENE P., *Fundamentals of Ecology*. Philadelphia: Saunders, 1953.

PENNAK, ROBERT W., *Fresh-Water Invertebrates of the United States*. New York: Ronald Press, 1953.

WAKSMAN, SELMAN A., *Principles of Soil Microbiology*. Baltimore: Williams & Wilkins, 1927.

WEAVER, JOHN E. and FREDERIC E. CLEMENTS, *Plant Ecology*. New York: McGraw-Hill, 1938.

WRIGHT, ALBERT HAZEN and ANNA ALLEN WRIGHT, *Handbook of Frogs and Toads*. Ithaca: Comstock Publishing Co., 1949.

XIII THE STARRY UNIVERSE

ABBOTT, C. G., *The Earth and the Stars*. New York: Van Nostrand, 1946.

ABETTI, GIORGIO, *The History of Astronomy*. Translated from the Italian by Betty Burr Abetti. New York: Schuman, 1952.

ALLER, LAWRENCE H., *Astrophysics: Nuclear Transformations, Stellar Interiors, and Nebulae*. New York: Ronald Press, 1954.

ALTER, DINSMORE and CLARENCE H. CLEMINSHAW, *Pictorial Astronomy*. New York: Crowell, 1952.

BAADE, WALTER and R. MINKOWSKI, "On the Identification of Radio Sources." *Astrophysical Journal*, Vol. 119, pp. 215–23; 1954.

BAKER, ROBERT H., *Astronomy*. New York: Van Nostrand, 1950.

BARNETT, LINCOLN, *The Universe and Dr. Einstein*. New York: Sloane, 1948.

BOK, BART J. and PRISCILLA F., *The Milky Way*. Philadelphia: Blakiston, 1945.

BONDI, HERMANN, *Cosmology*. London: Cambridge University Press, 1952.

BORN, MAX, *The Restless Universe*. Translated from the German by Winifred M. Deans. New York: Dover, 1951.

COUDERC, PAUL, *The Expansion of the Universe*. Translated from the French by J. B. Sidgwick. New York: Macmillan, 1952.

D'ABRO, A., *The Evolution of Scientific Thought from Newton to Einstein*. New York: Dover, 1950.

———, *The Rise of the New Physics*. New York: Dover, 1951.

DOIG, PETER, *A Concise History of Astronomy*. New York: Philosophical Library, 1951.

EINSTEIN, ALBERT, *The Meaning of Relativity*. Princeton: Princeton University Press, 1953.

EISELY, LOREN C., "Little Men and Flying Saucers." *Harpers' Magazine*, Vol. 206, No. 1234; March, 1953.

———, "Is Man Alone in Space?" *Scientific American*, Vol. 189, No. 1; July, 1953.

GAMOW, GEORGE, *The Creation of the Universe*. New York: Viking, 1952.

———, "Modern Cosmology." *Scientific American*, Vol. 190, No. 3; March, 1954.

GOLDBERG, LEO and LAWRENCE H. ALLER, *Atoms, Stars, and Nebulae*. Philadelphia: Blakiston, 1943.

HOFFMAN, BANESH, *The Strange Story of the Quantum*. New York: Harper, 1947.

HOYLE, FRED, *The Nature of the Universe*. New York: Harper, 1950.

HUBBLE, EDWIN, "Explorations in Space." *Proceedings of the American Philosophical Society*, Vol. 95, No. 5; October, 1951.

———, *The Realm of the Nebulae*. New Haven: Yale University Press, 1936.

JEANS, SIR JAMES, *The Universe Around Us*. London: Cambridge University Press, 1944.

JONES, H. SPENCER, *Life on Other Worlds*. New York: Macmillan, 1940.

KAHN, FRITZ, *Design of the Universe*. New York: Crown, 1954.

KAMP, PETER VAN DE, "The Nearest Stars." *American Scientist*, Vol. 42, No. 4; October, 1954.

KUIPER, GERARD P., "Note on the Origin of the Asteroids." *Proceedings of the National Academy of Sciences*, Vol. 39, No. 12; December, 1953.

———, "On the Evolution of the Protoplanets." *Ibid.*, Vol. 37, No. 7; July, 1951.

———, "On the Origin of the Irregular Satellites." *Ibid.*, Vol. 37, No. 11; November, 1951.

———, "On the Origin of the Solar System." *Ibid.*, Vol. 37, No. 1; January, 1951.

———, *The Sun*. Vol. I of *The Solar System*. Chicago: University of Chicago Press, 1953.

MÖLLER, CHRISTIAN, *The Theory of Relativity*. London: Oxford University Press, 1952.

PAYNE-GAPOSCHKIN, CECILIA, *Stars in the Making*. Cambridge: Harvard University Press, 1952.

RUDAUX, LUCIEN, *Sur les autres Mondes*. Paris: Larousse, 1937.

SANDAGE, ALLAN R., "A Survey of Present Knowledge of Globular Clusters and Its Significance for Stellar Evolution." *Mémoires de la Société Royale des Sciences de Liège*, Fourth Series, Vol. XIV, 1953.

SHAPLEY, HARLOW, *Galaxies*. Philadelphia: Blakiston, 1943.

STRUVE, OTTO, "Color Magnitude Diagrams and Stellar Evolution." *Sky and Telescope*, Vol. XII, No. 3; January, 1953.

———, "Pleione—A Story of Cosmic Evolution." *Ibid*, Vol. XI, No. 10; August, 1952.

———, "Pulsating Stars." *Ibid.*, Vol. XII, No. 5; March, 1953.

———, "Report from Rome, I and II." *Ibid.*, Vol. XII, Nos. 1 and 2; November, December, 1952.

———, "Spectra of Visual Double Stars, I and II." *Ibid.*, Vol. XIII, Nos. 8 and 9; June, July, 1954.

———, *Stellar Evolution*. Princeton: Princeton University Press, 1950.

———, "The Distance Scale of the Universe, I and II." *Sky and Telescope*, Vol. XII, Nos. 8 and 9; June, July, 1953.

———, "White Dwarfs, I and II." *Ibid.*, Vol. XIII, Nos. 2 and 3; December, 1953, January, 1954.

VAUCOULEURS, GERARD DE, "The Supergalaxy." *Scientific American*, Vol. 191, No. 1; July, 1954.

WHIPPLE, FRED L., *Earth, Moon and Planets*. Philadelphia: Blakiston, 1941.

INDEX

302

Water (see also Sea water)
  for desert animals, 182
  for desert plants, 194
  and epiphytes, 237
  erosion by, 42, 49, 52, 53
  force of, 35, 52
  freezing, 20
  on planets, 20
  properties of, 20
  in renewal of atmosphere, *67
  for sea animals and plants, 124
  solar energy stored by, 20
  from volcanoes, 40
Water flea, *254, 255
Water mite, *254, 255
Water snake, 254, *255
Water strider, *254, 255
Water vapor
  in atmosphere, 10, *11, 13, 64, *66,
    67, 69, 81, 82, 86
  and clouds, 79, 83

  and fog, 82
  rain formed from, 79
  sea formed from, 22
  and weathering of rock, 49
Waterfalls, *51, 52, 53
Waves, *34, *35
  action on land, *37, *38
  force of, 35
  height of, 34
  progress of, 35
Weasels, 117, 118, 252, *253, 264
Weather, 76–79, 85
  and air masses, *74, *75
  extremes of heat and cold, *85
  three zones of, 76, 77
Westerlies, 31, *74, *75, 77
Western states, geological features, 60
Whales, 124, 126, 130, *131, 139, 155
Whelks, *133
  egg case, *134
White Mountains, *56, 57

Wielandiella, 99, *100
Williamsonia, 99, *100, *101
Willow herb, *214, *215
Willows, *103, *181
Winds
  causes of, *74, *75
  and deserts, 178, *184
  erosion by, *54, *55
  and ocean currents, 31
  in storms, 78
  three major systems of, *74, 75
  in tundra, 203
  and waves, *34
Wolves, 121
  arctic, *208
Wood roach, 258, *259
Woodchuck, *253, 264
Woodland (see Forest)
Woodpecker
  downy, *252, 264
  flint-billed, *228

Worm snake, 258, *259
Worms
  in coral reefs, *153, *162, *166
  evolution of, *93, *94, *95
  fresh-water, *254, *255
  sea, *128, 135, 136, *145
  and soil formation, 258
Wrasse, 168
Wren
  cactus, *186
  quadrille, *229

Xenon in atmosphere, 68

Yaguarundi, *228, 229
Yellow-lipped tree snake, *229
Yellowstone River, *53
Ylem, 288

Zebras, 115
Zodiac, 272

ENGRAVINGS AND COMPOSITION
BY R. R. DONNELLEY & SONS COMPANY, CHICAGO, ILLINOIS.

PRESS WORK BY J. W. CLEMENT COMPANY, BUFFALO, NEW YORK
AND R. R. DONNELLEY & SONS COMPANY, CHICAGO, ILLINOIS.

BOUND BY R. R. DONNELLEY & SONS COMPANY, CRAWFORDSVILLE, INDIANA.

PAPER BY THE MEAD CORPORATION, DAYTON, OHIO.